B. Roebben, L. van der Tuin (eds.)

Practical theology and the interpretation of crossing boundaries

Theologie

Band 52

LIT

B. Roebben, L. van der Tuin (eds.)

Practical theology and the interpretation of crossing boundaries

Essays in honour of Professor M.P.J. van Knippenberg

LIT

Bibliographic information published by Die Deutsche Bibliothek
Die Deutsche Bibliothek lists this publication in the Deutsche
Nationalbibliografie; detailed bibliographic data are available in the
Internet at http://dnb.ddb.de.

BV2
.P73
2003x

ο 5 9 0 0 8 6 5 7

ISBN 3-8258-6617-3

© LIT VERLAG Münster – Hamburg – London   2003
Grevener Str./Fresnostr. 2   48159 Münster
Tel. 0251-23 50 91   Fax 0251-23 19 72
e-Mail: lit@lit-verlag.de   http://www.lit-verlag.de

Distributed in North America by:

Transaction Publishers
New Brunswick (U.S.A.) and London (U.K.)

Transaction Publishers
Rutgers University
35 Berrue Circle
Piscataway, NJ 08854

Tel.: (732) 445 - 2280
Fax: (732) 445 - 3138
for orders (U. S. only):
toll free (888) 999 - 6778

Table of Contents

Strategy

Introduction

Bert Roebben and Leo van der Tuin

The work of Tjeu van Knippenberg, who retired as professor of pastoral theology in the Faculty of Theology of Tilburg University on the 30th of September 2002, is characterised by the subject of the 'boundary'. The boundary forms the dividing line between two areas. On the one hand it acts as a form of protection, separating the strange from the familiar. When the boundary is crossed from the other side then this potentially forms a threat. Crossing over to the other side is a terrifying adventure. On the other hand the boundary is also a challenge. The desire to break new ground is the motive behind human existence. The other side of the boundary holds unknown horizons that want to be explored, that open up new perspectives, thus making the boundary the symbol for the ambivalence of existence itself. Science is also active on boundaries. After all, science exists in order to open up new horizons. Good thorough research is research that opens up new horizons.

Both aspects of the boundary, the existential and the scientific, are present in Tjeu van Knippenberg's work. His doctoral thesis *Dood en religie. Een studie naar communicatief zelfonderzoek in het pastoraat* (1987) [*Death and religion. A study into communicative self-analysis in pastoral care*] is about the most radical boundary to be experienced by people: death. It is an empirical study into the so-called 'meditatio mortis'. He studied the effects of a poimenic method based on the self-confrontation method from H.J.M. Hermans (*The Dialogical Self: Meaning as Movement*, 1993) on the attitude towards death and religion, in order to initiate internal communication of the participants on this. The boundary of death means the end of earthly existence and at the same time for believers it means hope for the beginning of an immortal life. Thus death can be a release for those who suffer in life. The idea of a self-chosen death is then present. For others, death is a threat because it means that everything comes to an end; they prefer to stand at the boundary and not to think about it.

Tjeu van Knippenberg accepted his chair in Tilburg in 1989 with an inaugural lecture: *Grenzen. Werkplaats voor pastoraal theologen* [*Boundaries. Field of activity for pastoral theologians*]. In this he outlines his approach towards practical theology. In line with Tillich he suggests that in theology the field of activity is the boundary area between Christian message and changing situation. Theology is a reflection on the situation based on the message so that the situation can be oriented towards the salvation proclaimed by the message. The boundary area of practical theology is that which lies between message and praxis, which is challenged by the message and by the praxis in which that message is or is not embraced. After all people's daily existence is more stubborn than the hope that is expressed in faith. The love experienced is more fickle than the Love that is God. Pastoral theology concentrates on the existential boundary that determines the basic structure of human life: the boundary of death and resurrection, as fact but also as possibility. Pastoral theology is interested in what people do, but also in what they are able to do, not only in actual religious acts but also in the encouragement of this behaviour.

Tjeu van Knippenberg's valedictory speech is called: *Verbroken verbinding. Zielzorg en levensverhaal [Broken bond. Cure of souls and life story].* In this the boundary is understood as the plane of fracture between transcendence and immanence, between the reality that is visible and in which we shape our life story, and the reality that is not visible and against the background of which we give our life story sense and meaning. The instrument with which we shape the coherence within us and with all that surrounds us is the soul. The soul is a boundary instrument that makes connections. Pastoral care is care for the soul. In their life story people repeatedly experience ruptures within themselves, between themselves and reality and between themselves and transcendental reality. The soul is the perfect image for the place where both within and on the outside, transcendence and immanence meet. In biblical language the soul is the breath of life that brings the human person to life and that in the action of breathing in and breathing out makes the connection between the inside and the outside: immanence and transcendence. In theological language the soul is the image of God in the human person, which makes it possible for him/her to say: I am part of the whole, of the whole within me and of the whole outside me. On its course of life the soul influences everything that happens to people. The cure of souls is the concern for people's life story. And this brings Tjeu van Knippenberg back to what has always been his subject of interest in his pastoral professorship: supporting people on their path of life or 'spiritual guidance'.

Van Knippenberg has developed the concept of spiritual guidance within the framework of the Tilburg research programme *Religious leadership and Christian identity.* He has written about it in many articles and ultimately in the book *Tussen naam en identiteit. Ontwerp van een model voor geestelijke begeleiding* (1998, reprinted in 2000 as *Tussen naam en identiteit. Een model voor geestelijke begeleiding*; translated in 2002 as *Towards religious identity. An excercise in Sprirtual Guidance*). In this book he is connecting to the age-old Western tradition of spiritual leadership. Living on the boundary demands guidance: you cannot care for your soul on your own. Pastoral theology is after all also aimed at the encouragement of religious communication. Pastoral communication gains the shape of 'reframing', which is to say framing reality within the self again and framing the self within that reality again.

In his other publications he follows two tracks. He concentrates on the content of religious communication itself, whereby subjects come up on this existential boundary: death, aging, melancholy, sin and meaning. He relates these topics to the development of the self and notes a fundamental ambivalence in them. Development is only possible when the self survives the tension between stability and change. The self is bipolar, is between a sense of security and openness, between boundary as closure and disclosure.

On the other hand Van Knippenberg follows the path of pastoral ministry with regard to the actual communication of these contents. Here he uses the concepts space and time. Within the boundaries of space and time people are on the way to their destination, they explore the boundaries, are traveller and host/hostess. They meet in the concept identity, having one's own name. If the order of space and time is disturbed then people go in search of meaning, of their identity, their own name. Having one's own name can then be connected to The name that transcends, supports and offers a future to the self and its death and temporariness. The pastor is someone on the boundary who mediates between the life story and the story of faith, between the individual and that which transcends the individual. It is in this way that the cure of souls and leadership are connected in Van Knippenberg's work.

This series of essays *reflects on* the boundary status of pastoral ministry. But it also wants to *reflect* the boundary status of good scholarship in practical theology. It aims at a disclosure of the potential of practical theology for contemporary boundary crossing ministry. In this series of essays we want to present to the reader the characteristic inter-disciplinary approach of the practical theology department of Tilburg University. Practical theology occurs in the continual interaction of theory and praxis, of hermeneutics and empirical research, of popular and academic, of theology and a variety of academic disciplines. Practical theology takes place òn the boundary with the other disciplines of theology and with the social sciences, on the boundary of church and society, of spiritual guidance and therapy, of education and spiritual development. Qualitative religious leadership means taking the lead in the search for, exchange of and expression of meaning, whilst being on the cutting edge of this multitude of boundary positions. It is to that end that the practical theologians of Tilburg and elsewhere accept the challenge to re-formulate their own sub-disciplinary approach of practical theology. The editors have challenged a number of theologians from the other theological disciplines in Tilburg to review and re-establish the boundaries of their own discipline in the perspective of practical theology.

The contributions have been grouped into three sections: context of, vision on and coping with boundaries. As far as the context is concerned, various contributions refer to contextual elements that indicate how contemporary pastoral ministry on the one hand and pastoral theology on the other are shaped today. The second part formulates the underlying vision with regard to boundaries: which innovative practical-theological tracks are being developed by religious leadership and practical theology, based on the experience of boundaries? How does this sensibility energise not only practical theology by theology as a whole? Finally there is the group 'coping with boundaries': which practical options can be recognised in contemporary pastoral care and pastoral theology? Which pastoral praxis is appropriate to which situation?

In the first contribution of the group 'context of boundaries', Leon Derckx explores the boundary between theory and praxis. He does this illustratively using the concept deadly sins. He develops an empirical instrument of research for measuring and evaluating the significance of these sins for the modern human person. He examines the extent to which this concept is able to clarify his/her concrete situation in modern society.

In a historical-systematic contribution Jan Jacobs, Dick Akerboom and Marcel Gielis examine the problem of the ecclesiastical ministry in the field of tension between service and authority. They approach the apparent differences on the basis of the Vatican II documents.

In his contribution Leo van der Tuin explores the boundary area of theology and ecology. In an empirical study he examines the extent to which education concerning the biblical view on nature influences the religious ecological awareness, and environmentally friendly behaviour of adults connected to this.

Marinus van Uden explores the boundary between healthy and unhealthy religious passion. In this passion the boundary between adaptation and defence is transcended, and people balance on the boundary of health and insanity.

Myriam Wijlens explores the boundary area between the priest and the professional lay person from a canonical perspective. She interpretes the relationship between both offices as being complimentary and based on mutual service to the world; each office has its own merits that do not compete against one another.

Hessel Zondag focuses on the task of the pastor in coping with traumas. Based on a traumatic event, a raging fire in a café in Volendam (the Netherlands), whereby many young people were seriously injured and mutilated and some died, he indicates how telling the story of what happened can act as a contribution to coping with post-traumatic stress.

In the first contribution of the group 'view on boundaries' Stefan Gärtner explores the significance of the boundary for poimenics by referring to Tillich. He views the boundary as 'locus theologicus'. When applied to pastoral care this means that the pastor concentrates on the boundaries that individuals experience in post-modern society, and that the individual learns to live in this boundary area between faith and society.

According to Jan Jans religious leaders play an important role in making connections with the transcendent dimension of reality and moral behaviour. He illustrates this with the parable of the Good Samaritan.

Wiel Logister shows that William of Ockham offers interesting viewpoints for the development of a communicative theology today. Encounter, temporariness and vulnerability are fundamental ideas in his philosophy. This philosophy wants to offer an answer to the fundamental questions that arise on that breaking point in time, among others inspired by the texts of Aristotle, discovered by Islamic scholars. Today as well the philosophy of religion faces such a breaking point.

Religion is a performative activity whereby, in this time of limited church involvement and limited participation in religious celebrations, there is ambiguity on the side of the person who, conscious of his/her disbelief, still participates in the celebration of the divine. Rein Nauta views this ambiguity as necessary and characteristic of the modern human person.

In his contribution Bert Roebben examines the challenge that lies in wait for church and faith in the modernisation of culture. This involves a transformation of Christian theological tradition, with the present-day quest for meaning in mind. The author is in favour of religious communication with young adults, because they are the ones who are radically involved in this quest – without being able to rely on religious socialisation and language from home.

Anton Vernooij sees in a special aspect of Tjeu van Knippenberg's work, his composing of liturgical music, an occasion to reflect on the importance of music as 'locus theologicus'.

The third group opens with Veerle Draulans' contribution. In her article she makes a contribution to the debate on the identity of the diaconate and the deacon. In doing so she emphasises the diaconate as being perfectly attuned to social commitment inspired by faith.

In their contribution Kristiaan Depoortere, Karlijn Demasure, and Anne Vandenhoeck go in search of a new liturgical form of the sacrament of reconciliation. They do this from the perspective of the perpetrator: in what way can this person grow when he/she, conscious of guilt and sin, asks forgiveness and reconciliation from the victim and God?

Ernest Henau examines the boundary area between religious leadership and the public media. In what way can justice be done to the legitimate expectations of religious leaders and the media at the same time? He describes the tension between the instrumental approach of the media by religious leaders and the viewer's desire for "human interest" programmes.

Sjaak Körver uses the concept professional biography as starting point for his contribution. On the basis of a report on supervision he shows that this concept is extremely usable in studying and making manageable the boundary between the individual and profession of the pastor.

Frans Maas makes use of one of Van Knippenberg's main concepts: spiritual guidance. In the context of Christian spirituality he asks and answers the questions: what is spiritual guidance, who is it aimed at and in what way does the guidance take place?

Karl-Wilhelm Merks discusses the concept of identity in the tension between interpreting it as drawing a boundary with regard to outsiders and belonging to a recognisable group. He emphasises the importance of identity bound organisations in a secularised society.

Pastors still spend most of their time on the liturgy, despite the differentiation in their ministry. In modern society this means that, according to Louis van Tongeren, in the training of the pastor not only should much attention be paid to the 'ars celebrandi', but also to the relevant tension between cultus and culture with regard to this.

This publication came about thanks to the valued co-operation of the Faculty of Theology of Tilburg University, who supported this work both morally and financially. The Congregation of Lazarists, Tjeu van Knippenberg's religious home base, provided a substantial subsidy for the realisation of this project. We also owe our thanks to LIT-Verlag in Münster (in the person of Dr. Michael J. Rainer) that was willing to include the book in its theological fund. Our special thanks goes to Mrs Nikki Idema, translator of most of the contributions, and to Mrs Caroline Jacobs, student assistant who dealt with the editing, corrections and lay out of the book. Finally we express our gratitude towards the various authors who have contributed to the success of this project. Their critical reflection on their fields of study based on the theme 'boundary crossing' resulted in interesting examples of innovative theological ideas. All this has lead to the completion of the tribute to their inspirer Tjeu van Knippenberg. They give back to him what they have received from him.

Tragic Life
The Deadly Sin as an Indicator of Actual Discontent

Leon Derckx

It was sometime in 1989. Nervous and with the necessary prejudices I took part in my first lecture at the Faculty of Theology in Tilburg. It was given by Professor Dr. Tjeu van Knippenberg. With much patience and attention he introduced us to the principles of practical theology. A discipline that pursues a 'continual methodical confrontation of actual human actions and the orientation to act as implied in Christian tradition' (Van Knippenberg 1989, 28). This thus means therefore that it balances on the boundary area of theory and practice.

A fascinating starting point that turned out to link up perfectly with my view on theology as a scientific discipline. During my training I have become more and more convinced that (theological) research should lead not only to the development and addition of nuances to existing theories, but that the knowledge gathered should at the same time be tested in a methodically responsible way for its power of expression and social relevance. Despite the fact that this view differs somewhat from the starting points of practical theology, both views are clearly aimed at empirical reality from a theoretical framework.

At the beginning of my own study especially, I regularly struggled with these views on science and theology. For example, I was soon faced with difficulties in processing theological concepts adequately in empirical research. The fact that the eight deadly sins were to play a major role in working out the problem formulated was certainly of importance. Apart from the scientific importance of these concepts, I whole-heartedly doubted the current value of these theological vices from the beginning. After all, did these categories not belong in a time when the church was prominently present in people's lives? It soon became obvious that the answer to this question could be both yes and no.

In my contribution to this special collection my aim is to emphasise the development of a sound research instrument for the measurement of the evaluation of deadly sins (in this case: pride, lust, greed, anger, gluttony, envy, apathy and melancholy). One of the first conditions to reaching this objective is to convince you on the basis of theoretical insights, of the current value of these theological categories. Therefore my ideas are in broad terms directed by two questions: 1) what makes deadly sins current and 2) to what extent is it possible to present these vices empirically?

After describing the seamy side of human development, I will pay attention to the possibility of considering the deadly sin as an indicator of actual discontent. I will contemplate questions such as: what actually are deadly sins, and why are they sinful? I will also explain in more detail the supposed current value of deadly sins based on a number of recent publications. Following this theoretical part, ways in which to present vices empirically are looked for. The conclusion will be that further research is desirable. The fact that the deadly sins appeal to the imagination of only a few does not mean that they have after all been disposed of as a diagnostic instrument.

1. The seamy side of human development

In order to find out what makes deadly sins current, I consider it useful to think shortly about the situation in which the people of today find themselves. Indeed, a broad description of developments that are taking place at present in (post)modern societies will possibly make the link with deadly sins (as an indicator of actual discontent) more plausible.

Research has shown that many European countries have to a large extent become individualised (Halman 1991). True this process has freed us from patronising institutions, but at the same time it makes a clear appeal on our ability to do things independently. In the meantime many enjoy the feeling of being free. It seems however that the space that has been gained for self-development has not unilaterally led to increased satisfaction in life. A similar argumentation can be applied to the relation between the level of prosperity and happiness in life.

Reality shows that spiritual well-being does not increase proportionate to an increase in the material standard of living. Having little or no money makes people unhappy, there is no doubt about that. But having too much money does not, probably against all expectations, lead to an increased feeling of prosperity and happiness. In any case, it appears that many people, despite the gains of modern times, experience a certain uneasiness. A sense of discomfort that is experienced by many in the form of loneliness, inner emptiness, apathy and constant feelings of meaninglessness (Nuber 1994). This ambivalence between prosperity and well-being provides food for thought.

There is, therefore an impression that life in an individualised society such as ours, is not only advantageous in terms of personal (choice) freedom, but that it also painfully confronts us with shortcomings; our own shortcomings that is! The security of a community in which status was dependent upon birth and trade is a thing of the past. Nowadays people are themselves to a large extent responsible for the success of their lives. One's own expectations and those of others are usually too high, whilst reality teaches us more than once that – despite our efforts – we do not have the supposed qualities and skills that enable us to realise our desired ideals. Apparently we are not the person we hoped to be.

It is possible that in the evaluation of individualisation too much emphasis was placed on the positive aspects of self-development, whereby the danger for possible disadvantages of what in principle was a valuable process were not stressed enough. In any case it seems that not only has individualisation led to an increase in self-development, but also to an excessive form of self-involvement (Taylor 1991). People set great store by the individual who corresponds to the ideals they dreamed of, instead of having an eye for the person who, in reality, manifests him/herself.

This gap between desire and reality is often confrontational. Because of an incapacity to deal with an insatiable desire for recognition and a confirmation of existence, modern man often hides his shortcomings behind a mask of pride and indifference towards him/herself and the environment. This mask is designed to offer protection against the unbearable thought of barely or not being noticed by others. This often also results in a threat to the appreciation of one's own existence. Apparently the reflection of the self through the eyes of another (Another) is a condition that is needed to be able to experience oneself and existence as meaningful (Burms 1992).

Up till now both philosophers and psychologists have proven to be capable of offering a contribution to the description and interpretation of the backgrounds of this human vulnerability (Baumeister 1987; Burms 1992; De Dijn 1998; Laing 1965; Sugerman 1976; Taylor 1991; Van Raalten 1965). However, we are interested in the contribution of theology in the clarification of the actual human situation. Who is modern man, and is it possible to interpret his actual discontent described theologically?

2. Deadly sins as an indicator of actual discontent

At a time in which people more than ever are driven by the desire for esteem and success, it is not natural to recognise one's own shortcomings. We enjoy praise for success, but prefer to deny every involvement when it comes to incapacity or failure. There are but a few who feel personally responsible for failing management, a serious disaster or a lingering problem in a relationship. Usually the splinter in the eye of others is pointed out, whilst the plank in one's own eye is ignored for as long as possible (Matthew 7, 3). One's own supremacy is rarely doubted.

The incapacity to recognise one's own shortcomings in for example the form of a confession of guilt, shows in actual fact just how sensitive the psychological constitution of people is. In any case it seems that people have a tendency to conceal their moments of failure from others. Not recognising the vulnerability of human life, and the ambition to display the ideal self-image that has been defined by the culture in which we live, causes us to live with half-truth. After all, besides the good and the perfect, shortcomings are also undeniably a part of our lives.

An important question now is whether the attitude of people described above can be interpreted theologically. Actually, what value would this issue add? There are enough psychological models available that offer a contribution from different perspectives to the clarification of the situation described anyway. What can theology add to these? For that matter, is theology of any importance in a society in which (parallel to increasing individualisation) the process of secularisation is rapidly taking place. Is the view of theology not something that is restricted to the experts? In any case, considering the time in which we live, they will have to make an effort to speak the language that coincides with the experiences of possible listeners. After all, it is only then that it will be possible to be heard.

In this respect the title of this section is remarkable and perhaps somewhat premature. Is it possible to take part in a social debate on actual discontent, if use is made of the deadly sins? Is there not so much resistance against these categories that theology is sure to be disqualified in advance as a serious discussion partner? Hopefully I will be able to persuade you otherwise in the course of this article. Let me start by considering the role deadly sins can play in the clarification of the life story. I will also mention two studies in which deadly sins are explicitly used as categories of actual discontent and existential uneasiness.

2.1. The deadly sin in the practice of confession

In the past the doctrinal authority of the Catholic Church has by stressing the confession of sins pointed out to us (sometimes more than we would wish for) the dark side of human existence. Not only was its psychological insight generally apt, the proposed therapy also had an effect. After all, in many cases the practice of confession was the perfect instrument for organising the personal life story from the viewpoint of human shortcomings (Van Knippenberg 2001; Nauta 1998). The confessor created an atmosphere of peace and gave the confessant the opportunity for breathing space. There was very little threat of losing respect following a confession. In the safety of the confessional box the mask of glamour could confidently be removed. Purification was the result.

The deadly sins played a major role in this type of structuring of the life story. They were conceived as being indications of intentions and behaviour that proved that man had lost sight of the right balance of life. The somewhat normative character of this expression will cause some to frown. After all, speaking of a 'right balance of life' implies a situation of wholeness. However, experience has taught us that many people who have temporarily lost balance, are fully aware that the path they are on at that time is the wrong one.

Thus most of us have a certain pre-understanding of the 'right' balance. It is believed that the deadly sins are able in this context to contribute to revealing irregularities on the personal path of life. A better insight in the nature of the wrong path (indicated with a specific deadly sin) makes it possible to re-evaluate the position that has been reached and to then consider taking an alternative route (for example through life in accordance with virtues). It is exactly this reason that makes it possible to consider deadly sins as an ancient diagnostic instrument, which can be used to typify human discontent.

2.2. Diagnostic value of the deadly sin

This view is supported by the findings of Backus (1969). In his book The Seven Deadly Sins: Their Meaning and Measurement he studies the suitability of the theological concept of sin as an area of psychological research. His starting point is the idea that the seven deadly sins can be interpreted as theoretical constructions that express a variety of human emotions, tendencies, choices and actions. More concretely, Backus asks himself to what extent the traditional deadly sins are a psychological constant with which, considering their age-long intrinsic stability, universal human character traits can possibly be specified. The results of his study confirm the suspicion that the descriptions given by theologians of the seven deadly sins are in actual fact general indications of shifts in human emotions. It is even possible to consider the deadly sins as 'primitive' indicators of psychopathology.

Capps (1993) chooses a different approach in The Depleted Self (1993). In order to find out to what extent Christians exhibit narcissistic characteristics, he carried out an empirical study amongst lay people and clergymen. He applied the deadly sins in his questionnaire, just as Backus did. Capps is convinced that the theological deadly sins are universal categories of existence that express undesirable attitudes, behaviour and threats that are characteristic of the situation in which people live (Capps 1987). In the evaluation of the data gathered Capps comes to the conclusion, referring to insights of Bursten (1973), that there are similarities between the evaluation of deadly sins, and the characteristics of the narcissistic personality (Halligan 1997).

These two studies confirm my belief that theology has a powerful instrument at its disposal that can be used to contribute to the debate in which uneasiness and vulnerability of modern man plays an important role. After all, the individual deadly sins have (still) not lost their expressiveness as age-old categories. Up till now they, for Backus and Capps in the form of psychological orientations on tragic life, are able to express human imperfection. I will come back to this later. For a thorough understanding it is, however, important to go into further detail on the meaning of deadly sins. So: what are deadly sins actually? Before I enter into this question, I will spend a little time on the essence of sin.

3. What are deadly sins actually?

The meanings that the Catholic Church has given to the concept of sin are in fact merely cautious nuances of a view on the moral nature of man, that was initiated by the Apostle Paul and later elaborated on by Augustine of Hippo. In this elaboration Augustine allowed himself to be inspired by 1) the story of Adam and Eve, 2) the idea that sin is an act of violence against a supposed divine order and 3) that this disorder can be passed on biologically (Farley 1990). This last paradigm especially has in the course of time lost much of its expressiveness. More and more people are questioning the idea that they are jointly responsible through inheritance for a mistake made by a human couple from the Old Testament. There is also more and more doubt as to the historical accuracy of the supposed existence of Adam and Eve. Rather they could be considered as the main characters in a mythological story about the blessings of paradise, and the indisputable human shortcomings that make an eternal stay there impossible; a theme that for that matter is central in several world religions, but which I will not discuss in the context of this article. After all, the main question is the extent to which deadly sins play a role in the lives of people nowadays. An important step in the direction of an answer is to look at that which will express the sin best. In order to do this I will briefly mention the interpretations of a number of authors. Following this, I shall mention the distinctions between sin and deadly sin.

3.1. The concept of sin in a broader perspective

Usually the theological concept of sin is used to express actions that are in defiance of a supposed holy cosmic order. This would thus be a (conscious) violation of divine laws and the moral code (Brink 1958). It is 'the forgetting of the divine' (Bolle 1977, 235) and the desire to make one's own decisions on life and death. Sin therefore corresponds to ignoring God's all-powerfulness (Bleibtreu 1993). The presumption of one's own greatness causes man to turn away from God and His creation.

Recent literature shows that some theologians have the desire to place the concept of sin in a broader perspective. They no longer connect sin exclusively with a broken relationship with God, but attempt to relate this concept to the actual situation in which people find themselves (Sievernich 1982). Most of them reserve the concept of sin to describe the general brokeness of human existence. Sin therefore not only indicates disobedience, disbelief and lawlessness, but also missing the mark, human shortcomings, wastage of given resources, straying and the fragmentation of the whole.

In this respect Plantinga (1995) speaks of 'shalom-breaking'. He aptly expresses in this way the disturbance introduced by man of the given unity. Through a belief in one's own supremacy, sinful man loses sight of reality and through this also of his/her destiny. Howsepian (1997) is even of the opinion that sinful activities are ultimately an expression of deep psychosis, whilst the controversial psychologist Laing (1965) interprets the concept of sin as an equivalent for 'madness'. It is in any case clear that these approaches lead to a continuing psychologicalisation of the concept of sin (Backus 1969; Capps 1993; Hiltner 1989; Lemly 1981; Schimmel 1997; Sugerman 1976; Tjalsma 1931).

Menninger also gives a non-theological interpretation of sin by considering it as a sign of the incapacity to actually give form to an individually or socially supported moral ideal. According to him sin is essentially 'a refusal of the love of others' (Menninger 1973, 19; Van Heijst 1995). Capps adds to this by suggesting that each sin is based on a personal decision and that it thus expresses a wrong attitude towards life (Capps 1987). Should this attitude actually be governed by feelings of discontent (as I mentioned above), and thus indeed cause people to tend to compensate the vulnerability experienced by striving for power, esteem and success, then sin is possibly a fitting image for the human shortcomings experienced (Ramshaw-Schmidt 1987).

This image can then be explained by regarding the uneasiness experienced as a result of the brokeness between the essence and existence of human life (Tillich 1959). Or to put it more clearly: man is apparently not who he/she was meant to be. This 'meant' betrays a professed model of successful human existence. From a Christian perspective this expresses the idea that man, as a supposed image of God, is called in word and deed to aid in the creation of God's Kingdom. Pannenberg (1980) is also of the opinion that man has a mission in life. However, man tends to forget his purpose as a result of which he lives according to his own judgement. In practice this usually means that he/she alienates him/herself from the light and rapidly ends up on the wrong path. The opportunity to build a relationship with God, oneself and with others is also seriously hindered because of this. Lonely and full of doubt man continues on his way; continually in search of opportunities to escape from fear. The excesses in Western societies, varying from the kick of cocaine to brief sexual contacts, could possibly be interpreted as attempts to find something to hold onto on the rugged path of life.

Blinded by the desire for power and esteem, but actually driven by feelings of fear and emptiness, man stumbles on. Fleeing for the opportunity to be who he/she really is (Nauta 1994). Thus it is possible to interpret sin as 'an apparent search for oneself, self-idolisation, radical independence (but) in reality: hostility and objection towards oneself and creation' (Haring 1959, 460). Perhaps the concept of sin can best be interpreted as the symbol of human brokeness. But what then are deadly sins?

3.2. Characteristics of the deadly sin

Many sins used to be classified according to the extent to which they were a hindrance to the realisation of being good and to justice. The number of offences, their seriousness and reprehensible disposition played a role in this. Besides these classifications sins were classed under seven categories of deadly sins. The addition 'deadly' can be cause for confusion and requires some explanation. After all, this does not necessarily express the supposed degree of intrinsic wickedness, but rather points out the influence of deadly sins on other vices.

According to the 'Dictionary of Theology' the deadly sin has a certain objective causality. This means that it has the characteristic of being able to steer other sins so as to reach a certain evil objective. Or to put it more precisely: a deadly sin is a sin 'that *by virtue of its own essence* [cursive lines as in original, L.D.] has the characteristic of being able to cause the undertaking of other *certain* sins as motives of these, because it is precisely these other sins that, also *by virtue of their own nature*, possess (an) aptitude for aiding or contributing to committing deadly sins, that is to say, to reach the individual objective of the deadly sins' (Brink 1958, 2271).

In order to create some structure in the multitude of vices, theologians have in the past compiled lists of circumstances that tempt people to sin most. Usually the uncontrolled pursuit of praise and honour is at the top of the list. This pursuit is usually described as pride and is often considered as the most influential sin (Brink 1958; Menninger 1973). The intemperate pursuit of the preservation of the individual counts as gluttony, whilst the disorderly pursuit of sexual pleasure is interpreted as lust or impurity. The excessive pursuit of, and one-sided acquirement of material goods or riches is registered as covetousness, and not realising a certain objective due to the physical exertion is the sin of spiritual half-heartedness, also known as apathy. The failure to compliment others out of fear of diverting the attention from one's own excellence corresponds to envy. Offering violent resistance to this is known as anger (Brink 1958; Capps 1993; Häring 1959).

In this presentation I have restricted myself to only seven deadly sins. However, according to Capps it is, based on tradition, justifiable to add an eighth deadly sin to this list, namely, 'melancholy'. For a precise description of the backgrounds and development of the number of deadly sins I refer to Capps (1987, 1993) and Backus (1969). I now want to concentrate on the question of what makes deadly sins sinful.

4. What makes deadly sins sinful?

An awkward question, more so because the concept of sin just as life itself is, as regards interpretation and meaning, always in motion. At a time when God is thought to be dead, it is for example no longer natural to connect (deadly) sins with guilt and penance. Now the traditional image of God no longer plays a part in the heads and hearts of modern man, breaking divine laws and rules is no longer a reason for reflection and repentance.

The fact that the role God plays in our Western society is becoming less and less evident does not mean that the concept of sin has also lost its power of expression. On the contrary even. After all, we have just seen that many theologians are convinced of the importance of deadly sins, and that they continue to succeed in relating the essence of deadly sins in an enlightening way to actual social developments. In the past decades the concept of sin has more and more often been considered as a symbol of the human incapacity to enter into a relationship with others, with oneself and (in view of the time in which we live) in the last place with God. This incapacity has ground in common with a situation that is often referred to using the (philosophical) concept 'alienation'.

The background can be explained using insights from anthropology. Usually alienation is used to express the field of tension that exists between a supposed essence of human existence and factors that stand in the way of a realisation of this essence. It is important to underline that the essence of human existence is not depicted as a static greatness; it is also not necessarily based on a divine ideal image (Dziewas 1995). Rather, it is the given socio-cultural or economic circumstances that restrict the further realisation of dimensions of human existence. So the alienation that can be a result of this is therefore related especially to the incapacity to be truly human.

It is this dichotomy between essence and existence that according to Tillich (1959) can be indicated using the concept of sin. During his journey through life man is distracted by many temptations, which have caused him to lose sight of his real destination. By speaking in terms of 'destination' a definite sense of life is actually insinuated. However, in an age in which the traditional beacons of faith are lacking, man is at the mercy of his own sense of direction. An underestimated task. In the desperation at not finding one's destination oneself, alternative routes are sought. Seven of these, in the form of deadly sins, are the main subjects of this article.

The unbearable confrontation with the finiteness of life has, partly under the influence of secularisation (understood as the process of the declining relevance of God in person and society), only strengthened the feeling of vulnerability. The idea of being supported by a good God has practically disappeared. In his pursuit of something to hold onto man has taken place on the throne that actually belongs to God. The loss of the right relations becomes a fact in this way of identifying with God. Man behaves arrogantly, thus giving the impression of being completely in control of life. However, more often than not the reverse is true. Global news and our personal worries are evidence of our undeserved pride.

Formulated in this way the seven deadly sins express the incapacity of people to cope reasonably with the gift of freedom. This incapacity is obvious in for example the excessive pursuit of material gain, the continual need for brief sexual contacts as a reaction to an intense lack of warmth and affection, the reluctance to be concerned about the welfare of others in an unselfish way, the persistent envy of the belongings of others and a disproportional anger that drowns this feeling of powerlessness. In short these are all wrong tracks that 'promise' us something to hold onto, but that in fact prevent us from being truly human!

5. The current value of deadly sins

Many people seem to be increasingly opposed to, according to present standards, the improper interference of religious authorities in the private life of citizens. Modern man aims towards autonomy and therefore no longer wishes to be burdened with irrational, and sometimes outdated opinions on human existence. The fact that the church's influence is dwindling does not mean that people have at the same time also stopped expressing religious ideas, feelings and desires. So man has not so much shut himself off from the religious dimension of existence but rather, from the sometimes distorted and absolute interpretation that religious institutions have given to this reality.

At the same time this opinion seems to relate to the reception of the concept of sin. After all, there is reason to suppose that this category, burdened by religious tradition, no longer appeals to the imagination of modern man. On the contrary. For example, in the summer of 2001 the popular weekly magazine 'Flair' published a series of articles on the seven deadly sins to find out to what extent these still played a role in the lives of its readers. At the end of each article one's own (sinful) position could be determined by means of a number of questions. Besides this example the concept of sin has up till now been the starting point for literary works, popular scientific studies, film, drama, the art of poetry and painting. A short exploration of the Internet is enough to convince you of the current value of this age-old category.

A careful translation to suit people's social environment is essential if the power of expression of the deadly sin is to be preserved (Van Heijst 1995). One of the ways of doing this is to try to detach the essence of sin from what in the meantime has for many become a meaningless ecclesiastic connection, and to then transfer this to a more existing context. Up till now several authors have succeeded in freeing the concept of sin from the sometimes aggravating moral connotations. Sin can then, as we have observed, be just as much connected to insights from psychology or anthropology for example. In order to prove the necessity for the (continual) updating of deadly sins I wish, in spite of the link with morality, to allow myself to be inspired by insights as these apply in ethics.

5.1. Limited eternity value

Ethics can, as a philosophical specialisation, be considered as a reflection on morality, which is built up of a set of values and norms related to these values. As far as the interpretation of norms goes, this is by definition dependant on time and space, making it impossible to formulate norms with eternity value (Dupuis 1993). It is quite possible that through developments in society people no longer recognise a norm and the way in which it provides an interpretation to the value behind it. Indeed this does not mean that the value on which the norm involved is based has lost its validity forever. Though it might be necessary to re-interpret this value (as an expression of what people find important), and to provide it with objectives to act or in other words norms that are probably better able to put the value at issue into practice (Jans 1992).

Just as moral norms are means of realising moral values (for example a just society), so are deadly sins categories that are used to indicate the way in which a moral and consequently psychological (Backus 1969) straying (for example the disruption of the relation of justness) can disadvantageously influence human life and welfare. Formulated in this way deadly sins appear, partly due to their negative emotional value, to be a good means of indicating the limits of human actions. Limits that if exceeded result in missing the straight and narrow or better still the right middle.

Despite the obvious aversion many people show on hearing the words sin or deadly sin, the doctrinal authority of the Catholic Church appears to be clutching onto the Pauline-Augustine description of sin (Catechism of the Catholic Church 1994, 1846-1876). According to Van Heijst (1995), 138) this contrast between concept and experience has led to a 'hermeneutic erosion' of the theological concept of sin. In relation to this Farley (1990) points to the importance of breaking open and carefully confronting the paradigms on which the traditional concept of sin is based with liberal, secular and psychological insights.

In order to make sure that the people of today feel attracted towards the corrective effect of deadly sins, it is important to realise the traditional interpretation of these. In doing this it is important not to slip back into the repetition of outdated statements. These belong after all to an age that is no longer ours. Modern (practical) theology is thus faced with the challenge of connecting the interpretation of the concept of sin with people's actual social situation. Empirical methods and techniques can be used to do this

6. The search for a sound instrument of research

We have seen that more and more authors have become convinced of the current value of the theological concept of sin. Some have already been mentioned, others are easy to find (Axt-Piscalar 1996; Dziewas 1994; Gestrich 1989; Peters 1994; Ramsay 1998; Sievernich 1982). Most of them confirm the idea that it is true that the continuing secularisation of our society has resulted in sin as a theological concept being less prominently present in people's lives, but that despite this it has not lost its diagnostic value for insight in oneself. A remarkable observation that in my opinion has very little empirical strength.

In my search for fitting literature I came across only two authors who involve the concept of sin in an empirical study. You have already become acquainted with them. The first, Backus (1969), asks himself in his study The Seven Deadly Sins: Their Meaning and Measurement to what extent the deadly sins can be understood as expressions of people's psychological characteristics. The second author, Capps (1993), makes a connection in his work The Depleted

Self. Sin in a Narcissistic Age between the rating of the concept of sin and characteristics of narcissistic vulnerability (as an expression of actual discontent). This vulnerability expresses the idea that hidden behind the self-satisfied attitude of the narcissistic person, there are feelings of doubt and uncertainty (Berthold 1996; Capps 1993; Lasch 1980; Lemly 1981; Sugerman 1976). Feelings that lead to shame and that are therefore preferably kept hidden.

In the past years both authors have in their own way inspired me in setting up a practical-theological study based on the relationship between deadly sins and existential uneasiness or discontent. In the theoretical area I have let myself be inspired especially by the insights of Capps (1993). If his findings concerning the presence of narcissistic characteristics in pastoral practice are correct, and shame and narcissism are indeed two sides of the same coin (Lewis 1995; Morrison 1989), then the question arises how pastoral care – that is aimed especially at the problem of guilt – can react best to a situation in which shame is involved. There are after all considerable differences in the way guilt and shame are experienced (Derckx 2001).

I myself am convinced that defining a problem selectively usually benefits the quality of research work. So instead of involving all the possible variables that play a role in the ideas of Capps in a further study (i.e. individualisation, guilt, shame, narcissism, deadly sins), and then on the basis of the information gathered developing an instrument for pastoral care in which not guilt but shame is predominate, I have decided to restrict myself (as PhD-student) to two concepts, that is: deadly sin and feelings of discontent. Hopefully this restriction on the research variables will benefit the quality of the whole. However, for this moment another restriction is necessary. In this article I will concentrate on the concept of sin only.

In compiling a questionnaire in which the assessment of deadly sins was most important I consulted Backus especially. At first the questionnaire compiled by him appeared to be good to use for my subject of research. However, a careful analysis of the items has led me to compose my own 'list of sins'. This made it possible to reduce the gap present between Backus' use of language and the supposed experiences of respondents. The starting point was the idea that a language that the chosen research population cannot associate with could have a disadvantageous influence the validity of a measurement.

The definitions given by Capps (1993) of the separate deadly sins have influenced me in putting them into practice. Contrary to Backus (and many others) Capps distinguishes not seven, but (in imitation of Cassianus 360-435 a. Christ) eight deadly sins. After a period of brainstorming I finally selected ten questions per deadly sin, and presented these in the form of a questionnaire to 260 students and 62 lecturers (incl. PhD students) from a Dutch faculty of theology.

6.1. Comments on the measurement (of interpretations) of deadly sins

The objective of this undertaking was primarily to gain insight into the usefulness of the items formulated in a relatively short period of time. By relating the scores of the students and lectures to each other I hoped to end up with four items per sin that I could use for further empirical research. The future measuring instrument for deadly sins would thus add up to thirty-two items.

The students were invited by letter to take part in a trial study of 'attitudes to life', and were asked to rate 80 questions on a scale ranging from 'totally agree' (1) to 'totally disagree' (5). On the other hand instead of being asked to rate statements, lecturers were asked to recognise deadly sins. They were given the task of putting a cross by the deadly sin that they felt was involved after reading an item. Definitions of the eight deadly sins were enclosed to help. In this way it became possible to determine to what extent an item actually referred to the concept of sin behind it.

Both groups were asked to put the completed list in a pigeonhole within three weeks. The percentages of response for students and lecturers were respectively 20% and 22%. An unexpectedly low response considering the congeniality of the questionnaires. In my search for a possible explanation for this high level of non-response I was helped by remarks on the lists returned. For example members of the university staff asked themselves to what extent particular items were actually the deadly sins in practice. It is possible that the prospective respondents of this research population decided not to take part for the very reason that deadly sins are not easy to recognise.

The reactions from students showed that some found it difficult to distinguish between the subject of research and the researcher. Most of their 'judgements' were very straight. Questions that for example involved the deadly sin 'lust' must, due to their sexist character, automatically stem from a male mind. The vulgar and offensive character of many of the questions apparently disturbed many students. This was for some of them a reason to hand in an empty questionnaire. There was also someone who compared me (as the compiler of the list) with an unreliable salesman who, out of self-interest, slyly attempted to mislead potential clients. Finally, another hoped with a certain sincerity that I myself had some idea of what the study should actually be about.

Some of the reactions were confronting and aimed at me personally. Yet I can imagine the aversion of the students particularly. The letter of introduction that was handed out together with the questionnaire did after all suggest that 'attitudes to life' would be the subject of research. I had neglected to mention that deadly sins acted as starting point for this. This was, however, a choice I made and not a coincidence. Indeed, I suspected that open use of the concept of sin, particularly because of the often-negative connotation, would possibly prevent prospective respondents from actually answering the questions (Capps 1993). This was obviously a wrong judgement.

The intrinsic negative character of deadly sins makes friendly and virtuous formulations impossible. It is therefore understandable that people get the impression that in assessing attitudes to life I concentrate one-sidedly on matters such as sex, money, envy, gluttony and such like. Further research is desirable in order to determine to what extent the reactions of the respondents are not expressions of the disgust at being confronted with personal deficiencies. This could be an indirect 'measurement' of deadly sins! Partly as a result of the particularly low response, I have decided not to carry out a detailed statistical analysis.

6.2. Results of the trial study explained

The above findings do not mean that the trial study has been done for nothing. On the contrary. It has after all provided me with useful information concerning putting deadly sins into practice. It is simply impossible to define the empirical strength of a set of questions from an office. In my discussion of the findings I will restrict myself to an analysis of the deadly sin that in view of the reactions received aroused most opposition from respondents. These were without a doubt the questions that were asked in the framework of the deadly sin 'lust'.
This deadly sin is described by Capps as (including a small adjustment I myself made) a manipulative and lustful attitude, whereby others are considered as an object (of lust) for one's own satisfaction in particular (1993, 49). In formulating the questions attention was paid especially to the degree to which they expressed indicators such as 'manipulation', 'desire', 'lust object' and 'self-interest'. Of the total number of ten questions presented to lecturers on lust, the percentage of recognition was 81% or higher. The question: 'I regularly try to placate others in order to get what I want' was clearly out of place with a recognition score of 33%. Questions with a score above 95% were for example: 'I would not like to give up my sexual fantasies and pleasures' (95%), 'I enter into some relationships for sex' (95%), 'I can hardly keep my eyes off beautiful men and women' (100%), 'I like watching films with erotic scenes' (100%), 'I sometimes fantasise about having an affair' (100%) and 'I am sometimes nice to my partner so that I can make love' (100%).
The definite selection of items arose by linking up the recognition percentage of lecturers with the scores of students. An item that on the one hand was connected by the majority of university staff with a specific deadly sin (in this case high recognition percentage), whilst on the other hand according to the data gathered from students there seemed to be a great connection with the way in which deadly sins were put into practice (in this case high homogeneity; preferably minimum alpha .80) could then, due to proved validity, be included in a questionnaire for future research. The following figure shows which questions were selected in this way.

Lust (according to Capps 1993)		Indicators
'A manipulative and lustful attitude, whereby others are considered as an object (of lust) for one's own satisfaction in particular'.		- Manipulation - Desire - Lust object - Self-interest

Questions	Recognition	Homogeneity index alpha .79
1. I am sometimes nice to my partner so that I can make love.	100%	--
2. I sometimes fantasise about having an affair.	100%	X
3. I like watching films with erotic scenes.	100%	X
4. I can hardly keep my eyes off beautiful men and women.	100%	X
5. I would not like to give up my sexual fantasies and pleasures.	95%	X
6. I cannot resist seducing others.	89,5%	--
Additional item		
7. I am regularly distracted by erotic fantasies during the day.	---	--

Figure 1.

It is clear that 100% of the university staff recognise the questions 1 up to and including 4 as the deadly sin 'lust' [...] as described by Capps. It is clear also that questions 2, 3, 4 and 5 result in a reasonably high Alpha (.79). This means that there is an obvious connection between the questions formulated and the sin construct behind these (1.00 is optimal). In selecting valid items for the purpose of further research it is on the basis of this combination of scores, reasonable to use the questions 2, 3, 4 and 5. True question 1 has a high recognition percentage, but together with the other items it causes a reduction of the Alpha. Also, many respondents dismissed this item because of its (according to them) particularly impertinent character. This qualification was not present in the other items.

Ultimately, in the framework of further research on the experience and rating of deadly sins, a different set of questions was chosen. Only two of the items (two and four) with a high recognition percentage and a convincing Alpha have been selected. The other two questions (one and three) have been replaced by items (six and seven) that when related back to the definition used of lust, in my opinion do more justice to the obsessive character of this deadly sin. After all it is not so much emotions whereby there is a desire to love the other that are involved, but rather the uncontrolled and compulsive pursuit of seduction and coarse eroticism.

7. Rehabilitation of the deadly sin: wrong path as a guide

In this article I have concentrated on the significance of deadly sins as the subject of practical-theological research. In doing this I started from the idea that theological research, besides a scientific relevance, should at the same time make a contribution to the clarification of the human situation in a given socio-cultural context. This desire to link theory and practice does in fact coincide with the intentions of theology in general and practical-theology in particular. It is the latter variety that sets itself the aim of repeatedly building a bridge between insights from the Christian tradition and people's concrete social situation. Because of the midway position that it occupies it is not by coincidence that 'the borderline' is used as a metaphorical indication for the workplace of those who implement this theological discipline (Van Knippenberg 1989).

Despite the opposition the concept of sin arouses in many people of today, it appears that this age-old construct has again become a subject of attention. Not only do theologians attempt to realise the concept of sin; psychologists, journalists, film makers and writers also allow themselves to this day to be inspired by categories that evidently hold a universal truth. The detailed report on deadly sins in 'Flair' surprised me most. As far as I am concerned this is a sign that the editors of this popular weekly magazine are also convinced of the current value of deadly sins. It does seem though that deadly sins have lost part of their religious strength. The fact is that they are used more and more often to express individual and socio-cultural wrongs or digressions. These are actions or convictions that seriously disturb the pursuit of well-balanced relations.

Due to the universal power of expression of deadly sins, it seems to me to be justifiable to aim for a kind of rehabilitation of these theological categories that still express forms of human shortcomings. One way of doing this is to make the deadly sin the subject of practical-theological research. In this article I have in brief reported a trial study of the recognition and rating of deadly sins. The results indicate that it is possible to gain an empirical picture of aspects of deadly sins. Further research is desired in which the development of a reliable measuring instrument should in principle be most important. Only then does it become possible to find out the extent to which deadly sins are actually expressions of psychopathology (Backus 1969) or of feelings of discontent experienced [...] by people of today (Capps 1993).

In his article 'Breathing-space in confession' (2000), Van Knippenberg argues in favour of the revaluation of the practice of confession. This opportunity provided by the church to bring order to one's life story from the perspective of a personal shortcoming appears (probably against all expectations) to connect well with the ever present need of people to evaluate the path of life that has been taken every now and then. However, it is unlikely that confession (just as the deadly sin) will return in its traditional form. There is too much opposition.

A realisation of the practice of confession whereby its essence is not lost is therefore desirable.

Use of deadly sins in this context could also be considered. After all these categories continue to have the ability to make a contribution to the clarification and evaluation of the actual path of life. Deadly sins can be applied here as gauging points that show us in which capacity our life has reached a dead end. Insight makes further consideration of alternative routes possible. It is because (some) consciousness of the personal situation precedes eventual change, that deadly sins can also be considered as 'self-confrontations' which stimulate us to life without straying and preoccupation.

References

Axt-Piscalar, C. 1996. *Ohnmächtige Freiheit. Studien zum Verhältnis von Subjektivität und Sünde bei August Tholuck, Julius Müller, Sören Kierkegaard und Friederich Schleiermacher.* Tübingen: Mohr (Paul Siebeck).

Backus, D.W. 1969. *The Seven Deadly Sins: Their Meaning and Measurement.* Michigan: University Microfilms.

Baumeister, R.F. 1987. How the Self Became a Problem: a Psychological Review of Historical Research. *Journal of Personality and Social Psychology* 52: 163-176.

Berthold, F. 1986. Theology and Self-understanding: The Christian Model of Man as Sinner. Pp.11-32 in *The Dialogue Between Theology and Psychology,* edited by P. Homans. Chicago/London.

Bleibtreu-Ehrenberg, G. 1993. Sunde/Schuld. Pp.288-296 in *Worterbuch der Religionspsychologie,* edited by S. Dunde. Gütersloh.

Bolle, K.W. 1967. Sin. Pp. 235 in *New Catholic Encyclopedia.* Washington.

Brink, H., eds. 1958. Hoofdzonde en Zonde. Pp. 2270-2273 and 5028-5056 in *Theologisch Woordenboek.* Roermond.

Burms, A. 1992. Autonomie: het ideaal van een narcistische cultuur. *Psychologie en Maatschappij* 58: 28-38.

Bursten, B. 1973. Some Narcissistic Personality Types. *International Journal of Psychoanalysis* 54: 287-300.

Capps, D. 1987. *Deadly Sins and Saving Virtues.* Philadelphia: Fortress.

Capps, D. 1993. *The Depleted Self. Sin in a Narcissistic Age.* Minneapolis: Fortress Press.

Derckx, L. 2001. Zonde en narcisme. De invloed van narcistische kwetsbaarheid op de hedendaagse religieuze communicatie. Pp. 114-130 in *Redden pastores het? Religieus leiderschap aan het begin van de eenentwintigste eeuw,* edited by K. Sonnberger, H. Zondag, and F. van Iersel. Budel.

Dijn, H. de 1998. Spiritualiteit en realisme. Pp. 9-27 in *Van zelfontplooiing tot spiritualiteit*, edited by H. de Dijn et al. Kapellen.

Dupuis, H. 1993. *Goed te leven. Reflecties op de moraal*. Baarn: Ten Have.

Dziewas, R. 1995. *Die Sünde der Menschen und die Sündhaftigkeit sozialer Systeme. Überlegungen zu den Bedingungen und Möglichkeiten theologischer Rede von Sünde aus sozialtheologischer Perspektive*. Munster: Lit.

Farley, E. 1990. Sin/Sins. Pp.1173-1176 in *Dictionary of Pastoral Care and Counseling*, edited by R.J. Hunter et al. Nashville.

Häring, B. 1959. *De wet van Christus. Een katholieke moraaltheologie voor priesters en leken*. Antwerpen: Standaard Boekhandel.

Halman, L. 1991. *Waarden in de Westerse Wereld. Een internationale exploratie van de waarden in de westerse samenleving*. Tilburg: Tilburg University Press.

Halligan, F. 1997. Narcissism, Spiritual Pride, and Original Sin. *Journal of Religion and Health* 36(4): 305-319.

Heijst, A. van 1995. Zonde als verstoring van verhoudingen. Pp. 138-153 in *Uit op geluk*, edited by K.-W. Merks and F.J.H. Vosman. Baarn.

Hiltner, S. 1989. Sin: Theological and Psychological Perspectives. Pp.23-36 in *Counseling and the Human Predicament. A Study of Sin, Guilt and Forgiveness*, edited by L. Aden and D.G. Benner. Michigan.

Howsepian, A. 1997. Sin and Psychosis. Pp. 264-281 in *Limning the Psyche. Explorations in Christian Psychology*, edited by R. Roberts and M. Talbot. Michigan.

Jans, J. 1992. De menselijke mens. De fundering van ethisch waarden en normen. Pp.17-24 in *Waarden in de vrije val? Over morele opvoeding vandaag* (Korrelcahier 5), edited by B. Roebben and R. Spijkers. Averbode/ Boxtel.

Knippenberg, M. van 1989. *Grenzen: werkplaats van pastoraaltheologen*. Kampen: Kok.

Knippenberg, M. van 2000. Op verhaal komen in de biechtstoel. *De Bazuin* 3: 18-20.

Laing, R.D. 1965. *The Divided Self: An Existential Study in Sanity and Madness*. Harmondsworth: Penguin books.

Lasch, C. 1979. *The Culture of Narcissism. American Life in an Age of Diminishing Expectations*. New York: Warner Books.

Lemly, S.E. 1981. *Narcissism and the Condition of Sin in the Theology of Paul Tillich: Implications for the Church and Christian Education for Young Adults*. Michigan: University Microfilms international.

Lewis, M. 1995. *Shame: The Exposed Self*. New York: Free Press.

Menninger, K. 1973. *Whatever Became of Sin?* New York: Hawthorn Books.

Morrison, A.P. 1989. *Shame. The Underside of Narcissism*. Hillsdale: The Analytic Press.

Nauta, R. 1994. De tragiek van de zonde: over het beeld van de mens bij Eugen Drewermann. *Kerk en Theologie* 45(2): 101-113.

Nauta, R. 1998. De biecht is een fantastisch instrument voor een narcistische cultuur. *De Bazuin* 81(14): 32.

Nuber, U. 1993. *De valkuil van het egoïsme Zelfverwerkelijking en eenzaamheid.* Baarn: Ambo.

Pannenberg, W. 1980. *Wat is de mens? De moderne antropologie in het licht van de theologie.* Baarn: Ten Have.

Peters, T. 1994. *Sin: Radical Evil in Soul and Society.* Michigan: Grand Rapids.

Plantinga, C. 1995. *Not the Way It's Supposed to be. A Breviary of Sin.* Michigan: Grand Rapids.

Raalten, F. van 1965. *Schaamte en existentie. Een onderzoek naar de plaats en de werking van de schaamte in de menselijke existentie in het bijzonder met betrekking tot het werk van Søren Kierkegaard.* Nijkerk: Callenbach.

Ramsay, N.J. 1998. *Pastoral Diagnosis. A Resource for Ministries of Care and Counseling.* Minneapolis: Fortress Press.

Ramshaw-Schmidt, G. 1987. De zonde: een van de beelden voor de menselijke beperktheid. *Concilium* 23(2): 10-18.

Schimmel, S. 1997. *The Seven Deadly Sins. Jewish, Christian, and Classical Reflections on Human Psychology.* Oxford: Oxford University Press.

Sievernich, M. 1982. *Schuld und Sünde in der Theologie der Gegenwart.* Frankfurt am Main: Josef Knecht.

Sugerman, S. 1976. *Sin and Madness: Studies in Narcissism.* Philadelphia: Westminster Press.

Tjalsma, P.D. 1931. *Zondebesef en zondeleer. Een psychologisch-dogmatische studie.* Assen: Van Gorcum.

Taylor, C. 1991. *De malaise van de moderniteit.* Kampen: Kok Agora.

Tillich, P. 1959. *Theology of Culture.* New York: Oxford University Press.

The Leading Role of the Ecclesiastical Ministry
Exercise of Power or Willingness to Serve?

Jan Jacobs, Dick Akerboom, and Marcel Gielis

1. Introduction

Shortly before the opening of the Second Vatican Council (1962-1965) the then bishop of Breda, Mgr. De Vet made a prophetic statement: "The ecclesiastical office should become a 'ministerium' instead of a 'dominium'". It is generally accepted that the Council has indeed interpreted the particular, that is to say the ordained office as being a service to Church and world. In a recent interview, however, Cardinal Simonis seems to dissociate himself from such views in his statement: "The Church is not a democracy; service is service to Christ as Lord of the Church". At first glance there is a fundamental contrast between the statements of both church leaders. In this contribution it is our aim to show – in the light of what the Second Vatican Council has said about the "power" of the ecclesiastical (ministerial) office – that this contradiction is merely ostensible. It is our opinion that ministry, which according to the Council is invested with a spiritual power given by divine providence in Christ, is a service to the church community and to the world. To put it precisely ministry exercises power, rendering a service to Christ as Lord of the Church and effecting His dominion. After all the dominion of Christ embodies the salvation of Church and world. In this contribution we shall explain the above proposition, which implies the difference between common and particular or special office.

In the first part of this article we sketch the theological and canonical problems concerning ministry, power and service as put on the eve of Vatican II. In the light of the above discussion we then research the Council doctrine on ministerial or hierarchical priesthood in its relation to the general or communal priesthood of all the faithful, on the power of the ecclesiastical office and on the ecclesiastical office as ministry. In doing so we base our opinion on the constitution *Lumen Gentium (LG)* and on the decrees *Christus Dominus (CD)*, *Presbyterorum Ordinis (PO)* and *Apostolicam Actuositatem (AA)*[1]. It appears

---

[1] For the original Latin text we use the editions of the separate council documents with the Dutch translation, published in 1964-1966 by the Katholiek Archief: *Constituties en decreten van het Tweede Vaticaans Oecumenisch Concilie*, parts II – XVI, Amersfoort: De Horstink, usually s.d. The first council document was published elsewhere: *Constitutie over de H. Liturgie. Text = Tijdschrift voor Liturgie*, 48 (1964), no. 1. For the English translation we use: 'Vatican II 1962-1965', in: *Decrees of the Ecumenical Councils*, ed. Norman P. Tanner, vol. 2: *Trent to Vatican II*, London: Sheed & Ward – Washington: Georgetown University Press, 1990, p. 815-1135.

from this historical-theological analysis of Council texts that Vatican II always calls the special ecclesiastical office a ministry, even though according to that same Council this office is characterised by a sacred power. Apparently the Council therefore sees no difference between the exercise of power and the willingness to serve. Finally in the third part – following a short overview of the various views concerning the distinction between common and particular priesthood – we will go further into the discussion on the relation of power and ministry as pursued in the first post-conciliar decade; in this discussion the paradoxical relation between 'power' and 'service' that Vatican II (in the line of renewed theological views) had introduced in the executive ecclesiastical function was cleared. Not only do we attempt here to shed new light on the way in which church leaders are expected to carry out their pastoral responsibility, but also to show which contribution can be made to the correct exercise of this responsibility on the basis of the history of church and theology [2].

2. The theological and canonical discussion on office, power and ministry before Vatican II

In order to gain insight in the discussion on office on the eve of Vatican II we can restrict ourselves to two authors: the ecclesiologist and ecumenical theologian Yves Congar and the canonist Klaus Mörsdorf. Both authors have engaged themselves in the problems of the threefold office and the power (or powers) in the Church. Both react to developments in church views that have taken place in the Catholic Church especially after the Council of Trent (1545-1563). Congar has, moreover, held an impressive plea for the view of the particular or hierarchical ministry as service.

2.1. The two powers of the ecclesiastical hierarchy

Since the Middle Ages two hierarchies are distinguished in the Church: the hierarchy of Orders and the hierarchy of Jurisdiction[3]. This distinction is connected to that between the two powers of the hierarchy: the power of Orders

---

[2] Cf. for parts 2 and 3 of this contribution: M. Gielis, 'Het diaconaat, het wijdingssacrament en het drievoudig ambt van profeet, priester en pastor', in: *Communio*, 26, no. 2-3 (2001), p. 144-170 (Special edition *Diaconaat en diaconie. Over dienstbaarheid en het diakenambt*, p. 64-90), and in particular p. 147-163 (67-83).

[3] Klaus Mörsdorf, 'Die Entwicklung der Zweigliedrigkeit der kirchlichen Hierarchie', in: *Münchener Theologische Zeitschrift*, 3 (1952), p. 1-16. Cf. J.Y.H.A. Jacobs, 'Van kerkvoogden naar kerkleiders. Bestuurlijke verwikkelingen in de Rooms-Katholieke Kerk in Nederland (1795-1853). Een introductie aan de hand van Romeinse archivalia', in: *Documentatieblad voor de Nederlandse Kerkgeschiedenis na 1800*, 53 (December 2000), p. 3-28, especially p. 6-10 and p. 21-24 on the power of religious 'leaders' in the Netherlands in the 17th, 18th and 19th century, viz. the apostolic vicars, the (inter) nuncios and the (auxiliary) bishops.

and the power of Jurisdiction. The power of Orders is given through ordination and involves participation in Christ's power to pass on God's grace to the faithful. The power of Jurisdiction (or pastoral power) consists of the power that is connected to an ecclesiastical ministry, to lead and guide the faithful, to promulgate laws and administer justice. On the one hand it is generally accepted that ordination is the foundation of the power of Jurisdiction, so that only someone who has been ordained is able to hold a ministry, but in some circles this is a disputed view. On the other hand the power of Jurisdiction has a regulating function with regard to the power of Orders, for example by assigning an area to someone within which he can practice his power of Orders. The hierarchy of Orders is described classically by Thomas Aquinas, when he discusses priesthood for the purpose of its relation to the Eucharist[4]. Because a bishop has no more power with regard to the Eucharist than a priest, priesthood (that of the ordinary priest) is the highest level in the hierarchy of Orders. Under the priest in this hierarchy come: deacon, sub-deacon, acolyte, exorcist, lector and doorkeeper. Priesthood, diaconate and sub-diaconate were (at least in the Western or Latin Church) the so-called major orders, the other ranks formed the minor orders. These orders and the corresponding ranks only had a position in the course that led to priesthood. Before the (in chronological order) first order, the ostiariate or the rank of 'ostiarius' or doorkeeper, was received, the future priest was accepted into the clergy by undergoing a tonsure. The bishop of course, who was qualified to ordain other priests, stood above the priest, but the office of bishop was considered as a major rank in the hierarchy of Jurisdiction, not in the hierarchy of Orders. Merely by virtue of his greater power of Jurisdiction the bishop appointed a certain area to a priest where the latter could then practice his official power (that was e.g. 'delegata' or 'vicaria') as parish priest, curate or chaplain. For that matter, the Roman Pontiff, as the highest in rank in the jurisdiction hierarchy, was clearly above the bishop, that is to say as the bishop of the universal Church.

A number of critical remarks can be made with regard to this picture of the hierarchical structure of the Catholic Church. In the course of time the distinction between both powers and hierarchies evolved into a separation. The rise and spread of the absolute ordainments (that means that for example priests were ordained without immediately being connected to a church in which they were able to practice their office) what was already forbidden by the Council of Chalcedon in 451, of course also played a role. That in the late Middle Ages a so-called 'Messopferpriestertum' existed, i.e. that many priests did nothing other than say mass for the deceased, is also only possible within a hierarchical system in which the power of Orders and that of Jurisdiction were separated.

---

[4] Thomas of Aquino, *Summa Theologiae*, suppl. , quaest. 37, art. 2 Cf. J.Y.H.A. Jacobs, 'De opgang tot het altaar van God. De structuur van de priesteropleiding in Nederland vóór en na 1853', in: *Documentatieblad voor de Nederlandse Kerkgeschiedenis na 1800,* 54 (June 2001), p. 5-27, especially 6-7.

The preaching of the Word of God and pastoral care were viewed as duties that arose from the power of Jurisdiction, which was held only by the bishop and not by the priest as such. Ultimately this separation between both powers and hierarchies led to the tendency to consider the Roman Pontiff as the source of all jurisdiction in the Church. The detrimental effects of this tendency became obvious in particular during the Council of Trent. In order to fight against absenteeism, the duty of residence was enforced upon the bishops. Those who supported this measure were of the opinion that the duty of residence was an obligation of divine law. However, this opinion supposed that the bishops received their power of Jurisdiction directly from God, and not via the Roman Pontiff. This was unacceptable to the Roman Curia that held to the conviction that the bishops received their power of Jurisdiction from the Roman Pontiff. Ultimately the Council managed to succeed in enforcing the duty of residence as a stringent moral duty upon the bishops, but it was forced to leave the issue of the divine law of this commandment open.

2.2. The threefold office of prophet, priest and pastor

The problem of the powers of the Church is very closely connected to the doctrine on the threefold office. In this doctrine one speaks not so much in the juridical sense about office(s). Instead it involves describing the task or function of Christ, the Church, the office holders or the faithful: the preaching of the Word of God (prophetic office or office of teaching), the celebration of the sacraments (priestly or liturgical office, or office of sanctifying) and the service of love in community forming, spiritual guidance, care for the poor and the sick and various forms of social and political commitments (pastoral, shepherdly, kingly or diaconal office or office of helpfulness)[5]. The theme of Christ's threefold function turns up every now and again in connection with the Church Fathers and the scholastic Doctors of the Church from the Middle Ages, usually in relation with the explanation of biblical texts on the unction of priests, kings and prophets. The reformer John Calvin in particular has made the theme interesting for theology by describing, on the basis of the threefold function, what precisely salvation through Jesus Christ means. At the beginning of the 19th century Catholic theologians included the theme of the threefold office in their ecclesiology, to describe the duties of the hierarchy. This led to the doctrine on the threefold office being connected to a doctrine on offices in the juridical sense. The power that is typical of the hierarchical offices was divided

---

[5] Yves Congar, 'Sur la Trilogie: prophéte – roi – prêtre', in: *Revue des Sciences Philosophiques et Théologiques*, 67 (1983), p. 97-115. Cf. on the threefold office also: M. Gielis, "Als het visioen verdwijnt, verwildert het volk". Beschouwingen over de identiteit van de katholieke school', in: *Communio*, 25 (200), p. 467-469; Jacobs, 'Van kerkvoogden naar kerkleiders', p. 21, n. 36; Jan Jacobs, 'Woord vooraf', in: *Boeken als bron. Opstellen aangeboden aan dr. Marcel Gielis*, Jan Jacobs (ed.), Tilburg, 2001, p. 5.

between three 'offices' or duties of the Church, which were distinguished as being the teaching authority, the ordination power and the governing power. Some theologians and canonists accepted only two powers, namely the power of Orders and the power of Jurisdiction, but then they split the latter power into teaching authority and ruling authority. In this point of view it was for example obvious that the preaching of the Word of God was a duty specific to the bishop because he was the one with teaching authority[6]. The task of teaching the Word of God was not actually the duty of the priest as such and even less so of the laity. It was only when the bishop appointed a priest as parish priest that he was assigned the task of preaching. The pastoral office, in the sense of the practice of love and of the willingness to serve threatened in this view to be completely lost in the exercise of governing power, so that for example the diaconal office was not conceived as being an essential dimension of the Church. As a result of this view, in which the duties of the Church stemmed from the powers of the hierarchy, the laity had no part in the fulfilment of the Church's duties.

The French theologian Yves Congar o.p., perhaps the most important pioneer of the Second Vatican Council and at the same time the person who had most influence on the realisation of the Council texts, showed from his first publications in the '30s great interest in the theme of the threefold office, due to their usefulness not only in Christology and Ecclesiology, but also in theological anthropology. In *Chrétiens désunis* (1937) he talks of the 'loi de l'incarnation' (law of incarnation), whereby the 'ecclesia de Trinitate', the Church that arises from the Holy Trinity through dogma, sacraments and offices becomes an 'ecclesia ex hominibus', a Church that is a community of people. His inspiration came from the 19th century German theologian Johann Adam Möhler according to whom faith, piety and love are expressed in dogma, liturgy and law. Thus we clearly meet here the theme of the threefold office, in the understanding that for Congar the ecclesiastical hierarchical office still takes the place of the experience of love that is concretised in the fulfilment of law. In the second part of *Jalons pour une théologie du laïcat* (1953) Congar discusses the part the laity play in the priestly, kingly and prophetical functions of the Church (whereby the kingly function again also involves the governing duty), and also in the communal aspect of the Church and in the apostolic mission of the Church (in the Catholic Action). In the hierarchy these positions are offices with 'power' attached to them. Members of the hierarchy and the laity act respectively 'ex officio' and 'ex spiritu'; in a paper from 1947 this was: 'ex missione' and 'ex spiritu'.

On the eve of the Council this complicated material from the doctrine on the threefold office was clarified by canonist Klaus Mörsdorf in a number of studies, the results of which have been laid down in a number of articles in the

---

[6] By virtue of his power of Jurisdiction, from which his task to proclaim stemmed, a bishop had for example the right to issue a catechism for his diocese.

second edition of the *Lexikon für Theologie und Kirche*, that was published round 1960[7]. Mörsdorf points out that in theology office is often spoken of in a significance that has nothing to do with the juridical interpretation of 'office'. This is in his opinion the case in what has since about 1800 in Catholic theology become the so fundamental doctrine on the threefold office and on the distinction between the priestly, prophetic and pastoral offices. Mörsdorf suggests that this division into three involves various duties, tasks or services, but not offices in the juridical sense of the word. He is strongly against the tendency to connect an individual 'power' to each 'office' (in the sense of 'duty'). According to Mörsdorf the power given by Jesus Christ, to the Church – and more particularly to the ecclesiastical hierarchy – with a view to the fulfilment of its duty forms in reality an inextricable whole, although conceptually it can be distinguished in the power of Orders and that of Jurisdiction. This dual power that has been assigned by Christ to the hierarchy concerns the fulfilment of the threefold duty of prophet, priest and pastor, and then in such a way that both powers participate in the fulfilment of each of these duties.

2.3. Ecclesiastical hierarchy as ministry

In his collection *Pour une Église servante et pauvre* that was published in 1963, but that included papers that had been published earlier[8], Yves Congar discusses the issue of the difficult relation between the 'traditional' view of ecclesiastical hierarchy as the authority that is invested with power(s), and the New Testamentary view of the ecclesiastical ministry as service. In a preliminary bible-theological chapter he proves that in the Gospels and in the Letters from the Apostle Paul, the exercise of authority within the Church is considered as a service ('diakonia') to the community. In the church historical second chapter Congar shows that Augustine fashioned the classical terminology concerning ecclesiastical authority, while he described the duty of the bishop as follows: "He edifies his people through his word and the liturgical service, whereby he is conscious of practising not a *dominium* or *potestas* but a *ministerium*"[9].

---

[7] See in particular Mörsdorf's articles 'Kirchenamt' and 'Kirchengewalt' in: *Lexikon für Theologie und Kirche, 6 (1961)*, col. 188-192 and 218-221. On Mörsdorf: Peter Krämer, *Dienst und Vollmacht in der Kirche: eine rechtstheologische Untersuchung zur Sacra Potestas-Lehre des II. Vatikanischen Konzils*, Trier: Theologische Fakultät Trier, 1973, in particular p. 73-86; Arturo Cattaneo, *Grundfragen des Kirchenrechts bei Klaus Mörsdorf: Synthese und Ansätze einer Wertung*, Amsterdam: Grüner, 1991; Myriam Wijlens, *Theology and canon law: the theories of Kläus Mörsdorf and Eugenio Corecco*, Lanham, Md [etc.]: University Press of America, 1992.

[8] Yves M. J. *Congar, Pour une Église servante et pauvre*, Paris: Les éditions du Cerf, 1963; in particular the first article 'La hiérarchie comme service', p. 13-96 is of importance here.

Nevertheless, in the course of church history power is understood more and more as a characteristic of religious leaders or those with authority, rather than something that belongs to a mission in the name of Jesus Christ. A priest is understood to be someone "who *governs* his parish, who has *regimen*, who practices the act of *regere*"[10]. Indeed on reoccurrence there was a reaction against this theology. Saint Bernard attempted, along the same lines as Augustine, to make it clear that an ecclesiastical office should not be interpreted as a 'dominium' or 'dominatus' (also called 'possessio' or possession), but that it should be viewed as a 'ministerium' or 'cura'[11]. The party in favour of reform, that wanted to interpret office as 'ministerium' remained, however, stuck in the same juridical attitude as the party it was against.

Congar is of the opinion that modern society, in which Church and world are no longer entwined, offers the Church a greater opportunity to be a true Church, that is to say a serving Church. In the chapter about the "Christian view on authority" he explains that this means that human relationships (slave – master, husband – wife) are experienced 'in the Lord', i.e. that "relationships between people or between the faithful and things – these are the relationships through which our life is woven on a horizontal plane of the world – are resumed or included in the vertical relationship of love that comes to us from God, and the vertical relationship of faith that goes from us to God". Such a "relationship then radically changes meaning. It is no longer a relationship with two terms, that face each other horizontally, but three terms, that are placed vertically. (...) Evangelical authority involves a relationship *sub et supra* (of subordination and authority) within a general relationship of service, that is attached to the quality of being Christian"[12]. The Church as a whole is service and all the faithful are servants, but "God calls some of his servants to become leaders in the service"[13]. Particular or ministerial priesthood must, according to the New Testament, clearly be situated in the church community[14]. Congar concludes that the whole church or all the faithful, "that superiors and subordinates serve God and man by professing that everything is mercy for all and through all, according to the rank in which God places each one of us. The superior definitely holds a position of authority, but in a brotherly community of service.

[9] Congar, *Pour une Église*, p. 47. It is pretty obvious that bishop De Vet also made use of this terminology in the statement made by him that has already been quoted.

[10] Congar, *Pour Église*, p. 58; cf. what Congar says about the overlapping of the image of the Church as Bride and as Body: p. 63-64.

[11] Congar, *Pour une Église*, p. 95, n. 26.

[12] Congar, *Pour une Église*, p. 84-86; quotes on p. 84 and 85. Cf. p. 91: "The relationship of government and subordination is transformed [by the Gospel or by Christianity]. It is always from and in the Lord".

[13] Congar, *Pour une Église*, p. 87. Cf. p. 136 where it is stated using a quote from Eph. 4, 12 that it is the duty of Christian leaders to "equip God's people for work in his service". (All bible quotations are taken from *The New English Bible with Apocrypha*).

[14] Congar, *Pour une Église*, p. 87-88.

(...) This expects from us all extremely profound conversion, not so much to an ethical ideal of unselfishness, because such an ideal is merely a result, but to God and to Christ as the only and absolute Lord: a *theo*-logale and *theo*-logical conversion"[15].

3. The Second Vatican Council on office, power and ministry

When we read the Council texts concerned in the light of the history of the doctrine on office, power and service, and especially in the light of what Congar and Mörsdorf wrote about this on the eve of Vatican II, it appears that the ecclesiastical teaching authority at the Council has included that which in modern theology has been put forward (especially the opinions of Congar) as an extremely valuable contribution to Catholic ecclesiology, but that the most recent developments of that period (Mörsdorf's distinction between offices and powers) were still not sufficiently incorporated into the Council texts[16]. The following analysis of texts on offices and powers from four Council documents, namely the constitution on the Church and the decrees on episcopacy, priesthood and lay apostolate, should clarify this. The constitution on the Church is taken as a starting point. It is a well-known rule in the explanation of the Council documents, also brought to recollection by the 1985 Synod of Bishops, that in the four constitutions supporting views are laid down, whilst in decrees particular offices, status or areas of action are elaborated on. The constitution on the Church is the oldest of the four Council documents discussed here: this constitution was issued during the third Council session in the autumn of 1964 (namely on 21 November 1964), whilst the three decrees mentioned were issued at various times during the fourth session in the autumn of 1965 (the decree on episcopacy on 28 October, that on lay apostolate on 18 November and finally that on priesthood on 7 December 1965).

3.1. The constitution on the Church[17] and the nature of particular or ministerial priesthood

In the first chapter of the constitution *Lumen gentium* on the Church the biblical images of the church have been listed. The second chapter discusses the Church

---

[15] Congar, *Pour une Église*, p. 92.

[16] This is not surprising in the view the Council itself (for that matter wholly in line with tradition) has on the task of ecclesiastical teaching authority. Bishops (and Council fathers) are as it were judges who pass judgement on that which theologians, who function as it were as lawyers, put forward. As is the case for judges in general, ecclesiastical teaching authority is to a great degree 'passive', that is to say dependent upon others who compose the files.

[17] Vatican II, *Lumen gentium. Dogmatic constitution on the church* (LG), nos. 10-12, 18-21, 24, 29 (nos. 24-27 on bishops, nos. 28-29 on the priests and the deacons); see also nos. 30-38 (on the laity).

as the People of God. In the first – more introductory – part the position of the Church in salvation history is discussed. The extremely fundamental second part of the second chapter characterises the People of God that makes up the Church as a priestly people (nos. 10-12). Two parts of the threefold office are hereby discussed. The first two numbers of this section (nos. 10-11) discuss the general or common priesthood of the People of God, the third (no. 12) discusses the prophetic task of this people. No. 10 determines that all those who have been baptised make up a holy priesthood, and then indicates the distinction between common and particular priesthood; this distinction is essential and not gradual. Particular priesthood (the ministerial or hierarchical priesthood, "sacerdotium ministeriale seu hierarchicum") has the advantage of a sacred power ("potestas sacra"). No. 11 discusses the practice of common priesthood in the administration of the seven sacraments. In the first section no.12 deals with the prophetic office and the sense of faith of the People of God in relation to the ecclesiastical teaching authority. True the whole People of God is gifted with an unmistakable supernatural sense of faith, yet it is dependent upon the leadership of the 'magisterium', that is to say the teaching authority that is practised by ecclesiastical hierarchy or particular priesthood. In the second section of no. 12 the Council points out that all sorts of charisms in the Church are more greatly widespread than the 'ministries' ('ministeria'), so that the faithful of all ranks can be suitable to practice various tasks and offices ("varia opera vel officia") in the Church; decisions concerning this are made by the leaders of the Church.

The third chapter of *Lumen gentium* (nos. 18-29) deals with ecclesiastical hierarchy or particular or hierarchical priesthood (official or ministerial priesthood), in particular the episcopate ("De constitutione hierarchica Ecclesiae et in specie de episcopatu"). Following an introductory number in which the doctrine of Vatican II on the episcopate is related to that of Vatican I on primacy (no. 18), the first part concerns the origin of the episcopate in the office of apostle (nos. 19-21), the second part the collegiality of the bishops (nos. 22-23), the third part the duty of the bishops (nos. 24-27) and finally the fourth part priests and deacons (nos. 28-29). In this third chapter of *Lumen gentium* the doctrine on the power of ecclesiastical hierarchy or particular or ministerial priesthood is elaborated. Already in the introductory number (no. 18) it is apparent that the reason for the sending of the apostles, who were invested with the power of Christ, was to teach as shepherds, to sanctify and to govern. No. 19 also talks of the power of the apostles to teach, to sanctify and to govern. The bishops, as successors to the apostles, are together with their helpers, priests and deacons, in the service of the church community, in which they practice the task of teaching, liturgy and government as chairmen and shepherds (no. 20). The bishops, assisted by the priests, represent Christ in a ministry that involves teaching, the administration of the sacraments and the growth of the community. It is clear that in these numbers the office of the bishops is described using the trilogy of the 'offices', but at the same time an attempt is made to indicate the specific aspects of the office of apostle and bishop; these offices are founded on a particular or hierarchical 'power' given by Christ, which enables apostles and bishops to act as His representatives. In no. 25, which concerns the prophetic office of bishops, this power appears also to include teaching authority ('auctoritas'). No. 27 that deals with the task of governing (the pastorate or pastoral or shepherdly office!), regularly mentions 'power' and 'authority' ('potestas' and 'auctoritas'). According to *Lumen gentium*, no. 28 priests also have power and authority, but this is subordinate to that of the bishop.

The power of the hierarchy is also mentioned a number of times in the fourth chapter, that deals with the laity. According to no. 32 the laity are as brothers of Christ also brothers of those who practice the threefold office with the authority of Christ[18]. In no. 35 on the prophetic office that is also practised by the laity, it is stated that the hierarchy proclaims in the name of Christ and with His power.

From the above it is apparent that the Council follows for a large part the line of tradition that considered that power(s) were typical of particular or hierarchical priesthood (almost always called 'ministerium' by the Council), to distinguish it from 'munus' that refers to an office in the sense of duty or task. This office is ministry as in the sense of service ('ministerium' or 'diaconia'). Number 24 especially is very clear with regards to this: "This office which the Lord entrusted to the shepherds of his people, is a true service, and in the Holy Scripture it is specifically called 'diaconia' or 'ministry' (see Acts 1, 17 and 25; 21, 19; Romans 11, 13; 1 Timothy 1, 12). The constitution on Revelation, *Dei Verbum* from 1964 also states in connection with ecclesiastical teaching authority that it is a ministry: "This teaching function is not above the word of God but stands at its service"[19].

3.2. The constitution on the Church and the duties of bishop, priest and lay person

Also in the description of the duties of the bishop in the third part of the third chapter the doctrine on the threefold office is used. According to the introductory number 24 it is the bishop's duty through preaching the Gospel, to bring all to salvation through the gifts of faith, baptism and the fulfilment of Gods commandments; it is also pointed out that the office of bishop is called a ministerial office in the Scriptures. In the description of the bishop's duties in the following numbers (no. 25-27) the doctrine of the threefold office is again mentioned: the bishops exercise teaching authority (no. 25) and have a task to

---

[18] *LG*, no. 32: "fratres habent eos, qui in sacro ministerio positi, auctoritate Christi docendo et sanctificando et regendo familiam Dei ita pascunt ut mandatum novum caritatis ab omnibus impleatur".

[19] Vatican II, *Dei Verbum. Dogmatic constitution on divice revelation DV)*, no. 10.

sanctify (no. 26; concerns the relation of bishop and Eucharist in particular) and a duty to govern (no. 27). The connection of the duty to proclaim with teaching authority and the replacement of an explanation of the pastoral office in the sense of exercising love and service by an explanation of governing duty are evidence that the 19th and 20th century theology, in which a separate power was distinguished for each ecclesiastical office, duty or function, still has an effect on the Council. Yet in the second section of no. 26 on the duty of sanctification the bishop's legislative duty with regards to the liturgy is discussed. This proves that both powers are employed in the fulfilment of one of the duties of the Church.

The fourth and last part of the third chapter of *Lumen gentium* (nos. 28-29) deals with the priests and deacons, who participate in various ways in particular or hierarchical priesthood which is granted in its fullness to the bishop. It is said of priests that they are ordained in order to preach the Gospel, to shepherd the faithful and to celebrate divine worship[20]. This fully describes the threefold office. The rest of number 28 only explains the prophetic duty and especially the priestly duty, that is to say the Eucharist and penance. Twice the Council mentions that by practising these duties the priests participate in the office of Christ. In the Eucharist they act "in persona Christi"[21] and represent the bishop in the local gatherings of the faithful. It is said of the deacons that they come at the bottom of the ecclesiastical hierarchy and that they are not ordained for priesthood, but for a ministerial office (= office of helper or assistant to bishop and priest)[22]. Ordination does, however, give them sacramental grace to practice their ministerial office ('diaconia'), involving liturgy, the proclamation of the word and the exercise of caritas. Here too we come across a beautiful description of the threefold office! The Council continues with a list of duties that a deacon can perform.

The chapter on the laity (the fourth) is important with regards to the problems of office, because it is mentioned a number of times that the laity may also practice certain services and/or charisms (no. 30: "ministrationes et charismata'), because in their own way (differing from priests and deacons) they also have a part in Christ's threefold office of priest, prophet and king, and in the duties of particular priesthood or ecclesiastical hierarchy that stems from this (nos. 30-32). Therefore they can be appointed through the hierarchy to practice certain ecclesiastical duties or offices ('munera ecclesiastica') (no. 33), that are then described on the basis of what for us is now the familiar 'trilogy' of priestly, prophetical and kingly functions (nos. 34-36). In connection with the prophetic duty of the laity it is stated that in an emergency (a situation where there is a

---

[20] *LG*, no. 28: "ad Evangelium praedicandum fidelesque pascendos et ad divinum cultum celebrandum".

[21] Cf. *LG*, no. 10.

[22] Cf. except Gielis, 'Diaconaat', p. 75/155 also p. 83/163 – 86/166.

lack of ordained office holders and in times of persecution) they also be able to practice certain sacred offices ("quaedam officia sacra") (no. 35).

3.3. The decrees on the office of bishop, priesthood and lay apostolate

A certain evolution has taken place in the decrees on the office of bishop, priesthood and the lay apostolate that were published approximately a year later than the constitution on the Church, in the sense that the descriptions of the 'munus triplex' are more precise and that the neo-scholastic doctrine on three powers that would correlate to the threefold office are mentioned less and less.
In the decree on the pastoral office of bishops[23] the responsibility of the bishops for the universal Church and episcopal collegiality is discussed first, followed by the duties of the diocesan bishops in their own diocese. The decree also talks about the circumscription of dioceses, assistants (besides assistant bishops and auxiliary bishops and the diocesan curia, the relation of the bishop to priests and the religious and to the various diocesan councils is also mentioned) and of the co-operation of bishops on the whole (synods, bishop conferences, archdioceses, bishops with interdiocesan positions, etc.). It is of course again in the description of the duties of the diocesan bishops that the Council applies the doctrine on the threefold office (nos. 12-16). Notably the description of each duty begins with the same expression: "In exercendo suo munere" ("When exercising their duty"). The three 'munera', duties or functions that are distinguished are: the 'munus docendi', the 'munus sanctificandi' and the 'munus patris ac pastoris'. The teaching or prophetic duty is first under the duties of the bishop, according to the Council, and involves proclaiming the Christian doctrine in various ways and using various methods including preaching and catechesis (nos. 12-14). In the discussion on the sanctification or priestly duty the Council states that in his diocese the bishop organises, encourages and monitors liturgical life, in which the Eucharist is central. Because the bishop has received the fullness of priesthood, priests and deacons are dependent upon him (no. 15). The pastoral duty – also called the 'fatherly' duty – includes gathering the faithful together in a community of love, and promoting in a broad sense not only the welfare of those who belong to the Catholic Church, but also of other Christians and those who are not baptised (no. 16).
In the decree on the ministry and life of priests[24] following a fundamental chapter on the position of particular or hierarchical priesthood in the mission of the Church and before a discussion on the relation of priests with regards to other office holders and the faithful, of the vocation of priest and of various aspects of the priestly way of life and spirituality, there is an explanation of the

---

[23] Vatican II, *Christus Dominus. Decree on the pastoral office of bishops in the church*, nos. 12-16.

[24] Vatican II, *Presbyterorum ordinis. Decree on the ministry and life of priests*, nos. 4-6.

priest's duties, whereby again the Council applies the doctrine of the threefold office (nos. 4-6). As in the case of the bishops the proclamatory, liturgical and pastoral ministry are hereby discussed in the same order. Priests proclaim in ways varying from sermon, catechesis, personal talk, etc. As far as their liturgical duty is concerned, priests are the administrators of baptism, penance, extreme unction and especially the Eucharist. They receive spiritual power for their other duties as well as for their pastoral duty, so that they are able to 'edify' the faithful and are capable of "the greatest humanity in the footsteps of the Lord" in their contact with their fellow men, and are able to answer for religious education, for the care for the poor and weak, youths, the married and parents (these last three sections of the population preferably in societies), the religious, sick and dying and for the development of a truly Christian community.

In the first chapter of the decree on the lay apostolate[25] the vocation of the lay to the apostolate is dealt with (nos. 2-4). It is true that Christ gave the apostles and their successors the duty of teaching, sanctifying and ruling in His name and with His power, but the laity also participate in these priestly, prophetic and kingly offices (no. 2)[26]. The lay apostolate is based on the connection with Christ (no. 3) that also forms the foundation for lay spirituality (no. 4). The second chapter of the decree concerns the duties ('munera') of the laity. In "the ministry of the word and the sacraments" ('ministerium verbi et sacramentorum'!) the lay apostolate is complementary to that of pastoral ministry (no. 6)[27]. The laity work in particular in the area of temporary order (no. 7).

We can make the following conclusion from this analysis of the Council texts on offices and powers. Despite the fact that the Council speaks on the one hand in *Lumen gentium* (from 1964) of a (one) sacred power, that falls to those who practice ministry ('ministerium'), in other words to the hierarchy, on the other hand it recognises an office of teaching that involves the prophetic office, and a power of Orders that involves the administration of the sacraments, whilst a discussion on the power of governing replaces that on pastoral or (in the

---

[25] Vatican II, *Apostolicam actuositatem. Decree on the apostolate of the laity*, nos. 2-8.

[26] *Apostolicam actuositatem*, no. 2: "laici, muneris sacerdotalis, prophetici et regale Christi participes effecti, suas partes in missione totius populi Dei explent in Ecclesia et in mundo"; cf. first sentence of no. 10 that is practically the same.

[27] *Apostolicam actuositatem*, no. 6: "Hoc principaliter fit per ministerium verbi et sacramentorum, speciali modo clero commissum, in quo et laici habent suas magni momenti partes adimplendas, ut sint 'cooperatores veritatis'(3 J 8). Hoc potissimum in ordine apostolatus laicorum et ministerium pastorale mutuo se complent"; "This happens principally through the ministry of the word and of the sacraments; this is entrusted in a special way to the clergy, but the laity also have a very important role to play as 'fellow workers... in the truth' (3 J 8). Here especially do the apostolate of the laity and the pastoral ministry complement each other." This quote brings with it numerous problems with regards to its interpretation.

Council's own words!) kingly office. Conversely, in the Council texts of 1965 we generally come across an explanation of the threefold office in which this theme is, more obviously than in the constitution on the Church of 1964 viewed as related to the Church's duties or the areas in which the Church is active, and not so much to offices (in the juridical sense of the word), to which a certain power is attached. The power of office holders is not discussed (in a dogmatic respect), because the Council fathers obviously were of the opinion that this issue had satisfactorily been dealt with in *Lumen gentium*.

3.4. Summary and critical comments

If we read the Council texts on the power of the hierarchy and on prophetic (teaching or proclamatory), priestly (liturgical) and pastoral (shepherdly, kingly or diaconal) office against the background of theological and canonistic tradition with respect these, then we notice that they are situated on the turning point in the history of these themes. Catholic theologians (Congar) and canonists (Mörsdorf) have, since the fifties, occupied themselves with a thorough renewal in the way these themes are dealt with, and an attempt to extricate them from the frightening opinion held of them in the era of neo-scholasticism (grosso modo 1850-1950), due to the confusion between offices and powers. In the new view, that was put forward by Mörsdorf especially, the doctrine on the three offices of prophet, priest and pastor was not interpreted in the juridical sense, but understood as a description of the Church's duties. Both powers fall to the hierarchy or particular priesthood and are applied in fulfilling each of the three offices or duties. The Council was unable to deal fully with what at the time was a fairly recent view. Nevertheless it is possible from this view to do justice to the Council texts and to gain a clearer picture of the intentions of the Council.

It is clear that the Council, with the help of the theme of the threefold office, that is not only practised by the hierarchy, but also by lay faithful, wishes to strengthen the position of the laity along the lines of Congar: the laity also belong to the Church and play an important role in the fulfilment of its tasks. This stems from the doctrine on common priesthood. A problem does arise in the Council's attempt to describe particular or hierarchical priesthood. True the Council emphatically confirms that there is an essential distinction between common and particular priesthood, but by describing the duties of both office holders (bishops, priests and deacons) and the laity with the help of the theme of the threefold office, this distinction threatens to fade. To a certain extent, the identity crisis that many priests experienced in the years following the Council, is probably connected to this vagueness in the Council texts. However, with the help of Mörsdorfs view it is possible to interpret the Council texts in such a way that, on the one hand, it becomes clear that the laity also fully participate in the fulfilment of the Church's duties and, on the other, the characteristics of particular priesthood can be more clearly understood. Following Mörsdorf we must then attempt to make a clearer distinction between offices (in the sense of duties) and powers in the Council texts, and in particular in *Lumen gentium*. Thus we are able to bring what *Lumen gentium* says about the power of priesthood into line with what we find in the decrees on the office of bishop, priesthood and the lay apostolate on the duties of both lay faithful and office holders.

When we read the fundamental numbers 10-12 of the constitution on the Church (on a priestly people and common priesthood) with Mörsdorf's opinion in mind, it appears that in *Lumen gentium* the Council thinks largely in terms of a theology that relates priestly power to the priestly duty (one part of threefold office in the sense of a threefold duty or function), and that it distinguishes a separate teaching power that is then connected to the prophetic duty. Within this frame of thought it is somewhat difficult to make a clear distinction between common or general priesthood and particular or ministerial priesthood. When we make clear distinctions between offices (in the sense of duties) and powers, then the meaning of these numbers becomes more obvious: true the lay faithful can practice all sorts of duties that are a part of the Church's proclaiming and liturgical office, on the grounds of common priesthood and their participation in the threefold office of Christ, but by virtue of the power invested in them by Christ, the holders of the particular or hierarchical office are for example, assigned to act as judges in matters concerning faith (traditionally speaking, but also confirmed by the Council[28]) and to fulfil the role of chairman in the liturgy of the sacraments. Along the same lines in the part concerning the duties of the bishops in the constitution on the Church (nos. 25-27) the governing power of the bishops, that is discussed at a time when it is expected that their responsibility for the pastoral or diaconal office will be dealt with (no. 27), should be viewed in relation to other offices or duties of the Church. The same applies to a discussion on teaching authority (the other part of the power of Jurisdiction) and the power of Orders, both of which are discussed in the same constitution in relation to the prophetic office and priestly office (nos. 25-26) respectively. Number 26 on priestly office already enters into the episcopal power of Jurisdiction with regard to liturgy.

The Council does cause a remarkable turn in the opinion on the 'sacred power' of particular or hierarchical priesthood. Whilst Mörsdorf still made a distinction between the power of Jurisdiction and that of Orders (at least conceptually), the Council never talks of different powers plurally, but it does mention divine

---

[28] Traditionally the exercise of teaching authority is described with the help of the idea of a judicial decision. Vatican II also makes use of this idea. *LG*, no. 25 states that the bishops "pro universa Ecclesia fidei et morum doctores et iudices sunt" ("are the teachers and judges of faith and morals for the universal church"). Cf. what is said in *Dei Verbum* on the bible interpretation that is subject to the judgement of the Church (*DV*, no. 12).

sacred singularly[29]. The Council wishes in this way to go beyond the doctrine of the dual hierarchy that since the Middle Ages was widely spread in the Catholic Church. According to the Council the central figure in the one hierarchy or in the particular priesthood – known in *Lumen gentium*, no. 10 as a ministerial or hierarchical priesthood ("sacerdotium ministeriale seu hierarchicum") - is the bishop: he is granted priesthood in all its fullness, that is to say the fullness of the power he exercises in the name of Christ and as His representative, as a service to the Church and to the world. Because the Council texts speak of one sacred power, the two hierarchies that existed together in the pre-conciliar Church disappear making space for the one priesthood, whereby the bishops, priests and deacons make up the separate grades (*LG*, nos. 28-29) or ranks. Priests and deacons participate as fellow-workers – respectively as representatives of the bishop and as assistants to the bishop – in the sacred power that forms the essence of priesthood, that is granted to the bishop in all its fullness.

Notably with regard to the office of bishop the Council speaks first of episcopal collegiality and common responsibility for the universal Church: as a college the bishops are the apostle's successors and they practise their office of governing in the Church (*LG*, nos. 23-24). Thus, as far as the bishops are concerned, the issue of absolute ordinations for example, disappears largely into the background. Should one wish to make a distinction between the power of Orders and that of Jurisdiction then one must argue that according to the Council both powers are practised by the bishops in the first place for the benefit of the universal Church. Within the episcopal college the bishop of Rome, the Roman Pontiff, emerges as the one whom for the sake of unity and solidarity amongst the bishops, holds a higher power of Jurisdiction, the primacy, the consequence of which is papal infallibility (*LG*, no. 25).

The members of the particular or hierarchical priesthood exercise their duties of prophet, priest and pastor on the grounds of a special sacramental grace that grants them a 'sacred power'. Thus in the opinion of the Council it is not the case that one of the functions of bishop, priest or deacon has especially to be connected to the prophetic, priestly or pastoral (diaconal) offices, however much the terminology used might give reason to believe this. The sacred power granted to them in the name of God implies that the members of the particular priesthood (deacons as well as bishops and priests) carry the responsibility for all of the Church's duties. This is obvious from the fact that in describing the duties of the bishop, priest and deacon the Council repeatedly makes use of the theme of the threefold office.

The Council applies the same to the description of the duties of the laity. On the grounds of their affiliation with Christ and their common priesthood through baptism and confirmation, ('sacerdotium commune fidelium' in *LG*, no. 10) the

---

[29] Wijlens, *Theology*, p. 56-57.

laity are also a full part of the Church, and also practise the duties ('munera') of the Church by means of various 'charisms', if necessary in 'officia' or 'ministrationes'. The 'offices' meant by these terms do not imply, however, responsibility for the whole; these include for both men and women alike for example the offices of catechist[30], theologian, leader in prayer, cantor, sacristan, pastoral worker, parish assistant, member of the pastoral team, pastoral youth workers, administrators for the church finances and of course numerous functions in the charity and social sectors[31]. Nowadays two of the offices that used (in theory) to be connected to the so-called minor orders, namely that of acolyte and lector are too practised by the laity, both men and women. In 1994 the teaching authority declared that what was traditionally known as the highest of these minor orders, that of acolyte, could also be practised by women.

4. Power and ministry in the post-conciliar discussion

The all in all clear statements made by the Council with regards to the pre-conciliar discussion on office, power and ministry did not have the effect that was expected. A fierce discussion was sparked off about the problems of the ecclesiastical office in the post-conciliar Church[32]. There were, and still are, two issues that are especially controversial: one is the difference between the

---

[30] Perhaps the 'office' of preacher could also be mentioned. The so-called 'official' proclamation (certainly the 'homily' or sermon on the readings of Sundays and festivals, that even before the Council were more or less the parish priest's responsibility) must, however, for the sake of its connection with the Eucharist be taken by an ordained office holder, thus a bishop, priest or deacon. However, a lay person may preach during prayer services.

[31] One controversial issue is to what extent the office of ecclesiastical judge can be practised by a lay person. According to the Ecclesiastical Code of 1983 an official principal acting as substitute for the bishop should always be a priest, or at least a deacon, but it is possible for the other judges to be lay people, although it is not entirely clear whether they practise their office by virtue of their own or of a delegated power of jurisdiction. From our point of view, in the first case an anomaly would arise on the basis of the Ecclesiastical Code of 1983.

[32] In the past years in German-speaking countries especially, a number of important publications have appeared: Guido Bausenhart, *Das Amt in der Kirche: eine not-wendende Neubestimmung*, Freiburg im Breisgau [etc.]: Herder, 1999; Gisbert Greshake, *Priester sein in dieser Zeit: Theologie – pastorale Praxis – Spiritualität*, Freiburg im Breisgau [etc.]: Herder, 2000; Judith Müller, *Im Dienst der Kirche Christi: zum Verständnis des Kirchlichen Amtes heute*, Regensburg: Pustet, cop. 2000; Jerzy Kochanowicz, *Für euch Priester, mit euch Christ: das Verhältnis von gemeinsamen und besonderem Priestertum*, Frankfurt um Main: Knecht, 2000; *Dienst im Namen Jesu Christi: impulse für Pastoral, Katechese und Liturgie*, ed. Helmut Hoping and Hans J. Münk, Freiburg (Switzerland): Paulusverlag, cop. 2001; Judith Müller, *In der Kirche Priester sein: das Priesterbild in der deutschsprachigen katholischen Dogmatik des 20. Jahrhunderts*, Würzburg: Echter, 2001. It is, within the scope of this article, of course impossible to discuss all the problems that are raised in these books. We are for example aware that the reproach of 'Christomonism', that is aimed by a number of these authors at a certain movement in the Catholic Church, could also affect our article; we hope to deal with this problem in future publications.

common and particular priesthood, and the other is the nature of the authority in the Church. The latter interests us most as it fits into the framework of this article on power and ministry, but considering that the first issue forms the basis of the second – we have after all shown that the distinction between common and ministerial priesthood lies exactly in the power of the hierarchical priesthood – we must briefly discuss it too.

4.1. The discussion on the distinction between common and particular or hierarchical priesthood

From our analysis of the Council texts it has become clear that, according to Vatican II, 'common' or 'general' priesthood of the faithful involves participation in Christ's threefold office of prophet, priest and pastor. Those who hold a hierarchical office or that of hierarchical priesthood have, through their ordination sacrament, received the power to share the grace of Christ with the faithful, and to guide them in the practice of threefold office. The faithful can only practice the duties that are involved in threefold office through the strength of sacramental grace, which they receive through the mediation and under the leadership of ordained office holders. The lay faithful can, on the grounds of common priesthood and a special charism, fulfil certain 'offices' and 'services' in the Church.

In the post-conciliar Church, however, views have been defended in which this distinction between ordained office holders who participate in the ordination sacrament, and the laity, who because of their charism fulfil certain offices, has faded. On the one hand Mörsdorf's view that the power of Orders is a condition for receiving the power of Jurisdiction is opposed by the Roman school (the canonists of the Gregoriana, among others Jean Beyer s.j.) and also by the so-called school of Navarra, that is to say canonists and theologians from the university of Opus Dei, that is situated in Pamplona[33]. In this movement it is argued that a lay person can also exercise the power of Jurisdiction. It seems to us that the arguments for this – besides the matter of lay judges, who have been admitted through the Code of 1983 – throw little weight into the scales: it is unacceptable that (as in the theory of the canonists of the university of Navarra) in the extremely hypothetical case of a lay person being chosen as Roman Pontiff and holding the power of Jurisdiction before his episcopal consecration, consequences are attached that put the clear pronouncements of Vatican II on the power of hierarchical priesthood at risk. That in the past certain abesses held some archdeaconry power does in our opinion not mean that the laity is able to have the power of Jurisdiction, but rather that those abesses (or their predecessors) were not lays, but that they had received the consecration of

---

[33] Cf. J. P. Beal, 'The exercise of the power of governance by lay people: state of the question', in: *The Jurist*, 55 (1995), p. 1-92.

deacon. Therefore this is not an argument for granting the power of Jurisdiction to the laity, but it is an argument for granting the consecration of the diaconate to women, certainly when they fulfil a leading function in the Church, as is undeniably the case with abesses[34].

On the other hand nowadays there is a tendency within the Church to more or less blur the distinctions between the hierarchical ministries of bishop, priest and deacon and the charisms of the offices of lay people. For example by dividing the hierarchical office, with its responsibility for the whole of the practice of threefold office, into the individual charisms of proclamation, liturgy, diacony and parish leadership. Peter de Mey, a dogmatician from Leuven, recently argued in favour of a charismatic leadership, the model of which he finds in the twelfth chapter of the first letter to the Corinthians, in which Paul speaks of the various gifts of the Holy Spirit[35]. According to De Mey it is also "not essential that the office of sanctifying and the office of governing be fulfilled by the same person". He believes his view is supported by *Lumen gentium*, no. 12, in which all the faithful participate in the prophetic office of Christ by practising "opera vel officia". Our analysis has, however, made it clear that this concerns 'offices' that should be definitely distinguished from the particular or hierarchical ministry. This is also evident from the end of the paragraph of *Lumen gentium*, no. 12 (that is not quoted by De Mey!), which states that those in positions of leadership within the Church have the right to pass judgement on the charisms.

4.2. The discussion on the nature and exercise of authority

Besides the matter of the distinction between common and particular priesthood, that of the nature of authority within the Church after the Council was also heatedly discussed[36]. A strong movement arose in the Church that, through the Council texts on office as ministry, felt authorised to make a stand for a way in which authority must be exercised in the Catholic Church, that

---

[34] The possibility for a diaconate for women is demonstrated in Gielis, 'Diaconaat', p. 86/166 – 89/169.

[35] Peter de Mey, 'Leidinggevend charisma. Over pastorale werkers en gewijde ambtsdragers', in: *Tertio*, 8 August 2001, p. 13 in a reaction to Stijn van den Bossche, 'Als bruid en bruidegom', in: *Tertio*, 1 August 2001, p. 12 who had pointed out an essential distinction that is founded in the ordination sacrament between office holders and the laity (pastoral workers).

[36] Cf. Henk Witte, 'Gezag in de kerk: in hoeverre van boven, in hoeverre van onderen?', in: *Geest en leven. Tijdschrift voor informatie, bezinning en gesprek*, 67 (1990), p. 175-183. On the problems of power in the church Kerk: *Macht, Dienst, Herrschaft in Kirche und Gesellschaft*, ed. Wilhelm Wever, Freiburg [etc.]: Herder, 1974; *Macht in de kerk. Over de legitimatie van macht en de veranderlijke vormen van machtsuitoefening in de kerk*, ed. James Provost en Knut Walf = *Concilium. Internationaal tijdschrift voor theologie*, 24, no. 3 (June 1988).

more or less correspond to that of modern democratic states. Already in the first years following Vatican II objections from philosophical as well as theological quarters were brought against such requirements: they were based on a wrong view on 'the willingness to serve'.

As far back as 1968 Louis Bouyer pointed out a misunderstanding on what the Council says about the service of the Church to the world as well as what it says about poverty, collegiality, ecumenism, openness for the world and aggiornamento[37]. In the post-conciliar era office holders themselves often took a wrong stand on the 'service' they were to render, so that they regularly failed in fulfilling their leadership role and allowed completely irresponsible reformations to be carried through[38]. With service to the world it was namely understood that the Church should no longer convert the world to the Gospel but that it should adapt itself to the world, in order to be able to better anticipate the needs that arose from this world; in doing so one had for example not to worry too much about the texts of that Gospel[39]. From then on the Church agenda was dictated by the world: service to the world meant that the Church was assigned its tasks from the world and not from the Gospel. This interpretation lead to a similar interpretation of ministry: according to many it was the office holders duty to ensure that the Church alleviated the needs of the world as well as possible. In a number of cases this has led to an overemphasis of the Church's diaconal duty[40].

---

[37] Louis Bouyer, *La décomposition du Catholicisme*, s.l. : Aubier-Montaigne, 1968, p. 21-26. Following the announcement that he will deal with the willingness to serve and poverty, Bouyer hints at the famous book written by Congar (which we have already discussed) by quoting in brackets what has become a proverbial saying ("L'Eglise servante et pauvre"); thus it is fairly clear that his explanation of the willingness to serve includes a critical dialogue with this book, which for that matter he fully agrees with (p. 23: "Comme l'a fort bien établi le Pére Congar"), but a wrong interpretation of which he wishes to oppose.

[38] Bouyer, *Décomposition*, p. 24-25: "Dire que les ministres de l'Église, à commencer par ses chefs, sont des serviteurs, cela donc en est venu à signifier qu'ils n'avient plus à prendre leurs responsabilités de conducteurs et de docteurs, mais à suivre le troupeau au lieu de le précéder. (...) Vatican II aura été suivi d'une démission quasi générale de l'Église enseignante". For that matter this concerns a 'service' that especially since Vatican II requires great expertise. In connection with this, Cardinal Danneels spoke at the most recent synod of bishops (Sept.-Oct. 2001) of an "ars definiendi et determinandi" on the one hand and an "ars persuadendi et communicandi" on the other.

[39] Bouyer, *Décomposition*, p. 25: "Mais le pire n'est pas là. C'est dans ce qu'on est arrivé à faire de l'idée que l'Église est au service du monde. L'Église, traduira-t-on, n'a plus á convertir le monde mais à se convertir à lui. Elle n'a plus rien à lui enseigner, mais à se mettre à son écoute. Mais l'Évangile du salut, direz-vous? N'en est-elle pas responsable tout entière pour le monde? N'est-ce pas de le lui apporter qui constitue l'essentiel de son service?"

[40] Parallel to this is a development that Valeer Neckebrouck, the missiology specialist from Leuven, has tirelessly protested against: the reduction of the mission to development aid on the grounds of what he calls the 'socio-focale' interpretation of Christianity. This one-sided interpretation has become more and more prominent in the Catholic Church too since the

A few years after the Council the Dutch philosopher Cornelis Verhoeven also wrote about 'the willingness to serve' that concerned the Church and that were certainly worthy of consideration[41]. He is extremely critical of the post-conciliar Church: "An institute like the Church, that indeed used to be a bulwark of power, is also not ready for a great conversion in its existence, when it will call itself a service institute. The willingness to serve can quite easily be a trick, the only aim of which is to get as many fingers as possible into as many pies as possible. Besides a means of gaining power it can also be a means of retaining its declining powers or hiding its hard core"[42]. Verhoeven connects the problem of authority and freedom (or of authority as ministry, of authority that brings about real freedom amongst its 'subjects') to that of mediation in the relation between subjects. On the basis of Hegel, Sartre and Levinas, Verhoeven points out that in the confrontation between two people which is not connected to a 'matter', it is immediately determined that one of the two is the master and the other the servant. It is only when people gather together round a particular 'matter' that freedom for all is guaranteed. Along the same lines as what he said about objectivity as a guarantee against the arbitrariness of authority[43], he suggests in his attempt to "clarify the relation between power and the willingness to serve" that: "authority is only of any value when it can make itself subordinate to real and great matters, and can convincingly rise above short-sighted viewpoints. To serve is to serve for a reason, to function. So to serve means to: commit authority to the interests themselves (...) Authority is

---

sixties. On the other hand Neckebrouck upholds that in missionary work "verbal preaching does in a certain sense have a status of priority" (*Het dubbele rentmeesterschap. Missionaire verkondiging en sociale actie*, Leuven-Amersfoort, 1994, p. 135). This is connected to the fact "that in that proclamation lies the most particular, the most specific and most irreplaceable task of the Church, in the sense that it is a task that is fulfilled only by the Church and that, should it fail in this it will not be continued by anyone else" (p. 137).

[41] Cornelis Verhoeven, *Zakelijkheid en ethiek*, Baarn: Ambo, 1971, p. 52-55.

[42] Verhoeven, *Zakelijkheid*, p. 54.

[43] Verhoeven, *Zakelijkheid*, p. 25-26: "The medium, the 'matter', deprives human contact of arbitrariness, which can result in a master-slave relationship. ... The matter is the impartial, objective medium that offers resistance to arbitrariness. Neither I nor the other, on which the attention is focused, is the source of morality, but the objective matter": p. 33-35: "It appears namely that human contact is only possible via the roundabout way on matters. ...The search for contact without the matter is a dangerous form of indulgence, certainly in cases when a lack of understanding and interest for the matter threaten to lead to disorder in the contact. ... And active participation can only stem from the matter. Participation without that justification is a passive, that is implemented by the balance of power that is necessary for the structure". Verhoeven discusses this in more detail in the next chapter, "The limits of power". He points out the danger of the structure becoming "an empty shell and a dead formalism" when it is separated from the 'matter'. Therefore it is in this context that the willingness to serve comes up as a masked form of the pursuit of power. Based on his criterion of 'objectivity' Verhoeven makes a number of interesting observations on change and historicity and on control, justification and responsibility, and finally on the ethics of the manager (that could just as well be the ethics of a Church leader!).

the willingness to serve because the willingness to serve is a form of superior insight, which is therefore authority. (...) Supervision is a willingness to serve in relation to a continually threatened matter"[44]. Many contemporary philosophers also hold Verhoeven's views. In her book about Jacques Lacan, Anika Rifflet-Lemaire points out that the latter also thinks a mediating third party necessary to guarantee the freedom of those involved in an inter-human relationship[45]. Vergote echoes these Lacanian views, but then applied to the significance of language and in particular of the Word of God[46]. S. IJsseling spoke of authority and freedom in exactly the same sense as Verhoeven[47].

In the same year that Verhoeven's book *Zakelijkheid en ethiek* appeared (1971), A. Spijkerboer published a booklet with extremely keen observations on politics, power and authority, people in authority and democratisation[48]. Spijkerboer suggests, just as Verhoeven does, that all authority is derived from (in the words of Verhoeven: is derived from the authority of the matter concerned). According to Spijkerboer such authority paradoxically leads to the real freedom of those over whom the authority is exercised. This authority makes an appeal to their insight in the matter concerned. Yet when this insight remains absent, true authentic authority, authority is derived from the matter itself, is also experienced by those who are subject to that authority as the brute, arbitrary exercise of power. In connection with the problem of democracy that can only work through decisions made by the majority, that are not guaranteed to be correct, Spijkerboer also refers to the requirements for the democratising of the Church. Unjustly according to him, in so-called 'democratic' decisions in the Church the question was never "asked whether 'the' will of 'the' parishioners sufficiently took into consideration what the church is and what its vocation is"[49]. According to Spijkerboer consequently the Church can never

---

[44] Verhoeven, *Zakelijkheid*, p. 55. That matter is the Word of God. Service to the Word of God is that which binds the members of the particular and of the common priesthood.

[45] Anika Rifflet-Lemaire, *Jacques Lacan*, Brussels, 1970, p. 42: "L'existence du médiat est ce qui va permettre à chacun de se repérer dans sa subjectivité distincte. Dans une relation immédiate, au contraire, la distinction du soi et de l'autre n'est pas nette".

[46] Antoine Vergote, *Interprétation du langage religieux*, Paris, 1974, p. 101: "Il n'y a pas d'accés direct ni à la propre subjectivité , ni à celle d'autrui. L'intersubjectivité se fonde sur l' 'entre-deux' entre moi et l'autre, et cet 'inter' consiste dans le monde commun, constitué dans l'intermédiaire. A ce monde appartient également le langage qui l'articule... les catégories de l'expérience et de l'empathie n'offrent aucune garantie contre les illusions subjectivistes, précisément parce qu'elles sont inaptes à poser l'altérité de l'autre". This concerns "la pensée dite personnaliste" (see p. 100). For an analysis of Vergote's book see M. Gielis, "'Gij hebt ons voor U gemaakt en onrustig is ons hart tot het rust vindt in U". Enkele aantekeningen betreffende de discussie over *Surnaturel* van Henri de Lubac', in: *Communio*, 26, no. 4 (2001), p. 310-315.

[47] Samuel IJsseling, 'Gezag en vrijheid', in: *Tijdschrift voor Theologie*, 9 (1969), p. 249-268. This article is the first in a special edition on *Christelijke vrijheid en kerkelijk gezag*.

[48] A. A. Spijkerboer, *Wat geloven wij werkelijk?*, Baarn, 1971, p. 57-67.

[49] Spijkerboer, *Wat geloven wij werkelijk?*, p. 64.

simply become a democracy; he suggests that the church is or should be a "Christocracy". It is in fact this view that Cardinal Simonis has made his own.

It is indeed clear that with the views of Verhoeven, Lacan, Vergote and Spijkerboer we have come close to what Congar remarked about an authority in service in his booklet *Pour une Église servante et pauvre*, that forms the background of the somewhat paradoxical doctrine of the Council on an ecclesiastical office, that is characterised by 'power', notwithstanding that it is a ministry. According to Congar the inter-human relationship that is the relation of authority, is not a bipolar but a triangular relationship: people in authority and subjects do not stand opposite one another, but form one community in Christ. Those in authority do not exercise their own authority, but 'serve' in order to enable Christ's authority to prevail. In the Catholic Church there are regulations for the extremely complicated combination of Scripture, Tradition, theology, sensus fidelium, reason and ecclesiastical authority (and Holy Spirit!) to put this 'Christocracy' into operation. Whether these regulations are always correctly applied is a question that must repeatedly be considered, also and perhaps in the first place, by church leaders with pastoral responsibility.

Can Faith Save the Earth?

Leo van der Tuin

Introduction: faith and the environment

The link between faith and the environment is not one that automatically comes to mind. What does faith have to do with the pollution of the environment? What is the relationship between the breakdown of our natural environment and faith in God? Faith primarily involves man, his redemption and salvation. Everything else in faith is subordinate to this. Environmental pollution and destruction are not concepts that can be found in the Catechism of the Catholic Church. The concept nature is only mentioned in connection with the law of nature and natural science. However, the concept environment refers directly to creation. The same applies to the lemma where there is also no clear reference to the threat to the integrity of creation through the actions of man. There is one instance of a reference to man's possible destructive management of creation (Catechism of the Catholic Church 373). All sorts of social issues are discussed in the Catechism: arms trade, war and peace, poverty, famine, drugs, tax fraud, politics. Ecological problems would certainly fit into this list, but instead they are casually mentioned as moral problems. In the part that deals with creation attention is paid to the possible abuse of mineral, vegetable and animal resources. But the attitude and views that are the basis of this abuse are not discussed in any detail. On the contrary, the view on creation is in no way related to the disturbance of the environment as a result of the way in which man considers himself. When problems concerning the environment are discussed then it is as moral problems and not as a fundamental problem relating to views.
It is this view with regard to nature that I wish to discuss in this contribution from catechetics. Tjeu van Knippenberg describes religious education as the form of pastoral action that is aimed at learning religious communication. He understands religious communication as 'the exchange of ultimate meanings that people give to their personal and social life, with in mind the development of an understanding within themselves as well as of one another, and within this with the cultural tradition of Christianity, which results in the involvement of sense and/or senselessness partly in relation to the Christian faith (Van Knippenberg 1987, 73).' Environmental problems affect us deeply in both our personal and social lives. They confront us with the limits of our existence, and also with the limits of our abilities. The way we treat nature we both live

in and are, affects the foundation of our existence and is as such the basis of the meaning we give to everything, of the ultimate meaning. It is in this boundary area that the practical theologian works, reflects on the sources of giving meaning (Van Knippenberg 1989). The biblical story of Creation is such a source, because it is not a story about the creation of earth but about its existence. In his affirmation of earth as creation man gives meaning to the ground beneath his feet. In a more recent book Van Knippenberg connects the idea of Creation with man's course of life. Created reality is after all the medium of the experience and meeting with God for the faithful (Van Knippenberg 1998, 160). The concept creation arises in theology when the question as to sense and meaning is involved. And the question as to sense and meaning does indeed arise in the situation of the earth being at risk.

In this article I give an account of a quasi-experimental educational study amongst adult church members. The object of this study was to find out to what extent the participants approach environmental problems from their (Christian) religious point of view on creation, and to what extent this can be influenced educationally. I start by presenting the situation as it is now in ecological theology (1), subsequently I point out the catechetical framework (2), following which I develop the method of questioning for the study and present the results of the empirical research (3). In the final section I discuss the answer to the question on the basis of the results (4).

1. Ecological theology

In the seventies and eighties of the previous century ecology was an important subject in theology. In the nineties attention waned. It was a subject that was discussed within ethics in particular (Altner 1974; 1989; Améry 1972; Auer 1984; Drewermann 1982; Hermans 1986; Manenschijn 1988; Moltmann 1985). The discussion itself was set off by a paper written by Lynn White that was published in 1967, and that later became famous: The historical roots of our ecological crisis (White 1967). In the paper White suggests that the Christian faith and the belief in the story of Creation especially is a factor in the development of environmental problems. This publication initiated a discussion on the contribution of Jewish-Christian theology to the alliance between science and technology, between studying and interfering with the natural environment (Améry 1972; Barbour 1973; Derr 1975; Drewermann 1986; Roscam Abbing 1976; White 1973). After all, this theology rejected pagan animism in which each tree, hill or spring was considered to house a spirit, so it was approached with respect. The Jewish-Christian view is characterised by the secularisation of the world, that is to say that none of reality is divine. God created the world, after which he withdrew from it by giving it to man to manage. Man is the guardian of the world and may use the world as he sees fit. Moreover, Jewish-Christian views are characterised by a linear view of time: history is connected to the future, time leads to the coming of the Kingdom of God. According to White both characteristics of this view provided room for a view of progress: the world is developing in the direction of more, bigger and better. Connected to the opinion of Creation whereby man is presented as an image of God, this has provided room for man's unbridled rule of all nature, whereby nature exists for the development of man without it being respected. In the course of history this has taken place in the form of the exploitation, pollution and exhaustion of nature. White argues for the reconsideration of the relation of man and nature based on Franciscan ideas. The key to understanding Franciscus is his belief in the virtue of modesty, not only that of the individual but of the modesty of man as a species. For him man is not the crown of God's creation and ruler over all living beings, not even a democratic ruler. The industrious ant is not an example to the lazy, and fire is not a sign of the union of the human soul with God: no, they are Brother Ant and Sister Fire, praising their creator in their own way, just as Brother man does (White 1967, 155). Franciscus preached to the animals and called on them to praise God. This fundamental equality of all creatures with regard to their mutual creator is, according to White, the spiritual foundation for a changed way of treating nature.

White's opinions have evoked many reactions, in an affirmative as well as a negative sense (Groot Wassink 1980). According to Ton Lemaire a society that wishes seriously to deal with environmental problems can no longer continue in the Jewish-Christian tradition (Crijnen 1989). After all, the faithful and the church discover themselves to be part of the problem and not only in the wonderful and gratifying role as a factor in the solution to the problem (Van Iersel 1989). In the following section I indicate that Christian ideas do hold possibilities for a different approach to environmental problems.

1.1. Two ecological value orientations

The interpretation presented by White of the biblical task of Creation is merely one of the possible interpretations. It is an anthropocentric view of this task. There is, however, also an ecocentric approach in interpretation history. In the following section I wish to explain these two approaches to the task of Creation in more detail. Anthropocentrism and ecocentrism are two fundamental ways of viewing reality. This view is related to man, to nature and to the norm with regard to dealing with nature that is connected to it.

1.1.1. Anthropocentrism

In anthropocentrism man is considered as being of central importance in reality. Man is the centre of that reality. Everything in reality apart from him is subordinate to him, the value of everything else is determined by the value it has for man. This value can be seen in terms of use, aesthetic pleasure and essential living condition. Nature within and outside man has no value of its own in the anthropocentric view, its value is determined by its value for man. Its value is that of a condition of existence: after all, nature makes it possible for man to live, man is man on the basis of his corporality. Nature also provides food for man and is for man a source of aesthetic pleasure, he finds beauty, peace and even religious experiences in nature. The norm for the way nature is treated is that of instrumentalism. Nature deserves protection that is equal to the practical value it has for man.

The anthropocentric view is a reaction to the cosmocentric view of the Greeks, that for a long time was typical of the West European view. In the cosmocentric way of thought reality is considered as a unity, as a structured, harmonious, beautiful and even sacral whole (Verstappen 2000). This unity is a part of the objective manifestation of reality itself, of which everything within that reality is a part. Or as Metz puts it: the archetype of understanding the conditions of being is mundane objectivity, the primary spatial availability, a condition (Metz 1964, 54-55). Nothing in reality derives its value from something else in that reality. Reality, nature, man and gods – are as a whole sacral and deserve respect. In the Christian view an initial reaction to this cosmocentric view can be seen. Man and nature are much more clearly distinguished from one another. Nature is distinguished from man, but is admired as a work of God and considered as a reference to God. However, only man is created in the image and likeness of God, which as such gives him precedence. Metz points out that the swing towards the anthropocentric way of thinking takes place in Thomas Aquinas's view (1225-1274). The primal condition of being is, according to Thomas, the typical human way of being, subjectivity. All other ways of being are interpreted from this subjectivity (Metz 1964, 56).

Anthropocentrism has since Descartes become a scientific way of thinking. According to Descartes nature has become the object and creation of human thought. After all man can question everything that exists. The only certainty that remains then is thought itself. That thinking and everything that is thought up in that thinking is subsequently the only thing that exists. Thus nature only exists in man's thoughts. This provided the opportunity for the experimental study of reality, first of nature, and then of man himself. Nature within and outside man is taken to be mechanical (Dijksterhuis 1951; Berger 1998). It is manipulated, changed, applied as an object of human actions for the fulfilment of human need. Nature becomes an instrument in the hands of man, it is approached instrumentally. The value of nature is defined by its value for man.

According to White this anthropocentric way of thinking is the basis of the Christian roots of present environmental problems. After all, the instrumental approach to nature has led to its exploitation, an unscrupulous exploitation that results in destruction, pollution and exhaustion. White points out that this started to happen from the moment that man began to employ nature on a large scale for his own food supply: first in agriculture, through large scale mechanical tilling of land and changes in the structure of the soil, later in stock breeding through the mass production of meat and milk. This can be characterised as the swing in the way in which nature was treated: first people lived off what nature has to offer, later nature is adjusted to suit the necessities of life for man. Industrialisation has only strengthened this process of damage to nature through exploitation.

There has, however, been a reaction to this exploitative way of treating nature in the anthropocentric way of thinking. In order to prevent pollution, destruction and exhaustion nature is approached in a more prudential instrumental way. Damage to nature is avoided as much as possible or unavoidable damage is repaired with the use of new technology. The anthropocentric way of thinking remains the same, nature continues to be of value to the extent that it is of use to man, damage is avoided where man is affected. Much of the immediate damage is moved to the future or elsewhere, for example the third world or the oceans. Old wildlife areas are made into residential areas for man, new wildlife areas are created elsewhere. In this anthropocentric approach the view on man and nature remains caught in a dualism of man and nature. Man and nature are each other's opposition, belong to different realities.

The anthropocentric way of thinking can also be found in the theological opinion on creationism. In number 343 of the Catechism of the Catholic Church the anthropocentric interpretation is expressed as follows: 'man is the highlight of the work of creation'. This is obvious in the order of the days of creation that go from the less to the more perfect. Although God loves all his creatures the Scriptures say: 'you are worth more than any number of sparrows' (Luke 12, 6-7). All other creatures are naturally destined for the communal well being of man. God created everything for man, the use of which is bound to moral laws, whereby the ultimate normative criterion is care for the quality of life of fellow man, including future generations (CCC 2415). At the same time it is stated that that which belongs to man may not belong to any other creature; one may not waste affection on animals (CCC 2418).

The anthropocentrism of the interpretation of creation of the Catechism also emerges in Christian doctrine that the definitive object of Creation is the salvation of man through Christ. 'God had the glory of the new creation in Christ in mind from the beginning' (CCC 280). Creation involves the salvation of man, his redemption and glory at the end of time.

Characteristics of anthropocentrism can be found in the Catechism: emphasis on the main value of man, the derivative value of the rest of creation and the instrumental contact with creatures.

1.1.2. Ecocentrism

As a reaction to this and under the influence of the considerable ecological problems that we have been confronted with in the past fifty years, philosophy and theology have developed a completely different view, a view in which the position of man in reality is no longer considered as opposition to non-human reality. Nature and man are considered together, as belonging to the same one and undivided reality: the ecocentric view. The development of modern physics is what initiated this view. Natural reality cannot be reduced to elementary particles that exist unrelated but is in itself a dynamic process of interrelated particles that in precisely these relations gain meaning. In this system-ecological view of the world spirit and matter, nature and man cannot be separated from one another. Here nature gains the meaning of the Greek phusis: the whole of reality as a unity as opposed to metaphysics (Van der Tuin 1999).

Each part of reality gets its position and meaning from the whole of reality, and therefore has its own individual meaning and value, an intrinsic value. This is not dependant on a particular centre, but on a position within the whole. It is a value that is not dependent upon attribution, but that exists from being. Each part of reality has its own unique position in that reality, is an irreplaceable part of it. It is in this relation in particular that it has its own value, which cannot be replaced. The unique significance of man is therefore also taken from man's position within the whole. This means that the actual position of man as a subject, providing active meaning in unity with the whole of reality is maintained. But man has no greater value than the rest of reality. Man is not of any greater value simply because of his intellectual qualities (Manenschijn 1988; Rodman 1977).

This intrinsic value of nature requires that it be treated with respect and attention (Blans 1991). This means that nature is maintained, and protected for the sake of itself, and not merely as an instrument in the hands of man. Respect means actions that are aimed at retaining integrity, stability and beauty. Respect implies showing justice and love with regard to the whole of nature (Schenderling 1999).

In the stories of Creation in Genesis there are elements that support an ecocentric interpretation of Creation. Again I will discuss this on the basis of the Catechism text. In the Catechism the whole of Creation is considered as a manifestation of God's glory (CCC 319). This means that each creature has its own goodness and perfection (CCC 339), has intrinsic value because God says of each of his acts of creation 'that it was good'. For man this means that he should respect the individual goodness of each creature (CCC 339). Everything exists in mutual dependence upon each other, each creature needs other creatures (CCC 340), there is solidarity amongst creatures on the basis of the fact that they all have the same Creator (CCC 344).

The characteristics of ecocentrism described earlier can be recognised in all of the above: reality as relation, the intrinsic value of each creature and the respectful treatment of each creature. Both these theological orientations on the view on Creation form the content of a catechetic treatment. In the following section the aim of this catechism is developed and justified.

2. Religious education for adults

Religious education is one of the ways in which the church gives form in its pastoral actions to its task of mediation in salvation. Therefore the general aim of religious education is on the one hand closely connected to this task of mediation in salvation, and on the other to the aim of pastoral actions. The aim of pastoral actions was described earlier in the introduction using Van Knippenberg's work, as the encouragement of religious communication (Van Knippenberg 1987). Catechetically this encouragement takes place in the form of learning religious communication.

It is the church's task to encourage salvation in the name of God (Rahner 1969). Pastoral action, in this case catechetic action is aimed at this task. Religious communication thus has the function of (ecological) action as fulfilment of the task of the encouragement of salvation by the faithful. In other words religious communication on salvation forms the spiritual orientation for (ecological) actions. Concentrating on the Church's task with regard to the environment, - to promote the wholeness of the earth, - learning religious communication in religious education is aimed at this ecological assignment. The object of learning religious communication is that it encourages this conduct by creating a spiritual foundation for it. Religious education is therefore: learning religious communication with the development and/or the strengthening of the spiritual foundation for (ecological) conduct in mind.

For the formulation of the objective of environmental catechesis I will now discuss in succession learning communication, the content of communication and actions based on this communication.

2.1. Learning to communicate

The formulation of educational aims in communicative terms is quite recent. This communicative turn in religious pedagogy is according to Feifel, characterised by the unity of understanding, attributing meaning and actions (Feifel 1987, 30-32).

In the first place communication involves understanding. I take understanding to mean the cognitive skills necessary in order to deal with content. These form the conditions for communication as the exchange of meanings. More specifically communication involves activities such as: learning to understand others and making oneself understandable for others; explaining what one means and learning to interpret what others mean; being able to ask for and give responsibility (De Jong 1990, 140). These activities imply cognitive skills: from the reproductive knowledge of and insight in the concepts that form the content of communication, to the skill to evaluate the consistency of concepts employed internally and externally (Bloom 1964).

Learning religious communication cannot, however, secondly, be reduced to learning these cognitive skills, as if it concerned cognitive skills with regard to concepts that are separated from some affective giving of meaning and sense. Understanding religious concepts means aiding in the execution of the experience of meaning that is expressed in these concepts. So here communication means connecting the experience of meaning that is expressed in religious concepts with one's own way of dealing with the question of meaning concerned.

Thirdly, religious communication refers to actions. Understanding and the attribution of meaning opens up new play areas for the imagination, in which at the very least a partly successful life based on faith is referred to. It is in exemplary conduct that understanding and the attribution of meaning reach completion. In other words: because religious communication involves the religious giving of meaning, taken from tradition as well as one's own view, learning it implies that the following are inextricably bound to one another: cognitive understanding, personal interpretation and actions. After all faith makes people think, initiates conversion and has to be done.

The catechetical task of learning religious communication concerning ultimate meaning involves the following:

- understanding, that is to say the acquirement of knowledge concerning ultimate meaning;
- the cognitive skills needed to be able to deal with that knowledge;
- the skill to relate that knowledge with one's own attribution of meaning concerning questions of life;
- the skill to view one's own actions on the basis of these meanings;

Thus religious education creates the conditions for the faithful that enable him/her to learn to participate in social communication concerning questions of meaning. This is not the immediate aim of catechesis but a transcendental aim. The interactive and social aspect of this communication is employed as a method in catechesis.

2.2. Content of communication

The content of communication is the ultimate attribution of meaning to one's personal and social life. This attribution of meaning is related to the man's fundamental existential questions. These so-called questions on life can be somewhat systematised as concerning the following areas of existence: the individual; the other and others; nature; space and time; suffering and death; good and evil. According to Schillebeeckx these areas constitute the co-ordination system of human existence: religion is about these questions (Schillebeeckx 1977, 674 et seq.). This religious communication makes use of central symbols and images of the various philosophical traditions. Hermans mentions the following with regard to Christian philosophy: God as Father; Creation; Sin; Mercy; Resurrection; God's Kingdom and Justice (Hermans 1993, 88 et seq.). The existential question that constitutes the content of communication in environmental catechesis is formed by the question as to the meaning of and treatment of earth.

In section one I discussed in detail the way in which this question is answered in modern views. In doing so I distinguished two orientations. The Christian symbol, in which the ultimate attribution of meaning is expressed, is the concept creation. This symbol is central in the content of communication in the framework of environmental catechesis. Thus in the first place learning concerns the various interpretations of this symbol, as expressed in the tradition of the Christian faith, in confrontation with the personal religious views of the students. Next learning concerns the attribution of meaning to nature that occurs on the basis of this confrontation, and finally it concerns the behavioural consequences this has for the way nature is treated.

Religious communication concerning the religious symbol of Creation thus implies: the acquirement of knowledge about the various Christian interpretations of the symbol that have been handed down and the skill in dealing with these; the exploration and explicit forming of one's own (religious) view; the formation of a relation between interpretations that have been handed down and one's own view, in order to reach the attribution of meaning; finally the skill to draw and think about the consequences for behaviour on the basis of this attribution of meaning.

2.3. Acting with the wholeness of Creation in mind

Learning religious education should provide actions with orientation. Based on the church's assignment it is the task of religious pastoral not only to encourage religious communication but also to encourage actions with the wholeness of Creation in mind, on the basis of an ecological orientation of this assignment. Thus I have made a strong connection between communication and conduct. Communication is thus deprived of its noncommittal character, as has already been mentioned earlier on in this section, because the content of this communication involves the appeal to actually act. Giving meaning on the basis of Christian interpretations of the concept creation means that the Christian actually testifies to the hope that Creation means. Learning religious communication in terms of cognitive and affective development provides actions with orientation in the sense of healing actions. This means that education aims at an intense affective involvement. Involvement that implies that students are prepared to make the value orientations that constitute the content of catechesis orientation for their own actions.

Following these reflections I reach the formulation of the general aim of environmental religious education: to teach students to participate in communication concerning the religious attribution of meaning to nature with cognitive and affective development in mind, in order to use this as orientation for their conduct with regard to nature. In other words: they acquire and strengthen their spiritual basis, formed by the religious attribution of meaning to nature, as orientation for the way they treat nature.

A catechetical treatment had been designed on the basis of this general formulation of an aim. The following section discusses this.

3. The quasi experimental study

3.1. The treatment

The above theological theory has been put into operation in an adult education program. The following concepts were used:

Anthropocentrism

a1 portrayal of man:
philosophical: man central, as distinct from the rest of nature
theological: man is the image of God
a2 nature view:
philosophical: derived from man, nature is owned by man, he rules over it
theological: monotheistic view of God as Creator. He is all powerful and absolute transcendent
a3 actions: rational instrumentalism (steward)

Ecocentrism

b1 portrayal of man:
philosophical: unity of all life, man does not hold a special position
theological: Creation as a manifestation of God
b2 nature view:
philosophical: intrinsic value of nature
theological: tritheistic view of God Creator who was permanently bound to his Creation from the beginning. He maintains it
b3 actions: respect (mandataris)

The cognitive aim of educational treatment is to encourage views concerning the connection of the belief in Creation and the way nature is treated. The affective aim is the increase of the affective openness for both theological ways of thinking (Bloom 1956). The aim to act lies in the perspective and concerns the strengthening of the relation between faith and conduct.

The aim to act requires further explanation. The way people act is influenced by various factors. I mention three of these: a means-aim factor, a socio-normative factor, a philosophical factor.

The means-aim factor and the socio-normative factor are taken from Ajzen and Fishbein's attitude-behaviour model (Ajzen 1987; 1988; 1991; Ajzen and Fishbein 1980; Fishbein and Ajzen 1975). The means-aim factor, called the cognitive factor, implies that behaviour is motivated by the aim one wishes to achieve with that behaviour, and the supposition of the expected effect that one will achieve with the behaviour. The socio-normative factor is related to the behaviour expected by the social environment and the importance one attaches to that social environment. The third factor, the philosophical, that is not included in Ajzen and Fishbein's model, is related to the values one applies related to the behaviour that best befits these values. The affective object of educational treatment is aimed at strengthening of this relation. In theological terms this concerns the development of a spiritual foundation for actions, in this case ecological actions. This foundation is developed intrinsically by both the orientations on the view of creation that were explained in the first section of this contribution. The aim is not the strengthening of one of either orientations, anthropocentrism or ecocentrism, as a motivation for actions but the strengthening of the philosophical orientation that is the foundation of both these ways of thinking as such as a motivation for actions. In other words the aim is to strengthen the bond between religion as a source of inspiration and participation in religious activities. A bond that other authors already suspected existed on the basis of survey research; this research, however, only covered church involvement and social activism that actually occur together (Hermans 2001, 91). A study on an intrinsic connection has not yet taken place. The other aims of treatment are formulated in cognitive and affective development with regard to the concepts that have been elaborated. The curriculum developed for the treatment includes materials and work forms like the instrumentation of set aims.

Subsequently the question to be studied is: what is the effect of a catechetic curriculum on two philosophically based ecological ways of thinking in terms of the cognitive and affective development, and the development of the spiritual motivation to act? The treatment took place amongst hundred adults. The control group, that did not receive treatment, was made up of thirty adults. Participants were presented with an extensive preliminary measurement, in which background variables were measured, and a numeration with the affective and cognitive variables, and environmental behaviour. Both groups included Roman Catholic and protestant adults who were involved in the church and had a secondary education, were from the social middle class and aged between twenty-five and seventy-five. The random sample is representative of those involved in the church in the Netherlands.

3.2. The results

The effect for the cognitive aim is .23. That is to say that the number of good scores in the re-measurement has increased by 23%. This percentage was reached by correcting the number of good scores of the experimental group before the number of good scores of the control group. The affective measurement showed that the total relation to thought orientations has only increased by .07 on a scale of 1-5. When split into the separate orientations this means that there has been a decrease for anthropocentrism of .14 and an increase of .07 for ecocentrism. These changes are minimal, but can be attributed to the so-called 'ceiling effect'. There was a great amount of involvement at the beginning of the experiment. This clearly involved people who took part in the treatment as a result of their deep personal feelings for the environment. Therefore a big change could not be expected.

The effect of the third aim was researched on the basis of Ajzen and Fishbein's model of 'reasoned behaviour' mentioned earlier. This involves measuring the philosophical orientation as an aspect of attitude and via an aim-means factor. The change in the model is too great to be able to incorporate a third separate factor, for this reason the philosophical factor was incorporated in the assessment of an aim that can be reached with certain behaviour. Thus the effect of the curriculum can be viewed especially in the strengthening of the relation between attitude, intended behaviour and conduct. Before the curriculum this relation was .48 and .30 respectively, afterwards a correlation of .73 and of .57 was measured. Quite an increase. In the preliminary measuring as well as the re-measuring this effect can be attributed to the attitude of ecocentrism in particular.

The result of the treatment in cognitive and affective terms is not particularly large, the effect is most obvious for the strengthening of the relation between philosophical views and conduct and this was the ultimate aim of the treatment. The treatment can therefore be considered as being successful in this respect.

4. Discussion

The aim of the quasi experiment was to investigate to what extent students can let themselves be guided in their actions with regard to the environment by their own religious spiritual background, and to what extent this can be influenced educationally. The experiment shows that religious education considerably strengthens the bond between the religious views and actual conduct of the students. Their behaviour does not change, but they are more inspired in their conduct by their religious views, they become more aware of their own religious background. Their knowledge of the view on creation also increases considerably, even though this was already strongly present.

From the beginning the participants in the experiment were deeply involved in the problems of nature, although these were certainly not the most important problems for their existence. The way they treat nature is extremely conscious and friendly. Their religious views could be characterised as being ecocentric rather than anthropocentric. This does not change much as a result of the educational treatment, although there is an obvious shift in their views. The greatest effect can be seen in the increase in the connection between religious views and conduct.

A second remark is related to the views themselves. It was supposed that both religious views could lead to environmentally friendly behaviour. This supposition has not been proved. In the preliminary and re-measuring the anthropocentric way of thinking is barely connected to (nature friendly) conduct of the participants. In the re-measuring this connection further decreases. Participants are inspired in their environmentally friendly conduct in particular by an ecocentric view of creation.

This leads to a third remark. Christian theology as a reflection of people's faith is considered as anthropocentric, and sometimes as androcentric theology. A theology in which (the man) man is the centre and the highlight of creation. This supposition is in any case not confirmed in this study. The participants show a clear ecocentric, and thereby also feministic view of creation and the position of man in creation.

This environmentally friendly view connected to environmentally friendly conduct, and this brings me to the fourth remark, provides no extra information for Lynn White's thesis, that puts the blame on the Christian view for laying the foundation for the ecological crisis that is threatening the existence of the world. This study shows that conduct that destroys the environment and the Christian faith are not inextricably bound, but that in the Christian view there are tendencies that reveal a different attitude with regard to nature and man's position in it. This study hereby confirms the conclusions that Ester and Seuren made earlier on the basis of empirical material, whereby the Lynn White thesis, put into operation as the relation between orthodox faith and environmentally friendly conduct, was falsified (Ester and Seuren 1992).

The catechetic experiment proves that environmental problems form an important issue for this group of practising religious and that they consider communication on this subject to be important. Not only are they prepared to communicate with others in the treatment about it, they are also prepared and able to take in new information and to connect this with their existing views. Catechesis contributes thus to the individual meanings people give to their existence and to the social relevance of these meanings because they make a closer connection between their social conduct and their faith. The observations already made by others are supported on this point in particular (Hermans 2001; Van Iersel and Spanjersberg 1993; Jeurissen 1993). However, further research is desirable, because the study only involved a reasonably small group.

The title of this contribution is: Can faith save the earth? This question has not come up as such in this contribution, also it cannot be directly researched and answered. However, the question has been approached indirectly. A strong bond between people's conduct with regard to their natural environment and their views on the foundation of their existence is indeed a contribution to the preservation of the earth. In other words: creation and environment belong together in people's faith and in the proclamation of the church to gather together. Only in this way can faith save the earth.

References

Ajzen, I. 1987. Attitudes, traits and actions: Dispositional prediction of behavior in personality and social psychology. *Advances in Experimental Social Psychology* 20: 1-63.

Ajzen, I. 1988. *Attitudes, Personality and Behavior.* Chicago: Dorsey.

Ajzen, I. 1991. The Theory of planned Behavior. *Organizational Behavior and Human Decision Processes* 50: 179-211.

Ajzen, I., and M. Fishbein. 1980. *Understanding Attitudes and Predicting Social Behavior.* N.J.: Prentice-Hall.

Albrecht, S.L., B.A. Chadwick, and D. Alcorn. 1977, Religiosity and Deviance: Application of an Attitude-Behavior Contingent Consistency Model. *Journal for the Scientific Study of Religion* 16, 263-274.

Altner, G. 1974. *Schöpfung am Abgrund: die Theologie vor der Umweltfrage.* Neukirchen: Neukirchener Verlag.

Altner, G. 1984. *Manifest zur Versöhnung mit der Natur: die Pflicht der Kirchen in der Weltkrise.* Neukirchen: Neukirchener Verlag.

Altner, G., eds. 1989. *Ökologische Theologie: perspektiven zur Orientierung.* Stuttgart: Kreuz Verlag.

Améry, C. 1972. *Das Ende der Vorsehung: die gnadenlosen Folgen des Christentums.* Reinbeck bei Hamburg: Rowohlt.

Auer, A. 1984. *Umweltethik: ein theologischer Beitrag zur ökologischen Diskussion.* Düsseldorf: Patmos.

Berger, H. 1998. *Ik noem het: God. Reflecties bij Luc Ferry, L'homme-Dieu ou le sens de la vie.* Tilburg: Tilburg University Press.

Bloom, B.S., eds. 1956. *Taxonomy of educational Objectives.* Book 1 Cognitive Domain, Book 2 Affective Domain. London: Longmans.

Boersema, J.J. 1997. *Thora en Stoa over mens en natuur. Een bijdrage aan het milieudebat over duurzaamheid en kwaliteit.* Baarn: Callenbach.

78

Bos, H. 1990. *Kerken in beweging voor gerechtigheid, vrede en milieu: deelname van de kerken aan het Conciliair Proces in kaart gebracht.* Nijmegen: KU Nijmegen.

Catechism of the Catholic Church 1994 Liguori : Libreria Editrice Vaticana (quoted as: CCC)

Crijnen, T. 1989. Cultuurpessimist, interview met Ton Lemaire. *De Tijd* 07-04-1989: 52-56.

Dijksterhuis, E.J. 1951. *Het wereldbeeld vernieuwd: van Copernicus tot Newton.* Arnhem: Van Loghum Slaterus.

Drewermann, E. 1981. *Der tödliche Fortschritt: von der Zerstörung der Erde und des Menschen im Erbe des Christentums.* Regensburg: Pustet.

Ester, P., and B. Seuren. 1992. Religious beliefs and environmental attitudes: an empirical test of the Lynn White hypothesis in fourteen nations. *Sociale Wetenschappen* 34(4): 20-40.

Fishbein, M., and I. Ajzen. 1975. *Belief, attitude, intention and behavior: an introduction to theory and research.* Reading: Addison-Wesley.

Groot Wassink, J. 1980. *Hedendaagse Franciscaanse spiritualiteit. Een handreiking aan ecologen.* Haarlem: Gottmer.

Hermans, C.A.M. 2001. *Participerend leren. Grondslagen van religieuze vorming in een globaliserende samenleving.* Budel: Damon.

Iersel, A.H.M. van 1989. Scheppingstheologie: een milieuprobleem? *Speling* 41(4): 13-20.

Iersel, A.H.M. van, and M. Spanjersberg. 1993. *Vrede leren in de kerk.* Kampen: Kok.

Jeurissen, R. 1993. *Peace and Religion. An Empirical-Theological Study of the Motivational Effects of Religious Peace Attitudes on Peace Action.* Kampen: Kok Pharos.

Kalbheim, B. 2000. *Sinngebung der Natur und ökologisches Handeln: eine empirisch theologische Untersuchung zu Motiven umweltschüützenden Handelns bei Kirchenmitgliedern und Nichtkirchenmitgliedern.* Münster: Lit.

Knippenberg, M. van 1987. *Dood en religie. Een studie naar communicatief zelfonderzoek in het pastoraat.* Kampen: Kok.

Knippenberg, M. van 1989. *Grenzen. Werkplaats van pastoraaltheologen.* Kampen: Kok.

Knippenberg, M. van 1998. *Tussen Naam en Identiteit. Ontwerp van een model van geestelijke begeleiding.* Kampen: Kok.

Manenschijn, G. 1988. *Geplunderde aarde, getergde hemel: ontwerp voor een christelijke milieuethiek.* Baarn: Ten Have.

Metz, J.B. 1964. *Christelijke mensbetrokkenheid: over de denkvorm van Thomas van Aquino.* Hilversum: Brand.

Moltmann, J. 1984. *Diakonie im Horizont des Reiches Gottes: Schritte zum Diakonentum aller Glaübigen.* Neukirchen-Vluyn: Neukirchener Verlag.

Moltmann, J. 1985. *Gott in der Schöpfung: ökologische Schöpfungslehre.* München: Kaiser.

Rodman, J. 1977. The Liberation of Nature? *Inquiry* 20: 85-95.

Schennink, B. 1992. *Blijven de kerken in beweging voor Gerechtigheid, Vrede en Heelheid van de Schepping?, deelname van lokale kerken aan de tweede fase (1989-1992) van het conciliair proces.* Nijmegen: KU Nijmegen.

Schenderling, J. 1999. *Mens en dier in theologisch perspectief: een bijdrage aan het debat over de morele status van het dier.* Zoetermeer: Boekencentrum.

Schillebeeckx, E. 1974. *Jezus, het verhaal van een levende.* Bloemendaal: Nelissen.

Spee, H. 1992. *Diaconie, een hartszaak: op zoek naar profielverdieping voor diaconaat aan de basis van de geloofsgemeenschap.* Kampen: Kok.

Tuin, L. van der 1995. Ecologische waardeoriëntaties: een filosofische en theologische benadering. *Bijdragen* 56: 387-428.

Tuin, L. van der 1999. *Catechese en diaconie. Een empirisch theologisch onderzoek naar de effecten van milieucatechese op milieubewust handelen.* Tilburg: Tilburg University Press.

Verstappen, B. 2000. *Ekklesia van leven. Een aanzet tot een discussie tussen theologische kosmologie en bevrijdingstheologie.* Zoetermeer: Boekencentrum.

White jr., L. 1967. The historical roots of our ecological crisis. *Science* 155: 3767, 1203-1207.

On Mental Health and Religious Passion

Marinus van Uden

In this contribution on mental health and religious passion we will first deal with the questions "What is mental health?" and "What is a passion?" Effective spiritual leadership will benefit from insights into these two concepts. We will connect passions with certain psychopathological phenomena, such as mania and obsession. In particular we will deal with obsessive-compulsive disorder, in which - so to speak - the powers of passion have been reversed. In this context we will also deal with the function of ritual. We will end with the questions how religious passions can be beneficial to mental health and how compassion is related to passion. Our view will be summarised in the statement: "Compassion should become the spiritual leaders' passion."

It could be postulated that passions are to be found in the domain between ecstasy and self-control. "Grootsch en meeslepend wil ik leven"('I want to live a grand and compelling life') is the first line of a poem by the Dutch poet Hendrik Marsman, "De grijsaard en de jongeling" ('The old man and the youth'). The young man does not want to heed his father's advice to exercise more self-control. He would rather be urged on in life by his passions. Passions are the driving forces in life. However, these forces can also endanger an individual's mental health and cause a great deal of trouble.

1. What is mental health?

In order to make the reader more aware of the relative value of definitions of mental health, we quote at some length from the book *'Kleine Psychiatrie' (Little Psychiatry)* by the Dutch phenomenological psychiatrist Jan Hendrik van den Berg (first print 1966, 37th print 1980, 278-279). In this text he revealed an important characteristic of mental health and made a connection with the importance of the passions:

"After all that has been listed so far with respect to human unhappiness, illness and disorder, we must answer the question what are the qualities characterising a human life that one could call a psychologically healthy one. The answer is difficult to give, not only because negative qualities generally are easier to describe ("Le bonheur ne se raconte pas" [Happiness doesn't talk]), but also because a description of positive qualities easily lends itself to one-sidedness and exaggeration. The best-known description is by Soddy (Congress on Mental Health, London 1948). According to Soddy, the attributes of mental health are the following:

1. Mentally healthy individuals meet the requirements of life without having to make big efforts.
2. Their ambitions are within the range of practical feasibility.
3. Healthy individuals have a clear insight in their own strengths and weaknesses.
4. Not only can they give help, they can also accept help.
5. They are resilient after failure and realistic after success.
6. They are capable of friendship and if necessary capable of aggression.
7. Nobody thinks they demand too much from their environment.
8. Their beliefs, their ways of thinking and all the things they value are sources of strength and life."

Van den Berg continues: "This list deserves respect. Nevertheless, with each successive attribute mentioned, the healthy individual becomes increasingly dull. What to think of individuals who live "without making great efforts", who have "a clear insight in their own strengths and weaknesses" and who "are resilient after failure"? We would like to urge them to start living. Yet the definition is meant for ordinary people living healthy lives. Maybe for people who are too ordinary? In any case, it is meant for the well adjusted. Is adjustment, then, the crucial attribute of mental health? This is often said. But we think non-adjustment is also an attribute of health. If this was not the case, all creative people and all kinds of risk-takers [all the people who are passionate, MvU] ought to be called unhealthy, while – in another sense – they are healthier than all Soddy's so-called healthy people. That's why we would like to propose a second list, not so as to correct the above list, but as a supplement to it. For one can be psychologically healthy in two ways. First according to the list cited above. Well-behaved family men and women meet its criteria. But there is another kind of mental health, the attributes of which are the following:

1. Mentally healthy individuals are willing to exert themselves in order to live to the point of exhaustion, destruction, and if necessary death.
2. Their ambitions surpass anything that can be realised.
3. They do not want to be preoccupied with themselves.
4. They are able to refuse to give help, and often refuse to accept help from others.
5. They are miserable after failure and delighted by success.
6. They are capable of renouncing friends and are inclined to aggressiveness.
7. People think they put their aspirations too high.
8. Because they think that truth in life is to be found in things that make life worthwhile, human and unrepeatably blissful. Because they are urged on between birth and death, these two extremes that keep them alive and make them realise that nothing is so suspect as complete peace of mind."

Here Van den Berg gives us a first insight into the relationship between mental health and passion. Both adjustment and non-adjustment are attributes of mental health. It could perhaps be said that in passion the boundary between adjustment and non-adjustment is transcended. One can loose oneself in passion without necessarily endangering one's mental health.

Another seminal author in the area of defining mental health is Han Fortmann. In the last volume of his principal work "Als Ziende de Onzienlijke" ('As Seeing Him Who is Invisible'; an allusion to Hebrews 11, 27) (1974), this Dutch psychologist of religion and culture has elaborately dealt with the relationship between religion and mental health. He started by expounding that, scientifically speaking, mental health is not easily definable. When we find a definition of mental health, we have to realise its relative cultural merits. What is strange and out of line in one culture may be an altogether normal way of behaving in another one. Therefore Fortmann pointed out that we have to consider the function behaviour represents for the individual rather than its external appearance.

Many definitions of mental health refer to a kind of a mixture as well as a balance of contradictory forces. As Freud once put it: 'Where id was, there ego shall be' (Freud 1933/1964, 80). An equilibrium between the drives in the id and the forces of the reality principle in the ego has to be achieved for the individual to be mentally healthy.

Fortmann himself gave the following formulation: "The ability (freedom!) to realise oneself (e.g. in work) and to lose oneself ... The term 'freedom' is not sufficient in itself. One should add that it is a freedom that functions in two ways: self-actualisation and surrender." (Fortmann 1974, 361). Mental disorder starts when individuals lose themselves in one of the two: in a boundless drive for expansion or in total apathy and indecision.

2. Passions and Psychopathology

How is this related to the concept of passions? What happens when people lose themselves completely in passion? Passions engulf people. Passions are states to which people have to surrender. But how does passion shift into psychopathology?

Where does grandeur deteriorate into an all-devastating pathos? And where does grandeur deteriorate into restrictedness and narrowness? In the first case we might speak of an exalted mania. The answer to the second question is: in depression and in obsession. These mental disorders, mania on the one hand and obsession and depression on the other, can be regarded as passions that are pushed outward, or pulled inward, respectively. What happens when passion becomes obsession? Let us deal in more detail with the obsessive variant.

Technically we speak of obsessive-compulsive disorder. We can think of mental states, like "pathological jealousy", where patients become fixated on their partner in an obsessive way. This partner cannot move one step without having to provide a detailed justification to their jealous companion. We can also refer to the irritating stalking of an ex-partner, idol or other person, of which we are hearing more and more nowadays. The worshipped idol becomes an obsession. Passion gets out of control. The "crime passionnel" too can be regarded as the result of an obsessive preoccupation with another person. For whatever reason, patients cannot ban this person from their mind, with all the terrible consequences emanating from this. These are passions transformed into obsessions and compulsions.

In the psychodiagnostic 'Bible', DSM-IV (Diagnostic and Statistical Manual of Mental Disorders), these compulsions are defined as follows under the heading of 'obsessive compulsive disorder' (code 300.3): 1. Repetitive behaviour (e.g., hand washing, cleaning up) or mental activities (e.g., praying, counting) that the patient feels forced to carry out in reaction to an obsessional idea, or sticking to rules that are rigidly applied. 2. Behaviour or mental activities are aimed at preventing or reducing suffering, or at preventing a certain event or a frightening situation from occurring; these kinds of behaviour or mental activities have no realistic connection to the events that have to be neutralised or prevented, or are evidently exaggerated.

The following case may illustrate this: Mr Fiedoor was referred for treatment with severe obsessive-compulsive complaints. He worked as an English teacher in a high school. His compulsions were increasingly becoming an obstacle to his normal functioning. According to the patient the problems had started several years earlier. At night, when he was in bed, he began wondering whether he had locked his backdoor properly. Ruminating over this, he was unable to fall asleep and finally he would decide to go downstairs to check. These safety procedures had to be completed with ever-increasing precision. He made a complete inspection round each night in a fixed order that allowed no deviation. This marked the beginning of an uncontrollable extension to areas in which he no longer felt secure. It often happened that, apart from locking his house, he also felt compelled to lock his car over and over again. Even more stressing was the fact that he was unable to tell from the outside whether his car was locked or not. There was no button visible from the outside. Things became even more disastrous when he started brooding about the question whether or not he had turned off his car radio. Then the car had to be opened again and the whole ritual had to start all over again.

3. Passion and Ritual

How to evaluate these and other rituals? Are we to conclude that all passionate ritual behaviours are unhealthy and meaningless?

In this connection we refer to Freud who, in 1907, pointed out the relationship between the obsessive ritual and the religious ritual. He emphasised the following similarities between the two phenomena: 1. The moral constraint that arises from failing to perform these acts; 2. The scrupulous ways in which both are performed; 3. The ways both are isolated from other daily activities; and 4. The fact that interruptions are forbidden in both.

In this line of thought Freud underlined the ill and unhealthy aspects of religious rituals. This has often led to the false conclusion that Freud has said: Religion is an obsessive disorder.

But is this the whole story? After all, Freud also clearly pointed out the differences between the two phenomena. He stressed the meaninglessness and the individual variation and the private character of obsessive acts in contrast with the collective character of religious ritual. With respect to the meaninglessness of obsessive acts, he stated that, although religious ritual is meaningful to the believer, this in fact applies also to the obsessive patient. What seems meaningless is not that meaningless in reality.

In Mr Fiedoor's case, his obsessive-compulsive disorder was closely linked to his fear that his wife would leave him. His complaints had started at the time when his wife was having an affair, of which he had approved within the framework of their so-called "open marriage". His obsession appeared to symbolise his need to control his wife in a situation that was beyond his influence. His love for his wife became blocked and was distorted into an obsessive-compulsive disorder. With a measure of passion that was out of control he tried to control his wife's passions. In other words: where initially there seemed to be a difference between religious ritual (meaningful!) and obsessive ritual (meaningless!), this case, when considered from a psychoanalytic point of view, indicates a similitude between the two. The obsessive ritual too is full of meaning. Which leaves the crucial difference between the two: the individual, idiosyncratic private character of the obsession versus the collective character of religious ritual.

Freud finished his argument with the following conclusion: "In view of these similarities and analogies one might venture to regard obsessional neurosis as a pathological counterpart of the formation of a religion, and to describe that neurosis as an individual religiosity and religion as a universal obsessional neurosis" (Freud 1907/1959, 126-127).

In this perspective, Freud admitted that religious rituals are not identical with obsessional states and he kept the possibility open that religious rituals can be healthy by limiting individual misery.

In our view, religious rituals contain a considerable healing force. Although more religious rituals existed in so-called primitive societies than in our industrialised society, several important religious rituals are still intact. They obviously meet a need. In the first place, religious ritual channels emotions, and is therefore beneficial to the individual's stability. It allows the expression of emotions that are not easily verbalised. Religious ritual uses well-proven channels, providing it does not overwhelm the individual. Secondly, religious ritual provides a frame of interpretation at the cognitive level, thus guiding the concrete life situation by attributing a specific sense and meaning to it. In religious ritual this is often a healing force, in obsessive ritual, however, passion leaves the track of a sacred obligation so as to become an obsessive obligation ("Van heilig moeten naar moeten moeten" – 'From a holy should to a compulsive should'). Hence, we could say that passions and strong emotions can be channelled as well as fashioned by religious rituals in a healthy way.

But is there not also another link between the religious domain and mental health? This link can best be framed in the following question: How can religious passion reduce psychopathological phenomena in a more direct way?

4. Religious Passion and Psychopathology

Intense religious experiences and conversions are known for their therapeutic effects. Let us now consider such an intense religious experience that appears to have had a positive effect on an individual's psychosocial well being.

We take an example from psychiatrist Gyselen's contribution to the study "Hoe menselijk is mystiek?" ('How human is mysticism?') (Gyselen et al. 1979). Gyselen described a 52-year-old patient's life and the positive effect of a certain mystical experience in the course of the psychiatric process.

"This turning point [in the patient's condition; MvU] occurs during a walk on a country road. 'Suddenly a weight fell off my shoulders. I felt light. The air vibrated and had a heart that was beating. The trees were my relatives. The bricks were living and trembling and were intensely coloured. Your heart beats to the rhythm of the vibrations all around. You feel one with all that is, and all that is, is good. The colour of the clouds gave me a feeling of peace, nature knew me intimately ... This event, I am inclined to say: this Divine event, maybe I'd better label it as a Divine intervention in the earthly existence of the man who I was at that moment. I can best describe it as a withdrawal away from my 'me' as I had always experienced it, while this other me was an onlooker at my person. This new me felt absorbed, no, felt part of Something who is cosmic, who is now and always will be. Something indescribably real. I remember now that I saw myself and that I was filled with aversion. And I also thought that in fact anyone who was interested could see me like this: full of sin, arrogance and vanity. And I understood that, in my intellectual zeal to understand everything rationally, I in fact wanted to be my own God. And then it seemed to me that I made a leap: a surrender to faith. The realisation that one doesn't really have to understand everything with one's reason but that one can live in peace and inner tranquillity, knowing with each and every fibre of one's body, that, since God is, everything is good. And that God is Life who supports me, me, and everything and everything. And that I know another word who is synonymous with Life: Love – Ardent. I think that this experience didn't last very long, maybe it was just a flash. Yet it was enough to enjoy a kind of tranquillity for months that I had never known before. A tranquillity that started by me seeing everything afresh ..." (Gyselen 1979, 17-18).

This patient described an intense experience in which religious passion played a big role and could block psychopathology. Gyselen concluded that the intense experience could be interpreted as 'an attack on the illness' and that, from a psychological point of view, this intense, religious experience definitely didn't make the patient more ill at all, but quite to the contrary, brought him closer to his true self.

Consequently, religious passions can really promote mental health.

5. The Role of the Spiritual Leader

In the process of mental health promotion, religious passions can play an important role. But they can also endanger mental health. In such situations the role of the spiritual leader becomes essential because a patient will need someone who is able to differentiate between psychopathology and religious experiences and who has an open attitude regarding the question whether a certain experience refers to "Something Beyond" or something else. Spiritual leaders should know about mental health and about mental health promoting emotions, passions and rituals. Only then can they be true spiritual leaders. They balance on the edge between spiritual direction and psychotherapy. Comfort and true compassion will be offered and found right here. Compassion should become these individuals' passion. "Religious compassion allows an individual to deal with the suffering of another person in an altruistic way. The basic affect is sympathy or empathy; the motivation is characterised by altruism; the corresponding behaviour is an attempt to alleviate suffering" (Van Knippenberg 1999, 211). This attitude is, of course, not the monopoly of spiritual leaders.

We now can summarise the themes touched upon earlier as follows. They provide and imply some guidelines to act upon in the area of mental health and religious passions.

1. Passion transcends the boundaries between adjustment and non-adjustment. One can lose oneself in it, without endangering one's mental health.
2. The derailment of passion can go in two directions: outward, into an exalted mania, or inward, into depression and obsession.
3. Passions are channelled and fashioned in rituals. In the religious ritual, this is often a healing process. In the obsessive ritual, passion has derailed and turns from a sacred obligation into an obsessive obligation.
4. Intense religious experiences resemble passions. Both can free people from an oppressive psychopathological domain.
5. Compassion should become the spiritual leaders' passion in order for them to really be able to help others.

References

Berg, J.H. van den 1980. *Kleine Psychiatrie.* Nijkerk: G.F. Callenbach.

Fortmann, H.M.M. 1974. *Als ziende de onzienlijke (volumes 1 and 2).* Hilversum: Gooi en Sticht.

Freud, S. 1907. *Obsessive Actions and Religious Practices* (Standard Edition, 1959, Vol. 9, 115-127). London: Hogarth.

Freud, S. 1933. *New Introductory Lectures on Psycho-Analysis* (Standard Edition, 1964, Vol. 22, 3-182). London: Hogarth [quotation in Lecture XXXI, 'The Dissection of the Psychical Personality', p. 80]

Gyselen, M. 1979. Mijn patiënt was meer dan ziek. Pp. 11-46 in *Hoe menselijk is mystiek?*, edited by M. Gyselen, P. Mommaers and J.J.C. Marlet. Baarn: Ambo.

Knippenberg, T. van 1999. Compassie: Over leiden en lijden. Pp. 205-219 in *Over Leiden. Dynamiek en structuur van het religieus leiderschap*, edited by H. Beck and R. Nauta. Tilburg: Syntax Publishers.

Leadership, Delineation and Complementarity
Laity and Clergy in Service to the People of God

Myriam Wijlens

"Leadership and (crossing) boundaries" are subjects central in the work of Tjeu van Knippenberg, whose work is honored in this *Festschrift*. When these subjects are reformulated as "leadership, delineation and complementarity" they also touch on questions arising from the increase of professional lay ministers and their relationship to clergy when they together stand in service to the people of God. After in the years preceding Vatican II the Liturgical Movement and the Catholic Action had made laity aware of their participation in the celebration of the Eucharist and the necessary consequences this should have in their actions in every day life, Vatican II affirmed the doctrine of the common priesthood of all baptized. Soon after Vatican II laity, therefore, increasingly took an interest in working not only in the world, but also within the Church itself. This led to questions about the cooperation of both clergy and (professional) laity, such as the appointment to a leadership position in a parish, or as a lay chancellor who grants dispensations, or as a lay judge.[1]

Those who have been engaged in these studies and discussions might have the impression that they have come to a halt: not much progress is made, it seems. Could the reason be that we are not asking the right questions? That then will be the subject of this study. After a short introduction in which I will clarify who we are talking about and thus identify the different "groups" existing in the Church, I will determine the questions that govern the current debates and see whether in light of Vatican II these questions need to be reformulated in order to understand lay ecclesial ministry, ordained ministry and the relationship between them in such a way that all ministry is a true service to the people of God.[2] Thus, the main question of this study is: Are we considering the issue of (lay ecclesial) ministry from the right perspective?

---

[1] Often pastoral theologians consider laity only on the level of parishes, hospitals or deaneries. However, leadership in the Church is exercised on the legislative, executive and judicial levels. Pastoral care is considered to belong to the executive domain, but lay persons are also active in the more administrative part of the executive power (such as in chancery offices) and in the judicial domain. As of 1971 diocesan bishops can appoint lay men to the office of judge. As of 1983 these offices are also open to lay women. However, lay persons can function only in a collegiate tribunal and the two other judges must be clerics. Recently, the question has arisen whether they can act as presiding judge in such a collegiate tribunal.

[2] While promulgating the 1983 *Code of Canon Law*, pope John Paul II emphasized that the newness of Vatican II should be the newness of the Code. Among the new insights he mentioned "the doctrine in which the Church is presented as the people of God (cf. dogmatic

1. Identification of the Different Persons

Theological reflections on laity and clergy and their cooperation are often based on the following division:

1. There are persons who are baptized and confirmed. With baptism they share in the threefold ministry of Christ. They are called to live their faith. In this group we find people who never actively live their faith as well as those who are very much engaged in the life of the Church or in the world. They would, however, not be commissioned by Church authority to do so, but would respond exclusively to their baptismal gifts.

2. There are persons who are baptized, confirmed and who are mandated by ecclesiastical authority to take on a specific task either within the community of faithful or within the world. At times they might have been granted an ecclesiastical office. In this group we may find persons who are mandated to represent the Catholic Church or the Holy See in international meetings, such as the World Conference on Women. This is a clear task set for a specified time, and it is clearly a task *in* the world. Other persons in this group are, for example, directors of religious education, lay judges, lay chancellors, professors of theology or of canon law, hospital chaplains, those who are appointed in virtue of canon 517, §2 [3] etc. This latter group is active within the faith community. In the Netherlands, these persons are called "pastoral workers." In the United States, this latter group is referred to as "lay ecclesial ministers." They are lay persons, who not only respond to their baptismal call, but who have also a place in the communion of the Church which is "submitted to the judgment and supervision of the hierarchy." [4] That is what the word "ecclesial" in lay ecclesial ministry refers to. Thus, it is not simply an activity undertaken on personal initiative.

Other characteristics of these persons are that they have obtained some education and are thus qualified and equipped for the tasks entrusted to them; the "mandate" they hold has been granted by the diocesan bishop or his representative. The tasks or office might have been conferred within a public ritual or liturgy, but this is not necessarily so. (An interesting example

---

constitution *Lumen gentium*, chapter 2) and hierarchical authority as service (cf. ibid. chapter 3)." John Paul II, Apostolic Constitution, "Sacrae disciplinae leges," *AAS* 75/2 (1983); English translation: *Code of Canon Law, Latin-English Edition, New English Translation*, Washington, DC: Canon Law Society of America, 1998, p. xxx. Further translations from the *Code of Canon Law* are taken from this edition.

[3] Canon 517 § 2 reads: "If, because of lack of priests, the diocesan bishop has decided that participation in the exercise of the pastoral care of a parish is to be entrusted to a deacon, to another person who is not a priest, or to a community of persons, he is to appoint some priest who, provided with he powers and faculties of a pastor, is to direct the pastoral care."

[4] Committee on the Laity, United States Conference of Catholic Bishops, *Lay Ecclesial Ministry: The State of the Questions. A Report of the Subcommittee on Lay Ministry*, (Washington DC: USCCB, 1999) 7.

might be the liturgical celebration in some German dioceses. Upon having completed a successful education as "pastoral workers," the diocesan bishop receives them within the context of a celebration of the Eucharist, into the "service of the diocese." In this ceremony, they promise obedience to the bishop and his successors and obtain a [civilly valid] contract for an indefinite time with the diocese. They also receive a mandate for their first concrete assignment to, for example, a parish or a hospital.)[5]

3. There are persons (men) who are baptized, confirmed and ordained. They can perform certain actions allowed by canon law. They can be deacons, priests, or bishops who although incardinated into a certain diocese do not hold a concrete office. In the terms of Vatican II, we would speak about bishops who are members of the college of bishops, but who have not yet obtained an office or do not any longer hold an office. It is the same for priests and (permanent) deacons: they are ordained and only subsequently they are assigned to a specific (pastoral) ministry.

4. There are men who are baptized, confirmed, ordained and who in the pre-Vatican II's and 1917 *Code of Canon Law*'s terminology have been granted jurisdiction. Often the power held is attached to an ecclesiastical office. Here we can think of functions such as parish priests, diocesan bishops, etc.

In the following sections I would like to make some remarks to this division.

2. Baptism in an Ecumenical Context

The four different sections give the impression that there is a clear distinction in the Catholic Church. But is this picture so clear? It seems that the division is based on the former ecclesiology which held that the Church of Christ is to be equated exclusively with the Roman Catholic Church. After all, it seems that we say that laity are those who are baptized (and confirmed). What does this say about those who are baptized outside the Catholic Church? They too are incorporated into Christ through their baptism and possibly received confirmation. They thus participate in the threefold ministry of Christ and, therefore, participate in the mission of the Church of Christ which is to proclaim the good news and to see to salvation. To be aware of the role of these Christians is not irrelevant, because there are offices in the Catholic Church that

---

[5] In the diocese of Basel the liturgical text used in the ceremony of June 12, 1993 shows great similarities to a kind of 'incardination', because the diocesan bishop and the lay person entered into a mutual commitment: the bishop promised to provide for a fitting position in the diocese, the lay person promised obedience to the diocesan bishop and his successors. Moreover, the spouses promised to assist their partners. Questions should be raised about the theological nature and theological and canonical implications of the content of these kind of celebrations.

can be and are *de facto* exercised by non-Catholics.[6] Such offices might be the finance officer or the notary. These baptized non-Catholics might feel called to work for the Catholic Church or to take part in the mission that the laity exercise in the world. I was recently asked whether a bishop could appoint an Orthodox priest to the office of judge for a marriage tribunal. The intention was to have this priest participate in a collegiate tribunal in which the validity of marriages entered into by one Roman Catholic party and by an Orthodox would be adjudicated. If this would not be possible, could he be appointed as assessor (c. 1425, §4)? [7] I believe these are areas where we have not thought about the canonical and practical implications of the new understanding of the Church, namely that the Church of Christ *subsistit in* the Catholic Church. Thus, the discussion about laity and clergy cannot forget to attend to the notion of the Church as well.

3. Cooperation and Complementarity

In the time preceding Vatican II the overriding model of understanding the Church had been that of a *societas perfecta*. Within this model there was a clear division between the power of orders and the power of jurisdiction. The power of orders was understood as a sacramental power for the communication *in persona Christ* of the saving grace of God to the individual members. The Church had also a social power in order to guide (and, if necessary, to coerce) its members along the ways of salvation. This power was called jurisdiction. Hence, the Church had two powers by the will of Christ and they were equally rooted in His will for the Church. These two powers were distinct in their nature, purpose and transmission.[8] Who could obtain power of orders or jurisdiction? Only clerics. However, before Vatican II a man became a cleric through the reception of first tonsure.[9]

With Vatican II this all changed. A major point at the Council was the question whether the bishops were mere delegates of the pope or were they

---

[6] Several tribunals around the world have baptized non-Catholic notaries. At times they are not even baptized. Thus, for example in some Indian dioceses it is rather difficult to find qualified Catholics to fill this position. Several judicial vicars in India argue that since the law concerning this office does not require (full) communion with the Catholic Church, and since the office requires skills of reading, writing, typing and honesty, the office can be filled with a non-Catholic person when a Catholic cannot be found.

[7] The question is interesting because the Catholic Church does recognize the power of priests belonging to an Orthodox Church "to bind and loose" in respect to the sacrament of penance (cf. c. 844, §2): these priests are validly ordained, but they are not in full communion.

[8] Hence, there were also two corresponding hierarchies. Canon 108 § 3 of the 1917 Code read: "By divine institution the hierarchy of orders consists of bishops, presbyters, and ministries; by reason of jurisdiction, of the supreme pontificate and the subordinate episcopate; but by ecclesiastical institutions other grades are also added."

[9] Thus there were the so-called minor orders and major orders.

representatives of Christ within their own dioceses?[10] The answer to that question would determine the understanding of powers in the Church. The Council did respond that the fullness of the sacrament of orders is conferred with episcopal consecration and that with it the three *munera* of sanctifying, teaching and governing are conferred (LG 21). Thus, there is one sacred power. When after the Council canonists had the task to draft a law, they were soon confronted with the new understanding, but also with the actual involvement of laity in the Church. Moreover, the term cleric was changed: not first tonsure, but ordination to the diaconate made someone into a cleric. To cut a long story short, a strong debate started leading to different schools of thoughts on the question whether lay persons could exercise jurisdiction or not.[11] The debate came clearly to the fore in two different terms used: whereas the final schema of 1982 for the *Code of Canon Law* determined that laity could participate (*participare*) in the power of governance, the promulgated text determines that they can cooperate (*cooperari*) in this power.[12]

After the promulgation of the Code, the discussion did not come to a halt. Indeed, whereas some do not want to see a doctrinal meaning in the change – and thus state that laity can participate - , others do see it as a change and thus claim that laity cannot participate, but can only cooperate in the power of governance. The well documented study by John Beal on the laity and the power of governance[13] reveals that the discussion on the subject seems to be stagnating. It appears that the different schools of thought are fixed in their positions and that once someone is familiar with a specific position it is relatively easy to predict what the answer to certain questions such as the dispensing power of the laity, or the capacity - in the theological sense - of a lay person to hold a position such as leading a parish as mentioned in canon 517, §2 will be.

---

[10] A major point had always been how a man who had not (yet) been ordained to the episcopacy could exercise power of jurisdiction once he was elected pope? There had been examples of this.

[11] Among the reasons for the development of different schools of thought lies the differing interpretation of history. History reveals that lay persons (e.g. abysses) did exercise jurisdiction in the past. Hence, those in favor of laity exercising power of governance invoke this in particular. The others, however, invoke in particular the doctrine of Vatican II which confirmed the one sacred power of the bishop. They state that this one sacred power would not allow for jurisdiction to be exercised without having the power of orders as well. John Beal provides an excellent description of the different schools in "The Exercise of the Power of Governance by Lay People: State of the Question," *The Jurist* 55 (1995) 1-92.

[12] Canon 129 reads: "§ 1. Those who have received sacred orders are qualified, according to the norm of the prescripts of the law, for the power of governance, which exists in the Church by divine institution and is also called the power of jurisdiction. §2. Lay members of the Christian faithful can cooperate in the exercise of this same power according to the norm of law."

[13] John Beal, "The Exercise of the Power of Governance."

After having studied the different arguments put forward by the different schools of thought, I started to wonder whether we have been asking the right question. What has been the question so far? I can see two issues: first, the different schools of thought all center not on the question of complementarity but on the question of cooperation of clergy and laity; secondly, in the context of that cooperation they focus around the question of ordination. Some scholars see ordination as an indispensable prerequisite to be able to exercise jurisdiction. They take recourse to the affirmation by Vatican II that there is a unity of the power of orders and of jurisdiction for the bishop and apply this therefore to all. Other scholars invoke historical arguments to state that the power of orders is not always necessary in order to be able to exercise jurisdiction. It should be noted that no matter from whatever side the arguments are put forward, "ordination" is a central point of departure.[14] Thus, whoever reflects on the issue responds to the question: Can those who have not received ordination exercise power of governance? Note, also that when speaking about laity, they are still very much seen as non-ordained. Therefore, the question is not: Does baptism and confirmation enable someone to exercise power of governance? Or, is being in full communion necessary to exercise power of governance?

This focusing on ordination in relation to powers and offices is also central in the 1997 instruction on the cooperation of laity and clergy.[15] The main question of this instruction seems to be: How can we do justice to the ministerial priesthood in light of the increased activities of laity within the Church? Is it surprising that these discussions focus on ordination? In light of history the answer must be "no." Since the middle ages, the understanding that the community is subject of the liturgy and that the proclamation of the Word enjoys an imminent importance in the community, was replaced by an understanding that there were two separate classes. There were clerics and there were lay persons. Gratian affirmed the existence of two differing classes

---

[14] I have the strong impression that discussions about holding an ecclesiastical office focus as well on ordination or its absence. Thus c. 228 §1 determines: "Lay persons who are found suitable are qualified to be admitted by the sacred pastors to those ecclesiastical offices and functions which they are able to exercise according to the precept of law." Yet, c. 274 §1 states: "Only clerics can obtain offices for whose exercise the power of orders or the power of ecclesiastical governance is required."

[15] Congretatio pro Clericis et aliae, Instructio "De quibusdam quaestionibus circa fidelium laicorum cooperationem sacerdotum ministerium spectantem," *AAS* 89 (1997) 852-877. The English translation on the Website of the Vatican renders this as 'Instruction on Certain Questions Regarding the Collaboration of the Non-ordained Faithful in the Sacred Ministry of Priests.' This translation sets different accents: *fidelium laicorum* is translated with 'non-ordained' and not with 'lay faithful'; *cooperare* is translated with 'collaboration.' The French translation provided on the Website is correct. The Dutch translation "Instructie over de medewerking van lekengelovigen aan het dienstwerk van de priesters," in *121-Kerkelijke Documentatie* 25 (1997) no. 8, 3-18 is correct as well.

(*genera*) of Christians. There were those who are set free for the divine service and who are devoted to contemplation and prayer. They are to stay away from worldly issues. These are the clerics and those who are religious. The other Christians are laity. The Greek word *laos* means in Latin *populus* (people). They are allowed to possess temporal goods, but only to use them; they are allowed to marry, cultivate the earth, go to court, bring their gifts to the altar, etc.[16] This differentiation is not just a moral one nor is it just a determination of competency. There is more to it; the true faithful are the clerics and the religious. The others are permitted to occupy themselves with worldly issues or temporal goods. The consequences of this division were that the laity were juridical excluded from true ecclesial affairs. Even though the juridical implications are to be seen in a specific historical context, namely the freedom and independence of the Church vis-à-vis the powers exercised by sovereigns, and henceforth it does not refer to the contemporary meaning of the word 'laity,' it nevertheless went into history as such.[17]

The division, according to Hervé Legrand, implies the approval of the identity and autonomy of the clergy vis-à-vis (the rest) of the community, which is declared incapable and incompetent with respect to matters of faith.[18] Whereas initially, the word clergy (*klèros*) referred to the whole community as God's heirs (Romans 8,17; Colossians 1,12), the word became thus reserved for a group in the Church. Due to criticism by the Reformation against this twofold division, the Counter Reformation reacted with a theology which would remain until Vatican II and which holds, according to Ton van Eijk, four characteristics. First, ordained ministry is understood as a faculty, or as a power, which in particular manifests itself in speaking the words of consecration (*de verba Christi*) in the Eucharist and in giving absolution in the sacrament of penance (*potestas consecrandi et absolvendi*). This power is conferred at ordination by consecrating bishops to the person who is to be consecrated a bishop and by a bishop to a priest (presbyter) or deacon. Second, the person exercises this received power *in persona Christi*. This terminology, which finds its origin in scholastic thinking, did not mean even in that theology that the

---

[16] Decretum Gratiani, C.12, q. 1, c.7.

[17] Ruud G.W. Huysmans, *Het recht van de leek in de Rooms-katholieke kerk van Nederland* (Hilversum: Gooi en Sticht, 1986) 11-13.

[18] Hervé M. Legrand, "La réalisation de l'église en un lieu," in Bernard Lauret / François Refoulé (éd.), *Initiation à la pratique de la théologie*, III. II (Paris, Cerf, 1983) 184 (la tendance à disqualifier religieusement les laïcs) and 186 (l'autonomisation des clercs et leur scission d'avec l'ecclesia). In his reflections Legrand points out that the theology preceding Vatican II saw ministry (and ordination) too much irrespective of the connection to the local Church (180-182) and to the working of the Holy Spirit. Vatican II did pay attention to the Holy Spirit and its working in the Church (*LG* 4), but its place remains modest according to Legrand (159-161). He writes that this has consequences for understanding ministry as well. He, therefore, proposes that ministry is reconsidered not only from a christological perspective, but also in the context of a *communio* ecclesiology.

ordained minister acts as if he replaces Christ. It did, however, obscure that he also acts *in persona ecclesiae*, and there is a danger that this terminology isolates it from this.[19] The christological foundation that is applied here appears also in that the ordained minister is spoken of as an *alter Christus*. It is not difficult to see how such a strong christological foundation for ordained ministry could easily underrate a spirituality for all Christians based on baptism. In this one sided christologically oriented theology of ministry, Christ, to whom all power (*exousia*) has been given, granted it to Peter and the other apostles. They in turn handed it over to the bishop of Rome and the other bishops. The latter granted it partially to the presbyters (not to the deacons though because they were not always destined for the priesthood). As a consequence of this the Church came to be understood as a pyramid of which the laity formed the large base. They are the ones who receive, who as Church are being taught (*ecclesia discens*) and are to be differentiated from the Church that teaches (*ecclesia docens*).

Thirdly, Van Eijk writes, this sharp differentiation between clergy and religious on the one hand and laity on the other hand did not just come about around the beginning of the second millennium. The development of a clergy and with it of a clericalization and consideration of offices in an hierarchical order started already around the fourth and fifth century. From this time, the offices and functions within the community are entrusted to a specific group in the sense that those are in a specific state of life (clergy) are placed into a specific order in relation to each other. This order is to be followed step by step and is seen as a career till one arrives at the final step, which is the office of bishop. Thus, there is a hierarchy of competencies and duties.[20]

Fourthly, already very early in history – between the years 180 and 260 – the power of the group of ordained ministers is typified as "priestly" and is thus considered in particular in relation to sacramental celebrations. The term "priesthood" refers to this, for the two other functions, namely to proclaim and to govern, disappear behind this terminology. Thus what in 1 Peter 2,5-9 is called the "people of priests" becomes the "people of the priests." [21] Van Eijk concludes that what is seen in this pre-conciliar theology of ministry is legitimate when taken each point on its own, but considered together there are

---

[19] See also Bernard-Dominique Marliangeas, *Clés pour une théologie du ministère. In persona Christi – In persona Ecclesiae.* Théologie historique, vol. 51 (Paris, Beauchesne, 1978). In this book Marlianges investigates the history of the terms *in persona Christi* and *in (ex) persona ecclesiae* as the great scholastics used them. He shows that in juridic terms this is equivalent to the term *nomine Ecclesiae* (p. 235).

[20] Van Eijk (*Teken van aanwezigheid*, 274) follows here A. Faivre, *Naissance d'une hiérarchie*. Théologie historique, vol. 40 (Paris, Beauchesne, 1977).

[21] As Antoine Faivre formulates it on p. 83 of *Ordonner la fraternité. Pouvoir d'innover et retour à l'ordre dans l'Église ancienne* (Histoire), Paris 1992: "Du peuple du prêtre au peuple des prêtres." (Cited by van Eijk, *Teken van Aanwezigheid*, 274).

some limitations. There is a rather limited foundation of ordained ministry in the (local) community of faithful, and it is being restricted to its priestly function.[22] Theologians call it a theology of an isolated Christ – representation, in as far as it has become isolated from the Church which is the whole body of Christ. Thus, there appeared an imbalance in the Church: the clergy were the actors, the laity the recipients of pastoral care. A lay person came to be understood as someone who is not a cleric. It was someone who belongs to the ordinary people and who did not belong to those who hold power and offices.[23]

This differentiation between laity and clergy based on the reception of orders is not in agreement with the Old Testament's meaning of the word *laos*. There *laos* was used in opposition to the *ethnè*, the pagans. Thus "laity" is an honorary title for those who have been chosen. In the First Letter of St. Peter we read: "But you are a chosen generation, a royal priesthood, a holy nation, a peculiar people" (1 Peter 2, 9). Hence, due to this commonly being chosen, all baptized belong to the people of God; and the division line is not between clergy, religious and laity, but between Christians and non-Christians.

Considering all of this, it is not really a surprise that when theologians and canonists hear something like "laity and clergy in complementarity," they almost instinctively reflect about cooperation – and not about complementarity – and that within this theological framework they indeed cannot state that laity can participate in the power, because of the theological premises. They focus on the question: How can lay persons cooperate in the work of the priests? A response is not difficult, but does not touch upon the question of the delineation and complementarity of laity and clergy.

Is the question about complementarity correct? Vatican II and several theologians after the Council show that the question is correct, because of the change in understanding the Church itself.

---

[22] Hervé Legrand describes this forcefully in his contribution "La réalisation de l'église en un lieu," in Bernard Lauret / François Refoulé (éd.), *Initiation à la pratique de la théologie*, III/II (Paris: Cerf, 1983) 181-193.

[23] There is thus a monarchical or pyramidal model of the Church. Edward Schillebeeckx writes that the monarchical model for the Church is theologically founded in 1) the predominance of a christology which forgets the influence of the Holy Spirit on the lowest level of the Church and 2) in the social significance of papal infallibility. In this understanding the pope becomes the representative of Christ in this world not unlike the governors were the representatives of the Roman emperor in distant places. The gift of the Holy Spirit for the lower level is changed into a faithful obedience to what the top of the hierarchy has decided and proclaimed. In this understanding laity are not subjects, that is carriers and makers of what the Church is, but they become objects of hierarchical decisions, preaching and pastoral care. This perspective, moreover, takes away from the other authorities (e.g., bishops and the community of faithful) their original Christian authority. Edward Schillebeeckx, *Mensen als verhaal van God* (Baarn: Nelissen, 1990) 216-217; English translation: *Church: The Human Story of God* (New York: Crossroad, 1990) 198-199.

4. Vatican II and the Notion of Complementarity

Vatican II made major changes in understanding the Church. In particular the history of the dogmatic constitution on the Church, *Lumen gentium,* reveals that the Council was aware that only one image for understanding the Church would be insufficient to explain its nature. Moreover, the Fathers decided that there is a need first to reflect on all the faithful as such, and subsequently to address the particular ecclesiological issues concerning the different groups in the Church. The Council affirmed a fundamental equality of all baptized, of all Christians, which precedes the subsequent important distinctions and transcends these distinctions. As we all know, Vatican II has clearly underlined these thoughts as it decided that the chapters on the hierarchy, the laity and the religious must be preceded by a chapter on the people of God. We should take notice of this, because the Council did not just recognize the position of the laity in virtue of baptism. It did do that, but it went even one step further. It positioned all the baptized together before making the distinctions among them. Thus, every Christian is an active responsible member of the Church. All baptized participate in the mission of the Church, which is "the coming of God's Kingdom and the accomplishment of salvation for the whole human race" (*GS* 45).

Why was the Council able to do this? Well, the Council accentuated that the Church which met and was built up after Easter should not only be seen as the Body of Christ, but also as the temple or community (*koinonia*) of the Holy Spirit. The post paschal texts that narrate how people were commissioned, reveal that Christ is still sending people, but this sending cannot be seen without considering the Holy Spirit and the local Church for and in which people are sent. Thus, in agreement with this approach, Vatican II made a turn from an almost exclusively christomonistic[24] approach to a perspective where the christological and the pneumatological line are kept together. This approach is important because in it the local Church holds a relevant position. Ministry is exercised with other ministers and it is done both for and within the whole community. Ministry is, therefore, seen in relation to a concrete community.

Vatican II situated ministry within the local Church (diocese) and within the parish. The Decree on the Bishops, *Christus Dominus,* reveals this when it describes the diocese / particular Church: "A diocese is a section (*portio*) of the people of God whose pastoral care is entrusted to a bishop in cooperation with his priests. Thus, in conjunction with their pastor and gathered by him into one flock in the Holy Spirit through the Gospel and the Eucharist, they constitute a

---

[24] "A Christomonistic model of the Church is one that identifies the Church exclusively with Christ without accounting for the presence and action of the Holy Spirit," Susan Wood, *Sacramental Orders, Lex Orandi* Series (Collegeville: Liturgical Press, 2000) 25.

particular Church." [25] The different elements listed here are not all of the same rank: the Church is gathered in the Holy Spirit who is the first "builder" of the community. There is the Gospel and there are the sacraments (the Eucharist is mentioned as the main sacrament, but it may not be dissociated from the other sacraments, in particular baptism). The pastor (bishop) stands in service of this all.[26] The *Code of Canon Law* has 'translated' this emphasis on the community for example in the title preceding c. 368: "Particular Churches and the Authority Established in them" and in the title preceding c. 515: "Parishes, Pastors and Parochial Vicars." These titles express that there is first the community and that in that community there is ministry. The canons describing a diocese and a parish do the same: "A diocese is a portion of the people of God which is entrusted for pastoral care to a bishop with the cooperation of the presbyterate [...]" (c. 369) and "The parish is a definite community of the Christian faithful [...]; the pastoral care is entrusted to a pastor as its own shepherd under the authority of the bishop" (c. 515 §1). Thus, ministry is to be understood from within the community.[27]

It should be noted that whereas there is an increasing debate on the ministry of the bishop within the local Church,[28] the question may be raised whether the discussions about lay ministry, also by canonists, is carried out within this new ecclesiology where not just baptism and confirmation are decisive – for that would again focus on individuals and their relationship with God – but where the community as such is the receiver of the different ministries.

As a model for such an understanding of ministries, the Church of Corinth (1 Corinthians 12,14) could function. It saw the diversity of *charismas* in relation to the same Spirit, the many forms of *diakonia* in relation to the same Lord Jesus Christ, and the many forms of activities (*energèta*) in relation to the same God. Essential in the letter of St. Paul is that there are many *charismas*, but one Spirit (12,4) and that this is all the work of the one and same Spirit who divides as He pleases (12,11). Unity and diversity are co-existing and the Spirit is the source of both. When unity and diversity coexist, unity cannot be uniformity; and thus, there must be diversity. The Holy Spirit grants a diversity of gifts that

---

[25] CD 11. English translation from Norman P. Tanner, *Decrees of the Ecumenical Councils* (London: Sheed & Ward, 1990).

[26] Hervé Legrand provides a detailed theological commentary to the different aspects and can show how the local dimension of the Church is of relevance as well as the working of the Holy Spirit and how (ordained) ministry is to be understood in this context. Legrand, "L'église se réalise en un lieu," 159-171.

[27] Such a perspective has far reaching consequences, for example, for the exercise of the office of diocesan bishop. I have attempted to outline them with respect to the legislative task of the bishop in my article: "'For You I am a Bishop, With you I am a Christian': The Bishop as Legislator," *The Jurist* 56 (1996) 68-91.

[28] Discussions about the theological and juridical status of Episcopal conferences are also expressions of this as is the recent active debate about the local and universal Church.

cannot be derived from each other. Yet, he connects them in that the individual gifts and its carriers are not left in isolation, but are related to each other in a community. As source of community, the Spirit is not a source of chaos, of anarchy; but is one of order, of structure and communication. Or to say it with the words of St. Paul, as he concludes this section in the letter to the Corinthians, "God is not the author of confusion, but of peace" (1 Corinthians 14, 33). Thus with the model of the Church of Corinth, we see that St. Paul emphasizes that there is a great diversity of *charismas* and that these *charismas* serve the community. It is also clear that there is, therefore, a true equality of all baptized which precedes the divisions.

The theologian Walter Kasper sees the different *charismas*, ministries and offices as complementary to each other. He takes recourse to the concept of *communio* to explain that there is a diversity in unity in them.[29] Thus the laity, he says, take actively part in the threefold mission of the Church. This should find expression in counsels and synods. However, Kasper emphasizes, Vatican II pointed out that the *communio* ecclesiology also requires that the biblically founded differentiation between clerics and laity obtains a new understanding.[30] The Council stressed the essential difference and not just a gradual difference between the common priesthood of all baptized and the ministerial priesthood. This does not mean that the ministerial priesthood is more intense or higher than the common priesthood. If that would be true, says Kasper, then clerics would be better Christians, and that is not the case. The common and ministerial

---

[29] Walter Kasper, "Berufung und Sendung des Laien in Kirche und Welt," *Stimmen der Zeit* 205 (1987) 579-593.

[30] In the Spring of 2002 a conference on ministry entitled "In Service of the Community" was held in Germany. Cardinal Lehmann held the opening lecture in which he emphasized the need for unity in diversity and diversity in unity within a communion ecclesiology. There is a unity in mission and a diversity in ministry. He admits that at times it might be quite a challenge to find the balance between the legitimate diversity and the necessary unity. He sees this confirmed in the decree on the Apostolate of the Laity: "In the Church there is a diversity in ministry (*diversitas ministerii*) but unity in mission (*unitas missionis*)" (AA 2). Thus, he writes, all should be aware that they are working for the same cause and that they obtain their competence and acknowledgement through their specific contribution. Hence, no one is competent for everything nor is anyone the sole competent person. Karl Lehmann, "Kirchliche Dienste, Aufgaben und Ämter im deutschsprachigen Raum: Chancen und Gefahren," in Sabine Demel, e.a. (eds.) *Im Dienst der Gemeinde: Wirklichkeit und Zukunftsgestalt der kirchlichen Ämter*, Kirchenrechtliche Bibliothek, vol. 5 (Münster: Lit, 2002) 16. It should be noted that when Lehmann uses the word *Ämter* he does not use it in the sense of *officium* but refers to ordained ministers. In German the word *officium* is translated with *Amt* as well. This may contribute to the confusion, because with *Amtsträger* common German parlour refers to ordained ministers exclusively. Lehmann proposes to restrict the use of the word "Amt" to ordained ministers and to use the word "Diensten" - which in Latin would be *minsteria* (added by MW) - for all others. Lehmann, "Kirchliche Dienste,"13.

priesthood differ not on the level of being Christian, but they refer to different vocations and missions within the communion of all Christians.[31]

Kasper points out that Vatican II intentionally omitted a theological definition of the laity and just provided a typological description. It said that the laity have not received orders, but to this negative qualification the Council added a positive element: they have a special task in the world. This task is now to be seen no longer in the context of a dualistic vision on the world and the sacred, but in the context of the explicit statement that the Church is *in* the world. Thus the world and the Church are closely connected. As the opening lines of *Gaudium et Spes* state: "The joys and the hopes and the sorrows and anxieties of people today, especially of those who are poor and afflicted, are also the joys and hopes, sorrows and anxieties of the disciples of Christ, and there is nothing truly human which does not also affect them." [32] This implies that the service of the laity in the world is not just a worldly matter, but it also carries an ecclesial dimension. The laity see to it that the questions and the experiences of the world are present in the Church and are made fruitful for the Church. Thus they bring some fresh air in the Church. At the same time, they should proclaim the faith in the world. Thus, the presence of the laity in the world implies that they participate in the sacramental character of the Church. Therefore, the pastors should provide the laity with "light and strength," should not patronize them and respect their Christian freedom and listen to the laity. The complementarity can thus be found in that the ministerial priesthood is to be of service to the common priesthood. Thus, Vatican II called for a partnership between priests and laity and spoke of a fraternal relationship between the shepherds and the faithful who are entrusted to their care. The priests are called to listen to the specific interests of the laity.[33]

---

[31] Lehmann states that the Latin text of *LG* 10 about the common and ministerial priesthood makes very clear that there is first a communality and only subsequently a differentiation. He emphasizes that ordained ministry cannot be derived from the common priesthood. The one who holds an office (*Amtsträger*) does not just stand vis-à-vis the community, but also lives in it. "Jeder Amtsträger und jeder, der einen Dienst in der Kirche ausübt, gehört zunächst radikal gleichsam zum Fußvolk Gottes und wird eines Tages nicht nach seinem Ämtern und Titeln, sondern nach dem gefragt, wie er gerade auch in seinem Dienst und Amt als Christ gelebt hat." Lehmann, "Kirchliche Dienste," 17-18.

[32] *GS* n. 1.

[33] The original is worth citing in full: "Es gibt also innerhalb der gemeinsamen Anteilhabe aller Christgläubigen an allen drei Ämtern Christi unterschiedliche Berufungen und Sendungen. Darin ist die *Differentia specifica* des Laien begründet. In ihrer spezifischen Berufung und Sendung ist ihnen das Amt nicht übergeordnet, sondern dienend zugeordnet. Anders ausgedrückt: Das Konzil hat zu einer partnerschaftlichen Verhältnisbestimmung zwischen Priestern und Laien gefunden. Deshalb hat es ausdrücklich von einem brüderlichen Verhältnis der Hirten zu den ihnen anvertrauten Gläubigen gesprochen und die Hirten ermahnt, auf die berechtigten Anliegen der Laien zu hören. Das ist ein Leitbild von Communio-Ekklesiologie und Mitverantwortung, das noch längst nicht überall der Wirklichkeit entspricht." Kasper, "Berufung und Sendung," 586.

What about the laity who work within the Church, for example the lay ecclesial ministers? Kasper points out that these ministries must be understood as founded in baptism and confirmation and not as derived from orders. These new ministries are neither a supply for nor are they in opposition to the priesthood. Thus, says Kasper, they may not be seen and dealt with as fulfilling a need for the time there is a shortage of priests. They make a positive contribution and are enriching to the ecclesiastical office; they are a sign that the ministry to the world and the ministry to salvation are not two separate entities.[34] Due to the new offices that laity hold, the pastoral activity of the Church will become more "worldly" in the positive sense of the word. The Church, says Kasper, needs this to be able to evangelize more effectively. On the other hand, the laity need priests who are familiar with the world because they are personally engaged in it.

If we now return to the main point of this study, namely, whether we are asking the right question we might have to admit that we might have to rethink some of the issues. In light of the above outlined considerations, it seems insufficient to take recourse only to a christological understanding of ministry.[35] On the basis of Vatican II, it might be necessary theologically to enter into a framework or model or paradigm in which we consider both the christological *and* the pneumatological model. Kasper would call for a use of the *communio* model. In that we might also be able to understand the position of the baptized non-Catholics and their gifts to the Church.

In summary the afore mentioned reflections reveal:
1. There are different ecclesiological models for understanding ministry in the Church. We must be attentive to the underlying models we select.[36]

---

[34] "Von grundsätzlicher Bedeutung ist, dass es sich bei diesen neuen Ämtern um Ämter von Laien handelt, welche ihre sakramentale Grundlage in Taufe und Firmung haben und welche darum nicht als Ausgliederung aus dem Sakrament des Ordo verstanden werden dürfen. Die neuen Ämter der Laien sind weder ein Ersatz noch eine Konkurrenz für die Priester. Sie sind darum auch kein notwendiges Übel wegen der zu geringen Zahl von Priestern. Sie sind ein positiver Beitrag und Zuwachs für das kirchliche Amt und ein Zeichen dafür, dass Weltdienst und Heilsdienst nicht zwei hermetisch voneinander geschiedene Bereiche sind." Kasper, "Berufung und Sendung," 588.

[35] Lehmann warns to attempt to consider offices (*Ämter*) and ministries (*Dienste*) theologically primarily within an ecclesiological context. He states that the connection with the Church is important and might have been considered insufficiently in the past. However, ecclesiology cannot provide exclusively a foundation of office (*Amt*) and ministry. Christology should hold its primacy position here before ecclesiology. An office holder, he writes, is a "vicar" never a "boss": officeholders (*Amtsträger*) are to make themselves free for Christ (p. 18). In the cooperation of the different charismas, offices and ministries, Lehmann also takes recourse to the Pauline model as presented in 1 Cor 12-14. Lehmann, "Kirchliche Dienste," 20-27.

[36] Susan Wood identifies four conceptualizations of the Church influencing the relationship between ordained ministry and the Church: a monarchical and hierarchical conceptualization;

2. Vatican II understood ministry to be located within the community. Laity and ordained have complementary gifts; they do not stand in opposition. They each enjoy their own gifts which should be delineated in the context of understanding different ministries as complementary to each other.[37]
3. The ministry exercised in the world is also an ecclesial ministry because the Church does not stand in opposition to the world, but lives in the world.
4. The gifts that ecclesial lay ministers bring to the Church are to be seen neither as a supplying for nor as standing in competition with the gifts that the ordained ministers bring, but they are to be considered and examined on their own merits.
5. The current law, in particular the issues expressed in canon 129, deals with questions concerning cooperation or participation. However, understanding lay and ordained ministry as being complementary to each other might lead to a new and fresh approach of understanding the cooperation between them.

Conclusion

This study focused around the question: are we raising the right issues in relation to professional laity, clergy, delineation and complementarity? Must we reconsider or reformulate the issues? With Vatican II the Church has entered into a new phase. The Fathers were able to look at the old in a new way, because with the help of theologians they were able to raise new questions. An attentive reading of the conciliar texts and even more so of the discussions of these texts, reveal that the Fathers set a train in motion, that they believed that the Holy Spirit guided them in doing so, but that they were also aware that they could not see all the implications of their teaching. We, the Church, are invited to enter into those same dynamics. Pope Paul VI referred to this attitude with

---

a eucharistic, collegial model representing the communion of particular Churches; the priest, prophet, and king motif that structures the concept of the Church as the people of God; and a theology of the Church as a sacrament of Christ and ordained ministry as a sacrament to the Church. She investigates the 1990 ordination rites and the theology they display. Susan Wood, *Sacramental Orders.*

[37] In a *nota* implementing the *Instructio* on the cooperation of the lay faithful with the ordained the Conference of Bishops of The Netherlands state that initially they as much as the faithful believed that laity were substituting for the diminishing number of clergy. However, they state, over the past 20 to 30 years they have discovered that many professional lay persons do not feel a vocation to the priesthood and are not working from the awareness that they are not priests. On the contrary, the bishops write, the ecclesial lay ministers have discovered for themselves and revealed to the community that they have their own specific call. The bishops evaluate this development and insight positively. Conference of Bishops of the Netherlands, "Meewerken in het pastoraat: Beleidsnota bij de 'Instructie over enige vragen betreffende de medewerking van lekengelovigen aan het dienstwerk van de priesters'," *Een-Twee-Een, Kerkelijke Documentatie* 27(1999) no. 8, 3-37.

the words: "novus habitus mentis", a new attitude of mind.[38] He invited students and professors of canon law to take on that new attitude of mind. There is no reason to restrict his invitation to canon lawyers; theologians, yes, the whole Church, is invited to accept it and be open to what the Holy Spirit might grant us.

---

[38] On December 14, 1973 he spoke to the "Course of Renewal in Canon Law" at the Gregorian University (cf. James I. O'Connor (ed.) *Canon law Digest* (Mundelein, Il.: St. Mary of the Lake Seminary, 1978) vol. 8, 100-101) and on February 4, 1977 he mentioned it again in an address to the Judges of the Rota Romana (cf. *Canon Law Digest*, vol. 8, 111).

Drama or Tragedy?
Coping with Stress as a Story

Hessel Zondag

The stories people tell about their own lives and that of others play an important role in Tjeu van Knippenberg's work (1998). In these stories people give form to their past and open up new perspectives to their future. The stream between past, present and future form the time dimension of the story. A second dimension of stories is that of space. Someone talks about other people and what other people think about the narrator, and someone talks about the places he was, is or expects to be in the future. The images of space often refer to those of time. It is in this way that people often use the metaphor of the path or the journey for the story of their life.

In his book *Tussen naam en identiteit* Van Knippenberg suggests that people rearrange events in stories so as to attribute meaning to them. It is easier to construct stories about some events than it is about others. Events that break through everyday life especially demand much of the constructing activity of humans. Stress is an excellent example of this. What do you do if your child suddenly dies? Popularly phrased 'how do you get over it?' What kind of story do you tell about it? These are the types of questions that are often asked of pastors. How are pastors able to contribute to coping with traumatic situations? And if I concentrate this question on the story of suffering then: how are pastors able to contribute to people telling their story of trauma in such a way that they can live with it, despite all the pain? In order to answer this question I will enter into more detail on 'stories', especially a number of important genres. Following this I will connect these genres with the theory on coping with trauma. To do this I distinguish three dimensions of coping with stress. I study how pastors are able to give form to coping with upsetting events and telling stories about suffering on the basis of a speech made by a pastor at a remembrance service. At the end of this contribution I discuss the dimensions distinguished in a broader theoretical framework.

1. Stories

According to the American social psychologists Gergen and Gergen (1983; 1986; 1988) stories are a method humans use to bring structure and coherence to what happens to them in life. In stories people connect events, so that life is not merely a succession of occurrences that have nothing to do with each other, but becomes a meaningful whole. Stories also enable people to give shape to space in a meaningful way; one situates places and people one knows in a mutual connection. That stories give meaning and direction to life does not necessarily mean that that meaning and direction automatically have a positive or pleasant character. Stories with a negative dimension also give meaning.

Stories help people to understand themselves and what happened to them in life. One could call this the 'explanative' function of the story. Besides this stories have a 'communicative' aspect; one wants to make life understandable for others. This can be done in the actual presence of others, but also in the presence of those with an imaginary character. Thus people can direct their stories towards figures from religious tradition or those who have passed away. The communicative and explanative function of stories is connected to one another. Often the nature of the event becomes clearer for yourself by telling others what has happened to you.

Stories have to satisfy three conditions in order to be able to structure the events of life (Gergen and Gergen 1983; 1986; 1988). In the first place they must include a point of evaluation, either positive or negative. A judgement in terms of good or bad, pleasant or unpleasant, desired or not, give events in the story direction. An example of a positive evaluation is the statement 'I consider my life successful'. The conclusion 'ultimately my life is a failure' is an example of a structuring with a negative point. A second condition is that one selects events in such a way that they have a relation with this aim. To stay with the example of a successful or failed life; this concerns occurrences that have something to do with success or failure in life. Someone who, midway through his life story begins to argue the extinction of dinosaurs not only risks being considered a bit strange, but also spoils the story he is telling. Finally, in a story one should make connections between events. This increases the coherence of the story. Stories in which coincidence dominates or in which someone performs a deux ex machina generally have little coherence. Connections are generally of a causal nature: each occurrence is the product of a different occurrence. It is in this way that people link events in a story to one another. This causality can have a determining character, which is the case if someone says 'I became a general practitioner because my parents wanted me to'. In the statement 'I became a pastor so I could be close to others' causality has an intentional character.

On the basis of the point of evaluation Gergen and Gergen distinguish three prototypical stories: progressive, regressive and stable. In a progressive story one structures events in such a way that a desired aim gradually comes within reach, 'things are improving'. A regressive story is the reflection of a progressive story; gradually one ends up at a negative point. This is the case in a story with the point 'my health is deteriorating'. Finally in a stable story nothing changes with regard to the point of evaluation, changes do not occur, 'life is okay'.

One is able to create more complex stories on the basis of these three types of stories. Stories in which stable, progressive and regressive elements alternate. Two of these types of story are of importance for this contribution: tragedy and drama. These two genres distinguish themselves from one another through their point of evaluation. A drama begins positively, then has a sudden low, after which the story ends positively. A tragedy also begins positively and has an unforeseen low that contrary to a drama forms the end of the story. In a drama one recovers following the low, a tragedy ends on a minor key. A drama consists respectively of progressive, regressive and finally progressive elements again, in a tragedy progressive elements are followed exclusively by regressive elements. In a drama a problematic development occurs that is overcome, in a tragedy one does not succeed in doing this.

2. Stories and coping with stress

The genres drama and tragedy can be used to explain the successful respectively unsuccessful or uncompleted coping with stressful events. With the perspective used here as starting point coping with stress is also a story. Coping can be described as a stabilising factor that helps people to adapt psychosocially in times of stress. It includes cognitive and behavioural efforts to restrict or eliminate stressful situations and the tension that goes with them (Holahan, Moos and Schaeffer 1996). A woman with a happy marriage is suddenly confronted with the death of her husband. Following a period of pain, sadness, loss and a desire for the lost, she slowly but surely succeeds in building a life without her husband. She continues to miss her husband, but the loss no longer overshadows her existence. This can be considered as a successful example of coping. The example shows that coping successfully does not necessarily mean that one does not suffer. This is a much too hedonistic perspective of coping. It would suggest that one was able to leave the negative result of a dramatic event such as the death of a loved one behind once and for all. This is not true, the pain caused by such an event will never go away. Coping successfully means that one is able to live with this pain, and that suffering does not have the last word in someone's life (Kleber, Mittendorff and Van der Hart 1997; Vossen 1992). The structure of a drama is easily recognisable in this process. A period of happiness is followed by a period of mourning that one recovers from. Should the woman not succeed in coping with the loss of her husband, that is to say that the loss of her husband continues to dominate her existence, then one can speak of a tragedy. She does not succeed in getting out of the abyss.

The question of the contribution of pastors to coping with stress can now be applied. How are pastors able to encourage the story people tell of their suffering in such a way that it ultimately gains the structure of a drama and not that of a tragedy? In order to clarify this I distinguish three dimensions of coping with upsetting events: a confrontational, a social and a mythological.

2.1. The confrontational dimension

In the period following his death the woman from the example is continually reminded of the loss of her husband. She sees an empty chair, a coat-stand with a coat still hanging on it, and she does the shopping for the weekend on her own now. Again and again she is confronted with the loss that causes her grief, pain and fear. When these emotions become too much for her she wards them off. She tries to put her mind to things; she turns the television on or visits a friend, and the pain is reduced. When the fear and pain have lessened she is able to allow the memories of her husband to return, after which the whole process repeats itself. This is an example of the characteristic pattern of denial and confrontation that is so typical of coping with stress (Horowitz 1979; 1986). The cycle repeats itself until memories and the emotions that accompany them no longer overwhelm the person concerned and she no longer wards them off.

Coping with grievous trauma takes a long time. This is because people do not usually question their opinions and expectations of themselves and the world. Their convictions are usually quite natural to them. If someone leaves a place and says 'good-bye', he assumes that others will acknowledge the greeting, which is generally the case. It is only when after a greeting someone notices a silence that they ask themselves whether there is anything wrong, the naturalness is then disturbed. These opinions and things that are a matter of course are also known as 'schemas' (Neisser 1976). These schemas are acquired in the course of life and are seldom well thought-out, expressed or systematised. That is why they have a natural character. They are essential for a good adaptation to the world, for dealing with information and acting.

In the course of life these schemas develop and expand. This development involves two processes, 'assimilation' and 'accommodation' (Piaget 1971). Assimilation is the taking in of information about the world within an existing schema. People take in new facts in such a way that these fit into their expectations and opinions. They approach the world in terms of an existing schema. Accommodation is the adaptation of schemas in order to be able to deal with new information. It is the adjustment of expectations and opinions that enable one to integrate new experiences and changing circumstances.

Schemas no longer function after an event that causes a lot of grief, and this disfunctioning explains why it often takes people a long time to cope with upsetting events. The woman who lost her husband as a result of an accident had expected to spend years with him and to have children. The accident thwarted this opinion on the future, it disturbed everything that was natural. Now she is a widow and must build a life on her own. How she is to do this is something she cannot yet imagine, she has to create new expectations. Therefore, the woman's old opinions are no longer satisfactory, but she has no new, adequate perspectives. If we formulate this technically one could say that the existing schema no longer functions, its assimilating function has been disturbed, and that the woman is faced with the task of accommodation, constructing a new schema. For the woman this could mean that she now considers herself as single, but that she might begin a new relationship in the future. Coping with stress is the construction of new, adequate schemas, in other words, coping is accommodation.

The confrontation with an upsetting event is important for accommodation. A confrontation makes people face the facts and 'forces' them as it were to construct new, adequate schemas.

An important part of confrontation, and also of coping with stress is attributing meaning to it (Kleber, Brom and Defares 1992). One of the ways in which the question as to the meaning of suffering can be answered is to look for the cause. Then people interpret meaning in a 'causal' sense. People want a clarification of the circumstances in which the traumatic event took place. The woman wants to know how the accident in which her husband died happened. However, in many cases people do not search for causes, but for the meaning of this event for their own lives (Baumeister 1991; Taylor 1983). One could talk of this as meaning in a 'consequential' sense. 'What is really important in my life now?' the woman who lost her husband asks herself.

Questions that concern the meaning of suffering confront one with that stressful situation and in this way contribute to coping with it. The confrontation with pain through the attributing meaning to it is an element of the process of accommodation. The attribution of meaning to misery is situating that misery. It does not seem to matter so much how meaning is attributed to misery, but rather that one succeeds in doing so. What is important is that someone with misfortune is able to do something with it in his or her life, a painful event should not continue to fling around in life like a loose stone.

2.2. The social dimension

People do not cope with trauma in a social vacuum, but in relationships with others. The recognition of sorrow contributes to coping with it. This recognition confirms people, a confirmation that precisely because of the stressful event was put at risk. After all, pain affects what is natural in life. It is in this way that recognition contributes to recovery and the normalisation of existence. On the other hand the absence of recognition restricts coping with stress. On their return to the United States, Vietnam veterans were barely recognised for their military past. In general they were given the cold shoulder, the result of which was that it was more difficult for them to cope adequately with the trauma of war (Silver 1985).

Social support from others comes in all forms (Flannery 1990). 'Cognitive' support especially is important. Cognitive support is for example the provision of advice and information. This information is important for setting new goals and creating new expectations. In other words, information aids in the creation of new schemas. Besides cognitive support, material support is important, for example in the form of finances. Material support can also be in the form of concrete activities, such as help in moving house. Friendship too – doing something with others, for example eating out or going to a movie – and emotional support in a narrower sense of the word - someone puts an arm round your shoulder when you're feeling down – appears to encourage a positive way of coping with upsetting situations. Other people's support can also have a negative affect. Sometimes the presence and influence of others restrain people when building a new life (Parkes 1986).

2.3. The mythological dimension

People who suffer often feel that their lives have stranded. Myths can offer a helping hand in sorting out problems (Van der Hart 1981). From the perspective of coping with trauma myths are stories about the cause and course of disaster. Besides these myths indicate what needs to be done in order to continue with life. One could tell the story about *The storm on the lake* to someone in need; the disciples were afraid that they would drown in the storm and Jesus told them to have faith and trust. Those concerned can learn to believe in a good outcome whatever might happen, from this myth. In this way people are not overwhelmed by the events of the moment, which contributes to the realisation of a good outcome. The bible story offers someone a model with which to confront the problems he or she has. Above all these myths offer frames of reference with which someone is able to give meaning to what happens to them in life.

Someone can include the story about their own suffering in a greater story (Gergen and Gergen 1983). Someone whose life is not going well can see this as part of the loss of society. The micro-story of one's own life is interwoven with the macro-story of society. Gergen and Gergen call this interweaving 'nestling' or 'multiple stories'. This enables people to consider their own religious life story or episodes as part of a greater religious story. The American-Jewish journalist Leon Wieseltier gives a good illustration of this when he explains how, when reading Hebrew texts from the Middle Ages in a quiet room, he feels that his own life story is bound with Jewish tradition (Krielaars 2001).

It is important to note that the confrontational, the social and the mythological dimension are closely connected. Myths are able to contribute to attributing meaning, that confronts people with the upsetting event, and it is in this way that the mythological and the confrontational dimensions are interwoven. If someone talks to someone else about his suffering they confront themselves in the face of the other with their stress, thus the confrontational and the social dimension are connected. Finally, myths are often told by others, thus linking the social and mythological aspect.

A speech at a remembrance service

How are pastors able in their work to contribute to coping with stress by taking into consideration the confrontational, social and mythological dimension? I studied this on the basis of the actions of a pastor during a remembrance service. The example used concerns the speech made on Friday the twelfth of January 2001 by Father Berkhout of Volendam at a remembrance service following a fire in a café in Volendam, whereby fourteen youths lost their lives. The fire raged during the celebration of New Year's Eve 2001. The remembrance service took place in the stadium of the football club FC Volendam and was attended by more than 20,000 people. Of the numerous wounded still in hospitals those who were able could follow the service on television. First I will render the speech made by Father Berkhout, following which I analyse it in the light of the dimensions distinguished.

'New Year's Eve, twelve o'clock, the bells of Volendam festively ring in the New Year. But a few moments later these joyful sounds are drowned out by the screams of young people in a panic and death agony. A message passes through Volendam at lightening speed "The Wir War is on fire". Our hearts shudder. Parents rush to the Dijk in desperation, in search of their children. On the evening of the first day we meet in homes to mourn. Numbed with grief and resignation. And it hurts. It hurts so much. We have no words. At the same time whole families wait in fear in the hospitals. In the week following a long funeral procession went through our village ten times. Ten times a young person. Ten times a father and a mother, grief-stricken. Ten times every youngster from our village, bound together in tremendous grief. This week I visited the hospitals of Brussels, Leuven, Liège, Aachen and Beverwijk, and I had already been to the university hospital in Amsterdam. Fifty youngsters bandaged from head to foot and kept in a slumber. Your heart breaks, you can't comprehend what you're seeing. And every single one of them comes from this village. Parents balance between hope and despair, each hour the situation can change. Some in our village ask "Father, why is God doing this to us?" Dear people, God is not doing this to us, truly not, He doesn't want young people to die. In a number of funerals we have listened to the story of the young man of Naim. A widow brings her only son to the grave. And then this is written. "Jesus have mercy on this mother". But that mercy is also anger, His heart turns when He sees this. A young person may not die, he/she has a whole life ahead. And He commands the bier to stop and says "Young man, arise." And He returns him to his mother. That is the will of God. God doesn't want young people to die. There is a great solidarity at this time, we support the families in which death has struck mercilessly. We are there for the victims and their fathers and mothers in the hospitals. And how must we go on, when life is back to normal, when the youngsters, hurt and injured are amongst us again. How are they to rediscover their position in our community? And where can we find the resilience and inspiration to continue to care for them?

In the past days I have thought a lot about my grandmother who was from Volendam and was born in the Zuideinde. As a boy I very much enjoyed visiting her, and I can still see her now, just as she was, just as your grandmothers are, sitting at her table, in her dress made of crêpe de Chine, a silver rosary within hands reach. And when I was with her she talked about the past, about her Volendam. She re-lived the year 1916 when the dykes burst and the village was flooded. She returned to the times of great poverty, the togetherness of big families, the warmth and security. She spoke of the love Volendam has for the Zuider Zee, and how that same sea often demanded great offers. How the bells tolled again as a sign of mourning for the village, and how people found comfort and strength in faith. And she told too of the fleet, how it was blessed by the priest on leaving the harbour. And she always finished with this lesson "boy" she said "whatever happens to you, always trust God, never let go of your faith". And what she said was the truth, because that's the way she experienced it.

In these past days we have seen that faith not only kept past generations going but it seems that we to draw strength from it. And this ancient faith will give us the strength to endure this ordeal, because God will not forsake us. It is the inheritance of the older generations that today, through our youngsters who have died and who are now lying in hospitals is passed on to us.

There are many young people here in this stadium and I would like to say something to you. It's like this, soon the youngsters that lie bandaged in the hospitals, I have seen them, almost all of them, will return to our community. And they are hurt, injured, have scars perhaps. And I have seen in the past days how you have been together, how you have supported one another, how you have been a great strength to one another. You were friends in good times, and be friends in difficult and bad times too if they come. And not for a week, not for a year, but they belong to your generation for as long as they live. And if you don't know where to get the strength from, remember then the old of Volendam, where they got their strength. We are bound to those in hospital, you can see me now. I want to greet you, I want to wish you luck. Fight, because we cannot do without you! And we hope to see you back here soon. And now I want to ask every person here in this stadium to clap for you, so that you may receive strength for the time ahead.'

A loud applause follows after which Father Berkhout prays the 'Our Father' and the 'Hail Mary'.

2.4. The confrontational dimension in the remembrance speech

In the speech made by the pastor of Volendam the confrontational dimension comes up. The priest emphatically reminds the people that there was a fire in which many died and were wounded, and that caused great sorrow. He reconstructs the fire as it were, now mentally. I pointed out earlier that this repetition is functional for coping with stress. In his speech the pastor confronts people with what happened. He talks about the fire itself, the desperation of the parents, mourning, pain, fear, speechlessness, grief, hope and despair, the disbelief at the sight of the wounded, and the question; how can the wounded rediscover their position in the community of Volendam?

Indirectly the pastor also brings up the cause of the fire. In this way he goes into the meaning of the fire, the causal sense. He does this in a particular way, namely he talks about who did not cause the fire: God. Father Berkhout absolves God as it were, God does not want young people to die, 'God doesn't do this to us', he argues, and he supports his defence with the story of the young boy of Naim.[1]

2.5. The social dimension in the remembrance speech

Aspects that refer to the social dimension also come up. The priest mentions namely that there is great mutual support in the village, and places this solidarity in a tradition by pointing out that the history of Volendam is characterised by mutual solidarity. I will come back to this, when I discuss the mythological dimension in his speech. The 'inclusion' of this tradition is obvious; people embrace the hope from that tradition that they will be able to be close to one another now too. Support is also clear from the questions the pastor asks about the future of the injured youngsters in the hospitals. How must they be received when they return? In this way he draws attention to the fate of these youngsters and shows his concern, thus recognising the position in which they find themselves. Father Berkhout asks that the victims be supported for as long as they live. In doing so he does something striking. He not only asks for support in a general sense, he also turns to an act of support. He does this by requesting an applause for those still in hospital, to give them heart.

2.6. The mythological dimension in the remembrance speech

The third dimension, the mythological, is also included by Father Berkhout in his speech. His myth takes place in the far past, in Volendam before the IJsselmeer Dam was built. The main character is his grandmother whom he visited as a child, and whose image he calls up vividly through the use of details such as clothing made of crêpe de Chine and a silver rosary. A woman just like the elderly people of Volendam probably remember from their youth. Perhaps their grandparents told them the same myths Father Berkhout heard from his own grandmother. In myths

---

[1] In his speech Father Berkhout does not enter into the meaning in a consequential sense. The fact that he is fully aware of this construction of meaning is clear from an interview in the Reformatorisch Dagblad (Ten Voorde 2001). In the article he says that one should reflect on the question of whether life consists only of going to parties. In connection with this he refers to the metaphor of stewardship.

threats occur: poverty and water. The water from the sea in which fishermen drown and that flooded the village after the dykes burst in 1916. Faith in God, where people found comfort and strength, and the mutual warmth and security are means of facing the calamity of water and poverty.[2] And those means from the past also work in the present, as in this day faith also 'gives the strength to endure this ordeal'. The pastor refers to powers for salvation that go beyond the human horizon; God. Father Berkhout's strategy of coping has a religious character.

The myth the priest tells can, with the terminology introduced above, be typified as a drama. Even though he does not mention a positive aim, by pointing out the means of overcoming stress he shows that it is possible to get over it.[3] At the same time he makes what happened to the people of Volendam in 2001 part of a greater historical myth, from the 'great' history of Volendam. In the terms of Gergen and Gergen (1983) this is a case of a multiple narrative form.

The speech made by Father Berkhout therefore includes all three dimensions. At the end of this analysis I wish to discuss briefly the succession of the three dimensions in his speech. In this one can see a notable repetition of the order: confrontation, social, mythology. Father Berkhout opens his speech with a confrontation (the fire and the immediate result), after which he continues with remarks that concern the social dimension (the solidarity in Volendam). Then the priest asks a question 'what are we to do when the injured youngsters return to Volendam?', following which he tells the myth about Volendam as it was in 1916. The mythological dimension functions as a 'vehicle' in order to answer the question 'what now?'. The myth itself also begins with a confrontation with an upsetting situation (poverty and floods), continues with social elements (warmth and security) and ends with the perspective 'God does not forsake people'. This means, which becomes clear in the myth, can help those of Volendam today. In the rest of the speech the order confrontation, social, myth is repeated once. First the confrontation again (youngsters in hospitals), then the social (supported one another), and then the myth (a reference to the Volendam of the past). Father Berkhout ends with two acts, one of which concerns the social dimension (a call for applause) and one the mythological dimension (prayer). The rhythmicity of the speech is therefore confrontation, support, perspective. First something dramatic happens to someone,

---

[2] God appears in Father Berkhout's story twice. As someone who does not want young people to die, and as someone you can trust in times of need.

[3] The speech made by Father Berkhout also belongs to the genre drama, there is a 'good' ending. In typifying his speech as a drama I must emphasise that the good ending is a prospect, the moment has not yet come. One expects a good outcome, the good ending is on the horizon. Because those who speak of a positive end do this at the point when the drama is at its worst. One could also say that the speeches put into words the hope that the story will develop into a drama and will not end in tragedy.

then solidarity follows in order to be able to bear the pain together, after which one puts suffering in a greater whole, whereby a certain transcendence takes place.

3. Drama and aesthetic distancing

The confrontational, social and mythological dimensions are all present in the speech made by the pastor of Volendam. I will go into more detail on the mutual connections between these three dimensions on the basis of the theory of Thomas Scheff (1977; 1979). This American sociologist suggests that coping with trauma requires a balanced combination of involvement and distance with regard to the event. He calls this 'aesthetic distancing'. One can accomplish this by entering into painful events, and at the same time distancing oneself from them. To be able to do this the person has to be a part of the traumatic event as well as a spectator of it. The involvement of others is essential to reaching this aesthetic distance. They provide a safe environment where people can allow stress, which eases the expression of pain. Scheff contrasts aesthetic distancing with 'over-distancing' and 'under-distancing', respectively too large and too small a distance. In over-distancing observation dominates, so the stressful event has no effect. Someone is a kind of stranger for himself or herself and does not allow the affective burden to sink in. In the case of under-distancing the stress is so overwhelming that one is unable to distance from oneself.

The relevance of the three dimensions distinguished can be argued further with the theory of Scheff. In the confrontational dimension stress is brought close and the social support and involvement of others encourage people to endure that pain. The myths make it possible to distance oneself from the stressful event. If pastors wish to contribute to coping with stress then they must do justice to the confrontational, the social and the mythological dimension. If they put too much emphasis on confrontation, then there is a danger of under-distancing; people are unable to distance themselves from their suffering. Too much stress on the mythological dimension brings with it the risk of over-distancing; one avoids pain, whereby the stress is not coped with. Under-distancing and over-distancing cause the story people tell of their suffering to become a tragedy, they do not recover from the traumatic event. If one succeeds in accomplishing aesthetic distancing, then the story about the stress can become a drama. A story in which suffering does not have the last word.

References

Baumeister, R.F. 1991. *Meanings of life*. New York: The Guilford Press.

Flannery, R.B. 1990. Social support and psychological trauma. *Journal of traumatic stress* 3: 593-613.

Gergen, K., and M. Gergen. 1983. Narratives of the self. Pp. 254-273 in *Studies in social identity*, edited by T. Sarbin and K. Scheibe. New York.

Gergen, K., and M. Gergen. 1986. Narrative form and the construction of psychological science. Pp. 22-44 in *Narrative psychology. The storied nature of human conduct*, edited by T. Sarbin. New York.

Gergen, K., and M. Gergen. 1988. Narrative and the self as relationship. *Advances in experimental social psychology* 21: 17-56.

Hart, O. van der 1981. Het gebruik van mythen en rituelen in psychotherapie. Pp. 16-32 in *Afscheidsrituelen in de psychotherapie*, edited by O. van der Hart. Baarn.

Holahan, C.J., R.H. Moos, and J.A. Schaeffer. 1996. Coping, stress resistance and growth: conceptualizing adaptive funtioning. Pp. 24-43 in *Handbook of coping: theory, research, applications*, edited by M. Zeidner and N.S. Endler. New York.

Horowitz, M.J. 1979. Psychological response to serious life events. Pp. 235-263 in *Human stress and cognition: an information processing approach*, edited by V. Hamilton and D.M. Warburton. Chisester.

Horowitz, M.J. 1986. *Stress response syndromes*. New York: Jason Aronson.

Kleber, R.J., D. Brom, and P.B. Defares. 1992. *Coping with trauma. Theory, prevention and treatment*. Amsterdam: Swets and Zeitlinger.

Kleber, R.J., C. Mittendorff, and O. van der Hart. 1997. Posttraumatische stress. Pp. 1-30 in *Handboek klinische psychologie*, edited by W.T.A.M. Everaerd, A.P. Bak and W.T.M. Berlo. Houten.

Knippenberg, M. van 1998. *Tussen naam en identiteit: ontwerp voor een model van geestelijke begeleiding*. Kampen: Kok.

Krielaars, M. 2001. Het antwoord op het leven ligt begraven in de traditie. Amerikaanse jood Leon Wieseltier over de waarde van rituelen bij een rouwproces. *NRC-Handelsblad*, 16 juni 2001.

Neisser, U. 1976. *Cognition and reality: principles and implications of cognitive psychology*. San Francisco: W.H. Freeman.

Parkes, C.M. 1986. *Bereavement: studies of grief in adult life*. London: Tavistock publications.

Piaget, J. 1971. *Structuralisme*. Meppel: Boom.

Scheff, T.J. 1977. The distancing of emotion in ritual. *Current Antropology* 18(3): 483-490.

Scheff, T.J. 1979. *Catharsis in healing, ritual and drama*. Berkeley: University of California Press.

Silver, S.M. 1985. Post-traumatic stress and the death imprint: the search for a new mythos. In *Post-traumatic stress disorder and the war veteran patient*, edited by W.E. Kelly. New York.

Taylor, S.E. 1983. Adjustment to threatening events: a theory of cognitive adaptation. *American Psychologist* 38: 1161-1173.

Voorde, G. ten 2001. Een schreeuw uit Volendam. Pastoor Berkhout: Ramp in café heeft dorp iets te zeggen. *Reformatorische Dagblad,* 5 januari 2001.

Vossen, E. 1992. Religieuze zingeving. Pp. 301-319 in *Zin tussen vraag en aanbod*, edited by B. Vedder, J. Jacobs, M. van Knippenberg, N. Schreurs and W. Weren. Tilburg.

Pastoral Care and Boundaries

Stefan Gärtner

Middle-class society enjoyed a quiet walk along former boundaries. By 1800, the old city walls of Vienna had been razed and turned into a promenade walk. Every Sunday, middle-class people would parade along the so-called Bastei, on the boundary between the old city centre and the endless rows of houses of the Neustadt. The same thing had happened fifty years earlier in Münster/Westfalen, where Franz von Fürstenberg had a garden promenade laid out on the destroyed outer city walls. Today still, strolling along old boundaries is a favourite pastime, not just on the former demarcation line between the two Germanies, which has now become a conservation area. This regular Sunday stroll is no longer a suitable metaphor for the type of boundary experiences we have today, however. The many demarcations that determine our way of life in postmodernity cannot be dealt with as easily as a former city wall.

Postmodern aesthetics plays with the boundaries between space and time, especially in architecture. In doing so, it shows us the perspectivity and the limitations of tradition and styles, crosses old boundaries and ideally creates something new from various elements. Yet, the same is often much harder to achieve for the individual, looking at his biography and way of life. The experience of many boundaries that are either imposed upon me or that I have to set myself, is not as easily assembled into a unity. On the contrary: The experience of otherness becomes the pre-eminent mode for the individual's unlocking of reality in present-day society (Grözinger 1995). Successfully shaping my life in the face of the many boundaries is no Sunday stroll.

1. A profession at the boundaries

In as far as theology tries account for Christian faith in the context of *the Signs of the Time*, it nowadays has to pay special attention to the subject of "boundaries". In the canon of theological disciplines, Pastoral Theology has a special commitment to this subject (Gärtner 2000). This is partly due to its history. The birth of Pastoral Theology took place during the Enlightenment, a time of profound boundary experiences for both church and theology. Both were faced with rise of autonomous reason. Christian faith would no longer be unquestionable, it now had to be comprehensible to be recognised as a free and personal choice. Intellectuals, and later on also larger sections of society, no longer took the church for granted. Therefore, it lost its unquestioned meaning.

The problem stemming from this limitation of the church's influence has led to the development of Pastoral Theology. It would become a discipline aimed at adapting theological insights to the new and changed practical situation. This entailed two things: First, it enabled the other theological disciplines to carry on without having to confront the change of paradigms the Enlightenment brought about. Secondly, it successfully established the position of Pastoral Theology within the canon of theological disciplines. It was set down as a pure, practical application of the insights of "true" theology, as a catalyst for mediating these insights to the acts of the faithful. Unfortunately, this application can still be found occasionally (Steck 1993).

Pastoral theology thus ended up on the margins of theology, i.e. its task was to take the pulse of the times. This meant a special engagement with the boundaries of church and religious life in its own time, for example with the changing boundaries between established church and state authority, or the differentiation of pastoral spheres of activity within church practice. It responded to the latter with an inner differentiation into separate disciplines (Poimenics, Catechetics, Homiletics etc.) that together constitute what is called Practical Theology. Conversely, the discipline itself has only promoted the subdivision of the pastoral into separate spheres of activity. This becomes problematic when the boundaries of one's own discipline are forcibly imposed upon reality to define it (Giri 1999). Therefore, the demarcation within Practical Theology should also be the subject of critical examination.

In as far as this discipline has always represented the margins of theology in a special way, it also considers itself to be inside theology as the entry point into practice. Practical Theology seeks to turn the Christian and religious acts of people in their current situations into a fertile ground for theology. In view of the current contexts of this practice, it is again faced with boundaries. For everyone is nowadays confronted with the challenge of shaping his/her life into an identity through the many boundary experiences. The same also holds true for the church as a communion. An *ecclesia semper reformanda* has to keep responding to new challenges and change in this postmodern age. This will not be possible without the experience of boundaries and breaks.

In view of this fragmentation and demarcation, (practical) theological theory and knowledge need to be justified. This means that, both because of its history and of the current position of Christian faith, the discipline should be placed at the boundaries and the breaks – "at the breaks between church and society, between culture and religion, between everyday experience and experience of God, between 'popular religion' and official church dogmatics, and also between experienced Christian practice and academic theological reflection." (Müller 1998, 137)

2. The boundary as a *locus theologicus*

The boundary is an important *locus theologicus*. Theology as a whole finds it-self at the boundary between Christian mission on the one hand, and changing situations and social realities on the other. We have seen that Practical Theology appears to be especially sensitive to this fundamental boundary, which differentiates into myriad demarcations. Moreover, it has developed a methodology to successfully operate at this boundary. It tries to mediate between said opposites and critically guide the real translation of these opposites into the religious acts (Van Knippenberg 1989).

To be able to further determine the boundary as a place for theology, we need to turn to someone who has made this the subject of his theology unlike anybody else has: Paul Tillich. This has rightfully earned him the status of "a guest of honour in the field of Pastoral Theology" (Van Knippenberg 1989, 5). This is not surprising, when we realise how Tillich has engaged with modern culture and the secular society of the twentieth century. It was his main desire to explain the traditions of Christianity to people of his day, and find clues in the experiences of their lives. His main interest was to find a correlation theological impetus for mediations on the boundary between religion and culture, to the extent that to Tillich, culture was the form of religion, and religion was the substance of culture.

Boundaries were also important to him for another reason: Tillich could and had to reconstruct his own biography as a "history of boundaries". "Boundaries" to him were a symbol of his personal and intellectual development (Tillich 1964, 9-57). "Auf der Grenze" from 1936 can be regarded as an attempt at self-assurance, in which Tillich tried to recover his form after his emigration to the U.S.A. - a crossing of a boundary that was much more of a radical change in 1933 as it would be in modern times. This was especially the case with the confrontation with two fundamental crises: First of all, having experienced the killing machine of the First World War, into which he was drafted as a chaplain in 1914, wholly unprepared after the sheltered existence in the parental home and during his theological education. The second biographical crisis would be his forced emigration caused by the National Socialist takeover in 1933, and the exile from his own country to another country whose language and culture were completely alien to him. No matter how different or alike our personal experiences may be to those of Tillich, his example nevertheless shows that the boundary can only be held as a position in theology, if one is sensitive to the boundaries in one's own biography (also in a theological sense).

Tillich himself has made the existential demarcation of identity his starting point for determining central symbols of Christian tradition as testimonies to the ultimate ground of human existence. In doing so, he presents the import of faith with a view to boundaries, albeit in such a way that these are not completely conquered, but rather that faith tries to provide an answer *to* this boundary being experienced. Therefore, it is a faith that goes hand in hand with despair, fear and meaninglessness, because it believes at the boundary to non-being, and endures it. This can be found in the three volumes of *Systematic Theology,* but most of all in his works on philosophy of religion (Tillich 1965).

All human experiences are tainted by the threat of non-being. Everyone is confronted with the force of meaninglessness, guilt and death, and is in danger of losing his or her courage to be (Tillich 1965, 41-68). Moreover, human identity fundamentally forms a confrontation that can be described in terms of three pairs of opposites. First, man is faced with the polarity of individualization and participation. This means he has to find a successful balance between his own wishes and desires, his plans, his idea of himself and his orientation towards community and his part in it. He carefully has to avoid extremes that cancel out the basic tension and focus on just one pole. Instead, the individual has to maintain a good balance amidst the constant conflicts.

The same can be said for the other two pairs of opposites that determine the basic structures of human existence, according to Tillich: The polarities between dynamics and form and between freedom and fate. My creative potential, the urge to recreate myself, to plan and rearrange the world creatively (dynamics), becomes hubris or idiocy without the limitations imposed by rules (form). Without normative form, creativity becomes chaotic and incommunicable. Likewise, a balance needs to be found between freedom and destiny: I can take my life into my own hands (freedom), yet I am part of history and of a context that determines my actions (destiny). I have to continually find a new balance between activity and passive endurance in interaction with the world.

Tillich situates these basic polarities of human existence on the level of essential analysis, but the force and threat of non-being breaks through on the level of the concrete existential actualisation of being. To him, existence is connected to the radical intensification of the effort to balance the three polarities described above. After all, this is where the real alienation of being by non-being really becomes clear, and *the courage to be* must show and prove itself in concrete life. This is where man has to fight for integration and balance, because he is confronted with the experience of guilt, loneliness, fear, tragedy, death and meaninglessness, in short: with non-being.

These are boundary experiences that form an essential part of every human life and therefore cannot be eliminated (Scherer-Rath 2001, 81-157; Leyener 1988, 53-86). In dealing with such non-being, man could see himself as competent to deal with these experiences. He cannot conquer the boundaries of his own identity, but he can act at these boundaries. The courage to resist guilt, fear, meaninglessness etc. and the actual success of these efforts are just as much part of human existence. Consequently, their aim is to constantly conquer the brokenness and threat of non-being. This is how man can achieve self-integration with a view to moral acting, self-creation with a view to culture and self-transcendence with a view to religion, with the latter to a certain extent encompassing the other two (Tillich 1965, 152-183).

This real conquest of the alienations by non-being will only succeed for a short moment in time, and only to a certain extent. Moreover, he experiences his own practical *courage to be* as based in his own existence. However, at the boundary of the utter threat of non-being, his experience points beyond the self and transcending individual possibilities. Therefore, man can act at the boundaries of his non-being, but this is also where his abilities end.

At this point, Tillich introduces the central symbols and traditions of Christianity. These show a God that reveals Himself as the source of unlimited courage and the deepest ground of man's *courage to be*. Man, who in spite of his competence in acting at the boundaries, ultimately experiencing himself as a stranger to himself and to God, feels definitely touched by this revelatory event. He can accept the event through faith, but in such a way that his position at the boundary between being and non-being is not abolished in the process. Rather, the experience of faith itself remains fragmented in time and history, and therefore needs a constant representation in a community (church).

On the whole, the God of Christian tradition shows himself to people at their boundaries, without eliminating these on earth. He is not the ready answer to all questions and alienations man has to suffer, but instead is introduced by Tillich in the passage through the manifold boundary experiences of being between being and non-being. The idea of God acquires its existential plausibility at the end, when man transcends his own efforts for identity and integration and an ultimate ground becomes apparent.

3. Boundaries in postmodern society

Our brief outline of Tillich's "boundary theology" has shown that his considerations are not just linked to his biography, but also to the moment in the history of thought at which they arose. In that sense, his initiative really is an attempt at contextual theology. The next question would be what the boundary as *locus theologicus* is *today*, in postmodern society. We are not interested in discussions concerning the contentious issue of the concept of "postmodernity" itself, however. "Postmodernity" is not used simply to mark the condition after modernity, but is understood as the cipher of a radicalised and dynamicized modernity, which has come to reflect upon its own conditions (Arens 1999, 16-18).

In Tillich's works, the subject formed the Archimedean point in its relation to the ultimate ground of being (God), in spite of the real threat by the alienating experiences of non-being. This enables man to act as a subject at the boundary after all. It would certainly lack nuance to speak of the *death of the subject* in postmodernity. A more precise description would be the „depotentialization of the ruling subject-imagination" (Welsch 1997, 316). This disenfranchisement follows from the disenchantment about broken promises and the *dialectics of the Enlightenment*, which gave the subject its autonomy and made it the focal point of reality.

Today, the implications of this concept of the subject are exposed as products of their time. The absolute singularity of the sovereign subject is exposed as fiction, and the unique guiding roles of man's consciousness and reason are put into perspective. Moreover, Michel Foucault reconstructed the modern turn to the subject as the history of ever-increasing control. Old certainties about man can therefore no longer be maintained. The opposite, a radical fragmentation of his existence now seems apparent: Man is no longer merely different from his fellow man, he is also different from himself. This means a radicalisation of the existential boundary experience in postmodernity.

However, the present also offers more opportunities to fundamentally avoid these experiences. Guilt and death are now among the very few taboos left in our society. Experiences of meaninglessness, fear and desperation mean little in the light of the norm of constant willingness and ability to perform. The boundaries of non-being will therefore have to remain hidden. Any penetration into reality will immediately have to be relieved therapeutically, instead of being used as a critical confrontation with the story of one's own life, thus using it as a new beginning (Luther 1992, 224-238). Nowadays, any boundary experiences will quickly be relieved. We live by the "commandment of normalisation" (Schieder 1994, 28).

This can be said especially for the public observation and appreciation of such experiences. Existential boundaries are still experienced as strongly as they were before. However, nowadays they have been pushed back into the private sphere. Whereas historically, religious ways of dealing with sin and guilt and the rehabilitation of the penitents were ritualised, in modern times the sacrament of confession has been removed from public life (Van Knippenberg 1998, 20-30). This can mean a reduction of the experience of sin and guilt for individual life.

In the same way, other experiences in dealing with non-being were and are still privatised further, both in the church and in public life. The mass media appear to play an important role in this respect, by reducing the concrete individual boundary experience and presenting a virtual horizon instead (Guggenberger 1997). Individual fate is thus drawn into an artificial space and unassailably encapsulated. This development can be seen both as a new form of breaking down boundaries and as globalisation. This does not just concern the media, but also other domains of postmodern society, especially economy. The transnational, yet one-sided economic cycle coincides with a medially communicated cultural homogenisation.

At the same time, as a counter-movement to these developments retreat and sheltering can be observed. The global eradication of boundaries results in a world that is increasingly difficult to comprehend. In reaction to this, individuals, groups and institutions retreat within supposedly fixed boundaries that offer orientation (Menzel 1998; Alsheimer et al. 2000). The problem of this interaction between globalisation and fragmentation/regionalization appears to be that they may be causally connected and mutually strengthening, but this coherence often remains hidden. The aim here would not be to establish new boundaries or retreat behind old ones in order to secure identity in an incomprehensible, globalised world as a regression, but rather to critically describe the coherence with the removal of boundaries in reality. Such a desideratum would accommodate the appreciation of fragmentedness in postmodernity, which forms the drawback of the hidden norm of *anything goes*. Social reality in a globalised postmodernity that has no boundaries is also *and at the same time* determined by new boundaries and fragmentations.

This is also connected to two other developments. On the one hand, social systems in postmodern society keep differentiating, according to the function they have in the larger scheme of things (Luhmann 1997). On the other hand, traditional concepts of unity with regards to the cohesion of these systems in society are losing their general plausibility. Previously, this merely applied to the religious canopy that spread itself over premodernity as a metaphysical protection and provided the dominant interpretation of reality. Now, it also affects economical, political and cultural developments. Faith in material progress and the healthy dynamics of political systems are faltering; there are no universal codes in aesthetics anymore. The boundaries of the manageable and planable become obvious. This also questions the prevalent dominance of economy over all other aspects of postmodern life.

Postmodern society thus presents us with a polycentric image. There is no longer *one* point, from which all aspects of self-determination of the individual and coexistence can be derived. Individuals, groups and organisations do still take such points of view – if this were not the case, all orientation would be lost. However, these constructions of reality are becoming more and more relative, because they only possess a limited import, and in spite of their claim, are no longer universal. This is typical of the strategic fragmentation of postmodernity: "The fact that all coordinating frameworks appear to be linked to specific contexts and corresponding interests and needs. In the light of this reality, postmodern relativism demonstrates the arbitrary character of any point of view, the fragmented multitude of traditions, language games and contexts, and with it the fact that relations between social groups and individuals will increasingly be dominated by strategic considerations." (Kunneman 1992, 82)

To the individual, it now becomes a challenge to compose his or her own way through life form a great number of possibilities. The ever-increasing differentiation leads to a structural *heretical imperative* (Peter L. Berger) in all sectors. The individual can no longer indubitably fall back on set traditions, for his individual judgement is at least challenged by the fact that others make different choices (De Lange 1995). Moreover, nowadays the individual is much more responsible for the consequences of his own decisions. He/she is increasingly less well protected from failure by a social frame of reference.

Accordingly, the development of an identity in postmodernity is an uncertain project with an open ending. Moreover, the decisions one has to take in the various aspects of life, are dominated by claims of postmodern society's social systems. This is especially true of economy and government. Decisions are taken for me, and in the process, my freedom to act and choose between various possibilities is limited. This exemplifies "that demarcations are usually acts of negation." (Wilfred 1999, 8) Besides, the competence to model my identity is severely limited by the reduction of the means available to me, my chances to an education, family circumstances etc.

In the end, we are all confronted with the fact that our individual decisions remain forever fallible. With every choice I make, I rule out other options, narrow my range and set new boundaries for myself. No matter what I choose and how I create my self-concept – I will always only explore a small part of reality, even though I am trying to find my orientation in view of the whole. The blind spot therefore becomes a permanent condition.

Therefore, the quest for identity is also determined by the structural fragmentation of reality in postmodernity. Individual identity has to be accordingly differentiated and provisional. "The differentiation and increased complexity of society, the constant change of correlations of meaning prevent the individual from building a constant and consistent identity. His identity will be as multifarious as his experiences. The individual has no other choice: he has to establish a 'multiple identity' for himself, if he wants to be able to find his way in this world." (Schieder 1994, 33)

4. Pastoral care in postmodernity: counselling at the boundaries

We have seen that Practical Theology has always had an excellent consciousness of boundaries as a result of its history and its methodology. Within this discipline, Poimenics is the specialism that is concerned with boundaries with respect to individual lives of people in postmodernity and tries to find and account for possibilities for pastoral care.

Tillich, who helped us find the phenomenon of the boundary theologically, has been very influential in pastoral care. His determination of the alienating boundary experience in human existence in particular, has been adopted, and his effort to demonstrate the meaning of life in Christian faith in dealing with these experiences has found a useful application in poimenic practice (Scherer-

Rath 2001, 172-175). The purpose of this exercise has been to communicate the life-force of the gospel as the founding perspective in the counselling of individuals or groups. Nonetheless, the fall back on Tillich has been an issue of much contention.

We are not interested in continuing this debate here. The discussions of the boundary experiences in postmodernity have shown, however, that the experience of non-being Tillich describes, has been radicalised to a certain extent, nowadays. Fear, tragedy, death and meaninglessness etc. are as virulent as ever before. These sad basic experiences are part of every life. However, the individual's ability to deal with them seems to be hampered by the conditions of postmodernity, as his identity can only be provisional and fragmented in the process. He no longer has, as it were, the solid footing to act at the existential boundaries. Instead, the quest for identity itself becomes a fundamental boundary experience. This is something that may already have become clear in the confrontation with non-being, but nowadays it has gained importance. "The decisive challenge to pastoral care for the individual in postmodernity consists therefore of his self-assurance. Pastoral care should focus on the individual and his doubts." (Schieder 1994, 36)

How should this be achieved practically? The aim of pastoral care is to counsel people at the boundaries of their lives, and *in* these experiences communicate the liberating gospel as a source of strength for each individual. What is meant here, is counselling at the boundaries, in order to support individual development in view of the boundaries of personal being and the ultimate conquest of these boundaries in the all-encompassing salvation of God (Gärtner 2002). To achieve this whilst taking into account the social conditions of the individual in postmodern society, the following fundamental focal points are (among others!) required:

1. The manifold experiences of non-being are radicalised in the life of people by the experience that the quest for identity itself is determined by many demarcations. Therefore, the quest for identity will only ever succeed in the fragment (Luther 1992, 160-182); the "Patchwork identity" (Heiner Keup) becomes normalcy. This fundamental demarcation does not need to be glossed over in pastoral care. It relieves me from the pressure of having to perfectly control my humanity. The experience of non-being is rather an essential part of the shaping of my biography.

2. Pastoral care will need to focus on certain aspects. In a time in which the church's resources and those of the individual pastoral workers are limited, some tasks will have to be dropped. When setting up pastoral care, a choice will have to be made; here again we find the marks of postmodernity. Should we choose to ignore this and try to do it all, we will do nothing right.

Against the backdrop of the gospel, choices like these in pastoral care can only end up being in favour of those most severely affected by the postmodern condition. Right from the start, those losing out in modernisation are hampered by their social situation in developing identity on the free market of ways of life. Pastoral care that takes the gospel as its starting point, is therefore not concerned with "care for bourgeois-Christian private Me" (Poensgen 1997, 161), but with finding those who are excluded from possibilities to shape their lives in complex and incoherent postmodernity.

3. Individual pastoral care place itself in an overall social context with such a choice. The boundary experiences of the individual are not personalised, even though it is individual counselling at the intrusion of non-being into the story of life that is at stake here. However, this starting point for pastoral care does not mean neglecting the social conditions of individual life. The intrusion of non-being in boundary situations will always be mediated by time, space, history and society (Van Knippenberg 1998). That is why, in pastoral care we need to investigate the fragmented experiences of identity of the individual for their causes: Loss of a job, bad health as a result of malnutrition, medial stereotyping of the roles of the sexes, loss of the private agenda because of the things forced upon us by others, exclusion from mobile society because of a handicap, marginalisation as a result of illegality and others.

4. Pastoral care as the counselling at the boundaries, therefore can also be critical of society. It is not easily satisfied with the expectations of the social mechanisms of postmodernity that mean to limit its function to social hygiene and social stabilisation. It would have to cushion the undesirable effects of these mechanisms – especially the economy -, in a social therapeutical way. Pastoral care can only meet these demands if it has first pulled out its critical sting of the gospel. In this sense too, pastoral care belongs to the basic diaconal practice of the church (Van Knippenberg and Nauta 1994, 139-141; Poensgen 1997, 161-163).

5. To ensure the credibility of such a social-critical continuation of individual counselling at the boundaries, pastoral practice has to rely on a symbolic anticipation of the conquest of the aporias of postmodern society in the church. When we ask for the social causes of a boundary experience in counselling the individual, this gains importance from the fact that pastoral care as an act of the church is part of an ecclesiological context, in which solidarity and justice truly live, and home is tangible. This, in turn, will build a social resonance for pastoral care. In it, we can start to experience the things that are often a permanent fixture in the lives of people.

This does not mean, however, that the church itself is a perfect society, and that the pastoral workers are its harbingers of a better world. Quite often, the mere form of its communities testifies to the opposite. The community of the faithful may have been promised the presence of the Holy Ghost, but as a community of sinful people, it only realises this promise in a very fragmented way. Nevertheless, it has to try to show in its practices, the same potential for hope that should be found in the personal biography of the individual in pastoral care. Because it knows its possibilities are reduced by human limitations, the church escapes the danger of uncritically following the commandment of perfection, which, in spite of real, experienced fragmentation is the secret norm of postmodern society.

6. The commandment of perfection also applies to the identity of the individual. Yet, at the same time, it is becoming less clear what exactly is perfect and normal. After all, any design for life is determined by the segmentation of social reality and the pluralisation of the possibilities. Pastoral care would have to "develop a culture of imperfection, which frees people from the inordinate and therefore unhealthy demand for perfection and the need to perform." (Scherer-Rath 2001, 33) The awareness that man is a sinner and that no human community can ever live up to its own pretensions, ensures that the real failure of human efforts for identity are not pushed aside for hasty answers. Instead, pastoral care at the boundaries is also about training people to use their talents in a controlled and humble way (Wiggermann 1999; Maas 1996). In experiences with non-being, we can always trust in God's possibilities, which will always be bigger than ours.

7. The awareness of one's own limitations and possibilities of God also regards the pastoral workers themselves when they consider their own competence. The "ability to restrain and distinguish oneself" (Schieder 1994, 39) are among the essential conditions for this job in postmodernism. This does not mean, however, that we should no longer try to train pastoral workers in the best way imaginable – on the contrary! The communication and acquiring of essential abilities will have to take into account that man's possibilities are limited in this field, however. This will mean a liberation from fantasies of power concerning the supposed range of pastoral care. It will also mean a liberation from the subtle lure of regarding clients as a discrepancy that needs to be corrected in order to fit into "normality" (Luther 1992, 224-238), or breaking them down even further before offering them the even greater salvation.

8. The abilities of a pastoral worker in postmodernity do not just include the ability to reflect on his own boundaries and talents, but also on those of the people that seek his counsel. A constant shift in perspectives is needed here, for

postmodernity has no general way of dealing with non-being. This is especially true of the Christian way of dealing with these experiences. Therefore, the pastoral worker needs to learn to counsel the individual in his boundary experiences from a distinct position. He will constantly have to use a double semantics, in as far as his distinctness cannot place the boundary experiences into a Christian interpretation. Consequently, sometimes only *one* conversation partner will put the boundary experiences into the perspective of the gospel – knowing that the promise of the gospel is for all people.

9. Christian faith will identify the ultimate ground for the ability to act at the boundaries of non-being as the loving God, who has ultimately revealed himself in Jesus Christ. It is the task of pastoral care to reveal this promise to the individual life stories of people in postmodern society, even when the person sitting opposite does not share this perspective initially.

Pastoral care that wants to counsel the individual in his never-ending process of the search for identity, will reflect on this process, knowing that the boundaries are not final. It will work from an eschatological hope for the lifting of all boundaries and the creation of true lives for all. This hope is a fundamental, orienting experience in the practice of Christian faith, here and now (Gruber 1997). The promise of the life to come forms the basis of the Christian way of dealing with boundaries in pastoral care. Its tries to reveal this hope in the individual life stories of people with their pasts and longings. This enables it to guard against "denying or pushing aside the fundamental fragmentedness of personal identity. Faith would mean living as a fragment, and being able to live as a fragment." (Luther 1992, 172) Pastoral care at the boundaries aims to teach people to live from such a faith.

References

Alsheimer, R., A. Moosmüller, and K. Roth, eds. 2000. *Lokale Kulturen in einer globalisierten Welt: Perspektiven auf interkulturelle Spannungsfelder* (Münchener Beiträge zur Interkulturellen Kommunikation 9). Münster et al.: Waxmann.

Arens, E. 1999. Was heißt in der entfalteten Moderne an Gott glauben? *Bulletin ET* 10: 15-24.

Gärtner, S. 2000. Pastoraltheologie? Praktische Theologie! Die theologische Disziplin an den (Um-) Brüchen. Pp. 320-336 in *Katholische Theologie studieren: Themenfelder und Disziplinen*, edited by A. Leinhäupl-Wilke and M. Striet. Münster et al.

Gärtner, S. 2002. Zwischen Schweigsamkeit und Sprachgewirr. Gottes-rede in der Moderne. *International Journal of Practical Theology* 6: 64-83.

Giri, A.K. 1999. De grenzen van disciplines: het heroverwegen van theo-rieën en methoden. *Concilium. Internationaal tijdschrift voor theologie* 35(2): 64-71.

Grözinger, A. 1995. *Differenz-Erfahrung: Seelsorge in der multikulturel-len Gesellschaft* (Wechsel-Wirkungen 11). Waltrop: Spenner.

Gruber, F. 1997. *Von Gott reden in geschichtsloser Zeit: Zur sym-bolischen Sprache eschatologischer Hoffnung.* Freiburg im Breisgau et al.: Herder.

Guggenberger, B. 1997. Grenzenlose Technik - Wiederaneignung des Raums. Pp. 148-159 in *Grenzen-los? Jedes System braucht Grenzen - aber wie durchlässig müssen diese sein?,* edited by E.U. von Weizsäcker. Berlin.

Knippenberg, M. van 1989. *Grenzen. Werkplaats van pastoraalthe-ologen: Rede in verkorte vorm uitgesproken bij de aanvaarding van het ambt van hoogleraar in de pastoraaltheologie aan de theologische faculteit Tilburg.* Kampen: Kok.

Knippenberg, M. van 1998. *Tussen naam en identiteit: Ontwerp van een model voor geestelijke begeleiding.* Kampen: Kok.

Knippenberg, M. van, and R. Nauta. 1994. Diakonie als zielzorg - vraag en aanbod. Pp. 139-158 in *Weg van de kerk: Reflecties op „De pastorale arbeid in de negentiger jaren" van bisschop H.C.A. Ernst,* edited by J.A. van der Ven and A.W.J. Houtepen. Kampen.

Kunneman, H.P.J.M. 1992. Een tegendraadse filosoof: Theo de Boer en het postmoderne relativisme. Pp. 67-85 in *Filosofie aan de grens,* edited by H.P.J.M. Kunneman and T.C.W. Oudemans. Assen/Maastricht.

Lange, F. de 1995. *„Legio is mijn naam": Het pluralistische zelf als thema in de theologie* (Kamper oraties 7). Kampen: TH U Kampen.

Leyener, T. 1988. *Konkrete Kontingenz: Zur Theorie einer wachstum-sorientierten seelsorglichen Begleitung der Kontingenzerfahrung in Grenz-situationen* (Europäische Hochschulschriften Reihe XXIII Theologie 341). Frankfurt am Main et al.: Lang.

Luhmann, N. 1997. *Die Gesellschaft der Gesellschaft.* Frankfurt am Main: Suhrkamp.

Luther, H. 1992. *Religion und Alltag: Bausteine zu einer Praktischen Theologie des Subjekts.* Stuttgart: Radius.

Maas, F. 1996. Met grenzen leven: Over de deugd van gematigdheid. *Tijdschrift voor geestelijk leven* 3: 247-261.

Menzel, U. 1998. *Globalisierung versus Fragmentierung.* Frankfurt am Main: Suhrkamp.

Müller, H. 1998. Kontextualität als normative Kategorie in der Praktischen Theologie: Plädoyer für die Weiterführung einer Debatte. *Jahrbuch für kontextuelle Theologien* 6: 136-154.

Poensgen, H. 1997. Alles ist Fragment: Kritische Anfragen zu Konzepten heilender Seelsorge in der Pastoral. *Theologisch-praktische Quartalsschrift* 145: 155-167.

Scherer-Rath, M. 2001. *Lebenssackgassen: Herausforderung für die pastorale Beratung und Begleitung von Menschen in Lebenskrisen* (Empirische Theologie 3). Münster et al.: Lit.

Schieder, R. 1994. Seelsorge in der Postmoderne. *Wege zum Menschen* 46: 26-43.

Steck, W. 1993. Der lange Schatten der Pastoraltheologie: Wissenschaftstheoretische Reflexionen zu Funktion und Struktur der gegenwärtigen Praktischen Theologie. *Pastoraltheologische Informationen* 13: 93-121.

Tillich, P. 1964. *Auf der Grenze: Aus dem Lebenswerk Paul Tillichs.* München et al.: Evang. Verl.-Werk.

Tillich, P. 1965. *The courage to be.* London/Glasgow: Collins.

Welsch, W. 1997. *Unsere postmoderne Moderne.* Berlin: Akademie.

Wiggermann, K.-F. 1999. Mit Scheitern leben: Zu einer Praktischen Theologie der Lebensbewahrheitung sub contrario. *Zeitschrift für Theologie und Kirche* 96: 424-438.

Wilfred, F. 1999. Ter inleiding - De kunst van het omgaan met grenzen. *Concilium. Internationaal tijdschrift voor theologie* 35(2): 6-12.

Religious Leadership
from the Perspective of Moral Theology[1]

Jan Jans

"It is the task of moral theology to explain how, according to our Christian revelation, our relationship to God affects us in all the dimensions of our person" (Janssens 1990, 94).

Introduction

Long ago, somewhere in the beginning of the sixties of the twentieth century, two brothers were having a theological discussion on the sin that their elder sister committed by receiving holy communion less then one hour after she had been eating something. Maybe influenced by the then famous Maline Catechism that they were taught and had to learn by heart at school and by the sometimes subtle distinctions of neo-scholastic casuistry which perhaps their teachers reflected, they already advanced to a distinction between 'one hour before the beginning of mass' and 'one hour before the actual communion'. While they were pondering the effect of this distinction on the gravity of the sin committed, their grandmother intervened. As an authentic religious leader she declared: "God is not having a watch".

Many years later, somewhere in the eighties while I was doing research on the discussions of the "Papal Commission for the study of the population problem, of the family and the regulation of births" (1963-1966), these wise words of my grandmother came to my mind again. For, when one of the religious leaders of this commission declared a change of the existing teaching on contraception to be absolutely impossible, because then the church would have condemned so many innocent people – the ones that confessed contraception and were therefore refused absolution –

---

[1] An earlier version of this paper was published in Dutch as: Leiden als Helpen. Een moraaltheologisch perspectief. Pp.163-175 in: Beck, H., and R. Nauta. 1999. *Over Leiden. Dynamiek en structuur van het religieus leiderschap*, Tilburg: Syntax. The current revision and expansion is to an important degree the result of the lecture and subsequent discussion that I was able to deliver to the staff members of the Faculty of Theology of Fort Hare University (South Africa) during my stay with them in October 2000, made possible by a grant from Tilburg Faculty of Theology.

unjustly to hell, one of the lay women present replied: "Monsignor, do you really believe God has carried out all your orders?" (McClory 1995, 122).

1. Pinpointing the problem

The point of departure of this contribution about religious leadership from the perspective of moral theology is the position that the singularity of religiosity can be described as the meaningful connection with the transcendent dimension of reality. In general, I consider the result of such a connection to be religious faith. Religious leaders, then, are those persons who lead the way into these kinds of meaningful connections. Therefore, they can also be characterized as 'ministers of faith'. Still speaking very generally, it depends on the more precise content of the meaning with which one gets connected through faith[2], if and how this content will or should be related to one's ethical behaviour.
Of course, the proper content of a particular faith may or may not correspond with the factual ethical behaviour of its faithful. However, religious leaders of a faith that does thematize ethical behaviour are confronted with the question to what a degree they are implied in formulating and implementing such a relationship between transcendent meaning and moral behaviour.

Moral theology can be described as the systematic reflection within the catholic variety of christian faith on such a relationship between transcendent meaning and moral behaviour. The following description of Klaus Demmer is dear to me: "Moral theology is the scientific study of God's salvivic activity on behalf of humanity, which in its significance for ethical behaviour is worked out and reasoned about" (Demmer 1989a, 10). This description is dear to me because it focuses the attention on the real specificity of christian faith, which – notwithstanding it being 'christian' faith – is first and most faith in God. That which I up to now described as 'the transcendent dimension of reality' turns out to have a personal name, or following Exodus 3,14, to proclaim its identity using a Verb that urges towards response and activity. If religiosity is a general human phenomenon, then christian faith in God is a particular version thereof in which a central component of it's proper content thematises the relationship between faith and ethics. This is exactly the point at which moral theology is situated and its own task therefore is to develop the practical meaning of Gods salvivic activity. This moral theology is 'christian' because it considers the peculiar jewish faith in God of Jesus of Nazareth, the behaviour that is in line with this faith, and the theology that reflects this as God's revelation of/and salvivic activity. In other words: those who in this Jesus not only recognize a reli-

---

[2] In the back of my mind, there resonates the word of Alfred North Whitehead: "[God] has been named respectively, Jehovah, Allah, Brahma, Father in Heaven, Order of Heaven, First Cause, Supreme Being, Change. Each name corresponds to a system of thought derived from the experiences of those who have used it" (Whitehead 1967, 179).

gious leader, but are also confessing him to be God's anointed one – the *Messiah* or the *Christos* – have to take up the task to thematize theologically his preaching about the Kin(g)dom of God in its ethical relevance then and now.

For true 'ministers of faith', however, such moral theology is not at all without obligations. After all: those who are leaders in religious matters stand amidst the concreteness of today and although the ethical answers of yesterday, yesteryear, yester century and yester millennium can and in many cases will be inspirational, they are no blueprint. To put this matter a little more sharply: fidelity to the tradition does not consists in its mere repetition but in the continuation of its own dynamism[3]. If in Jesus the Christ, God's salvivic will for the whole of humanity became revealed, and if the responding faith of believers expressed itself in their ethical behaviour, then the task of religious leaders of today and tomorrow is to proceed in such a way that this process of grace offered and responded to, can find continuation. Christian religious leadership, therefore, cannot economize on this task, and therefore it needs the input and support of moral theology.

In the fulfillment of religious leadership understood in this way, two intertwined themes seem to me to be of crucial importance. The first is that if religious leadership wants to mediate in the relation between christian faith in God and ethical life, then an insight into the very character of morality is a necessary pre-supposition. The second is that down into the field of applied normative ethics, there is always - if only implicitly - a certain image of God present, which because it is at the same time the very foundation of a teaching, must be scrutinized in terms of its ethical plausibility (Jans 2001). The background of these themes and the reason for they being intertwined, is the perichoresis – to be understood as a 'resounding in each other' - of christian faith and ethical reason, aptly expressed by Demmer: "Faith and [ethical] reason challenge each other, they perform each in their proper way a maieutical function" (Demmer 1989b, 72).

2. Human dignity as the cornerstone of morality

Morality is a universal human datum. It consists in the particular type of behaviour in which human persons are lead by their acquired insight that something has to be done because it is good and other things have to be avoided because they are evil. Morality is therefore tied to the notions good and evil, not as abstract ideas but filled in by the content of 'humane' and 'inhumane'. Of course, about such concrete filling-in, there exists a wide variety of convictions and corresponding behaviour. Nevertheless, the *conditio sine qua non* of whatever morality is the janus-like reality

---

[3] This thought is expressed very aptly by John Mahoney in his appreciation of the Second Vatican Council: "Vatican II ... has produced a new edition of the catholic tradition" (Mahoney 1987, 302).

of 'freedom/responsibility'. An apt way of expressing this is the notion of human dignity.

In our contemporary society in which it seems that ethics is abundantly with us through the mass media, this term seems to be very susceptible to inflation. However, I hope to turn it into hard currency again by the following definition, which is the very first sentence of *Dignitatis humanae personae*, the declaration of the Second Vatican Council on religious freedom, issued on December 7th, 1965: "A sense of the dignity of the human person has been impressing itself more and more deeply on the consciousness of contemporary man [*sic*], and the demand is increasingly made that men should act on their own judgment, enjoying and making use of a responsible freedom, not driven by coercion but motivated by a sense of duty". The importance for my theme in this article is that religious leadership that wants to mediate between faith and the moral development/activity of the faithful, must take this human dignity as its measure in order to avoid ending up in the pitfall of moralism.

Time and again, the uneasy tension between human freedom as appeal and human responsibility as answer, can lure both moral and religious leaders into short-circuiting this tension by falling back on a moral discourse which precedes the human person and the contents of which are superimposed on human agents. The cornerstone of such an 'ethics' is therefore no longer the tension-filled human dignity, but a pre-given obedience in which there is no room left for duty-to-be-assumed. Especially in combination with – or possibly inspired by – voluntaristic images of God, this approach inevitably leads to the end of ethics[4]. The permanent antidotum for this pathology is a clear consciousness of the constitution of human dignity from its intrinsic bonds between factuality, anthropology and morality and the unabandonable role that the human person plays in these connections. Again in the background stands the work of the German moral theologian Demmer (Demmer 1980; 1989a, 16-19; 1989b, 119-154; 1991, 69-81; 1999, 98-131; 2000, 65-71). He pleas for a differentiation – both difference ànd connection – between the three levels of facts, their general anthropological interpretation and their praxis-relevant normative working out. One way of illustrating this differentiation is the shift with regard to reason and truth.

First of all, on the level of facts one can speak about registering or receptive reason in which the empirical facts carry the foundation of their validity in themselves. Therefore, objective truth is a matter of factual consensus, which comes about by the use of measurements and instruments, which remains almost independent of the subject using them (example: the gold-price of *a ring* at my finger).

---

[4] Next to this genuine theological approach, there are also other approaches which tend towards the same conclusion: for example in philosophy F. Nietzsche's *Jenseits von Gut und Böse* (1885-86); in psychology of behaviour B.F. Skinner's *Beyond Freedom and Dignity* (1971); in sociobiology E. Wilson's *Sociobiology: The New Synthesis* (1975).

With the explicit involvement of the subject, the transition is made to the second level, which is established by valuative or hermeneutical reason. Thereby, facts become seen in the light of their significance for a successful or good life, of which the general contours are outlined by a projective truth about humanity. As with any hermeneutics, such discernment also stands amidst the dialectics of receiving and establishing: in its reception of empirical facts they are not just taken for granted but precisely valuated by anthropological pre-suppositions (example: the expressive or symbol-value of *a wedding ring* at someone's finger). In this, the content of such an anthropology itself is also dialectical, because it is really a truth 'of' humanity: the insights about meaning and significance that are vocalized in it, are a project which must show itself to be plausible by its opening up of humane perspectives of being and acting.

Exactly in the concretization of this truth of the human person is the third level situated. Here, reason is rightly designated as ethical or normative, because the insights of valuative reason which have the character of a project or appeal, effectively àre taken up: what appears on the second level in general as 'worthwhile', now effectively – and therefore always and again partially - becomes dedication and action (example: the concrete meaning of *this wedding-ring* at my finger with everything that this implies in the terms of a reciprocal covenant). Therefore, on this level we can talk about practical truth which coincides with personal participation into acquired insights through a judgment of conscience.

Another way of indicating both the interaction between these levels and the indispensable place of the human person in his/her responsible freedom as *conditio sine qua non* and tailpiece of morality is the trio 'nature' – 'culture' – 'person'. *Nature* stands for the ensemble of observable reality (our subjectivity, embodiedness, materiality, intersubjectivity, sociality, religiosity, historicity and equality/unicity)[5]; *culture* stands for the meaning of this factuality as grasped or comprehended by its participants (for example: the human person as the adequate and integral unity of these components); and *person* stands for the working out by humans which are making this culture becoming true according to their possibilities and expectations, and according to their conscientious insights.

A conclusion from this might be that the proper kind of moral leadership – both within and outside of the context of religious leadership – is first and most a service to the building up and formation of such a layered judgment of conscience. At the same time, this will prevent that such a 'great story' about the good life becomes an heteronomous story about humanity, by which real and concrete persons are not so much challenged or lured into responsibility to be taken up, but reduced to obedience. However, in discussing specific religious leadership, one cannot leave aside the proper input of a faith in God both on the level of the anthropological frame-

---

[5] I will return to these categories in the final part of this article.

work of meaning, which is outlining the contours of moral identity as on the level of concrete formation of conscience and subsequent personal acting.

3. The always included Image of God

In order to avoid a possible misunderstanding: in no way I am pleading for a two-stock reflection in which ethics would be the general and easy to access ground floor and religiosity some kind of – optional - first floor. On the contrary: building on Karl Rahners theology of the 'supernatural existential', I join the thesis of Demmer: "[Christian] faith is no *superadditum* to common human nature, but a human is originally a religious being and his/her ethical rational insight is always standing within the horizon of some faith which does not remain outside of such insight" (Demmer 1989b, 72). For Christian religious leadership, this means that the whole issue of ethical ministry is and cannot be a side-issue, but that it must be developed from the very content of the faith confessed. Again in the words of Demmer: "The urgent question (for the work of moral theologians) is what faith contributes to human self-understanding, to the meaning of our existence and behaviour" (Demmer 1989b, 72). Here, I also refer back to the quotation from Janssens that I choose as the general motto of this contribution or alternatively to the even more succinct statement of John Mahoney: "Moral theology is faith seeking expression in behaviour" (Mahoney 1987, 340).

Now it seems to me that it benefits religious leadership to develop the significance of this horizon of faith both in more general as in more specific terms, with paying special attention to the image of God present[6]. A general analysis can forward two elements, namely that Christian faith and morality are content wise consonant with one another, and secondly that Christian faith 'dynamises' the ethical intentionality. Earlier in this article, I referred to morality as that kind of behaviour that follows from the acquired insight in good and evil, given content by the notions of humane and inhumane. Now it seems to me that it belongs to the core of Jesus' gospel – literally the good news – about the coming kin(g)dom of God, that he proclaimed this God as human-oriented love[7]. Put more forcefully: the golden thread which according to me goes through the whole of the biblical scriptures – and by which isolated periscopes can be examined – is exactly this revelation of the 'associated God': "In his acting and his speaking, Jesus clearly proclaims a God who is ethically qualified. This is expressed in the tradition by 'God is love'. Accordingly, an ethical category is used to speak about God. God is not just something or somebody, but can only be love. In Jesus who takes sides of paltry people, a God is shown who

---

[6] "If the moral life is defined as the sum of fitting responses to a reality defined by God's being and God's acting, then everything, in a sense, hangs on the way we understand that prior action and being" (Meeks 1998, 176).

[7] Janssens (1990, 98-103) is developing this under the headings of "God reigns through merciful love" and "Gods reigns through solicitous love".

associates with humans in their smallness and suffering. This is the *associated God*" (Burggraeve 1994, 29). Such a view is inspired by the theological narrative of the birth of Jesus in the gospel according to Luke. I am referring here of course to the passage in which the angels sing a hymn following their announcement to the shepherds of the *eu-angelion* that "a saviour is born", specified as "*christos*, the Lord". This hymn is a real exegesis of the event announced and it reveals the consequent relation between God and humankind, clarifying how God from now on stands towards humanity: "Glory to God in the highest, and on earth peace among men with whom God is pleased" (Luke 2,14). Some translations - and manuscripts - give a significantly different rendering: "on earth peace among men of good will". In this way God's peace is restrictively understood as only given to those who are (already) of good will, which only seems possible in the upstairs-downstairs model that I rejected earlier on. However, by understanding God's peace as announced to the whole of humanity (see Luke 2,10b: "good news of great joy to all the people") in a definitory way, meaning that in God's eyes human beings are *as such* of the kind that God is pleased with them, the problem of a possibly difficult relation between God's glory – which we confess in faith - and human persons' well-being – which we confess in ethics - is from the outset on prevented. Also inspiring is a seemingly off-handed remark by Thomas Aquinas in his *Summa contra Gentiles* (III, 122). In his disquisition on the sinfulness of sexual relations between unmarried people (*fornicatio simplex*), he replies to the thesis that this wrongs God and is therefore sinful, by stating: "God is not offended by us except by what we do against our own good".

The second point is the dynamical relation between Christian faith in God and ethics[8]. If one can conceive of Christian faith in God as the answer that a human person is giving to the 'vertical' or 'transcendent' dimension of reality offered to him/her, and if one can conceive of ethics as the responsibility of human beings over against each other in the 'horizontal' or 'immanent' dimension of reality, then it turns out that this God is served in feeding the hungry, quenching the thirsty, receiving the foreigners, clothing the naked, caring for the sick and consoling the depressed (Matthew 25). More in general and at the same time more radical, Christian religiosity and human responsibility are really implicated in one another, as becomes clear in the famous parable about what happened on the road between Jerusalem and Jericho (Luke 10, 30b-35). In many cases, the real point of the parable is missed, because the shift remains unnoticed between the original question of the scribe: "But who is my neighbour" – a question about the delimitation of others over against me – and the final question of Jesus: "*Which of these three*, do you think, *to has become*

---

[8] I am influenced here by the work of Paul Ricoeur: "My proposal is to say that the Gospel *reanimates* this whole dynamics [of ethics] from its very point of departure on. I think that one is going the wrong way in asking what values, imperatives or laws, possibly new, the Gospel is adding" (Ricoeur 1975, 333).

neighbour to the man who fell into the hands of the robbers?", a question which refers to the unescapable subject-character of ethical commitment. Consequently, Christian faith in God becomes the dynamics of the ethical interest because the *metanoia* which brings one in faith before God, makes him/her effectively into the neighbour[9].

I would like to end this general section with an additional remark. In the reflection of many religious leaders and their theologians, the ethical realm is all to often first en foremost formulated in terms of imposed obedience. The foundation hereof is a vision of God's creation, claiming that the existing order of things reflects God's creative will and that therefore his creatures have to respect this order without any further ado. To the degree, however, that human knowledge, skills and the related process of valuation are increasing – and furthermore some events are causing a real theological crisis as in the case of the earthquake that destroyed Lisbon on the first of November, 1755, leading to the so-called theodicy – the necessity appears to deal with ethics in terms of responsibility-to-be-taken-up. The relation between Creator and creature is no longer thought of by way of hierarchy, but more as analogy, in which humans understand and value their increasing knowledge and skills no longer as infringements on a god-given order, but as expression and development of God-given talents, for which they themselves have to assume the responsibility. Let me at the same time use the occasion to state my case against the hyper-modern type of restauration which claims to unmask such responsibility as human arrogance and pride – the deadly sin of *hybris* – and which suggests that only a mute-making heteronomy contains real salvation.

These themes of congruency and dynamism could also be worked out by concentrating on the image of God in fundamental moral theology on the one hand (Römelt 1988; Demmer 1993) or on the service of moral theology to humanity on the other hand (Vidal 1990; Burggraeve 1994). But it is also worthwhile – especially from the perspective of applied ethics – to reflect in dealing with particular cases on the image of God that always in some way or another is involved. I restrict myself here to eight deliberately pointed thesis, following the eight anthropological components which I already mentioned before[10].

---

[9] I have developed this to some degree in *Zichzelf als naaste* (Jans 1997)

[10] "To consider the human person in an integral and adequate way, account must be taken of the person's fundamental aspects or dimensions. I discern eight such essential dimensions: 1. The human person is a subject, not an object as are the things of the world. Since the person is called to self-determination, he or she is a moral subject, deciding on all his or her doings in conscience and consequently in a responsible way. 2. The human person is a subject in corporeality. Our body forms part of the totality we are: what concerns our human body affects our person. 3. Because of the materiality of our body, our being is a being-in-the-world. 4. Human persons are essentially directed towards each other. 5. Not only because of our openness to one another are we social beings, but also because we need to live in social

1 That the human person is a moral subject correlates with a theology of conscience which following the model of participation and God's indwelling takes shape and thereby turns away from any voluntaristic model of subjection.

2 That the human person is a corporal subject correlates with a theology of embodiment which for example in the area of health care shows itself in the balance between quality of life and sanctity of life without giving in to antagonistic images of God leading to 'demarcation line disputes'.

3 That the human person is a material being and can only realise him/herself by making use of the inherent possibilities and limits of materiality correlates with an ecological theology which sees creation as the field of co-creation and does not decree that some areas are beyond ethical reflection as belonging to God's prerogative.

4 That the human person is an interpersonal being correlates with a theology of sexuality and gender which sees in the covenant of life and love the source of human fertility on which God's blessing rests without an authoritarian casuistry of isolated acts.

5 That the human person is a social being correlates with a theology of liberation which places God's love for the needy on the foreground and which does not give into an acclaimed parity between factual structures of injustice in both society and church and Gods plan about our living together.

6 That the human person is open towards God correlates with a theology of God's universal initiative of salvation which is the horizon of God's concrete way with people, in which real unicity such as in Jesus of Nazareth is not a transgression but the beginning of eschatology.

7 That the human person is an historical being correlates with a theology of history in which ethical truth is seen as a project entrusted by God to humanity and which refuses being short-circuited by an unaffected, immovable and nontemporal imposed order.

8 That human persons are at the same time equal to one another and unique individuals correlates with a theology of creativity which holds every single human person in high esteem as image of God and invites him/her to become God's likeness – a grace-filled goal towards which religious leadership can and may assist.

---

groups with appropriate structures and institutions. 6. Human persons are fundamentally open to God, and it is the task of moral theology to explain how, according to our Christian revelation, our relationship to God affects us in all the dimensions of our person. 7. Human persons are historical beings since they are characterized by historicity. 8. All human persons are fundamentally equal, but at the same time each is an originality, a unique subject" (Janssens 1990, 94). For a recent reformulation and development, see Selling 1998.

4. Concluding remarks

In my concluding remarks, I would like to return to the scene in the Gospel according to Luke, chapter ten and ask about the religious leadership of the various characters involved. First of all, there is no doubt about who is the central character of the whole (Luke 10, 25-37) of the pericope: Jesus, reverently addressed by the scribe/lawyer who is about to test him, as 'Teacher'. This scribe is treated in a very benevolent way and twice he is given the advice of emulation: the first time rather encompassing as a result of his own formulation of the approved double commandment put together by him from Deuteronomy and Leviticus, the second time pinpointed after his correct answer to Jesus' question about who became the neighbour, with the ringing admonition "Go and do likewise". The road to conversion and thereby even possible religious leadership is opened for him by this advice of the obvious leader, Jesus.

But what about the characters of the parable? Leaving aside the robbers - even theological acrobacy cannot turn them into something remotely akin to ministers of faith -, and the nursing innkeeper, we have to ask about the nameless man who went down from Jerusalem to Jericho, the priest, the Levite and the Samaritan. The robbed one remains passive: he literally is the 'direct object' of the other's activity, but plays no role himself. Things change dramatically with the priest and the Levite: one can assume official religious leadership of the both of them, and although it can hardly be the case that they were ignorant about Deuteronomy and Leviticus, there status and knowledge did not prevent them from intentionally "passing by on the other side" upon seeing the half dead victim. Maybe it was even their own image of God and the corresponding notion of what it means to serve this God, that lead them to take the narrated distance and thereby practically to invalidate the mentioned double commandment from the inside out.

But, finally, what about the Samaritan: is he a religious leader? Interestingly enough, the parable tells us nothing about his relation with God - analogous to what we learn about those addressed with "Come, you that are blessed by my Father, inherit the kingdom prepared for you from the foundation of the world" in Matthew 25,34b -, but there is absolutely no doubt about his moral emotion followed by his concrete and very physical help. Furthermore, the parable extends his intervention by narrating the efforts he makes to ensure some continuity in the care of the robbed man by stand surety for him at the innkeeper.

But even this is not the full story. For those who apprehend the content of the double commandment to love both God and neighbour - put together by the scribe and approved by Jesus - as the very relation between faith and ethics, they will not only agree with their non-contradiction, but also with their mutual reciprocity. In and by becoming neighbour shines through the looked-for ministry of faith and therefore the ethical life can aptly be depicted as being a mystagogy: "an initiation in the mystery of God who remains hidden" (Beemer 1993, 101).

References

Beemer, T. 1993. Het geboorterecht van de berooiden en de verborgen God. Pp. 92-107 in *Om het geheim van God. Moraaltheologie in de jaren negentig*, edited by R. Houdijk. Heerlen.

Burggraeve, R. 1994. *Tussen Rome en leven. Essay over een ethiek van het haalbare opgetekend door Ilse Van Halst.* Tielt: Lannoo.

Demmer, K. 1980. *Sittlich handeln aus Verstehen. Strukturen hermeneutisch orientierter Fundamentalmoral.* Düsseldorf: Patmos.

Demmer, K. 1989a. Das Selbstverständnis der Moraltheologie. Pp. 9-25 in *Grundlagen und Probleme der heutigen Moraltheologie*, edited by W. Ernst. Würzburg.

Demmer, K. 1989b. *Moraltheologische Methodenlehre.* Freiburg et al.: Universitätsverlag/Herder.

Demmer, K. 1991. *Die Wahrheit Leben. Theorie des Handelns.* Freiburg im Breisgau: Herder.

Demmer, K. 1993. *Gottes Anspruch denken. Die Gottesfrage in der Moraltheologie.* Freiburg et al.: Universitätsverlag/Herder.

Demmer, K. 1999. *Fundamentale Theologie des Ethischen.* Freiburg et al.: Universitätsverlag/Herder.

Demmer, K. 2000. *Shaping the Moral Life. An Approach to Moral Theology.* Washington: Georgetown University Press.

Jans, J. 1997. Zichzelf als naaste. Pp. 227-236 in *De passie van een grensganger. Theologie aan de vooravond van het derde millenium*, edited by K.-W. Merks and N. Schreurs. Baarn.

Jans, J. 2001. Het uur van de waarheid. Over consensus en dissensus in de moraaltheologie. Pp. 198-210 in *Over moed. De deugd van de grenservaring en de grensoverschrijding*, edited by H. Beck and K.-W. Merks. Budel.

Janssens, L. 1990. Personalism in Moral Theology. Pp.94-107 in *Moral Theology. Challenges for the Future*, edited by C.E. Curran. Mahway.

Mahoney, J. 1987. *The Making of Moral Theology. A Study of the Roman Catholic Tradition.* Oxford: Clarendon Press.

McClory, R. 1995. *Turning point.* New York: Crossroad.

Meeks, W.A. 1998. The Christian Beginnings and Christian Ethics: The Hermeneutical Challenge. *Bulletin ET* 9: 171-181.

Ricoeur, P. 1975. Le problème du fondement de la morale. *Sapienza* 28(3), 313-337.

Römelt, J. 1988. *Personales Gottesverständnis in heutiger Moraltheologie auf dem Hintergrund der Theologien von K. Rahner und H.U.V. Balthasar.* Innsbruck-Wien: Tyriola.

Selling, J. 1998. The Human Person. Pp. 95-109 in *Christian Ethics. An Introduction*, edited by B. Hoose. London.

Vidal, M. 1990. Die Moraltheologie als Dienst an der Sache des Menschen. *Theologie der Gegenwart* 33: 3-19.

Whitehead, A.N. 1967. *Science and the Modern World.* New York: The Free Press.

Starting Points of a Communicative Theology in William of Ockham

Wiel Logister

Many believe that the loss of Christian understanding of life and Christian culture starts with Ockham (1280-1350). He is regarded as an anti-metaphysicist and an epistemological relativist. Since he supposedly undermined the ontological basis for the *adequatio rei et intellectus*, he gave room to modern epistemological scepticism that resulted in the loss of meaning and belief in God. In the last decades, however, the opinion on Ockham has changed quite a lot. In his own way he did go into the challenge that rose, when by means of Islamic scholars a number of new texts by Aristotle end up on the desks of Christian theologians. Notions known from time immemorial like causality, principles, necessity and essence got a new meaning. As Thomas Aquinas, Duns Scotus and others, William of Ockham struggled fiercely with this problem. In a broader sense this is also about *anagkè, ma'at, karma, fate, arbitrariness* on the one hand and grace and freedom on the other. In the Bible we see a God who wants to make history with people, sharing with them freedom and creativity. This God is full of the spirit of affection and care, arising out of his inexhaustible creative phantasy. Not fate or necessity determines finally life, but the way God involves human beings in his creativeness. According to recent research, this was also the focus of Ockham. In my eyes he offers interesting insights for a communicative theology.

1. The concern of Ockham

The final years of Ockham's life are dominated by his struggle with John XXII, who had condemned the thesis that a church with possessions cannot be the true church of Christ. In a good Franciscan manner Ockham emphasizes "that Christ and his Apostles in their life on earth did not possess anything in property, neither as individuals nor as a community" (Miethke 1994, 213). Poverty is the basis of the right relation to everything and everyone. Only then we can let each other be. The viewpoint of John, however, breathes the atmosphere of almighty power; he makes the order-founding impulse of God into a massive worldview. Ockham writes: "John XXII teaches and proves, that everything happens out of necessity, because all has been predestined by God. A determination of God cannot be blocked or obstructed. That is why he thinks explicitly in his bul *Quia vir reprobus*, that Christ in his humanity could not renounce temporal kingship and power over the things of this world. Otherwise he would have broken the regulation of his Father. On this ground the Pope also contends the distinctions made by theologians of the absolute and ordered power of God. On the same ground he says also, that God necessarily - by no means contingent - had destined the elected for eternal life. So he beliefs clearly, that everything happens with necessity" (Ockham 1994, 213).

According to Jan Beckmann the orthodoxy trial against Ockham in Avignon "in der Sache" had nothing to do "with the conflict on papel jurisdiction" nor with the controversy on poverty, in which Ockham together with other Franciscans defends that Christ and the apostles neither together nor separately owned anything and that this should be the case for the church as well (Beckmann 1985, 23). I wonder if Beckmann is right. I recognize in the linguistic and logical work of the young Ockham the same intuition and concern. The importance that he attaches to the virtue of poverty in later years, explains what he had in mind all along. A life of poverty accords with his theory of communication and with his considerations on philosophy of science.

Ockham wants to speak about God carefully and not just identify God with something else. That was also the concern of Duns Scotus before him. According to Scotus God is the destination of the human person, rather than already present in him or her, with a presence that has only to be discovered, if necessary with supernatural help. The participation in the divine nature has to be born and realized in a life-long process in confrontation with the Word. In the course of our life we do not unfold a nature given in advance, but engage in communication with others and the Other respectful of each other's freedom. Ockham radicalises this point of view. He sharpens the distance between one and the other, between perceiver and the perceived, between origin and final destination, between human beings and God. Not to cause scepticism, but in order to highlight the exciting adventure that life is in general and the God-human-relationship in particular. He emphasizes the distance between "Ich und Du" to make the encounter all the more exciting. Nevertheless he increases the demands of "it is necessarily this way and not another" in justification of the epistemic and ethical relationship towards the other in order not to forget that this relationship is not self-evident and not-necessary, but is based on freedom and respect.

From the desire to communicate with the world around us and with others we cannot derive the nature of what surrounds others and us. We are always heading for it, while a distance remains. The other remains the other and God is infinite. We pick up signals from them and attempt to put these into words as clearly as possible and to comprehend. But this does not completely bridge the gap. We can decrease the distance but with this nearness the respect for the freedom of others grows at the same time. Therefore the appeal not to rule over others remains necessary. That calls for a spirituality of poverty, of letting be. As soon as we are given an inch, we often take a mile and do not allow others to be themselves. This "incurvatio in seipsum" renders all possession into a precarious undertaking. That is what the controversy on poverty in the Franciscan movement is about. Within the scope of this Franciscan spirituality Ockham studies the range of our terms and concepts. In his early work, it is true, he does not make this link explicitly. But also in his later work the question remains how we deal with reality and experience it. He considers the groping nature of words and concepts characteristic for our situation.

2. The process of cognition

Confronted with something, someone, a concept, an affect, an expectation or an idea, I have an intuitive link with this singular matter. To Ockham intuitive cognition means that I truly make contact with others in their singularity and that I am able to communicate with them, but not that I gauge them from within. "The outcome is that the term 'idea' is not an absolute name, but a connotative name, more precisely a relative name"(Biard 1999, 77). This cognitive intuition shows a certain analogy to the act in which God creates the singular, namely not as an application of eternal ideas, but exactly as the singular.

The first act in my encounter with the other is: "he, she, it exists, is there." Therefore the statement "this is" does not concern something universal, but this concrete singular thing. The is-statement wants to point out the being-there of this particular thing in its concreteness. The is-statement is not meant to connect the singular with something universal that is supposed to be higher in value or meaning. "We meet here a basic principle in the metaphysics of Ockham: to be means to be different... The universal concepts are indebted exclusively to the activity of the intellect. They are concepts in the form of intellectual intentions; with their help the intellect tries to be sure on reality" (Beckmann 1985, 93; 98). When I come to a judgement about the who and the what of the other, not only the intellect but also the will and thus the ethical responsibility are involved according to Ockham. Thanks to the Spirit of God I thereby have this ability and I possess the cognitive power. In this way God creates me in his own image and likeness. Jesus Christ is the image in its fulness. I abstract to come closer to this concrete singular being, not to classify it under something universal. In this act of abstracting I do not confront the concrete being with "species intelligibiles" present in the mind, as if I had prior knowledge of this or that reality (for example based on my participation and theirs in the uncreated being). Ockham thus rejects the existence of such universals. "The universalia are not substance and do not belong to the substance of the singular, rather they only declare the substance of things as signs" (Ockham 1970, 254). "The intellect does not make the singular thing to an universal, but it subsumes the singular thing among his categories" (Beckmann 1985, 111). "Semantically this means, that universal concepts as signs signify something universal (namely a more or less great number of individual things), but not a real universal (because in the individual things there is nothing that is universal)" (Beckmann 1985, 123). This is in flat contradiction with the opinion of the idealists, who accept that the intellect imitates only the reality and uses universal predicates, while there is universality in the reality of things.

We explain only by way of is-sentences the terms that we use. In this premise we put our first groping determination of the singular (John is a human being) in relation to the experience that we have of similar beings. Based on this we call attention to a certain aspect of John, without it immediately being obvious how, what and who John really is. Our conclusion does not finish my looking at John but it starts it again. We have caught sight of what John is and does in his uniqueness, and attempt to map this out more clearly by way of new reasoning. We are not allowed to stop thinking due to insolent laziness, pleased as we are with our own intelligence.

Ockham speaks of science, if the steps towards the eventual judgement or proposition about this or that are indicated and taken in a precise order. In science it is up for discussion if statements and/or judgements about this or that are brought about in the right way and can be verified step by step. "Solae propositiones sciuntur" (Ockham 1970, 134). I have to put remarks and feelings into propositions or is-sentences; only then do I leave my spontaneous sentiments in order and does it become possible to judge my knowledge. Constantly the awareness remains in this process that I am speaking and asserting; that way ill-considered self-evidences can be cleared out of the way. Theology and other scientific disciplines want to "specify the signification of the used terms, evaluate the truth of the sentences, define the (variable) status of the conclusions" (Biard 1999, 16-17).

Continuously Ockham is concerned with alertness and carefulness in dealing with myself, with the world around me and with God. He fears rash self-evidence. He is afraid that we rule over life with no respect. In that case we are in fact possessed and behave as someone who is possessed. Scared to lose my grip on life, scared to lose power. That we become lonely because of it, we hardly realize. We try to drive out demons only by the power of Beelzebub, by attempting to get control. But that is more of the same. Then respectless behaviour towards others and lack of self-knowledge only increase. Does the iconoclastic tradition not relate to this tendency to get a grip on everything, to mould and get a handhold? Doesn't the iconoclastic tradition turn against any form of absolutism that does not respect the other in his uniqueness?

Every statement about someone else has to result in my expressing honour and respect and acknowledging his or her freedom. Speaking and acting thus become a precarious affair. It might even make me scrupulous! But I have to address myself and others; I have to relate to others and myself. Because life presents itself, looks for communication, asks for acknowledgement and invites one to walk along for a while. Respectfully relating to others and other things asks the utmost of my freedom, implies radical obedience and at the same time appeals to my creativity. Behaving responsibly almost requires the humanly impossible. It can only be accomplished in a spirituality of poverty.

Ockham does not want the me-you-relationship to be blocked by something we put between ourselves as some sort of higher reality. That starts with the relationship between things and animals and culminates in the relationship with people and with God. I have to prevent my is-sentences from coming between me and others. They are propositions, literally "proposed". They are always open to improvement and have to be appropriated with wisdom and deliberation. I have to keep trying to speak of others with respect for their being and freedom. Language and other forms of expression are aesthetically sound, only if they serve this communication in freedom and respect between me and others. Ockham does not rule out my ability to truly know the reality of myself and others. However, that succeeds only when communication is established in freedom and respect.

That is also true for my own nature and being. I cannot account for it by something outside myself. I am free and not the prisoner of my surroundings. When I act, I act; I have to accept that responsibility. I do not act in the name of paternity or nationality, but I am a father or a Dutchman on the basis of my own possibilities and responsibilities. Ockham agrees with the opposition against the saying "The fathers ate unripe grapes, and the children's teeth are set on edge". He makes much of everyone's personal responsibility. I may not underestimate this being-while-acting of myself and others.

3. Culture as offer

All this does not make Ockham a Philistine. He doesn't want to banish all language, science, technology, art and tradition (devotion, liturgy) for fear of them coming between me and the reality of myself and others and preventing communication. He does however turn against the tendency to give culture an indisputable position, to consider its authority self-evident and put it on an unquestionable pedestal. Culture of a high order is characterized by the strength to prevent its own idolization. It should not claim to be the ultimate reflection of pure external ideas "rationes intelligibiles" that subsequently start regulating and ruling life with so-called logical or rationalistic relentlessness. Ockham shows how careful logic really is. "The strong disputative character of medieval philosophy brings, that logic is very busy with the linguistic and semantic conditions and consequences of scientific argumentations.... Always stronger the theory of language, of signs and their meaning joins logic, so that from the midst of the thirteen century logic and semantic hardly can be separated" (Beckmann 1985, 64-65). To what degree logic had degenerated in modern scholastics, became obvious when theologians educated with this logic could not deal with rediscoveries in the philosophy of language.

World and culture are not full of God's presence just like that. No one can take this for granted. They do not participate directly in God. Thus they should be transparent and not claim a special position or grace. If they claim so, they will soon start behaving as owners or rulers over God as well as over other people. Shrinking from this resembles the attitude of Dante (1265-1321), Eckhart (1260-1327) and Nicholas of Cusa (1401-1464). Each of them relates this in his own way to the sacramental-hierarchical view of Christianity and church. Sacraments and authorities are not static incarnations of God. Ockham does however come to the insight, following the transubstantiation theory, that large transformations can take place in created reality. The transformation of bread and wine during the Eucharist is analogous to the radical way in which the humanity of Christ subsists in the Word of God. It is possible to efface oneself radically for the sake of others. Culture can participate in this. But cultural heritage may never be viewed and experienced as incontrovertible authority.

It is true that I am helped by Scripture and other authorities, but the standard for my actions is what I should do according to my own insight and judgement. I cannot shift this responsibility onto them. An authority that takes over or eliminates my responsibility does not show respect. Politicians and other leaders make their largest mistake when keeping or bringing others in a state of dependence. When this happens, authorities in church and state become accomplices of the devil. Jesus however is a true leader from a Christian viewpoint. He is called the Word and the Wisdom, because he brings others to insight, creativity and responsibility. He is not a leader, a prophet, a wise man or rabbi without respect for others. On the contrary, he makes others independent.

4. Ockham as a metaphysicist

If metaphysics is not put on a par with the idea that reality is supported by eternally immutable ideas, one cannot deny Ockham a certain metaphysical sensibility. Therefore caution is needed, as Kurt Flasch puts it "What the world did loose in metaphysical glory, thinking did regain in radicalism and acting in latitude" (Flasch 1987, 451). Ockham is neither an empiricist for whom life consists of facts and figures, nor spokesman for a one-dimensional positivism. He regards reality as a space in which communication in freedom and respect really matters. Empirical observations do not get around to that. The transcendental nature of humans is nothing more (and nothing less) than the possibility to communicate with all that is in a conscious, free and responsible way. Metaphysics is concerned with that possibility; it differs immensely from sciences that only observe and describe facts. This communication reaches into the nature of God, even though I can only fathom God's works (*potentia ordinata Dei*) and not penetrate the Secret of God (*potentia absoluta Dei*). "Non propter diversitatem potentiarum in Deo, sed propter diversitatem locutionis ... sit dicendum quod Deus posset aliqua de potentia absoluta, quae numquam faciet (Ockham 1974, 234). The term "potentia absoluta Dei" indicates that God does not create "de necessitate", but "contingenter" (Ockham 1974, 231). Against this thinking in terms of necessity of some medieval aristotelians "potentia absoluta Dei" wants to guarantee God's freedom. Contrary to assertions of Hans Blumenberg, this has nothing to do with a God of despotic arbitrariness and unreliability. "Potentia ordinata Dei" turns against that conclusion. God's word is reliable and without contradiction. Granting there is much space to read between the lines. We can not understand all of God's ways (like the election of Jacob and the rejection of Esau). God's word does not offer a complete view of life. It teaches us, that we should live without wanting to dominate.

Thus the goal is not to fathom the O/other, but to meet and to cherish in a way that differs radically from the mentality of possessing, using, dominating, ignoring. Put differently, in terms of biblical wisdom: "Keine Bemühung um ein theoretisch in sich geschlossenes Weltbild, kein ideales Menschenbild, auf das hin der Mensch über sich selbst hinaus geführt werden soll, keine wissenschaftliche Systembildung, viel eher eine spürbare Zurückhaltung gegenüber übergreifenden Erklärungsversuchen; demgegenüber ein unabgeschlossener und auch unabschließbarer Dialog über Welt und Menschen auf Grund eines Wissens um die Ambivalenz der wahrgenommenen Phänomene, Vorrang des (u.U. kontingenten) Geschehens vor jedem 'Logos' usw. Aber sind das nur Negativa? Stand nicht hinter dem allem ein grundlegendes Wissen, das Israel im Bereich der ihm gegebenen Möglichkeiten und auch der ihm gesetzten Grenzen praktizierte? Daß sich nämlich die Wahrheit über die Welt und den Menschen nicht zum Gegenstand unseres theoretischen Erkennens hergibt; daß ein verläßliches Wissen nur im vertrauendem Umgang mit den Dingen zu gewinnen ist; daß es eine große Weisheit ist, von dem Versuch abzustehen, ihrer begrifflich Herr zu werden, daß es vielmehr weise ist, den Dingen ihr zuletzt doch immer rätselhaftes Wesen zu lassen, und das hieße, ihnen Raum zu geben, selbst aktiv zu werden, um durch ihre Sprache den Menschen zurechtzubringen"(Von Rad 1970, 404-405).
Even more emphatically than Pannenberg Ockham would say: "Die Bindung metaphysischer Reflexion und Rekonstruktion an die Endlichkeit und Geschichtlichkeit der Erfahrungssituation, von der sie ihren Ausgang nimmt, lässt sich nicht überholen, sondern nur aufklären" (Pannenberg 1988, 19). By no means the contingent worldly reality may be looked upon with contempt. Therefore I should not become detached, since God reveals Himself in it and stands up for it. As a result I should not react by speculating but by reasoning, in thankful doxological praise for God as the "gründende Grund des Seienden im Ganzen" (Pannenberg 1988, 11). But with caution, since terms like 'Grund' and 'Ganze' easily divert attention from the concrete or the singular.
Confirmation of God's omnipotence is nothing other than respectfully submitting to the fact that God's works excel in communication in freedom and respect. God can communicate in an ever-creative manner. The language of faith expresses this explicitly by crediting God with mercy, compassion, forgiveness and encouragement. In theology these doxological or evocative terms are converted into propositions. In these propositions or is-sentences the horizon of doxology becomes subject of dia-

logue, in order to encourage new creativity to burst out and erupt. Then questions arise like: What exactly is said or meant here? What does this imply for concrete situations? Those who listen well to Scripture and Tradition in the "communio sanctorum", leave self-evidence behind and come to new reflection and communication. Not in order to create something new at any price, as if new automatically means better. We are often impressed by the wealth of comprehension and expression of previous generations and therefore we like to safeguard it. Not by conservatism, but because of vigilance.

5. Faith and evidence

Ockham agrees with what the church professes doxologically about God. His question is: How can we translate doxology in a scientific way? Can we clarify in an orderly fashion what we profess as believers about the nature and the horizon of life and God? That is not a new question, but it is posed more fiercely than ever in the academic environment to which Ockham belongs. First he states that we may not conceive God in terms of necessity. We have to allow for this realisation in language and understanding. Thus we have to acknowledge that there are limits to our rational explanations of the meaning and the reasons of the world. Theological knowledge is not based upon necessities and does not concern an incontrovertible state of affairs, but concerns a contingency that is connected with freedom. The only necessity that is defended by theology is that we participate by grace in the freedom of God and offer others room to live from there. In following God we have to creatively surround the world with freedom and respect and thus establish shalom.
Who believes, concerns himself with the ways of God who acts in complete freedom and after his own good will. That is why Ockham hesitates at Anselm's phrase: "Credo ut intelligam". To him it suffices that God's acting in freedom is without contradiction and not necessarily impossible; I do not have to fathom it from within or have to be able to explain it. Thus he wants to prevent "that human science with her claim for necessity and universality brings into God some necessities and thus fails to understand the absolute freedom of God ... A theology, that strenghtens to dogmatics and restricts God's freedom, looses the title to be a scientifically legitimated Godtalk" (Beckmann 1985, 148). That God acts without contradiction we can see. However we cannot design how God should act from our notions about non-contradiction, order and disorder. In retrospect we speak of non-contradiction and order, in gratitude.
What is called God's humanity in the language of faith, Ockham translates with the scientific term "potestas ordinata". With this he indicates among others that charity is without contradiction. It is possible therefore to relate to God and each other in an orderly fashion, respecting the singular being and freedom of others. As a creature of God every singular being is in principle good and precious; it deserves respect in advance. Experience teaches us that we have trouble bringing ourselves to do this;

we become tyrannical, trespass and attempt to subject others. We should however not shout ourselves down and not indulge in this type of behaviour, but know when to stop. We have to take ourselves and others seriously. In this respect Ockham asks especially about myself: "Who am I? How do I think? How do I act?" Not to strengthen my egocentrism, but to come to insight about the way I deal with others. What I say about God has to be in line with the way God speaks to me. I have to keep examining my insights. How are they brought about? Can they be justified? Do they do justice to the way that God speaks? In God's Word we discover a trace of God. Don't we run off with it? Don't we pull conclusions that are too fast and too far-reaching? Do we draw the right conclusion, such as the importance of freedom and respect? Ockham has great respect for traditions or dogmas of the church, precisely because they have come into being by praying and imploring. To him they are not merely hypotheses. But neither are they dogmas in the modern sense. They cause us to think because of the spiritual poverty in which they were conceived. That gives rise to gratitude. But they are human words, notions, and language. They keep giving rise to thought on the condition that the thinker displays the same spiritual intensity.

This determines the status of hope. First we hope that our insight in God's humanity is correct. Subsequently we approach the future with it "until he comes". We imagine what God's future will bring without absolute insight into the nature of God's charity. The terms, expressions and images of hope that live within us we have to surround with reserve, without obstructing the trusting abandonment to God. This reserve should not end up in speculations about predestination that are pushed too far. Ockham puts his trust in God's humanity and does not limit God's mercy, without calculating.

This approach fits in with the emphasis on the viatorical nature of human existence. Our world is not founded in an order that encloses all singularities. A communication process is in progress, in which we should participate together and individually in freedom and respect. Revelation does not plug all the holes in our understanding, but wants to help us to live in communication. It comes to us through people who are radically poor, who know how to become the servant of others and guard the tendency to rule in the name of subservience. Through them God hands us wise insights and challenging examples, that we may not expand to a worldview in which everything has been filled in and determined. God's word leaves room for free will and creativity. Everybody has to search for his own destination, inspired by the freedom that God offers and that Jesus found in his receptiveness characterized by a spirituality of poverty. God's will does not stand in the way of autonomy, as long as it listens to the commandment to "love God ('s word) and others as myself". Life is not determined by necessities. We have to reflect critically and be open to what is and happens around us.

This point of view is having a hard time in a culture that demands absolute certainties and guarantees. It is at right angles to the way in which revelation has been understood and theology has developed during past centuries. That order in the world is not based on immutable structures and positivist regulations, but is the beginning and the end of the acts of God and the standard for the relations in creation. It does not concern an arbitrary God (as Blumenberg states), but a God who opts for communication in freedom and respect. The desire for all-encompassing totalitarian systems is diametrically opposed to the notion of a cloud of not-knowing. To keep that notion alive, Ockham deems a spirituality (and practice) of poverty necessary. The church should resist the tendency to reason in an apodictic way. In the church our words and actions are surrounded by silence, in order to let the wise word of God sound and his concealment be respected. That fails if the way that John XXII views poverty and possession, gains ground. In continuation of this, Ockham raises protest against theologians who strive for an absolute knowledge and inconvertible conclusions. Theological research about the content and the meaning of God's word and our experience thereof, or put differently, attempting an orderly theology, may not result in a system of necessities. We have to realise that our talking about God originates from the free initiative of God, in which not all of God's godness is revealed. Put in a Jewish way, we only know the *aleph*, the first letter of *ani* (I am). Theology therefore is not scientia in the sense of Aristotle. That is: the word of God does not offer us the principle with which we can reason logically. God refuses flatly to be God in the way that we (sometimes, often) long for a God. In this sense Ockham seems rather a Jewish than a pagan-Christian (Logister 1997, 77-83).

6. Christian existence

Ockham does not fill reality with ideas or ideal worlds that would explain what I, you and we are and do. Thus he wants to keep us from not taking ourselves and others sufficiently seriously. I am able to perceive myself, the world around me and God the way we are (truth), to respect our positive possibilities (goodness), to prevent conflicts (unity) and let everything shine in its own right (beauty). Transcendentalia are not well-defined domains. In the communication between me and others truth, goodness, unity and beauty have to be realised again and again. Possibly with words and images, rituals and standards from the past. Provided that I appropriate them consciously and attentively and take responsibility for them myself, critically reflecting whether they are not carriers of "verzerrte Kommunikation" (Habermas). What the transcendentalia imply today and tomorrow I do not learn by staring at the heavens, but by looking at myself and others in a spirit of poverty and acting subsequently. In this I can learn much from those before me who have occupied themselves with truth, goodness, peace and beauty. However, I am and I remain responsible for what I say and do. The same is also true for Jesus. He is not the incarnation of a pre-existent Wisdom or Logos, but judges truly, acts justly, makes peace and makes everything find its lustre. Ockham refuses to substantialise Wisdom, Logos etc. He does acknowledge an "order of origin" between Father and

Son, "but in no way he enters into the divine essence (placing her as the first) or into God's wisdom" (Biard 1999, 71).

During the Eucharist Christ comes present again as witness of God's humanity for the entire world. In radical poverty Christ meets God and people without hybrid claims. Thus as the Son he shares the nature of the Father and of us (*homoousios*) and is the image of who God wants to be for us and how we may be and become human beings. He is this without laying claim to possession. In the way he communicates, lustre arises that lifts others up and encourages them. Any place where the name of Christ is celebrated, true communion and communication arise and the kingdom of freedom, that is the kingdom of God, breaks through in all areas of life. In that kingdom one allows the singular nature of the other to blossom and institutions no longer arise for the sake of those institutions nor for the sake of its servants. In his explanation of the transubstantiation Ockham says that bread and wine are fully determined by Christ who holds them, without him behaving like the owner. The ability to be determined by another that characterises the being of bread and wine and even more freely the being of Christ, should also determine the person who becomes one with Christ during Holy Communion.

Christ shows his nature in the fact that he lets others be, that he liberates them from fixation on certainty (that eventually results in fixation on chance and fate) and stimulates them to look around in open creativity. He opposes a plurality that stands in the way of unity or shalom, but his ideal of unity is also at right angles to euro- centrism, imperialism and totalitarianism. Nevertheless it is not a perspective that evaporates constantly. The appeal to devote to God with all the heart, all the soul and all the mind has a tenor with respect to content: equality of all people, respect for each other, offering each other space. It supposes kenosis. This kenosis is "id quo magis cogitari nequit" or the absolute moment, which is not negotiable, which cannot be relativated. Kenotic existence should become the breadth and length and height and depth of life (Ephesians 3,18). It is the ground, the foundation, the rock that enables nations, cultures and religions to relate without imperialism. In that sense I read the Second Vatican Council: "But whatever truth and grace are to be found among the nations, as a sort of secret presence of God, this activity frees from all taint of evil and restores to Christ its maker, who overthrows the devil's domain and wards off the manifold malice of vice" (Ad Gentes 9). The deeds and words of Jesus are the exemplary form of this kenosis.

In the Christian divine ordinance freedom goes hand in hand with poverty, i.e. with not ruling over each other, not trapping each other in necessities. Jesus shows how people may offer each other room and thus become children of God. His radical openness is not without structure. It has a law, a line, and dynamics: letting be. This law should be the yeast in every dimension of life. In the name and the space of God this becomes possible. The qualities or characteristics that we attribute to God, relate to this offering of space. They indicate at what the creative possibilities of God are directed and what is intended by them. Believing is stepping into the space of all those possibilities, even though at first sight an abyss or the loss of all certainty threatens. What happens to me, if I depend upon the grace and the mercy of others? Christian truth unfolds from the promise that this threat does not have the last word. Who enters the space of grace and mercy and of communication that arises there, gains life.

The Christian vision of reality and life gets into a tight corner, if I put myself forward in order to win a position and establish my Ego. This "incurvatio in seipsum" is diametrically opposed to the shalom that Jesus wants to establish in the name of God. That Ego demands clarity, because otherwise it feels threatened. Clarity is a basis for ruling and exercising power. Because others cause a break in that desire, they become a threat. Biblical faith emerges in another space and has a different horizon. My destination gets another horizon. Listening to the O/other and letting him be, become fundamental. In that communication dawns what truth is and how it enters life. Kenosis, poverty, letting be, not clinging to imperialistic ideas about God and truth belong to the core of Christian divine ordinance. Any claim to truth should relate to this. It is the heart of the "hierarchia veritatum" and the "articulus stantis et cadentis ecclesiae". We exist thanks to a potentia that lets us be. Claims of truth that are contradictory to this, are untrue, false, heretical. Contingent beings, however, easily yield to the temptation to start thinking and acting imperialistically. The claims to truth that they propose then are, theologically speaking, perilous. Ockham stresses the frailness of culture and tradition, also in church. All too easily they are taken for granted as foundation and become something like "potentia absoluta". In Ockham's opinion one not only makes oneself all too comfortable that way, but also gets trapped in rigidity. Communication in freedom and respect has to be realised again and again. Tradition can assist in this, but Ockham recognizes in much of tradition and in living the tradition the possessive mentality of John XXII. He cannot protest too much against it. Because it is God himself who cherishes liveliness, freedom and communication and who creates human beings to communicate with them that life and that freedom. The knowledge, the insight and the life that well up from it, only remain authentic however in a setting of radical spirituality of poverty. This insight of St. Francis has been defended by Ockham against John XXII. Karl Rahner said once that the Christian of the future has to be a mystic. Ockham pictures the Christian as poor. Poverty is the core of his mysticism and of his view of Christianity with a future.

References

Beckmann, J.P. 1985. *Wilhelm von Ockham*. München: Verlag C.H. Beck.
Biard, J. 1999. *Guillaume d'Ockham et la théologie*. Paris: Du Cerf.
Blumenberg, H. 1996. *Die Legitimität der Neuzeit*. Frankfurt: Suhrkamp.

Flasch, K. 1987. *Das Philosophische Denken im Mittelalter von Augustin zu Macchiavelli*. Stuttgart: Reclam.

Goldstein, J. 1998. *Nominalismus und Moderne*. Zur Konstitution neuzeitlicher Subjektivität bei Hans Blumenberg und Wilhelm von Ockham. Freiburg/München: Verlag Karl Alber.

Logister, W. 1997. *Een dramatische breuk. De plaats van Israël in de eerste eeuwen van het christendom*. Kampen: Kok.

Miethke, J. 1994. Ockhams Politische Theorie. Pp. 209-232 in *Dialogus*. Auszüge zur Politischen *Theorie*. W. Ockham. Darmstadt.

Ockham. 1994. *Dialogus*. Auszüge zur Politischen Theorie. Ausgewählt, übersetzt und mit einem Nachwort versehen von Jürgen Miethke. Darmstadt: Wissenschaftliche Buchgesellschaft.

Ockham. 1970. *Opera Theologica II*. New York: St. Bonaventure.

Ockham. 1974. *Opera Politica*. Manchester: Universitas.

Pannenberg, W. 1988. *Metaphysik und Gottesgedanke*. Göttingen: Vandenhoeck.

Rad, G. von 1970. *Weisheit in Israel*. Neukirchen-Vluyn: Neukirchener Verlag.

Spectator and Participant
About the Necessary Ambiguity of Celebrating the Divine

Rein Nauta

Church attendance has dwindled down. When people go to church it is usually for a special event rather than a regular service. They participate in a religious service when a niece is married or an uncle has died. Some are reminded then of times gone by. Once again they sing the songs from their youth, or smell the scents of the past. However, for younger generations in particular a church has become an unknown building, and what takes place there unfamiliar. Perhaps the royal weddings and funerals as watched on TV are the most common shared religious experiences of a people that has lost its taste for the divine. The well-chosen words that express the public ambivalence concerning the choice of a partner are widely appreciated. The public at large is confronted with its own sadness when the sermon acknowledges the melancholic sacrifice of a stranger who became a royal husband and father. The ritual and ceremony, the music and the hymns that are sung help to create the aesthetic distance that helps to express emotions that otherwise would have remained hidden. These public moments of joy and sorrow in the ritual settings of the passages of life constitute perhaps the only shared exploration of the transcendent in a society that has become thoroughly secular.

Those who in our time and in our part of the world still go to church usually only do so once in a while. For them the church service has also become something of an exception. Church attendance is the result of a well-considered decision. It is surrounded with expectations concerning the edifying effect. The service has to be special if disappointment is to be avoided. Something has to happen.[1] Participation must be instrumental for a spiritual experience of some kind.

1. Paradoxical participation

Where once religion was a matter of course, was a part of us just as the air that gives us life, it has now become an alternative way of spending free time, a possible way to spend Sunday, in competition with numerous other, more or less

---

[1] In a contribution to the collection "De Madonna van de Bijenkorf – beweging op de rituele markt", I entered into more detail on the need for the eventful, the special and the exceptional, the unique as characteristic for the interest in old and new rituals. Every wedding is lovely, every celebration should be a once-only. In my introduction in the psychology of religion: "Ik geloof het wel", I explain how all sorts of religious activities, including conversions, show a rational structure in which expectations on the effect are of a decisive significance.

attractive ways to do so. This has led to a remarkable paradox in church involvement: where expectations rise, participation falls. Or in other words: the more importance there is attached to the church service, the greater the chance that people will attend less often, because disappointment is also more frequent and more serious. Such expectations have to do with the fulfilment of a certain nostalgia for the good days of former times, for confirmation and acceptance, the desire for a life that is free of everyday suffering. It is because church attendance has become a matter of choice that expectations concerning the result, the effect, determine whether one shall go or not. And that result is a reason for disappointment in more cases than one. Instead of instilling hope and trust, uncertainty and doubt are confirmed in the experienced disappointment. Although longing for a good word, what they hear consists of platitudes and unintelligible pious talk. In the hope of a better life, people are confronted with what perhaps used to be good, but the significance of which has now worn out. What is possibly the worst about this paradox of hope and disappointment is that people no longer feel at home with those they meet in church. After all, typical of each group and therefore also of the religious community is a tendency towards homogenisation, towards uniformity. People take part because they feel as though they fit in with those who are already there.[2] If this is not the case, then people leave again. The development towards a community of "our type of people", and the concomitant process of zapping participation, are characteristic for the instrumental nature of involvement and commitment. The development of each community into an in crowd, of a select group of members that are happy with each other results in a form of homogeneity that shuts the group off for the outside world, and that unconsciously but unavoidably concentrates on the inside, on the own little club and its internal affairs.

2. Confrontation with the transcendent

The casual visitor who decides once again to go to church hopes for a spiritual confrontation, an uplifting experience that will lighten the day. A barrier to such an experience is not seldom the congregation present in worship. For the occasional believer, the person seeking for the transcendent the regulars present are recognised as different. They do not coincide with what one would like them

---

[2] I explained this somewhat humiliating idea that religious communities also are more determined by their affectivity than by conviction in an article in the magazine Praktische Theologie. Religious communities form themselves round religious leaders and adopt characteristics that can be related back to the person of the leader. The Christian church as Jesus Christ's movement is clearly recognisable as an example. Within this differences between monastic communities and religious orders are still recognised as being defined by the person and the spirituality of the founder. In daily life this means that the identity and appeal of parishes and congregations is always a derivative of those who, formally or informally, fulfil leading roles and positions.

to be. In many cases the occasional visitors of any church service feel themselves to be an outsider. Therefore the service that invites participation can only be seen as a spectacle. Where solidarity and unity are expected, thus distance and judgement dominate. But perhaps it is the case that such an outsider position and its related attitude of criticism and relativity are right and fitting for those who are estranged from what was once familiar.[3] Perhaps the position of observer and its inherent perspective of distant commitment are particularly suitable for those who are in search of healing and salvation while being estranged from the salvific tradition.

This detachment, this balancing in between hope of enlightenment and fear of disappointment, seems to a certain extent, however, to concern all those who still go to church. Is not everybody a spectator in a certain sense, full of doubt about what the show will bring and with only a gleam of hope of a good ending? Perhaps this ambivalence and ambiguity create the aesthetic distance that is a necessary condition to sort out the spiritual effect that one so desperately desires. Every church service, as a confrontation with the Other, unavoidably involves something strange, is offensive to the rational mind, but sometimes exciting. It is the comprehension of this tension, which makes us open to the sacred that goes beyond and encompasses any individual being.

3. Two illustrations

Characteristic of this ambivalence is perhaps the doubt that overcomes us when participating in Midnight Mass. These services in particular are the ones in which strangers join with those who already know about the miracle. Midnight Mass should be beautiful, entertaining, up to date, familiar and unique. Invited by a friend who is the local pastor in a village near Groningen, facing wind and rain to get there, I took part in the Christmas Eve celebration in his parish. Despite all the warmth and well-meant welcomes, I was overcome by a feeling of being a spectator and outsider. Reflecting on this disappointing experience however I came to the conclusion that to avoid the superficial kitsch of such a nightly celebration - singing of peace on earth and good will in everyman, this feeling of alienation and estrangement might be safeguarding the integrity of the occasion.

---

[3] The American psychotherapist and anthropologist T.J. Scheff analyses how the cleansing function of drama – a play, a novel, a film that carries one away and that gives one the feeling that it has helped one to learn to understand and interpret one's own problems better – always requires the right aesthetic distance. It is the distance the merits of which you learn at a very early age when your mother plays peek-a-boo with you. If she shows herself too soon then it isn't a game, if she stays away too long then the fear of her disappearance gets the upper hand, but if the timing is good (the right aesthetic distance has been accomplished) there is the sound of a relieved laugh when the mother shows her face again. Every drama requires such tension. Church services too, understood as liturgical drama, require this detachment.

The church, dating from the late 19th century and in dire need of essential restoration, was hideously decorated, hot and stuffy. A group of well meaning but out of tune singers sang lengthy arias and choruses from the Christmas oratorio and the Messiah, a saxophone quartet played intermezzos in between the readings and the sermon. The minister, wearing a cassock over his woolly jumper gave a modern, political interpretation on the story of Christmas. Although this was interesting, I had the feeling that he spoke on a different wavelength than the one the listeners had tuned into. At the end of the service all those who had helped received flowers as a mark of appreciation, and the sexton was applauded for the application of the Christmas decorations. Although to be an outsider to such an event might be more in tune with the original situation where marginal shepherds were among the first to hear the glad tidings, the aesthetic distance I experienced that night to what was celebrated left me more lonely and doubtful than when I entered that church on this sacred night.

Where difference in taste led to distance too large to be helpful in experiencing the holy, language as a distancing device worked better in that respect. Like the time, in a different village, when the service was held in the local dialect, a language in which I think God speaks so loud that I can better understand Him. Although I myself was not born in Groningen, my wife has taught me to understand the language. It is direct and simple. It is a language that avoids big words, and therefore particularly useful for the expression and understanding of feelings and emotions. An organ made by Arp Schnitger, was beautifully played. All joined in singing the traditional Christmas hymns in the local vernacular. The minister gave a traditional explanation of the gospel. Peace on earth. It was a service not to be forgotten. It reminded me of what it was like when as a child I went with my parents to the candle light service on Christmas Eve. The gospel was alive. Hope was installed.

4. The temptation of simplicity

Such a relation of distant involvement, of critical commitment, of doubtful participation is in itself stable but is susceptible to the powers that want to reduce this ambiguous position to a less complicated stance. However such a reduction seems to me to be a temptation that can lead only to ruin if complied with. These reductive powers are centrifugal because they – just like in a centrifuge – force the parties related to one another, church and churchgoer, faith and doubt, apart. Churchgoers are spectators, in anticipation, distanced, critical with regard to what happens in the church service. A ceremony that nearly always fails expectations and ends in disappointment. Insiders - the faithful believers, the pastor– will repress their doubts and hesitations. They will try to reduce the ambiguity of the ritual service by selectively capitalizing on community, happiness, joy and grace. Outsiders are warmly invited to take part. They should feel included in the circle of those already present. The church emphasises togetherness, wants others to be participants. This cordiality shown can easily degenerate into forced conviviality, into artificial harmony, surrender to that which already is and which perhaps will always remain so. Where the hesitative spectators have for a moment ventured in, they react to this overwhelming takeover by fleeing as fast as possible. Their hesitation was there for a reason. Cordiality is not what was sought, lack of bravura not the reason to keep their distance. This rebound results in yet more frantic attempts by the insiders to make the outsider feel at home – that is at home in a way that this congregation defines as home. The result of which is that the stranger feels even stranger.

The spectator, who only doubtfully, hesitatingly, searchingly observes what is happening, is distinguished by the senses of eye and ear, critical, searching modalities. Everything that is seen is kept at a distance, everything that is heard is tested for genuineness and conviction. The church that hospitably opens itself to outsiders, appeals especially to the structures of hand and foot. A hand is reached to those who do not yet participate. Those outside are invited to travel along. "Come, go with us and do as we do". The really existing Church is determined by movement and action. The hesitant observer, the casual visitor however has the tendency to lean back. The position of the spectator is one of peace, quiet, of reflection and attention. When the congregational actor and the religious observer are left to fend for themselves, both could deteriorate, loose themselves in exaggeration. But related to one another they should hold each other in a certain balance: if spectators participate sometimes, they introduce some distance to what seemed to have become a social club of faithful insiders. By taking into consideration the desires of critical and doubtful outsiders, the church is able to see itself through new eyes. And it is sometimes alarmed at what it sees.

5. Ambiguous celebration

Where actors and spectators meet something of the ambiguity remains that is hidden in what has become too familiar. It is this ambiguity that refers to the mystery that fills us with fear but that also approaches us as a power that cares and supports.[4] A religious celebration, festive or serious, makes everybody, though perhaps reluctantly, a sharer in this secret. Sometimes it seems as though

---

[4] The former administrator in Netherlands East Indies and later Governor of Netherlands New Guinea, J. van Baal, writes in his dissertation, conceived whilst staying in Japanese internment camps: Over wegen en drijfveren van de religie, insistently about this existential problem of being a part, fellow actor, and separated, spectator. In his "Boodschap uit de stilte", he remembers how overwhelming the silence is in his journeys through the jungle. "It is a silence with power. Those who open themselves to it, listen and submit to it, can suddenly be confronted with an all-embracing power that cannot be explained in words. It does not frighten but fills us with wonder" (p. 39).

both spectators and participants offer resistance to a confrontation with the religious mystery. Actors, insiders wish to control the effect of their gathering too emphatically, and the spectators, observers, outsiders have too great a critical desire for something unique, something special. In their mutual distrust spectators and participants should guard each other from such seductive distractions as fashionable poetry, pathetic music, or kitschy art. The desire for the special and unique should be unmasked as an arrogant resistance against tradition, as a defensive plea for self worth. The anxious conservatism of the plea for harmony and fundamental truths should on the other hand be exposed as a lack of faith in both God and man. A religious celebration – vespers on a weekday, a baptism, a children's service – is not a spectacle, not a show, not theatre. But as a ritual praxis it should be permeated by a permanent confirmation of what is not seen or heard and of a denial of what shows itself and allows itself to be heard. The liturgical gestures and words point beyond themselves to first speakers and first movers. At the same time all of this is surrounded by doubt and disbelief. Perhaps it is this ambivalence that gives the celebration its transformative potential. Even for a detached, critical spectator the significance is reflectively unveiled through uncertainty. Religion is a performative activity. It can only realise the practice of faith as an act of surrender by those who in celebrating become conscious of their disbelief. As such the position of spectator is necessary, to really be able to participate in celebrating the divine.

References

Baal, J. van 1947. *Over wegen en drijfveren van de religie*. Amsterdam: Noord-Hollandsche Uitgeversmaatschappij.

Baal, J. van 1985. *Boodschap uit de stilte*. Baarn: Ten Have.

Nauta, R. 1995. *Ik geloof het wel*. Assen: Van Gorcum.

Nauta, R. 1997. Rituelen als decor - over het geheim van de leegte. Pp. 73-94 in *De Madonna van de Bijenkorf*, edited by P. Post and W.M. Speelman. Baarn.

Nauta, R. 2001. Mensen maken de kerk – over de identiteit van de gemeente. *Praktische Theologie* 28, 25-40.

Scheff, T.J. 1977. The distancing of emotion in ritual. *Current Anthropology* 18, 483-505.

Scheff, T.J. 1979. *Catharsis in healing, ritual and drama*. Berkeley: University of California Press.

Religious Communication in Modern Culture
The Case of Young Adults

Bert Roebben

Introduction

Theology is moored in time and space. Roman Catholic theology in the Netherlands and Flanders is trying to find its way in today's culture, forty years after the Second Vatican Council. Much of what was considered to be the promise of a new and grown-up church and in which especially the Netherlands served as a model for these dynamics of renewal, has stranded on the resistance of conservative forces in the church. This is painful for many who are active in the church. This pain is, however, of no concern to young adult students in theology departments. The struggle of the church with her self-understanding ever since the Second Vatican Council, has passed them by simply because they are less than forty years old. The disappointment of unkept promises, the "blues" of the eighties and early nineties ("things should be different in the church, but they can't be") (Michiels and Roebben 1994) is wasted on them. They would rather like to know what is driving religiously convinced people, i.c. Christians, to experience and answer present-day questions in their own specific way. Christian churches are confronted for the first time in their history with a generation of young adults who have been hardly religiously socialized at home. Young theologians are voicing this experience of their contemporaries. This situation is food for thought.

What Jan Bluyssen, former bishop of 's-Hertogenbosch (Netherlands) already wrote in the eighties "after the great church abandonment", is applicable more than ever to religious communication in modern culture. From a catechetic concern he writes in the late eighties: "We are not in the need of believers who worry day in day out about how for heaven's sake they can go on with *this* church. Nor do we need believers who fearfully mourn the losses of the church. Young people who see their elders deal with their Christianity in such a strained manner, or see them struggle so painfully with the questions of our times, will hardly be tempted to join the Lord and his church. What we need first and foremost is people who give evidence of a well-tested and deep-seated faith in God" (Bluyssen 1989, 195). Practical theology can reinforce this question, place it in a new time frame ("joining the Lord and his church" might have meant something different in the eighties than it does in 2002) and reflect on it theologically. In any case the request for authentic religious communication in our society and for the presence of the Christian tradition is prominent. Theologically educated young adults (between eighteen and twenty-eight years old) in the Netherlands and in Flanders, engaged in higher education, intermediary relations in church and society and in all sorts of volunteering, show these dynamics.

In this essay I would like to systematize these dynamics as follows. In the first section (problem definition) I will indicate in what manner traditional religious institutions try to deal with the pressure of modernization in society. The point that I am making is that churches do not know how to deal with these developments. They appear to be unable to convey their traditions of meaningful life to future generations. In the second section (analysis) I attempt to go beyond the perspective of the crisis of tradition and I opt to corroborate the creative powers in a modern society in its search for meaning from a religious perspective. I analyze the process of 'interactive search for meaning' of contemporaries and offer some critical notes in the margin. As a practical theologian I would like to offer insight in the ways churches might react, now that they are confronted with new challenges. This will be done in the third section (perspective). I believe that churches should set themselves up as mature dialogue partners 'in religiosis'. They should dare to bring their language of meaningful life in a critical interrelationship with the way life is experienced nowadays. This assumes new priorities where religious socialization, communication and leadership are concerned. At the end of this contribution (section four: strategy) I make a plea for religious education of young adults. More than ever before, religious socialization of children assumes educating young adults as future parents in matters of religious communication.

1. Problem definition: society under the pressure of modernization, churches under the pressure of tradition

Present-day society is pressured to modernize. This is a development with deep-seated historical roots. Its analysis is complex. Karl Gabriel, the German sociologist of religion, interprets this as follows: de-traditionalization concerning frameworks of values and meaning causes people to fall back on themselves to give meaning to their lives (Gabriel 1991, 69-88). The supply at the 'meaning-seeking-market' is broad, there is no shortage of religion and search for meaning. People have to steer by their own compass to make responsible choices from this supply. Ever since Enlightenment traditional religious institutions have lost more and more of their function of orientation in moral and religious symbolization. A systematic approach of this situation by re-confessionalization and denominational segregation (or 'pillarization') in the Netherlands and Flanders (especially in the educational and health care sector in the nineteenth and twentieth century) has not been able to turn the tide. The

Netherlands and Flanders became more and more secularized. Research of sociology of religion has confirmed this trend (Dekker, de Hart and Peters 1997; Dobbelaere, Elchardus and Kerkhofs 2000).

Along with this de-confessionalization the de-traditionalization has progressed even further and faster than before. At many levels of society institutionalized religious traditions have lost their "good grounds" to find acceptance for a religious stance concerning existential questions and the transfer of faith. There is a crisis of tradition. The process of religious 'tradere' (Latin for passing on) itself has become problematic, sometimes even lost. The relation faith-life is characterized by correlation weakness, or even a breach in correlation. Young people wonder pityingly: "What is it that religious people talk about? What are they getting upset about?" Attempts by theology to re-establish the plausibility of a religious perspective on every day life deal with the same crisis that institutionalized religions are experiencing. The tradition crisis is to be felt deep into the reflexive layers of religious institutions.

In this section I proceed as follows. First I define four problem areas concerning religious communication (two ecclesiological and two religious educational ones) that offer insight in the given that churches nowadays do not know how to offer a meaningful learning route 'in religiosis'. Subsequently I refer to two explanation models for this situation out of the sociology of religion. Finally I indicate what concrete actions churches undertake nowadays in order to deal with the given circumstances.

1.1. Four problem areas

1.1.1. First of all, it is true that virtually no *substratum of experience* corresponds to the traditional religious socialization of the church anymore. People do not identify with the church anymore, they do not understand its language anymore, do not know what it wants to express with its symbols and sacraments. If young people, for example, do not know of the effectiveness of salvation (*opus operatum*), how can they be expected to engage in the sacrament of confirmation out of a personal involvement (*opus operantis*) (Roebben 1999). When this religious mooring disappears, so does the social relevance of faith. People continue to belong to the church by means of baptism, but (virtually) no religious praxis, experience or practical insight in the liberating dynamics of the gospel corresponds with it.

The official church finds its influence in the life of believers shrinking and attempts to win them back by entrusting religious socialization to the family in a gesture of generosity. It no longer claims to be the originator, but positions the center in the 'home church' and its permanent religious initiation. The former secretary of the Council for Family Ministry in Flanders, Paul Deleu, has seriously criticized this development: "The greater the established secularism, the greater the expectation of the churches with respect to the family. As if secularism has stopped at the threshold of the home church. By thinking about the family in this manner one does not really approach it for its own worth, but as the carrier of frustrated church expectations". And this leads to the paradox: "One can proclaim that the family is an in-between that can evangelize and be evangelized, and still ignore the specific experience of the evangelizing family" (Deleu 1988, 52). So, the attention is shifted from occasional catechesis in church towards a permanent evangelization in the home church, from church initiative towards support of religious education at home, but the concern remains the same: to close the gap between church and world and to strive for the highest possible degree of participation in the life of the church.

1.1.2. In line with the above, authors like Erich Feifel and Walter Kasper (1987), Karl Gabriel (1991), Franz-Xavier Kaufmann and Günther Stachel (1980) and Volker Drehsen (1994) have phrased interesting thoughts about the *crisis of credibility of the church* in a postmodern society. The church stands in its own way if it makes people responsible for personal belief on the one hand, but does not permit the development of dissenting views or praxis on the other hand. People are leaving the church while they are kept in their place because of a traditional socialization idea (Drehsen 1994, 48-55). The church is faced with an immense educational dilemma, according to Drehsen: either it persists in its infertile attitude of being in the right until it has become totally unworldly and sectarian, or it takes up the challenge of the 'Tradierungskrise' and turns it into the focus of mature religious communication itself. In another analysis Drehsen states that as a result of this situation the church is no longer capable of formulating the true religious questions of modern people. Ever since the process of secularization has started, it has not taken advantage of the return of religion in many new colors. That is its ultimate tragedy: people cannot find their way in the church, it conveys little to them, because it conveys little 'about' them. They do not feel heard in their quest for religious self-clarification, in their efforts to deal with the contingencies of life in a meaningful way. The church is struggling in its heart of hearts with its 'religiöse Integra-tionsfähigkeit' (Drehsen 1994, 8), with the question of how to 'authenticate and communicate' its religious message within a modern world that is confused and self-confident at the same time.

1.1.3. Another element in the explanation of the absence of successful religious socialization by the church is of a socio-pedagogical nature and has to do with the *educational uncertainty* of parents and educators. They hesitate to continue to raise their children within a Christian perspective. Either they have dropped out in the opinion that the message of the church has lost its credibility in their eyes or they lack the nerve to point out the religious dimension of life to their children altogether. Many parents do not have their children baptized in the opinion that they should leave them free to make the decision themselves later in their lives. They assume that an education devoid of value judgments and religion is possible, or in other words that the perspectives of life and faith are completely incompatible. The church and its message does not appeal to them, it does not arouse their interest, therefore it has nothing worthwhile to offer, according to their reasoning.

Other parents are all too happy to see their child initiated in the full life of the church by way of the first communion or confirmation without realizing that this implies engagement. They shrink from questions about this half-heartedness, stay away from catechetic introductions for parents but drift along on the flow of what is socio-culturally taken for granted. If children are no longer aware of the scope of, for example, confirmation and only concentrate on the festivities and presents and parents cannot or dare not voice an alternative (not even a generally sacral, a religious or non-materialistic perspective), then it is to be expected that this process only enlarges the educational embarrassment of parents. The youthful perception of reality (being in fashion, on top of the latest trends, flexible) becomes the norm. Parents are unable to deny their children the celebration annex festivities surrounding confirmation, because it would make them lose face with their friends. In these confusing times children frequently lack grown up 'biographical advisors', adults who have in mind something other than a certain degree of material habituation and a lukewarm identity (Roebben 1994; 1995).

1.1.4. A final explanation arises from the radically *different experience of being young* nowadays. Adolescence differs structurally from the way it was some forty years ago. It is no longer viewed as a storm-free transition period from childhood to adulthood (between the age of twelve and eighteen), but as a turbulent and independent period in which adolescents create their own biography and attempt to gain insight into the dynamics of their own story, identity and person (Schweitzer 1993; see also Roebben 1997). Nowadays being young means that one has to learn to deal with the fact that as a future (young) adult one will have to live continually in a situation of transition. One will have to take an honest and integrated standpoint in the postmodern experience of 'social mobility'. In addition to that, the onset of adolescence has been accelerated (earlier than twelve) and the period of schooling prolonged, so that the entrance into the world of adulthood, employment, partner choice and raising a family has been postponed. This definition of young adulthood (caught in the paradox between personal and professional insecurity and huge societal expectations) will later in this essay function as a starting point for a renewed reflection on religious communication with young adults. Many of them are dwelling in an existential vacuum after their experiences with congregational catechesis and religious education at school. The challenge of working with young adults is huge (Schweitzer 1993, 79).

All this, according to Friedrich Schweitzer, has drastic consequences for religious socialization, for example for confirmation. This no longer serves to demarcate the passage into adulthood, it has lost its social impact as a moment of initiation (Schweitzer 1993, 77-79). The sacrament of confirmation can therefore no longer be legitimized theologically from this viewpoint. Furthermore, the prolonged biography of youth entails that those who join in children's and family services become progressively younger (80) and that the young adult (or post-adolescent) parents with small children of today feel that they belong to that generation segment of 'youth' with its typical experience of life. This new situation implies an important task for youth ministry that in this context has to work with young people mainly on 'moral/religious self-clarification' and building of identity against the background of a blurred society (85).

1.2. Two models of explanation

In sociology of religion in the past forty years at least two models of explanation have been developed (Ebertz 1999; Ziebertz 1999). One speaks of the *secularization thesis*: religion in general and the churches in particular are no longer the overarching 'meaning-prompters' for culture and society. They have lost their impact in several domains of human life. Nowadays people self-confidently search for meaning. The term 'functional differentiation' applies here: within the complexity of life its domains have become disconnected. They have grown apart more and more and have started to lead their own life. Religion is but one of those domains, conveniently next to and apart from the others, just like for example relationships, raising children, education, work, leisure, sports, etc. Additionally, in sociology of religion one speaks of the *modernization thesis*. Traditional religious institutions have indeed lost their influence; however, at the same time former churchgoers and their contemporaries are freely and unrestrainedly searching for meaning in their lives. Individualization is the keyword of modern culture and this carries over into the area of religion. De-traditionalization has the effect that people no longer find inspiration for their own way in life in traditions as passed on by religious institutions. Living authentically means that one can and dares to steer by his or her own compass. Pluralization is the result of this development: numerous religious options that can be combined indefinitely (syncretism) are available in modern culture. One can speak of a 'reli-market' – where a person can offer his own life project as ware and where the customer can get a bargain and determine whether and how much religion one takes home. "Could you make that a little more, please?"

Because of the disappearance of the great narratives that build a context of meaningfulness, people have been left to their own devices. They are in each other's charge, but at each other's mercy as well. After all, individualization can also pressure people: "I *have* to be free and authentic". It carries the risk of being lived, because the task of making choices time and again is felt as too much of a burden. Paradoxically our freedom becomes a constraint. "I determine" becomes equal to "I am determined". The building blocks of freedom have become nothing other than monoliths, organically fitted into what the market requires. Added to this can be the fact that the promise of modernization of culture as a project of meaning seeking is often not fulfilled. The 'meaning-seeker-without-compass', the person who has freed himself from enslaving traditions, often enough chokes on the experience of contingency and ambiguity, an experience that not only characterized human life in the old days, but still does today. The promise of the makability of our own life and of life as a self-directed project, which is what modernity is all about, often dead-ends in itself. Since no one can direct the contingent circumstances of his or her own life, especially not the last circumstance: death. The core of the human self is "not available". And that is disturbing to modern people. The French sociologist of religion, Danièle Hervieu-Léger argues as follows: "The structural tension in the experience of modernity stems from the fact that it simultaneously produces the expectations it is supposed to satisfy and the feeling of helplessness arising from the awareness that it provokes of the world's opaqueness. The affirmation of the reign of man [sic], his autonomism, his all-powerfulness, breaks down at the very moment and in the very mechanism through which it was made" (1990, 24).

Religion can serve the purpose of contingency management. People can experiment with alternative medicine and meditation. They join eager groups that offer the opportunity of contact with what goes beyond everyday reality. After abandoning the church, they knock on the doors of private caregivers who design religious rituals for key moments in life. Popular religion is booming. In the overheated sorry-culture confession is called upon again. The 'new-religious longing', according to the Dutch systematic theologian Anton van Harskamp (2000), is developing in many ways in the tension between the individualization of meaning and the awareness of its ultimate unavailability.

1.3. Three possible reactions

This situation could be a temptation for churches to welcome the 'new receptivity' with open arms and to functionalize it in view of new membership.

They could focus exclusively on the new and new-religious longing to undo their own anemia and to adapt to what is marketable. And there is the temptation of the 'snuggle strategy', of cocooning in the conviction of ultimately being in the right. This option has a variation that is milder: that of re-profiling what is typically Christian, in view of a more forceful testimony in the world of meaning-seekers. The German sociologist of religion, Michael Ebertz, distinguishes three possible reactions: the option of self-complacency (with the corresponding strategy of closing rank – since the world is in the wrong), the option of self-regulation (with the adaptation strategy – since we have to get through these difficult times) and the option of self-direction (with the development strategy – which are the opportunities for learning and change in this situation?) (Ebertz 1999, 140-141). He makes a plea for the third option and strategy. Only then churches can become sacrament of salvation for the world. Since that is what they are meant to be, according to Ebertz.

There is much uncertainty in church circles about how to deal with religiosity outside the church. One thing is for sure: the dynamics *ad intra* (what does modernization of religion mean for a community of believers?) and the dynamics *ad extra* (what can churches mean to modernized contemporaries?) need to remain connected. Self-absorption of the church on the one hand or its clearance sale to culture on the other hand does not serve any purpose. In the research project 'God in the Netherlands' this ambivalence is recognized, but at the same time one remarks that it is not easy, from a church political point of view, to keep these two motions together. Choices have to be made, according to this paper (Dekker, de Hart and Peters 1997, 117-123). This process of prioritizing calls for profound analysis.

2. Analysis: the longing for religious orientation in modern culture

For a modernized perspective of religion 'creative perception' is necessary. In the analysis one needs to be courageous in order to look at reality differently. The present-day crisis of faith might be an optical illusion: maybe churches are so focused on certain developments that they are unable to see the new ones (Tieleman 1995). What is happening to a modern community of faith, is it comparable to the sinking of the Titanic, a fortress of power that is perishing and desperately casting life-boats from where one wistfully looks back at what is gone forever? Or is it something else: is today's culture more like a sea of meaning on which many drift about without any sense of orientation, in search of a perspective of meaningful life; as an open space of discovery of meaning out of whose depths the Christian story emerges next to other fragmented frames of reference; as a collection of disparate pieces of wreckage, that remind us of a rich and dynamic past, to which the meaning-seeker can cling?

2.1. Kairologic analysis

The first scenario, a disaster scenario, refers to the secularization thesis of the former paragraph, the second scenario, an emergence scenario, refers to the modernization thesis. Emergence points at the positive act of coming up for air, of recovering one's breath. At the same time it points at the urgent nature (*emergency*) of this analysis: who spends too much time mourning the lost glory will be unable to see through the tears that people in their vitality are already busy looking for a new *modus vivendi*. Modern theology should keep an open mind for this development and should be open to the signals of the young who have no experience of the struggle that the church has gone through in its Titanic-stage. Schematically both scenarios yield the following ways of being-church. For the time being they help us to look at religiously loaded reality in a clear and original way.

Disaster Scenario	Emergence Scenario
Ideological	Spiritual
Moralistic	Enthusiastic
Imposed	Self-directed
Top down	Contextual
Retrospective	Innovative
Self-glorifying	Self-criticizing

In practical theology a kairologic awareness is present: the practical theologian can choose a hopeful perspective for assessing a situation, because he or she is convinced that it concerns a *kairos*, an inspired moment for a new and critical praxis (Englert 1992). This *kairos* is founded in the conviction that reality does not shut tight once and for all, but remains open as a meaningful and humanizing event that can be assented to and interpreted by people. Viewing the current situation as a 'crisis' and considering practical theology as some sort of 'science of crisis' does little justice to the search for truth of people today and to the freedom of the coming of God in the middle of this process of searching for truth (to use the words of the theology of hope). The term 'crisis' presumes a deficiency, something that is lost. It sounds wistful and threatens to play down what is new and trying to break through in time. The term *kairos*, on the contrary, has a positive meaning. It refers to the trust in the fullness of reality, as it is intrinsically comprehensible for contemporaries and contains 'opportunities to learn and change' (Ebertz, par. 1.3).

2.2. Interactive search for meaning

Every person searches for meaning, develops dynamics for his or her life, consciously or subconsciously. Whenever those dynamics are interpreted as a finality with an origin and a goal, one speaks of a philosophy of life; this in its turn can be filled in an explicitly religious or prophane way. As is argued above, search for meaning is a syncretic event nowadays. Young people are dealing flexibly and unrestrainedly with what is pre-given, with whatever they happen upon. The pleasure of *surfing* (exploring), *fiddling* (taking apart) and *sampling* (mixing) of moral and religious convictions and life patterns often in different settings at the same time, is more important than the final result. The latter is difficult for young people to envision as a matter of fact, because things were not thought out or planned in advance. Two Dutch youth researchers, Jacques Janssen and Maarten Prins, speak of the primacy of action over reflection and of annexing religious traditions as a 'toolkit of symbols' (2000, 12) in that process. And especially: "the building-schemes can only be made after their buildings have been completed" (2000, 11). Older people tend to feel insecure with such a 'balancing identity'; but the young feel like fish in the water. Cell phones and chat-boxes on the internet are favorite media for them to undertake action, to develop patterns and ways of thinking on the go – in and through the interaction with peers, without building-schemes, purely for the pleasure of exchange. Action to them is inter-action, dynamics and involvement.

Also religious language games do not escape this enthusiastic process of annexation. Young people are abundantly experimenting with religion. The attraction of crossing the boundaries of reality, the utopia and the relationality of religion appeals to them. Older people can be shocked by this annexation of religion in youth culture and view it as a lack of respect. But in the mean time it is really happening: "the irreverent spiritual quest of generation X" (Beaudoin 1998). Numerous music clips contain religious connotations and artifacts. There are sites on the internet that offer an alternative (Christian) worship (see e.g. http://web.ukonline.co.uk/paradigm/index.htm). Youth channels are deliberately taking a religious stance and are aiming at some kind of democratization of religion. Examples of this development abound. One of them is especially eloquent. It was picked from the program Republica on Studio Brussels, a Flemish youth radio station. It has a section *'Van god los'* (cut off from god) in which streetreporter Peter Derie addresses young people in the street and asks their opinion about a variety of religious topics. Lieven Vandenhaute, the host of *Republica*, motivates his decision to tackle religion as follows: "Religion is no nonsense. It is an essential part of human beings. In *Republica* we have fun talking about everything that makes life worth living: theater, books, sports, fitness, fashion – only religion we safely ignore. Why would I stay away from it, when it is truly fascinating? Religion is one of the major realizations of human beings – I am not the only one who thinks that way – and postmodern people are slowly realizing that they should not throw away the child with the bathwater, that if we push religion out of our daily thinking, it surfaces elsewhere in the form of an addiction to shopping, for example. A credit card becomes heaven on earth. But religion is always there. You show it out of your house by the front door and it sneaks back in through the back" (Hens 2001).

What functions as a general principle in construction of culture, functions in the construction of religious meaning as well. "No matter how fast the young can run, their elders will catch up with them" (Jacques Janssen). Retro-socialization (Roebben 1997, 334), or the fact that adults often imitate the disrespectful behavior, options and patterns of youngsters, is also the case here. In the *main stream* culture religious elements resurface. God and religion are allowed to be topics again in popular radio and television programs, if coming from unexpected sources. The internet is crowded with religious sites. After eroticism, religion is the most popular topic. After the eleventh of September 2001 the interest in religious information has leapt forward (thus www.beliefnet.com). People want objective information about other religions, but more profound than that, there is a need for a language to tackle one's confusion at the level of religious orientation. One example is striking. On the website of Reata Strickland, a teacher of religion in Buhl (Alabama, US), an 'Interview with God' can be read (www.reata.org). On a nice summer day this lady coupled some nature shots with profound views of life and assembled them as a dialogue between God and human and placed them on the internet. After four days it turned out that half a million people had visited her site. The interview has been translated in twelve languages by now (medio 2002) and she receives thousands of reactions with personal stories, questions, suggestions every day.

An important aspect in the development of the interactive search for meaning is its commercialization. The 'dissemination' (Ebertz 1998, 148-149) and democratization of religious matters in modern culture is of interest to marketeers. They are always looking for new trends that can be marketed. Just like commercials play with the ecological and ethical sensitivity of potential buyers (think of 'green products', the 'clean clothes'-campaign and cars with 'controlled performance') (Van Gerwen 1995), the market goes along with the present-day longing for religious orientation in the search for meaning. Coca-Cola is a terrific example of this. In its clips it makes use of young people who have mock religious experiences in nature and in friendship. This company employs a dazzling and contemporary *styling* to voice the more profound longing of young people to launch its message ... "Enjoy Coca-Cola". A deep longing for community, for a firm basis, etc. is picked from the collective memory of modern young people, thematized, pictured seductively and subsequently neatly filled in materially. I suspect this multinational of having the know-how of professional theologians at its disposal in the marketing-department!

2.3. Critical evaluation

It is true that our contemporaries are looking for firm ground, an existential mooring for their search for authenticity. They are able to find this in religion. It is true that the plurality of life makes people long for fulfillment and wholeness, something that can already be found in religious encounters and communities of all sorts (Van Harskamp 2000). It is true that young people are making a challenging track in this process: the development of their identity is taking place in a culture that is searching for an identity itself (Mette 2001). However, should we not place some critical notes in the margin concerning this development? Three aspects require our attention – because they illicit criticism from a Christian-theological perspective, and because they are food for thought to explore new horizons of religious communication at the same time.

The first comment has to do with the aspect of esthetical use or 'glamorization' of religion. Everything gets linked to everything. Elements picked from different religions, are gathered and collected in a patchwork quilt. Nothing is holy in itself. The attraction of religion lies only in the attraction of this process of taking into use. Therefore it cannot be claimed that young people are totally isolated from religious language games. On the contrary, in their search they rearrange old frames of reference. They fall back on chunks of religious socialization from the old days. The question that surfaces, however, is the following: Does it go any further than just attribution, does the basic religious experience of those terms mean anything to young people? In other words, is it only the functional aspect of religion that remains (attribution), religion aimed at making the contingency of life tolerable and exciting, and not the substantial meaning of religion (experience)? And is the substantial role of religion at all possible without being anchored in a community of faith? Or even: is a new type of religion developing, one that is completely self-directed? A new type of religious self-awareness, making use of the affirmative language of religions, but reworded in a completely individualized re-composition?

A second problem is linked with this: Assuming that religion is designed for search, in which the experience of searching itself takes priority over finding, how can the aspect of action of such a venture be studied? If it is true that "the building-schemes are made after their buildings have been completed" (Janssen and Prins 2000, 11), how can the designers be approached? Young people want action, rather than reflection. They do not ask for the meaning of things, they use the meaning. They recreate a chaotic and confused jumble of impulses into a livable whole. Do the young handy-men know what they are doing, what they are getting into? May we speak of a new habitat, one that is held together by shoestring, but viewed more closely a source of inspiration for the young themselves? And could this be a rich experience to them, beyond traditional religious substances?

Next comes the question: is it true religion that is involved here? True religion articulates the relationship between the life of human beings that is visible and what transcends it. It takes a position in the tension between existential self-management and ultimate perspective, or the tension between individualization of meaning and the awareness of its ultimate non-availability. However, the new religious longing threatens to continue the myth of self-realization that is so characteristic for our day and age. It leads people to expect that they will be able to escape the ruthlessness of time by following a merciful alternative under one's own steam. This already hard existence becomes even more burdened: One has to realize his or her own salvation. In true religion a person is urged to be guided by the wisdom of predecessors, who struggled in their own way with the same questions and were able to find parts of answers. Religion leads people into a symbolic order that can liberate them as a person.

Here one could also remark: is religion taking on a fundamentally new appearance? Is the substantial element abandoned in preference of the merely functional aspect? Is the break in culture complete in the sense that people can only be approached as far as the profane aspect of religion is concerned? Will there be a religion without God before long? The Dutch theologian Anton van Harskamp claims that in the mean time we should wait for God – now that He is 'out of the picture'. His colleague, Erik Borgman, wonders if God will reveal himself in a new shape or that God will never be okay again (2000). Apparently theologians admit that there is no way around these difficult questions any longer. Religion is being used by people (for their own salvation) – and that is contrary to an important characteristic of religion in general and Christianity in particular: religion will not be used, that is not what it is for. Religion is gratuitous, something that indeed confirms human deliberations, but transcends, questions and challenges them as well.

3. Perspective: churches as mature dialogue partners 'in religiosis'

An embankment of the longing for religious orientation in our present-day culture can be discerned. People do not stay impassive in their quest for meaning in complex times. This longing is ambivalent and calls for clarification. For the practical theologian who considers it his/her job to perceive culture in an intensified theological perspective, this means a challenge to open up new horizons of religious communication. The questions are numerous: How will believers evaluate this situation theologically? How do they view themselves? And how will the theological tradition be revitalized? Which role do churches claim in this process? In this section I will indicate several crucial dimensions of a church community that is critically interpellating and recognizably involved in life, a church that neither turns away from nor gets lost in this epoch.

3.1. Reading the 'signs of the times' - beyond pastoral crisis technology

With the kairologic perspective (par. 2.1.) I have chosen for the hopeful analysis, averse to pastoral panic and hectics. I assume that the future of traditional religious institutions lies in a day to day willingness to be open to the culture and to trust culture to be a place of religious confrontation and deepening. Too much pastoral activity shuts off this possibility and suffers of self-complacency (Ebertz, par. 1.3.), of the illusion that nothing is wrong and that everything should continue along the old and familiar tracks, embellished with the newest tricks of 'pastoral crisis technology'. However, when the deeper and supportive layers of ministry are barely touched upon in the work itself, people who are searching for religious orientation will turn away from it. Since ministry can give the impression of ruthlessness: full of itself, disconnected from the deep longing in culture, and even worse, cut off from the source of life that inspires it.

If, however, the ministry knows how to master the art of listening at the new-religious longing and wording it in the language in which it is anchored itself, the opportunity for new things will arise. This tension between inside and outside, refreshing itself at its own sources of faith in view of a better understanding of religious revitalization of culture, this mutual transformation of Christian tradition and cultural context, is pre-eminently the task of Christianity today. The "critical interrelationship" of text and context, of theological tradition and present-day culture, on the basis of the story of grace of Christianity (in a nutshell: God who cares about the well-being of people, who declares his solidarity in the person of the living Jesus, to make people become fully human, united and merciful towards each other and their world) is the task of Christians today: as study and as engagement. This calls for a fundamental choice of openness of the churches towards the signs of the times. The metaphor of the 'inn' could be helpful: the church could be an inn where people can find rest and friendship, where they can jump in to be part of the table community (Hendriks 2000). The table is the central source of this happening, but not for members only. It is an attractive source for many people who enter the tavern. The table is connected to the stream of grace inside the house, on the basis of which the management of the tavern decides to open up its doors every day and decides to be responsive for the quest for meaning in contemporary culture.

3.2. Support for religious socialization in families

Religious socialization in a postmodern context can no longer be viewed as an offer that is already defined in time and space, but it will rather have to be considered as a *lengthy and interactive process* in which the critical education of the young, the skill to find their way independently in a dynamic environment and to word their own point of view, should be the focus. The fact that the young go a different direction from what their predecessors had hoped for in the beginning, is inherent to the possible outcome of that process of socialization. The crux of the matter is that acquiring one's own identity can be viewed as a religious process and can therefore be the content of religious education. The initial religious sensibility is then no longer the starting-point of a systematic explanation of religion and faith, but the theme itself of this learning process.

How will this process remain sufficiently socially coherent? In my opinion this will imply a permanent communication among all parties involved. Erik Vossen, a Dutch religious educationalist, has eminently proved before how this communicative view of religious socialization can take place within the family. First of all it presumes sufficient attention for the initiation aspect of the socialization: "The religious development of children is to a large degree a social learning process, in which learning goals and content are determined by the parents (either consciously or subconsciously) and in which they supply the actual 'learning material' by way of the examples set by their own practice. Those parents who truly want to guide their children towards a personal deliberation of their religious orientation and thereby offer their own believes and praxis as a starting-point, will have to concretely initiate their children" (Vossen 1989, 128-129).

This is not indoctrination, according to Vossen, this an aspect of development: "(Since) we have no other choice than to follow a strategy of transmission and making-familiar for young children, if we want to hand them enough material in order to make their own critical choice later on. What matters is, how we handle this already laid foundation later in the religious education" (124). Of great importance is how religious practices (like evening prayer and regular talks about faith – practices with a highly socializing value) are framed in a general openness for the life of parents and children. What sticks in the experience of young people is the willingness of adults to justify what they do and do not do. The best way to learn is the confrontation with adults who are not yet 'finished' or have 'been there', but who want to learn and grow, and who want to involve their children in this learning process (Hutsebaut 1995, 17-38). This 'communicative initiation' within the family seems to be a major challenge for vigorous communities of faith. Here the religious socialization of children acquires new dynamics, namely from the religious communication with young adults. This way a new meaning can arise, as a self-discovered 'horizon' of meaningful and authentic life, that is worth passing on, communicatively to fellow travelers and intergenerationally to one's own children. This way a new language will originate, anchored in private life experience and mastered in personal involvement (Maas and Ziebertz 1997).

3.3. Religious communication in a language that is concerned with life

How can such a language come into existence and be confirmed? How can the social stratum in which the request for religious orientation is made, grow into a new language experience for communities of faith? The need is great and many immediate 'Ersatz' solutions can be thought of. For example the churches could present the Christian faith as a radical anti-story, represented as a leap into the dark, as an option – as "go swim by yourself in the abysmal deep of the deposit of faith". Churches could charm people to take the step towards full identification with Christian faith. One could speed up the process of joining by skipping the cultivation of the longing. One could aim for a uniformly accelerated motion in the direction of the creed. The tender societal stratum, like a vulnerable riverbed, however, would not be able to handle this. The water is hardly deep enough to catch all those who might jump. And modern people will not be persuaded to let their life story be determined by the comments of others. They want to be the architect of their life story themselves. What they cannot appropriate will never become clear to them.

The Flemish dogmatic theologian Peter Schmidt has made an impressive analysis of the loss of meaning of religious language, when it is no longer sufficiently supported by contemporary human experience. The problem of the comprehensibility of faith in the church can be avoided perfectly well, according to Schmidt, "by curving back on oneself mentally". That is the way it often happens. Spiritual leaders are friendly, cooperative where others are concerned, but avoid expressing the "truth of faith" (Schmidt 1993, 87). "A lot of attention is paid to the interior decoration of the fortress of faith. The fact, however, that the drawbridges have been drawn, thus keeping anyone from entering, is a problem that one would rather not pay attention to" (90). And Schmidt continues by saying: "If the communicated content of faith is true in a totally different way than the way it is expressed, why should it be expressed that way? The language game used, cannot be converted into another anymore" (97). All that can still be done, is soulless repetition and imitation. In other words: A religious language game that ignores the religious longing in which it could be embedded, becomes esoteric and devoid of meaning. Those who lead in church no longer understand themselves what it is they believe and in which they feel obliged to guide others. That is the worst that can happen to a community of faith – that it has nothing left to say, not *ad extra*, not *ad intra*.

3.4. Towards new forms of religious leadership

"After the Second Vatican Council the church has paid too little attention to education of its audience", Mgr. Alfred Daelemans, former director-general of the Flemish Secretariat of Catholic Education once confided to me in the early nineties. I think that indeed a major part of the depression in the Roman Catholic church in particular has to do with this. Laymen feel attracted to the *aggiornamento* of the council. Attention was paid to their active participation in church, liturgy, catechesis and ministry, but too little was invested in educating and encouraging them at the intersection of faith and culture. There were some good initiatives; but no lay theology. For concrete questions from everyday life (intimate relationships, raising children, work relations, tension family-work, etc.) a normative way of speaking of the church was available, but that was miles away from the actual experience and words of regular searching believers (Luther 1992). The Canadian Dominican J.-M. Tillard thinks that, with regard to searching contemporaries, the church has adapted or hidden itself too much – as it were "entre le magistère des mass media et le magistère de la chair ecclésiale". No real confrontation has taken place with the intelligence of the faith in daily life, the church has not been able to show younger generations what the authority of faith means to those who are in tune with their own experience, according to Tillard (1997, 14 passim).

In this context the importance of new forms of religious leadership should be mentioned. In a complex society like ours, in which many alternatives are present (par. 2), a need for authentic identification figures exists, people of flesh and blood who live the 'Verbindlichkeit' of a religiously inspired life project in the double sense of the word: they feel obliged to live it and they feel connected with it. Erik Vossen has pointed out before that "current culture [makes] Christianity insufficiently explicit to enable young people to make sense of religious-Christian examples" (Vossen 1986, 250). Many examples and ideals are shown, but they are often so exalted and idealized (think of Mother Theresa, Oscar Romero, a.o.), that a critical confrontation frequently leads to frustration. There is a need for a real life and 'semantically explicit' (Vossen) religious leadership that is 'food for thought', that can be disputed, questioned and tested. This can also be an inspiration to concrete spiritual leaders such as parents and educators; they can be pioneers and maybe heralds of a new and realistic justification of faith. All of this presupposes guidance, education and support of parents and educators. Since in confrontation with their children their own questions, lamentations and inability surface. Religious socialization of children can, as stated before, no longer leave out a critical retrospective view of the story of faith of the adults themselves. Religious socialization and its justification (from a meta-perspective) in religious communication are intertwined (Roebben 2001).

4. Strategy: the option of religious education with young adults

A new generation of young adults is lining up, who have had no or hardly any religious socialization (see par. 1.4). Moreover this generation is an easy prey to the current pressure of modernization. The idea of the directability of life, work and love is imprinted in them in many different ways. They are the primary targets of advertising and marketing. In addition to that they are expected as young employees or managers, as young lovers, as young parents, as young homeowners, etc. to fulfill their social 'duties' and make responsible choices. To endure all this and keep it together they 'use' religion, esthetized and self-directed. Their search for meaning is interactive: pick up whatever fits your life project. For this they appeal to the 'expertise' of the church.

Their cultural context is a *kairos*: not to steer them into church in view of the future and the vitality of the community of faith, but to bring them in touch with the flow of grace that streams from the religious tradition of Christianity as a possible answer to their longing for a final orientation, or at least as a clarification of their questions concerning this. This answer is not a mere blind to take away the pain of daily contingency management, but a critical eye-opener to review their own life project and make it tolerable. Gérard Defois, bishop of Lille, calls this 'wide angle ministry'. Michael Ebertz speaks of 'communication ministry' (1998, 144-145). The large group of interested, who seem to be looking to approach the church, are not left out at the gate. They are invited to move into the space between the inside and the outside of the church, in the passage between culture and faith.

This openness is not a form of church expansionism, but a contemporary understanding of how Christians can be present in the world. Their presence in society is no longer monolithic, their message not to be taken or left. They can be inspiring on the road to the truth, a truth that in accordance with human life consists of many facets. The times of the massive 'opposite' of Christianity have passed; the temptation exists of withdrawing with like-minded in a 'snuggle strategy'. I wonder if that suffices – evangelically speaking. Can Christians take the liberty of losing their flexibility and of being put off to the side? For the time being quite a few people are still in and out of the church. Often they come into contact with it through traditional pastoral activities: a funeral, a marriage, a baptism, the first communion and confirmation of their children. All of these activities, however, are diminishing (especially marriage) or are experienced as being without a meaningful future (especially confirmation). The traditional forms of social presence of faith are dampened down further. How will the story of faith become visible in the future: authentically, sensibly and evangelically flexibly?

In line of the above I make a plea for religious education of young adults. Instead of continuing to invest the available energy in the catechesis of children (first communion and confirmation at an early age), the church could ask itself f how it can serve the longing for religious orientation of young adult contemporaries. Partly this is done already in connection with the sacraments of marriage and of the baptism/first communion of children. At parents' evenings one notices that young parents like to pass on something of value in the moral and religious upbringing of their children, but that they usually lack the words. Their anthropological experience of birth and parenthood does not get enough response and religious interpretation from the highly sacramental message of church baptism. And when young children grow up and start asking questions about life, young parents are often at a loss for answers or an attitude of answering (Schweitzer 2000). In the meantime – i.e. now that it is still not clear what to do with the catechesis of sacraments – it seems very important to me to involve the parents as much as possible in the religious education that is part of the sacrament (of their children).

There are other ways, however, to address young adults from the sidelines. I think of encounter groups (for instance in higher vocational education and universities), of intervision groups of young people in the same profession (for instance new nurses, teachers, etc.) and other intensive meetings (like summer camps) and forms of cultural service of churches to young adult meaning seekers (through websites, publications, information evenings), etc. This calls for a different kind of engagement of the church: it offers its own house and its own expertise as a forum, as a space in which the process of searching of young adults can grow and be enriched.

It is not about actualizing or adapting the Christian message, but about rereading of the particular context of young adults from the perspective of the gospel. Often the 'process of revelation' starts with opening the senses, with learning to read one's own life again, with reconnecting with one's own sources of imagination and creativity. Because it is shocking to see how much goodwill, how much desire to live a truly good life (in relationships, at work, during time off, etc.) is undone by the media, hard work and hyped up relationships at the age of young adults. Many of the small stories are trampled by the big story of the market. The gospel can refute this ruthlessness and show images of truly good life. Fact is that young people cannot be talked into anything. If they are unable to see for themselves how an old story is capable of uprooting the self-evidences and/or brokenness of their story, nothing happens. If the flow of grace does not come from the inside, can be rediscovered and worded from their own experience of longing for grace, nothing happens. The social riverbed is present, it should be broadened and deepened by encounters with contemporaries and wise insights from the past. However, the question is: will there be enough people left in churches who are willing and able to inhabit this meeting place in an inspired and sensible way?

Epilogue

These reflections fit in the broader perspective of renewed attention for adult religious education. In the Dutch and Flemish dioceses many initiatives have arisen during the past five years. It is realized that no longer all salvation is to be expected of religious education of children. In addition to that, religious communication takes on a different hue in a society of choices, especially that of personal engagement. I conclude here that these initiatives take many forms corresponding to concrete local needs and requests.

It was my intention mainly to make clear that the new generation young adults, just like the currents one, has the right to a personally appropriated experience of faith. However, the complexity of this experience in the given circumstances is much greater for future adults. That is the reason why this kind of work is even more exciting than it already is with 'normal' adults, but paradoxically also relaxing, since nothing has to be proven.

References

Beaudoin, T. 1998. *Virtual Faith: the Irreverent Spiritual Quest of Generation X*. San Francisco: Jossey-Bass.

Bluyssen, J. 1989, *De vele wegen en de ene weg*. Baarn: Arbor.

Borgman, E. 2000. Zoeken naar het zelf of wachten op God? *De Bazuin*, 10 november 2000.

Dekker, G., J. de Hart, and J. Peters. 1997. *God in Nederland. 1966-1996*. Amsterdam: Anthos.

Deleu, P. 1988. *De kinderen zijn vrij. Over gezin, kerk en geloofsopvoeding*. Tielt: Lannoo.

Dobbelaere, K., M. Elchardus, and J. Kerkhofs. 2000. *Verloren zekerheid. De Belgen en hun waarden, overtuigingen en houdingen*. Tielt: Lannoo.

Drehsen, V. 1994. *Wie religionsfähig ist die Volkskirche? Sozialisationstheoretische Erkundungen neuzeitlicher Christentumpraxis*. Gütersloh: Kaiser Verlag.

Ebertz, M.N. 1999. *Kirche im Gegenwind. Zum Umbruch der religiösen Gesellschaft.* Freiburg/Basel/Wien: Herder.

Englert, R. 1992. *Religiöse Erwachsenenbildung: Situation, Probleme, Handlungsorientierung* (Praktische Theologie Heute 7). Stuttgart: Kohlhammer.

Feifel, E., and W. Kasper. 1987. *Tradierungskrise des Glaubens.* München: Kösel.

Gabriel, K. 1991. Tradition im Kontext enttraditionalisierter Gesellschaft. In *Wie geschieht Tradition? Überlieferung im Lebensprozeß der Kirche* (Quaestiones Disputatae 133), edited by D. Wiederkehr. Freiburg-im-Breisgau.

Gerwen, J. van 1995. Ethiek als profiel, ethiek als koopwaar. Het Gentse communicatiebureau 'Imagine'. Pp. 71-90 in *De vis heeft geen weet van het water. Ethiek tussen berekening en zorg,* edited by J. Taels. Kapellen.

Harskamp, A. van 2000. *Het nieuw-religieuze verlangen.* Kampen: Kok.

Hendriks, J. 2000. *Gemeente als herberg. De kerk van 2000 – een concrete utopie.* Kampen: Kok.

Hens, T. 2001. Eerst seks, dan God. Het lieve leven van Studio Brusselman Lieven Vandenhaute. *De Standaard Magazine,* 9 november 2001.

Hervieu-Léger, D. 1990. Religion and Modernity in the French context. For a New Approach to Secularization. *Sociological Analysis* 51: 15-25.

Hutsebaut, D. 1995. *Een zekere onzekerheid. Jongeren en geloof.* Leuven: Acco.

Janssen, J., and M. Prins. 2000.'Let's reinvent the Gods'. De religie van Nederlandse jongeren in een Europese context. *J* Tijdschrift over jongeren* 1(4), 4-14.

Kaufmann, F.-X., and G. Stachel. 1980. Art. Religiöse Sozialisation. Pp. 117-164 in *Christlicher Glaube in moderner Gesellschaft* (Band 25), Freiburg/Basel/Wien.

Luther, H. 1992. *Religion und Alltag. Bausteine zu einer Praktischen Theologie des Subjekts.* Stuttgart: Radius Verlag.

Maas, J. and H.-G. Ziebertz. 1997. Over breukvlakken en bruggehoofden: religieuze opvoeding in het gezin. *Tijdschrift voor Theologie* 37(4), 384-404.

N. Mette 2001. Identity before or identity through familiarization with plurality? The actual discussion concerning school based religious education in Germany. Pp. 217-244 in *Religious Education as Practical Theology. Essays in Honour of Professor Herman Lombaerts* (ANL 40), edited by B. Roebben and M. Warren. Leuven/Paris/Sterling.

Michiels, R., and B. Roebben, eds. 1994. *Kerk op-nieuw. Variaties op het hedendaagse kerkgebeuren,* Leuven/Amersfoort: Acco.

Roebben, B. 1994. To Initiate into a World of Difference: A Design for Dynamic-Integral Values Education. *Louvain Studies* 19: 338-349.

Roebben, B. 1995. Do We Still Have Faith in Young People? A West-European Answer to the Evangelization of Young People in a Postmodern World. *Religious Education* 90: 327-345.

Roebben, B. 1997. Shaping a Playground for Transcendence. Postmodern Youth Ministry as a Radical Challenge. *Religious Education* 92: 332-347.

Roebben, B. 1999. Youth ministry in and beyond the church? The sacrament of confirmation in the Roman Catholic Church as a testcase. *Journal of Beliefs and Values* 20: 51-59.

Roebben, B. 2001. Religious education through times of crisis. Reflections on the future of a vulnerable school subject. Pp. 245-272 in *Religious Education as Practical Theology. Essays in Honour of Professor Herman Lombaerts* (ANL 40), edited by B. Roebben and M. Warren. Leuven/Paris/Sterling.

Schmidt, P. 1993. Verstaan we nog zelf wat we zeggen? Over de mededeelbaarheid van de geloofstaal. Pp. 87-103 in *Geloof en cultuur. Christen-zijn in het Europa van morgen*, edited by J. Claes and J. Kerkhofs. Averbode/Apeldoorn.

Schweitzer, F. 1993. Der Wandel des Jugendalters und die Religionspädagogik. *Jahrbuch für Religionspädagogik* 10: 71-88.

Schweitzer, F. 2000. *Das Recht des Kindes auf Religion*. Gütersloh: Gütersloher Verlagshaus.

Tieleman, D. 1995. *Geloofscrisis als gezichtsbedrog. Spiritualiteit en pastoraat in een postmoderne cultuur*. Kampen: Kok.

Tillard, J.-M. 1997. *Sommes-nous les derniers chrétiens?* Québec: Fides.

Vossen, E. 1986. Religieuze vorming in een gerationaliseerde kultuur. *Praktische theologie* 13: 235-254.

Vossen, E. 1989. Geloofsopvoeding als probleem. Een visie op doel en kondities. *Praktische theologie* 16: 115-133.

Ziebertz, H.-G. 1999. *Religion, Christentum und Moderne. Veränderte Religionspräsenz als Herausforderung*. Stuttgart/Berlin/Köln: Kohlhammer.

Music as Locus Theologicus

Anton Vernooij

One of the tasks that I, as a professor occupying an endowed chair in Liturgical Music at the University of Tilburg, have set myself is to proclaim where and whenever possible that theology and music are inextricably bound to one another, or to put it more precisely, that God and music are one, that God speaks a musical language, and that someone who practices theology uses tools that in many respects are similar to those from musicology. The bible is to a large extent a hymnbook, the content of which can only be done justice to when declaimed or sung. In my opinion a lack of musical feeling is for the theologian, and in particular an exegete, a serious handicap. He reads the Scriptures with the eyes and especially the ears of a musician: he hears the word of God and then sings it out. Is it possible for an exegete to understand a bible text without declaiming it first, without sensing the rhythm of the original language, without fathoming the poetic setting of the text?

It is probably this that makes Tjeu van Knippenberg a good theologian, because he has a feeling for music. He is the composer of 13 of the "31 Liederen voor afscheid en rouw" (*31 hymns for farewell and mourning*), published in 1995.[1] His leaving the Faculty of Theology has provided me with the opportunity to consider the past thoughts of theologians on the origin of music. This turned out to be more than I expected. The 'theologians' therefore had to be altered to 'some theologians'. I have tried to find out (1) how theologians have sought after the divine origin of music and (2) after the ancient tension between music from heaven and music from earth. Finally (3) I attempt to describe some of the qualities that have traditionally been attributed to music by theologians. Because the article is so short this has forced me to be selective and especially not to work exhaustingly.[2]

1. Music and creation

Theology from the Middle Ages has linked up the conscious practice of music with the order of creation. It did this on the basis of Pythagoras' theorem on the

---

[1] Reen, T. van (lyrics), P. Dogge, T. van Knippenberg and M. de Nobel-Andriessen (music). 1995. *Hierna: 31 liederen voor afscheid en rouw. Om te zingen – om te zeggen*. Baarn: Gooi & Sticht.

[2] The most important literature for this contribution was the work of Herbst 1997. Various quotes were taken from this article. I myself did the translations, or took them from the KBS translation, 1995 edition.

close relations between musical and astronomical structures. The numerical relations within music and between heavenly bodies were according to Pythagoras very similar. In his opinion musical harmony reflects the secrets of the cosmos, which has been arranged by God 'according to size and number and weight' (Sap. 11, 20). According to the ancient Greek theory of the *musica speculativa*, as expressed by the theoreticus Boethius (MPL 63, 1167) in particular, the theory of music is based on the idea that music is not in the first place an expression of human culture, but that it is a gift of God, that was given to His Creation by him from the beginning. Church father Augustine connected this theory with the biblical theory of Creation, and the religious idea that stemmed from this of a *creatio ex nihilo* by God: 'Where else would all this come from, than from the highest and eternal Beginning of numbers, equality and order? If you let this stem from earth it will amount to nothing. In this way only did God create earth, it has come to be from nothing' (MPL 32, 1192).

Later, in all his church reforming acts the extremely musical Martin Luther was unwilling to give up this classical foundation of music: 'Those who study the material will discover that from the beginning of the world God gave this art to everybody and all and that he helped to create it' (ML 50, 368). True Luther goes beyond the *musica speculativa* from the Middle Ages in his theology of music by not only connecting the creative character of music with the ontologically given structure of things, but also with Christ's work of salvation, that has after all finally given man free and correct use of creation. He also places the practical study of music above the *musica theorica*, with all the consequences for worship, the practice of teaching and teacher training (ML 5, 6248). For Luther music and the word of God have in common that both should be heard. 'Fides ex auditu'. The word of God is actually sung and therefore proclaimed in the language of the arts. Somewhere in the Italian Abruzzo I remember reading on the edge of a twelfth-Century pulpit a warning to the one who was about to preach the word of God 'Tu qui magna canis, fac ne tua vox sit inanis...': You, who are about to preach the magnalia Dei, make sure your voice will be heard...'. I can recall that in the rest of that reasonably long text the 'inanis' was explained in an ethical sense: there had to be a connection between the 'canere' and practising God's word in daily life. For Luther hearing was more important than seeing: *Ocularia miracula longe minora sunt quam auricularia*: 'The wonders, that take place before our eyes, are much smaller than those we perceive with our ears' (ML 44, 352). Theology and music were very closely connected, and when it came down to it Luther had a preference for music: *Primum locum do Musicae post Theologiam* (ML 30/2, 696). It was on the basis of this that the Lutheran tradition enriched itself with a great store of church music: Hymn collections, choral versions, spiritual concerts, motets, cantatas, oratories and organ music.

Traditionally theologians have occupied themselves with the question of whether music is a gift of creation or the work of man, or perhaps both. As long as the church continued in this respect to think in terms of Augustine and followed the *musica speculativa* of the Middle Ages, music undisputedly remained a gift of God. Under the influence of humanism especially the question was no longer approached unanimously, and it was also approached in a less confessional way. In the first half of the twentieth century music was once again founded on the laws of nature, under the influence of a review of old traditions. However, this did not mean that there was a return to the *musica speculativa* of the Middle Ages. For the age-old connections made by theology and the dogmatic restrictions on music that were a result of these, had for a long time played a role in the church only.[3] People were still convinced of a certain structural analogy between cosmos and music. Music, as some thought, was an expression of a higher order that could not be fully defined. In the introduction to his symphony *Die Harmonie der Welt* from 1951, the composer Paul Hindemith (1895-1963) states that in his new symphony he tried 'die Weltharmonie zu erkennen und die Musik als ihr tönendes Gleichnis zu verstehen' ('to identify the harmony of the world and to interpret music as its (the world's) image in sound') (quoted in MGG-I, 6, 445). For Karlheinz Stockhausen (* 1928) the similarity between musical vibrations and those in the cosmos means 'daß in der klingenden Struktur göttliche Ordnungen wahrnehmbar werden' ('that the structure of sound is based on a divine order') (de la Motte-Haber 1995, 235). As from the sixties of the twentieth century, under the influence of Eastern spirituality finally the relations between the universe, sounds and overtone frequencies are applied as openings to the divine, which at the same time clear the way to finding one's own identity.

2. Music on earth from heaven?

It was bound to happen that as a result of the briefly described creation theology of music the origin of the latter would also be sought in the angels in heaven, who had on the birth of Christ already made it known that the lively practice of music also played a role in heaven (Luke 2, 13-14). Music is also viewed as a continuation of heavenly angel music and the future hymn of saints. The Christian art of the Middle Ages and the renaissance especially depict angels as extremely musical creatures, who ever give added lustre to the appearance of the divine on earth with song and string music. In the Old Testament God is encouraged in his work on creation by cheering angels: 'Who set its (the world) corner-stone in place, when the morning stars sang together and all the sons of God shouted aloud?' (Job 38, 6-7) and in Psalm 148 'all his angels...all his host...his loyal servants' were called to praise the name of the Lord. The fifteenth century painters of the Apocalypse, the brothers Hubert and Jan van Eijk,

---

[3] Cf. for 'Catholic' opinions on music in the church, for example the rules given by the Council of Trent, and the motu-proprio *Tra le sollecitudini* (1903) from pope Pius X.

show us in their *Adoration of the Lamb* what the apostle John saw and heard in his mind: 'it was the sound of harpers playing on their harps. There before the throne…they were singing a new song' (Revelation 14, 2-3). According to the *Instituta patrum de modo psallendi sive cantandi* (eleventh century) the old church fathers learnt liturgical music directly from the angels ('hunc modem cantandi ab Angelis didicerunt'), who in their heavenly practice were experienced in this: Cantantes et psallentes in conspectu sanctae Trinitatis & sanctorum Angelorum' (Gerbert 1784, 1-8). Church reformer Luther automatically found it very hard to accept this speculative theory of music aimed at the angels, due to his dismissal of angel worship and therefore of the theory of angels: 'Denn das ist Abgötterey, Und solche Ehre gehöret Gott alleine zu' ('then that is idolatry, only God deserves such an honour') (ML 50, 210). The new song, that once shall sing the glorified creation, 'before the throne', was a great source of inspiration for seventeenth century Lutheran composers of church music in particular. Michael Praetorius (1571-1621) described music 'als einer schönen herrlichen Gabe Gottes / und die ein Vorbild und Gleichniβ ist der himlischen Music / wie die heiligen Engel Gottes mit dem gantzen himlischen Heer ihren Schöpffer / in einer lieblichen Harmonia stetigs ohn unterlaβ rühmen und preisen' ('as beautiful and glorious gift of God/ that is an echo of the heavenly music / with which God's holy angels together with all the heavenly host/ honour and praise their creator continuously in sweet harmony') (Praetorius in Gunlitt 1959).

Heavenly angel music on earth: the traditional opinion of the Roman Catholic Church on church music can be summarised in this way. According to the Second Vatican Council 'by way of a taste of what is in store for us we may be involved in the heavenly liturgy, that is celebrated in the holy city of Jerusalem [...] until He, our life, appears and we together with Him will appear in glory' (Fortmann 1967, 5). The community character of liturgy also finds its true foundation in the heavenly community around God's throne: 'Inner unity is strengthened by the uniting of the voices, the beauty of the holy causes the spirit to be raised more easily to the heavenly, and the whole service becomes an even more splendid portrayal of the liturgy of the holy city of Jerusalem' (Musicam Sacram 1967, no. 5). It takes the power of music to realise this heavenly glory on earth. Pope Paul VI expressed the opinion of his predecessor Pius X during a speech to the participants of the tenth international congress of church choirs in 1970: 'It is thanks to music that the splendour of God's face shines upon the community that has gathered in the name of God; hearts exult more easily through the spiritual power of art, to a purifying and sanctifying meeting with the magnificent reality of the holy. Music creates the best conditions for the celebration of the secret of salvation and participation in its fruits' (Acta Apostolicae Sedis 1970, 224). In turn Pius X relied on the church father Augustine, who in his *Confessiones* on music in the church says that 'few things are as suitable to fill the soul with pious emotions and kindle the passion of divine love' (Van Der Meer 1957, II, 50).

3. Music and theological ethics

The theory of creation concerning the essence of music has, besides its origin, also greatly determined the objective and the meaning of music. Up till the rise of humanism the general objective and value of music has been defined from this viewpoint. When church and 'world' separated, church music automatically gained its own sacral values. The latter were defined in relatively consistent terms. It was only as a result of secularisation that in the second half of the 20th century traditional differences between the sacral and the profane disappeared, causing the relation between these two concepts to change.

The boundaries between 'creative theological' and ethical interpretations of music have always been very vague. After Augustine the principle of numbers and order from Sap. 11, 20 was applied in order to encourage the love of God. 'Ad Dei amorem provocatur anima ex numerorum et ordinis ratione quam in rebus diligit' (MPL 32, 1186). Adam von Fulda (1490) goes one step further by making a direct connection between harmonic numerical relations and ethical values: 'The right numerical relation in (musical) harmony naturally forces people as it were into justice, reasonability and compliance with authority' (Gerbert 1784, 3; 335).

There are also examples in the bible in which music has a less positive effect. The Old Testament connects the harp and lute in particular with less exalting activities. Man, who is separated from God, often makes music. 'Shame on you! you who rise early in the morning to go in pursuit of liquor and draw out the evening inflamed with wine, who have no eyes for the work of the Lord, and never see the things he has done' (Isaiah 5, 11-12). The eloquent prophet Amos did not hold those in the higher circles of his time in high esteem: 'You who loll on beds inlaid with ivory [...] feasting on lambs from the flock and fatted calves, you who pluck the strings of the lute and invent musical instruments like David [...] but are you not grieved at the ruin of Joseph' (Amos 6, 4-6). In the city of Tyre music was connected with prostitution, that is, judging by the beginning of a song that was so well known that Isaiah quoted it: 'Take your harp, go round the city, poor forgotten harlot; touch the strings sweetly, sing all your songs, make men remember you again' (Isaiah 23, 16). The abuse of music in the city of Tyre is so manifold that God mentions it in relation to the city's destruction: 'So I will silence the clamour of your songs, and the sound of your harps will be heard no more' (Ezekiel 26, 13). In the book of Daniel music is used in idolatry: 'O peoples and nations of every language, you are commanded, when you hear the sound of horn, pipe, zither, triangle, dulcimer, music, and singing of every kind, to prostrate yourselves and worship the golden image which King Nebuchadnezzar has set up' (Daniel 3, 5).

One could ask oneself whether in the Old Testament a difference can be distinguished between 'wrong' and 'right' instruments. Did the instruments in themselves have a neutral significance, and did the negative or positive judgement of them depend more on their use, on the dances and automatically on the texts that accompanied these dances during the making of music? When David danced in front of the Ark it was considered an act of shame (2 Samuel 6, 15). However, it was not the dancing in itself or the use of 'harps and lutes, of tambourines and castanets and cymbals' that caused reproach, but rather the lack of clothes the king was wearing at the time. Michal, Saul's daughter, reproached him 'What a glorious day for the king of Israel, when he exposed his person in the sight of his servant's slave-girls. But David answered: But it was done in the presence of the Lord' (2 Samuel 6, 20-21). The instruments mentioned were also used in the temple, although it appears that as a rule particular instruments were used, including the trumpet: 'He posted the Levites in the house of the Lord with cymbals, lutes, and harps, according to the rule prescribed by David, by Gad the kings seer and Nathan the prophet; for this rule had come from the Lord through his prophets. The Levites stood ready with the instruments of David, and the priests with the trumpets' (2 Chronicles 29, 25-26). The history of church music shows us that the sacredness of instruments is based on custom and tradition, which results in exclusiveness, but that this sacredness is determined more by the character of the music an instrument produces rather than by the instrument itself. In the Old Testament therapeutic powers were also attributed to music: David's harp playing was able to free Saul from the evil spirit that tormented him; 'And whenever a spirit from God came upon Saul, David would take his harp and play on it, so that Saul found relief; he recovered and the evil spirit left him alone' (2 Samuel 6, 20-21).

In the Scriptures music is made for the praise and honour of the Lord from the psalms through to the Revelation of John. Besides this the ethical ambivalence of music is much emphasised in the Christian tradition. The fact that music is made in both worship and idolatry, that it proclaims praise to the Lord as well as lawlessness, and that it can even incite violence, is recognised more clearly by theologians the less they base their ideas on the traditional theology of creation, and on the *musica speculativa* from the Middle-Ages.

In the old church theologians thought little of the ecstatic music of the heathen cultus. There was also a continual struggle with the effect of music in liturgy. The fact that people with a special feeling for the language of the arts could in this respect become at odds with themselves is proved by the extremely musical church father Augustine in his *Confessiones*: 'Once the lust of the ear had me firmly in and under its hold: but you have parted me from it and freed me. Yet I admit that even now I am little absorbed in the sounds that make your proclamations so alive, when sung by a sweet and trained voice; not because I desire to remain stranded in them, no, I want straight away to rise above them [...] Often that physical pleasure deceives me [...] Then emotions will not come to their senses in such a way that they are willing to wait patiently in second place, but precisely for the sake of reason deserve to be allowed in, try to be ahead and to take charge. In this way I sin, unconsciously […] and I hesitate between the danger of lust, and my salutary experience; and, even though I do not wish to present an irrevocable statement, I do feel most for approving the custom of singing in church' (Van Der Meer 1957, II, 58-59). With his opinion on the significance of music Thomas of Aquinas is on familiar ground by emphasising the psychological meaning of music for worship: Consonantiae musicae immutant hominis affectum, […] inde est, […] quod in omni cultu aliquae consonantiae musicae exerceantur, ut animus hominis excitetur ad deum' (= Music changes people's mood, […] the result being that […] music is always made in worship in one way or another, to turn man's soul to God') (In Psalmos 92).

4. Conclusion

In the above it is mentioned that in our present culture the relation between the concepts sacral and profane has changed. Thanks to the younger generation, that is no longer initiated in traditional religious rites with their characteristic music and instruments, music, that used as such to be profanely barred from the church, seems to be able to function excellently. Nowadays the concept sacredness is less applicable. Sacral music, made by man and aimed at God, is not the most important thing for the new generation, but rather hymns and instrumental music that are able to function within the community service. It would be naive to think that in our time therefore the traditional ethical objectives of church music, determined by tradition and more and more often confirmed, are definitely out of the picture. True church fathers and theologians were always children of their time – what else would they be? – but they have again and again distinguished the characteristics of music made by man for religious acts and rituals, which are universal and therefore of a permanent nature. Characteristic of our time is therefore not the disappearance of the feeling or the need for sacral music, but a new relation between the sacral and the profane. Consider in this respect the many recent ritual studies on the sacredness and ritualism of music made outside the church.

Many see, in connection with these incultural developments, a danger in the role music plays in society in general. Music has become a natural part of people's lives. Silence has become a thing of value. As a result of this people are careless with the way in which they use music. Music is also listened to more, rather than actively made. We now have an auditive music culture (Sabbe 1996). Finally, less and less people are willing to make the effort to approach music with an active, inquisitive, curious and open mind. The listener wishes to delight in recognisable and pleasant harmony and dynamics. Naturally all of this has consequences for the quality of music in liturgy. In church to, people would rather listen to music than make it themselves. Back in 1962 Theodor Adorno complained about the passive behaviour of the people of a consumer society concerning music: 'Wenn die Funktion der Konsumentenmusik [...] von keiner Erinnerung an Übel und Tot überschatteten Lebensbejahung [...] aufgeht, so hat sie die Säkularisierung jener theologischen Konzeption vollendet und sie zugleich in ihr zynisches Widerspiel verkehrt; das irdische Leben selber, so wie es ist, wird einem ohne Leiden gleichgesetzt: doppelt trostlos, weil dies Gleichung - nichts ist als kreisende Wiederholung, abgesperrt vom letzten Blick auf etwas, was anders wäre'('If the function of consumer music [...] has absolutely no connection with a realisation that life is overshadowed by pain and death, then the secularisation of that theological idea has been accomplished, and moreover, completely turned round; in life on earth, as it is, all suffering is denied: this is twice as disconsolate, because this comparison is merely a blatant repetition, shut off from a last glance of something that is perhaps different') (Adorno 1962, 53-54). For Adorno music can therefore only be credible when it can provide an answer to the suffering and differences in society. H. Schröer talks in this respect of a 'Musica crucis, die Realismus des Leidens und Hoffnung [...] zeichenhaft verbindet' (a 'musica crucis', that meaningfully connects the reality of suffering and hope') (Schröer 1981, 64).

A fine task awaits theology, namely a study into the relation between music, religion and society.

References

Acta Apostolicae Sedis. Roma: Typis Polyglottis Vaticanis.

Adorno, T. 1962. *Einleitung in die Musiksoziologie*: zwölf theoretische Vorlesungen. Frankfurt am Main: Suhrkamp.

Busa, R. 1980. *S. Thomae Aquinatis opera omnia: ut sunt in indice thomistico additis 61 scriptis ex aliis medii aevi auctoribus*. Stuttgard-Bad Cannstatt: Frommann- Holzboog.

Fortmann, H. 1967. *Constituties en Decreten van het Tweede Vaticaans Oecumenisch Concilie*. Amersfoort: Katholiek Archief.

Gerbert, M. 1784. *Scriptores ecclesiastici de musica sacra potissimum*. Sankt Blasien (=GS)

Herbst, W. 1997. Musik in der Kirche. Pp. 715-727 in *Die Musik in Geschichte und Gegenwart*. Bährenreiter: Kassel. (=MGG-II 6)

1883-1954. *Martin Luthers Werke: kritische Gesamtausgabe*. Weimar: Böhlau. (=ML)

Meer, F. van der 1957. *Augustinus de* zielzorger: een studie over de praktijk van een *kerkvader*. Utrecht: Het Spectrum. (Volume I and II)

Migne, J. 1844-1864. *Patrologiae cursus completus, series latina*. Paris. (=MPL)

Motte-Haber, H. de la 1995. *Musik und Religion*. Laaber: Laaber-Verlag.

Musicam Sacram. Instructie van de ritencongregatie van 5 maart 1967 over de muziek in de heilige liturgie. 1967. Hilversum: Gooi and Sticht.

Die Musik in Geschichte und Gegenwart (old edition). Kassel. 1949-1986. (=MGG-I)

Die Musik in Geschichte und Gegenwart (new edition). Kassel. 1994- (=MGG-II)

Praetorius, M. 1614-1619. *Syntagma Musicum*. Wolfenbüttel.

Sabbe, H. 1996. *"All that Music!" Een antropologie van de westerse muziekcultuur*. Leuven/Amersfoort: Acco.

Schröer, H. 1981. Musik als Offenbarung des Unendlichen? In *Humanität-Musik-Erziehung*, edited by K. Ehrendorf. Mainz.

The Permanent Deacon as 'The Go-Between'
Religious Leadership in Search of a Specific Identity

Veerle Draulans

Introduction

More than thirty-five years after the decision of Vatican II to assign the permanent diaconate independence as a separate office in the Catholic Church, the debate on its individual profile or specific identity is still undecided.[1] There are traces of the two different arguments for the permanent diaconate at the time of the conciliar debates, in the way in which permanent deacons actually carry out their task nowadays: the deacon could be either a welcome assistant to the priest in the practise of spiritual care or pre-eminently the person who is responsible for social commitment based on faith (Nissen 1991; Hoefnagels 2002, 135-136).

The aim of this article is to offer a stimulative contribution to the debate on an individual diaconal identity, fitted into a more global approach in which the general diaconal task of all faithful is central.

The article is set up as follows: in the first section I will consider the question of which building bricks tradition supplies for the thought process on the identity of deacons. In which way did ancient Jewry justify social commitment? What does the analysis of the Greek word 'διακονια' teach us? Tradition is not only sanctifying, but neither are the characteristics of a context. The question is which criteria do we have nowadays, despite the particularities of a specific context, to critically test and evaluate diaconal actions. These criteria are discussed in more detail in the second section. In the third part the question of identity is discussed by means of specific questions: what is the profile of deacons nowadays, who do deacons want to be, what do others say about the profile of deacons? Finally, in the fourth part I formulate a number of pillars that in my opinion are fundamental for the process of reflection on diaconal identity.

Before starting I would like to make the following introductory remark: as a woman it is somewhat strange to write about an office in which neither I nor my

---

[1] This article is a renewed version of a lecture held at the national deacon day that took place on 28 September 2002 in Hilversum, to celebrate 'twenty-five years of permanent deaconate' in the diocese of Haarlem.

fellow-women are allowed to take part in the Catholic Church. Viewed from this angle I write this article as a complete 'outsider'. Of course, this is not a drawback... a number of important scientific paradigmatic shifts have taken place as a result of critical questions put by 'complete outsiders', and these people have as such stimulated various scientific disciplines, as we have already learnt from T. Kuhn (1962) in his inspiring study 'The Structure of Scientific Revolutions'. Furthermore, I cannot find a single element in the following building bricks for a diaconal identity that can plausibly legitimise the exclusion of women from this office. I do not wish to elaborate the debate on the desirability of a permanent diaconate for women in this article. I wish only to support Schüssler-Fiorenza's thoughts that a permanent diaconate for women without them being able to hold all offices of leadership again creates inequality (Schüssler Fiorenza 1998).[2]

1. Building bricks from tradition

September 2002 marked the beginning of 'the year of the diaconate' in the Catholic Church in Belgium. Up till June 2003 various sections of the Catholic Church will spend time thinking about and working on "a spirituality of service". Particular attention will be paid to four themes: 1) the use of the fruits of the earth or ecological care, 2) waiving the burden of debt of the poorest countries and the justifiable division of the earth's resources, 3) hospitality and the cohabitation of cultures and religions, and 4) peace and democracy (De zending van de christenen in de wereld. Verklaring van de bisschoppen van België 2000). Each of these are socially and politically sensitive themes, that lead to serious differences of opinion amongst Christians too. Sometimes the faithful propose that the church tackle themes that actually belong to the area of action of new social movements. Churches would do better to keep themselves occupied with 'real' themes concerning faith or with the quality of the liturgy, according to critical remarks made on religiously inspired social commitment. These options have, more than the opponents or hesitating spectators on the side-lines suspect, roots in an old yet inspiring tradition.

1.1. Jewish inspiration: chässäd, tsedaqua and chemilut chassadim in rabbi-nical literature

Which human-friendly tasks or acts agreeable to God are described in Talmud literature and in the post-rabbinical Halacha as 'chemilut chassadim' (mercy, something geared to opening up the opportunities of life)? In the framework of this article I restrict myself to a brief list and am aware that in doing so I do not do justice to the broad range of views and passages from the bible that could

---

[2] For an overview of this debate see among others www.womenpriests.org

possibly colour this dry list. For this I refer to the K. Müller's thesis, *Diakonie im Dialog mit dem Judentum. Eine Studie zu den Grundlagen sozialer Verantwortung im jüdisch-christlichen Gespräch* (Müller 1999). The author abundantly illustrates the fundamental meaning of the following religiously inspired acts: taking in strangers, bringing up orphans, caring for the poor and widows, accompanying the bride down the isle on her wedding day, visiting the sick, burying the dead, offering comfort to those who grieve. These seem to be completely different actions, yet a clear communal thread can be recognised in them, in particular doing right, giving people the right to live (tsedaqua).

One of these actions undoubtedly requires an explanation: accompanying the bride down the isle on her wedding day. This is an explicit symbolically charged action: those who dress the bride for the wedding, those who bring the bride and groom together and bless the bridal couple, thus illustrate the way God as Creator meant people to be: rational creatures, directed at partnership and living together. But other elements also play a part: the experience of joy at a wedding and the provision of the minimum of material goods for poor and needy bridal couples. Moreover the symbolism of marriage is often also the symbol for God's covenant with people and with the whole of creation (Müller 1999, 96-99). In Hosea 2, 20-21 we read for example the following verses: "Then I will make a covenant on behalf of Israel with the wild beasts, the birds of the air, and the things that creep on the earth, and I will break bow and sword and weapon of war and sweep them off the earth, so that all living creatures may lie down without fear. I will betroth you to myself for ever, betroth you in lawful wedlock with unfailing devotion and love; I will betroth you to myself to have and to hold, and you shall know the Lord."

Every society is dynamic and undergoes changes in the social, political and economic sphere. The Roman occupation meant an extremely fundamental change in the way of life of the Jewish people, and put a lot of pressure on symbols, customs and insights. Consider for example the destruction of the temple in the year seventy. The existing system of social care was also affected. The literature from that era reflects the changed social needs and interprets the deeds of 'tsedaqua' in eleven areas of action: feeding the poor, clothing the naked, freeing the imprisoned, caring for travellers/hospitality, providing a trousseau for brides with little capital and support in widowhood, legal support for orphans, the provision of a house, maintenance for the older generation, offering perspective in life to the younger generation, caring for the sick and the weak, arranging a funeral for the poor.

K. Müller searches for the element that connects these forms of service to man and religion and concludes the following: "tsedaqa meint das verbindliche und verlässliche In-Kraft-Setzen der Levensrechte des Mitmenschen." (Müller 1999, 221) "In-Kraft-Setzen", make strong… it puts me on the track of a term from feminism that is very dear to me: empowerment.

1.2. The Greek concept 'διακονια' as the foundation of reflection.

The second important element in the search for 'diaconal identity' can be found in a different geographical area of the ancient world. If the Jewish inspiration put each Christian on the track of the foundations for a general diaconal consciousness, the following reflection sooner offers stimulation for a specific thought process on the identity of the deacon as a leader. The Greek language supplies us with the word 'διακονια' How should we interpret this word? And can a terminological debate stimulate thoughts on identity?

In his book *Diakonie zwischen Mensch, Kirche und Gesellschaft*, Haslinger gives a classic – in the sense of currently generally accepted – etymological interpretation of the term 'διακονια' (Haslinger 1996, 117-124). 'διακονια' is derived from the Greek verb διακονεω, which is said to refer to the human activity of 'serving'. In profane language-usage, διακονια is said to refer to a form of inferior labour, such as, for example, dishing up, which was usually slave labour. It is highly remarkable, says the author, that it should be precisely this term which is used in the Christian tradition to designate one of the most distinctive dimensions of this tradition: Christian-inspired aid to fellow human beings. Apart from that, the resemblance between the secular dishing up and the Eucharistic event of a meal-service par excellence is no accident. The New-Testament concept of διακονια, however, must not be interpreted as if serving implied a dependent relationship or one of 'inferior versus superior'. Such relations are indicated in the New Testament by the words δουλοσ or δουλοω. According to Haslinger this difference indicates that the New-testament concept refers to a voluntary servitude, free of all power-relations.

Caritas has a totally different etymological origin. It refers to the Greek αγαπη and aims, in the first instance, not at a human activity but at the love of God for human beings. God's love for human beings evokes a human response, a commitment to his fellow-man, since men are created in God's image: 'Ubi caritas et amor, ibi deus est…'. On the basis of religious arguments such as, especially, the thought of imago Dei, men are convinced of fundamental human equality, inviting them to fight discriminatory situations in which human dignity is violated.

Anyone who associates the two kinds of aid with these two terms, creates a false opposition. The terms 'caritas' and 'διακονια' point to quite different aspects of the Christian religion, but presuppose each other and need each other to put the Christian faith into practice in an authentic way. It is highly remarkable that in his opus magnum H. Haslinger refers not once to the work of the Roman-Catholic Australian exegete, J.N. Collins. The least one may say about the results of Collins' research is that they have given the διακονια-debate a new, polemically coloured élan, and also stimulated the discussion about the deacon's tasks. In short, his position is the following: neither the classical Greek profane language nor the New Testament give convincing reasons for a present-day broadly accepted interpretation of the 'διακον'-word-group as designating a humble service to the destitute. On the basis of his large-scale research, he concludes that διακονια and διακονος are directly connected to 'messages' and to 'being sent'…

"In der Antike hingegen bestand die Diakonia aus dem Auftrag einer Autorität, und dann ging der Diakonos, ob er nun eher als Bote oder eher als Agent auftrat, daran, diese Vorgabe zu erfüllen. (…). Die frühen Christen ernannten einige aus ihr Mitte zu Diakonen, nicht weil diese an den Tischen der Armen oder am Altartisch aufwarteten, sondern weil diese die persönlichen Vertreter des Bischofs waren." (Collins 1994, 67-68)

In his work *Diakonia. Re-interpreting the Ancient Sources*, Collins recon-structed, with a very precise and extensive linguistic analysis, what the ancient Greeks meant by διακονια. For this he analysed a broad range of texts, papyri and inscriptions, covering a period from 500 BC till 300 AD. The conclusion of his synchronic study is that the signification of the διακονια-term is remarkably consistent over a period of nearly thousand years of classical Greek, and hardly points to a connotation of διακονια as service in the meaning of menial labour. Plato's writings mention the διακονος as the 'go-between', "a person who takes things from one place to another", the action being "an operation carried on between two parties by a third party." (Collins 1990, 79-80)

In the second place, Collins studied the use of the διακονια word group in various pericopes of early Christian writings, obviously against the background of the insights gained during linguistic studies. For example, what is the meaning of Mark 10,45, a verse of profound interest for a 'classic' Christological legitimation of diakonia as servant-like acting: "because the Son of Man did not come to be served but to serve and to give his life as a ransom for many." Who will be served by the Son of God? What 'service' is He offering? (Collins 1990, 250-251) .[3]

The analysis of some verses in which Paul uses the word διακονος (1 Corinthians 3,5; 2 Corinthians 6,4; 2 Corinthians 11,23) also leads Collins to the conclusion that there are clear affinities between Paul's language use and an διακονος interpretation, in conformity with the profane Greek usage. Paul considers himself to be "a go- between": he has to deliver a special message in the name of somebody else... Collins speaks in terms of "spokesmen and messengers of heaven". The 'diakonos' is someone who holds an eminent position with regard to religious matters. It is not just a humble task that can be carried out by anybody, but a specific, honourable position, reserved for certain people: there is after all a mandate attached that was received by someone from a authoritative person of a higher rank (Collins 1990, 258-259).

Collins is convinced that the distorted διακονια interpretation has become firmly entrenched in recent decades, so that correction will be no easy matter. For example, in the 19th century, German Protestant (Inner Mission) groups founded the diakonia with the express purpose of being servants who, coming from the church, helped the destitute and the poor. The emphasis on humble service provided them with a plausible theological legitimation (Collins 1994, 65). I do not wish to elaborate this historical reconstruction. The emphasis on διακονια as an honourable, eminent task connected to a mandate that someone received from someone of a higher rank is what is important for this contribution. Collins concludes that this 'go-between position' is certainly a specific position, reserved for certain Christians and not automatically meant for everyone.

With this latter statement he draws a distinction between the general diaconal task of every Christian on the basis of his or her baptism and the office of deacon, as a specific office. The statement may not be interpreted as a legitimation for the exclusion of woman from the office of deacon, because Collins is extremely clear on that point: there is not a single theological ground that legitimises that exclusion.[4]

---

[3] "Thus, Mark's Son of Man is serving, or, better, ministering under God. In laying down his life, he is carrying out the sacred commission or *diakonia* he had received from God." Collins, J.N. 1995. A Ministry for Tomorrow's Church. *Journal of Ecumenical Studies* 32 (2): 171.

[4] " On an authentic view of ministry, the exclusion was simply wrong and has become unjust. (...). That is, early Christians chose to base essential ministry on the conviction that the word of God is communicated to men and women with equal force and clarity, and is then to be communicated to others by those among them, whether male or female, who are faithful hearers and honourable bearers of its import." (Collins 1994, 260-261)

A logical next step would be to examine the way in which the first Christian communities gave shape to their ethical driving spirit and how the church fathers legitimised the service characteristic of the Christian faith theologically. But this analysis would put me too much on the track of the past. There is one element that I would explicitly like to mention, namely the way in which the Eucharist and the sharing of elementary goods with the poor were fundamentally connected in the early Christian communities. The foundation for this was the conviction that two kinds of proclamation were necessary: the proclamation of the Word and the testimony of actions, in which an evangelical moving force gains shape wordlessly and yet powerfully. This joining of proclamation and social-charitable care in the early Christian churches was expressed amongst other things in the title given to the bishop: "Pater pauperum, Father of the poor" (Mette 1993, 116).

2. Criteria as test for relevant and liberating diaconal actions today

The past is, however, not strictly normative for our actions nowadays. A question that is equally important is which criteria we are supplied with in order to test diaconal actions of today for their relevance and liberating character. The search for such criteria confronts us with a specific difficulty: such criteria have to be sufficiently general in order to remain applicable to a broad range of diaconal activities, but on the other hand they may not remain purely theoretical. Three key concepts, that I will explain systematically, can in my opinion function as such a touchstone, namely integrity, equality and solidarity. I shall briefly explain each of these concepts.

2.1. Integrity

Integrity refers to a characteristic that all human beings should possess. It explicitly implies that a liberating praxis of diaconia shoud incorporate the various dimensions of life. In his well known book *Christ, the Christian Experience in the Modern world* (Schillebeeckx 1977, 671-683; Schillebeeckx 1980; Schillebeeckx 1989) (in the Dutch language the title refers to justice and love, salvation and liberation) the Roman Catholic theologian Edward Schillebeeckx, amply explores the question as to 'What is fundamental for human life?'. He does not search for an existing, complete, universal ideal about liveable humanity, as if there is merely a single theory on it. "In any case, 'humanity' is an abstract term. It exists only in very diverse cultural forms, although this may be on the basis of a fundamentally identical biogenetical substratum. Any hegemony of a definite culture is therefore pernicious, because it is tainted with 'regionalism' and imperialism" (Schillebeeckx 1982, 23). Schillebeeckx gives serious consideration to a number of basic conditions of human life, which he considers to be the conditions for realising human salvation.

Relation to one's own body and to nature
The first anthropologic subject Schillebeeckx reflects on considers the way in which men and women relate to their body and to nature. People need to recognise and respect the limits of their own corporality. In addition, human domination of the ecological environment needs to be seriously restricted. Schillebeeckx pleads for greater awareness of the intrinsic link between man and the surrounding cosmos. People cannot be reduced to a ratio. Moods, fantasy, instincts, love, etc., are integral components of the authentic human being. Genuine corporality demands activity as well as contemplation, eroticism, enjoyment and playful carefreeness.

Human beings as a fellow person
To be a human being means to be a fellow person. The relational dimension of human life manifests itself from the very first moments of life. The fundamental orientation towards other people enables us to transcend our own individuality. In Western countries, loneliness is considered to be one of the main social problems. Loneliness implies an impossibility to optimally experience the relational dimension of life.

People live in a network of social structures
People live in a complex whole of social and institutional structures. These structures partly constitute one's personality. Too often people tend to look upon social structures as being unchangeable. They forget that these structures are the result of concrete events and historical developments. Consequently, structures cannot claim universal or general validity. Structures or institutions that are unjust or enslaving, wherever they occur, must be changed.

Time and (geographical) space
All people live for a specific time and in a specific geographical space or culture. Both elements, time and environment, strongly influence the way people experience their lives. It is much to their credit that liberation theologies and feminist theologies urge us to be permanently aware of our situationally determined life-styles.

Theory and praxis are intrinsically connected
Human hermeneutics aimed at understanding meaning and significance cannot be separated from actually striving for a better world. This interconnectedness of theory and praxis is so fundamental to a theologian like Schillebeeckx that he goes into it explicitly in a separate section.

Ideas about the future, vision
People experience their humanity against the background of a specific utopian conviction that gives their lives meaning and direction. They search for a kind of substantial rationality. This utopian conviction can be religious or ideological, non-religious. It gives coherence to all things that happen in a person's life and acts as a source of inspiration. Often, the hope for the future is supported by the belief that people cannot fully realise this utopian ideal by virtue of their human energy alone. This anthropological condition points to a transcendent reality in human life.

Synthesis of these six dimensions
Schillebeeckx states that salvation and healing can be realised if attention is paid to the above mentioned six anthropological dimensions. That is why he considers the synthesis of these dimensions as an autonomous, fundamental ideal. One cannot give preference to one or two of the six anthropological dimensions. All six together form a basic pattern for human existence. Nor should any of these anthropological dimensions be considered less important than any of the others. The whole is meaningful precisely because of the balance between the six dimensions.

2.2. Equality

The notion of 'equality' has been the subject of many discussions, also among theologians and church leaders. In the world of citizenship (e.g. the Universal Declaration of Human Rights) all people are equal in theory. It proclaims the ideal of free citizens participating in social and public life on a basis of equality. The notion of 'equality' in an existential sense means: each person is fundamentally equal to all others. This existential meaning is inviolable.

However, are people not equal to each other merely in a formal and abstract way? More than anything else, real life shows us where people are not equal to each other: educational opportunities, possibilities on the labour market, character traits, etc. Putting all the emphasis on equality causes the side effect that the attention for differences is obscured. Groups of people have great mutual differences: just as little as 'the' group of men exists, does 'the' group of women exist. Race, economic situation, religious or philosophical conviction, age, etc. make for differences.

2.3. Solidarity

Solidarity is a third, important concept, which is closely connected to both other terms. A diaconal praxis based on solidarity excludes paternalistic relationships between the person asking for help and the person who provides help. A diaconal praxis based on solidarity makes both persons in this relationship participate in each other's humanity. Besides, solidarity enables people to go beyond the particularity of one specific situation of assistance. Solidarity means that people do not remain within the bounds of their specific problems and that they become aware that many problems can be reduced to common causes: "Where, in what kind of situations, human dignity is violated?"

3. An individual identity as deacon today?

Both the information on tradition, given in the first section, and the criteria used to test liberating diaconal actions from section two, offer inspiration for a global analysis of the general diaconal task that is typical of all faithful. Of course deacons share in this general diaconal task, but this only accentuates the demand for the specificness of their office. In this third section the question as to the individual identity is central. Can one, considering the multitude of tasks that deacons carry out, speak of a common identity of a group of deacons? And if so, is it possible to define essential elements?

Deacons are able, in my opinion, to stimulate thoughts on identity with the help of three questions: 1) who are we?, 2) who do we wish to be?, 3) who do others say we are? In the following section I wish to formulate a number of notes or reflections on these three questions.

3.1. Who are we?

On first sight it seems as though this question can be answered clearly, professionally and descriptively with numerical information on age, year of ordainment as a deacon, paid or non-paid tasks, family situation, etc. But numerical information also has its restrictions and usually does not inform us on the way in which people experience the way they function in a particular organisation or community. A different type of questioning is required in order to gain such information, for example by means of a number of depth interviews or a written questionnaire. This is an extensive and exciting field of research. Another angle of approach is to find out deacon's priorities: these priorities give an impression of the way in which deacons give actual shape to their identity.

3.2. Who do we wish to be?

The questions 'Who are we?' and 'Who do we wish to be?' have to do with what I would call 'self-attribution'. Although those involved answer both questions themselves, the answer to the 'who are we?' question does not necessarily coincide with the answer to the 'who do we wish to be?' question. On the contrary, often fantasy (who do we wish to be?) is not the same as reality (who are we?). But however different, answering the question 'who do we wish to be?' is an enriching experience, because in doing so future perspectives and aims are expressed.

The above mentioned anthropologic constants, described in the second section as a touchstone for liberating diaconal actions, can also function as a source of reflection here. Well-balanced people try to experience the various dimensions of being in harmony, without neglecting a single element or emphasising one element more than the other. Indeed this simple principle applies to each person. In my opinion leaders may be expected even more so to aim for a balance between these dimensions. The way in which the constants described can function as instruments of critical reflection on the individual identity of the deacon is shown in the following examples that were elaborated in each case in duplicate. Attention has been paid to the personal attitude and disposition as well as to the more general content of tasks.

Relation to one's own body and to nature
Do leaders listen enough to the signals sent out by the body? Signals that sometimes indicate that it is time to slow down before it is too late? Self-care is an important concept that was, for a long time, also neglected in religious circles due to the incorrect assumption that self-care would imply egoism. Of another order, but just as meaningful is the socially critical task of deacons with regard to this first anthropological constant. For example the choice made by the Belgium bishops to make 'the use of the fruits of the earth or ecological care' a subject of reflection. The social assignment can also be interpreted in a completely different way: deacons make it their task to assist sick people as individuals. But they also have to voice cultural criticism vis-à-vis society and the dominant social ideal of the young, unviolated, sports-person like body. Theologically speaking, it might be clear that sick or disfigured people also represent the image of God.

Human beings as a fellow person
Is enough attention paid to the relation to the direct environment? Many deacons are married. Are work and family in balance? How does one react if children who are growing up do not like their parent's obvious religious connection? In which way does being a deacon colour the partnership? Of another order is the question as to the way in which this dimension can be interpreted in the setting of a task and the actual exercising of an office. Most deacons are fully aware of the serious social problem of loneliness. It is very important not to disconnect the attention for the individual human being from larger, complex social structures. Loneliness refers to a lack of personal contact. But the quality of relationships also needs to be reflected: e.g.: in this context, violence experienced in families deserves attention.

People live in a network of social structures

Is enough attention paid to the way in which institutions and structures influence diaconal work? Typical of diaconal work is that social as well as religious structures and institutions exercise an influence on functioning. Yet I argued that structures are the results of concrete events and historical developments. Structures or institutions that are unjust or enslaving, wherever they occur, must be changed. It will be clear that we are now entering into the political dimension of diaconal activities.

Time and (geographical) space

Is enough attention paid to the significance of being a deacon here and now? The first permanent Roman Catholic deacon in the Netherlands was ordained a quarter of a century ago in Haarlem. Times have changed since then. Religious and social feelings too. What did remain consistent, and has perhaps in the meantime even been accentuated is the concern for the provision of diaconal care in an unpatronising way. The challenge not to work from a (western) paternalistic model of charity and social assistance that thwarts the true emancipation and liberation of the people asking for help, remained the same over all those years.

Theory and praxis are intrinsically connected

The attention paid to the relationship between theory and praxis holds a clear message for deacons: a rigorous split between theoreticians, the 'thinkers', on the one hand and the 'workers in the field' on the other is something to avoid. Yet reality shows that it is often very difficult to organise a constructive dialogue between the two groups. Some people give priority to the area of 'doing' or 'action' to such an extent that they consider in-service training and even simply reading a newspaper or a book as a waste of time.

Ideas about the future, vision

People live on the basis of a sense perspective. This anthropological condition points to a transcendent reality in human life. Diaconal aid is obviously permeated by this conviction. The belief in a transcendent reality urging people into social action constitutes the very dynamics of deacony. Yet, we need to reflect on the question how in a secularised world Christian-inspired social action deals with the many existing systems for attributing significance and meaning to life and existence. Nor can we afford to turn a blind eye to different opinions, differing theological viewpoints and motivations that move people within one and the same denomination into social action. This dimension also evokes the question as to the personal spirituality of the deacon. Where is this spirituality nourished? What are the main elements of this spirituality? In what way is spirituality in balance with regard to the other dimensions of leadership?

Synthesis of these six dimensions

Sincere people try to give shape in their actions and their 'being' to these various dimensions in a balanced way. As has already been mentioned, one may expect such a search for integrity and balance from leaders especially. In the meantime the word 'leadership' has also been mentioned a number of times. Do deacons consider themselves as 'leaders'? Is 'leadership' part of the diaconal identity? Why yes, why no?

3.3. Who do others say we are?

Who do others say we are? This question concerns externally attributed characteristics and conceptualisation. People are sensitive to conceptualisation and, whether they like it or not, this externally attributed identity plays a role in the priorities and aims people set themselves. The answer to this question confronts, however, with the multitude of expectations that, with regard to deacons, can be formulated from various angles. Partner, children, colleagues, friends, people for whom diaconal work is carried out, those jointly responsible for the parish, priests, the bishop, the magisterium... [5] all these groups of people can formulate diverse ideas about the question as to who deacons are and what they should do. Are deacons, implicitly or explicitly, aware of the ideas and expectations of these various groups of people? And of the way in which this diversity of ideas, implicitly or explicitly, is contributory to their experience of identity?

4. A number of pillars of the diaconal identity

It is clear from the above information what, in my opinion, the spearheads in the search for a specific identity of permanent deacons are. In connection with the Jewish tradition of chässäd, tsedaqua and chemilut chassadim an explicit social orientation on man and society/ecological environment forms a main element. It is precisely in this that the specific of the 'go-between' function that Collins describes on the basis of his linguistic analysis can be situated: in exercising office the deacon shares in the authority of the principal, the episcopus, who in the person of the deacon also gives shape to his task as 'pater pauperum'. The anthropological constants offer a double touchstone: on the one hand one can check the extent to which the deacon as a person exercises the (leadership) office evenly and harmoniously, and on the other whether enough attention is paid to the various dimensions that are connected to actual problems. In the following section I will go into this basis foundation in more theological detail.

---

[5] Vatican Documents: Ratio Fundamentalis institutionis diaconorum permanentium & Directorium pro ministerio et vita diaconorum permanentium. 1998. (www.deacons.net/directory/joint.htm)

4.1. Again: balance

As a rule the concepts proclamation (kerugma), liturgy (leiturgia), community (koinonia) and the willingness to serve (diakonia) are mentioned as ecclesiological fundamental categories. A church community may, in my opinion, expect from deacons that they pay particular attention to making sure that full justice is done to this service dimension, organised in separate activities as well as integrated into proclamation, liturgy and the shaping of a community. "Proclamation should go together with breaking and sharing just as breathing in and breathing out together make one breath." (Dehaene 2002, 1) This does not mean that the deacons are solely responsible for the diaconal dimension so that the rest of the religious community can bask in a kind of 'shift-of-responsibility mentality'. Of course it is the task of each leader to make sure there is a balance between these four religious fundamental elements. But besides general tasks and those that apply to everyone, spearheads of attention and care can also be defined. In politics these are sometimes called 'watchdog positions'. Our tradition offers us a better image: watchmen on the bulwarks surrounding the city. Deacons pay particular attention to guarding the service dimension.

4.2. "Your name is passion for righteousness" [6]

This sentence can be considered as the thread through the many texts from the Old and New Testament that offer us a biblical-theological foundation of diacony. Passion for righteousness may be expected of every Christian, and I consider it to be an essential characteristic of the identity of deacons in particular. Passion for righteousness in the service of the Kingdom of God can lead to a conflict situation with prevailing laws, norms and values in society. In the extreme this can even lead to the question of whether civil disobedience is permissible. Living and working on the fracture area of church and society characterises the identity of deacons.

4.3. Presbyterium and diaconate as distinguished offices

A third pillar in the search for the individual identity of deacon's links with the early Christian idea about the bishop as 'pater pauperum'. Furthermore Vatican II has clearly stated that presbyterium and diaconate should in a distinguished way share in the mission and task of the one religious-sacramental office of the bishop. Presbyterium and diaconate are not thus structured in a hierarchical relation as higher/lower, but are equal to one another as two distinguished

---

[6] IPB-secretariaat, eds. 2002. *Uw naam is hartstocht voor gerechtigheid. Krijtlijnen voor een kerkelijke diaconie vandaag en morgen.* Brussel: IPB-Halewijn. Cfr. "to know Thee is the whole of righteousness", as we can read in the Wisdom literature (Wisdom of Solomon 15,3).

offices. The individuality of the diaconate can be indicated from the 'pater pauperum' conviction, in particular the bishop who was responsible for service to the destitute, the oppressed, strangers and marginalized people. The deacon is the perfect person to assist the bishop in exercising these tasks (Greshake 2000, 167-169). I wish to connect this idea with Collins' 'go-between' proposition: the deacon is the one who is sent with a special task, to areas that are sometimes more difficult for the bishop to reach … In exercising this task the deacon is not merely 'the help', responsible for (inferior) service tasks, but the one who actually shares in the authority of the bishop.

4.4. Koinonia as context and motivation

Schillebeeckx's anthropological constants clarify among other things that being human is by definition being human communally. Naturally this applies to the faithful. Theoretically this communal dimension is indicated on the basis of baptism. Building up a religious community requires energy, time and care, just as people should invest in friendships and relationships with their fellow men. The communal aspect is the starting point of a religious image in which the permanent diaconate functions (Kasper 1999). And at the same time there is the reason for existence within the communal dimension. Thus koinonia is at the same time context and motivation.

4.5. Spiritual anchorage

When diaconal spirituality is discussed, the willingness to serve is usually fully emphasised. The component action is given an explicit Christologically legitimated emphasis. But how can one avoid people collapsing under the 'weight of ethics' that rests on their shoulders? The way mercy is considered, the promise of divine salvation, forms a fundamental component of diaconal identity and can preserve from this 'collapse under the weight of all that still has to be done'.[7] Despite all the well-meant effort it is not possible for people to solve all the evil that exists in the world. The realisation that we have been promised salvation creates room to breathe despite the awareness of permanent evil (Burggraeve 2000, 78-83; 159-198). The realisation that we have been promised salvation provides us with room to enjoy, despite all the work that awaits us. But one cannot manage without enjoyment and without self-care.

---

[7] "Theologisch gesprochen ist es der 'eschatologische Vorbehalt': Ich stelle die aktuelle Situation, eine konkrete Entscheidung, eine perspektivische Planung, auch meine eigenen Ambivalenzen in so einem Entscheidungsprozess in den 'Horizont Gottes'; trotzdem muss ich entscheiden, aber ich tue das im Bewusstsein eines weiteren Zusammenhanges und mit dem Vertrauen, dass Gott auch über unsere Begrenztheiten hinaus wirksam sein kann. Das relativiert alle Allmachtsphantasien und das hat zugleich einen entlastenden und befreienden Aspekt" (Wolf 2001, 66).

4.6. Nourishment from the liturgy

The religious conviction that we have been promised divine salvation is expressed and symbolised in the liturgy. In relation to this R. Burggraeve convincingly describes the salutary meaning of 'merciful actions' in the tension between 'ethical actions and the awareness of human limitations'. Deacons have, based on the specific task they have been set in society, a special assignment in this area. They are able to present themselves in their merciful actions as 'go-between', as the one who builds bridges between church and society. A merciful gesture 'somewhere on the shop floor' is then nourished from the specific task they have been set in the liturgy.[8]

4.7. Plea for imagination and creativity

The search for an individual identity and profile for permanent deacons, for example in their relation to pastoral employees, requires creativity. Imagination is needed in the search for new candidates for the office of deacon as well as in working out a desirable and optimal job definition. W. Kasper describes an inspiring practise in the diocese of Besançon. The search for new candidates for the office of deacon is given a serious parish-oriented interpretation. The various parishes were asked to make a context analysis, and in doing so to pay particular attention to registering the social focus of their diaconate. Once the specific needs had been registered, they were asked to go in search of people who, based on their social conscience and in combination with their professional competence, would be able to contribute to solving the social needs within that area. In other words: people were purposefully approached and at the same time confronted with the possibility of the permanent diaconate. Possible candidates are given a year of 'considering time'. Those who, after a year of consideration, positively accept the invitation are able to start the course leading to becoming a permanent deacon (Kasper 1999, 162). In my opinion this approach is evidence of a creative search for a contemporary interpretation of the 'go-between' identity.

---

[8] "Deze goddelijke, genadevolle zegening is direct een uitnodiging om zélf ook zegenend op te treden. En deze algemene ethische opdracht kan zich onder meer verbijzonderen in alle vormen van intermenselijke en sociale zorg, hulpverlening en welzijnswerk. De genade van de zegen, die ons te beurt valt, wekt in ons de roeping, het ethisch appèl anderen zegenend te benaderen" (Burggraeve 2000, 161).

Conclusion

The aim of my contribution was to offer a number of pillars as a foundation for a thought process on the specific identity of permanent deacons. Pillars are an essential part of a construction; without pillars there is no bridge, no connection between two banks. It is partly on the basis of the pillars described above that permanent deacons, in combination with the religious community and other office holders, are able to give shape to their 'go-between' task, their bridging function between church and society, driven by the firm conviction that God's name is passion for righteousness.

References

Burggraeve, R. 2000. *Ethiek en passie. Over de radicaliteit van christelijk engagement.*Tielt: Lannoo.

Collins, J.N. 1990. *Diakonia. Re-interpreting the Ancient Sources.* New York/Oxford: Oxford University Press.

Collins, J.N. 1994. Die Bedeutung der Diakonia – eine persönliche Erfahrung. *Diakonia Christi* 29(1-2): 51-71.

Collins, J.N. 1995. A Ministry for Tomorrow's Church. *Journal of Ecumenical Studies* 32(2): 159-178.

Dehaene, T. 2002. Editoriaal. Ga aan Johannes vertellen wat gij hoort en ziet. *IPB-Transparant* 5(2): 1.

De zending van de christenen in de wereld. Verklaringen van de bisschoppen van België, nummer 26. 2000. Brussel

Greshake, G. 2000. *Priester sein in dieser Zeit. Theologie-Pastorale Praxis-Spiritualität.* Freiburg/Basel/Wien: Herder.

Haslinger, H. 1996. *Diakonie zwischen Mensch, Kirche und Gesellschaft. Eine praktisch-theologische Untersuchung der diakonischen Praxis unter dem Kriterium des Subjektseins des Menschen.* Echter: Seelsorge Echter Verlag.

Hoefnagels, P. 2002. De diaken als 'bewogen beweger'. Theologische verkenningen rond de diaken in liturgie. *Tijdschrift voor Liturgie* 86: 135-148.

IPB-secretariaat, eds. 2002. *Uw naam is hartstocht voor gerechtigheid. Krijtlijnen voor een kerkelijke diaconie vandaag en morgen.* Brussel: IPB-Halewijn.

Kasper, W. 1999. Der Diakon in ekklesiologischer Sicht angesichts der gegenwärtigen Herausforderungen in Kirche und Gesellschaft. Pp. 145-162 in *Theologie und Kirche,Bd. 2,* edited by W. Kasper. Mainz.

Kuhn, T.S. 1962. *The Structure of Scientific Revolutions.* Chicago: University of Chicago Press.

Mette, N. 1993. Theologie der Caritas. Pp. 115-138 in *Grundkurs Caritas,* edited by M. Lehner and W. Zauner. Linz.

Müller, K. 1999. *Diakonie im Dialog mit dem Judentum. Eine Studie zu den Grundlagen sozialer Verantwortung im jüdisch-christlichen Gespräch.* Heidelberg: Universitätsverlag C. Winter.

Nissen, P.J.A. 1991. Het Tweede Vaticaans Concilie en het herstel van het permanent diaconaat. Pp. 301-319 in *Kerk in beraad. Opstellen aangeboden aan prof. dr. J.C.P.A. van Laarhoven bij gelegenheid van zijn afscheid als hoogleraar aan de Katholieke Universiteit Nijmegen,* edited by G. Ackermans. Nijmegen.

Schillebeeckx, E. 1977. *Gerechtigheid en liefde, genade en bevrijding.* Bloemendaal: Nelissen.

Schillebeeckx, E. 1980. *Christ, the Christian Experience in the Modern World.* London: SCM Press.

Schillebeeckx, E. 1989. *Christ: the Experience of Jesus as Lord.* New York: Crossroad.

Schillebeeckx, E. 1989. Christian Identity and Human Integrity. *Concilium* 18(5): 23-31.

Schüssler Fiorenza, E. 1998. "Vrouwen moeten een plaats hebben in het centrum". *De Bazuin* 81: 22-24.

Vatican documents: Ratio Fundamentalis institutionis diaconorum permanentium & Directorium pro ministerio et vita diaconorum permanentium. 1998.

Wolf, B. 2001. Diakonische Identität und Spiritualität. Persönliche und institutionelle Aspekte. Pp. 61-71 in: *Spiritualität in der Diakonie. Anstösse zur Erneuerung christlicher Kernkompetenz,* edited by B. Hoffmann and M. Schibilsky. Stuttgart/Berlin/Köln: W. Kohlhammer Verlag.

The Story of the Perpetrator
Conflict Negotiation, Restorative Justice, and Gratuitous Forgiveness through Sacramental Reconciliation

Kristiaan Depoortere, Karlijn Demasure, and Anne Vandenhoeck

1. Defining subject and method

The purpose of our research was to identify some steppingstones on the path to a renewed liturgical form of reconciliation. The focus of much of the recently published literature on reconciliation is the inner growth of the victim towards forgiveness (e.g., Monbourquette 2000; Basset 1997; 1999; Lascaris 1999; Burggraeve 2000). Despite the interesting nature of these publications, they only serve our cause indirectly. In this contribution, we focus on the perpetrators and their personal experience in a liturgy of reconciliation with God and fellow humans within the context of a religious community. We applied some of the new data reported in the literature dealing with the victims to the situation of the perpetrator. How do perpetrators grow towards an awareness of guilt and sin? How do they attempt to repair the evil they have caused? How do they ask the victims and God for forgiveness and reconciliation? Consequently, in our study we did not look into the inner growth towards forgiveness of the victims, nor did we make a distinction between normal and unhealthy feelings of guilt. Little reference is made to Paul Ricœur's phenomenology of guilt, or to common guilt without a personal perpetrator.

Our pastoral-theological method is to analyze, to evaluate, and to formulate some strategic proposals for change (among other authors: Knobloch 1996, 93-99). First, we analyze the current situation of ritual forgiveness and reconciliation. We will describe the "end of the third penitential regime" (private auricular confession) in the Roman Catholic Church and the current vacuum that surrounds sacramental reconciliation. Secondly, we evaluate the situation and confront these facts with the most remarkable conclusions on forgiveness and reconciliation from the fields of history, theology and other human sciences (psychology, philosophy, counseling, criminology). These conclusions are the foundations for our third part: an attempt to develop a model for a "fourth penitential regime" (De Clerck 1983).

2. Analysis of the third Penitential Regime – the current vacuum

Some people claim that the confessional ruined their youth and was the cause of many frustrations. But others remember the joyful experience of being forgiven. Hearing God answer through the priest cleared and quieted their conscience. The anonymity of the confessional contributed to honesty. The strict guarantee of confessional secrecy created a sense of safety and confidentiality (under the patronage of Saint John Nepomucenus, executed in 1393 in Prague because of his refusal to breach confessional secrecy). The confessor could be asked for advice. Confession gave the person an opportunity for regular self-evaluation. The catechesis in those days mostly proclaimed a good balance between the images of God as a Judge and as a merciful Father. An objective analysis of the catechisms confirms this.

There were, of course, weaknesses and disadvantages in the third penitential regime. Indeed, confessions frequently centered on the sixth and ninth commandment (dealing with sexuality). Too little attention was paid to the victim and her or his surroundings. "I sinned against You, my God" overshadowed the "I sinned against you, my fellow human". Especially after the Council of Trent, the emphasis was on inner contrition and not so much on penance. Restitution was mentioned, but did it concern the validity of the sacrament in its very essence? Too often the attitude was "we forgive and forget", which in many cases led to repression of guilt. The complex emotional state of the perpetrator/sinner was not sufficiently taken into consideration. Reconciliation was based on will power and the confessor was not challenged into conflict negotiation. The sinner was seldom referred to counseling, therapy, or … to the police. Spiritual guidance was mainly religiously inspired but hardly in a professional way, despite the efforts, in Flanders, of the Jesuit priests Raymond Hostie and Louis Monden to inspire this professional attitude back in the sixties (Hostie 1963; Monden 1964). The sometimes objectivist and juridical approach to guilt and sin amplified the already heavy anxieties of some penitents.

One can find an actual vacuum around sacramental reconciliation in Northwestern Europe today. The most fundamental cause for this lies in the loss of a personal relationship with God and the correlative evaporation of a sense of guilt, which Paul Ricœur describes in *The Symbolism of Evil*. It can be assumed that it was this evolution that gave birth to new liturgical forms of confession (services of reconciliation which offer opportunities for personal or communal confession), but none of them were really successful. At this point, personal confession only happens in places of pilgrimage and in some churches of religious orders. Reconciliation services usually only take place in Advent or Lent in parish churches. But the experience of hospital chaplains and pastors involved in critical situations points out that many people live with a repressed sense of guilt that comes to the surface in times of crisis (the guilt that stays after abortion, or after making a last will meant to punish recalcitrant children and grandchildren, …) These experiences demand further creative reflection.

3. The input of history and theology (evaluation I)

In the present section, we shall gather elements from the history of reconciliation, the ecumenical movement, theological ethics, sacramentology, ecclesiology, dogmatic theology, and pastoral theology. The question is: Can these elements become the building blocks for a new model?

3.1. The history of the sacrament of reconciliation teaches us that in the first millennium there were a diversity of rituals for reconciliation. This variety was narrowed down when the seven sacraments were theologically outlined. One form received the monopoly of a sacrament; the others were downgraded to "sacramentals". The fact that only a priest could perform sacraments enhanced the monopoly of one form. However, in addition to the official sacrament, a kind of private confession in the context of spiritual guidance (not necessarily by a priest but by a monk, inspired by the example of John Cassian) continued to exist throughout the Middle Ages in Western Europe and in the Orthodox Churches (Van Knippenberg 2000, 25).

The history of sacramental reconciliation is not a smooth one, as described in an eminent way by Cyrille Vogel (1982). No other sacrament underwent so many changes in its liturgical form. At first there was the so-called canonical or antique penitential regime with a strong emphasis on the social and ecclesial aspect of penance. The conditions for reconciliation were hardly bearable and this type has fallen into disuse. After a vacuum of at least two centuries, a second penitential regime was born: Celtic Christianity inspired the so-called tariff penance that provided an objective, measurable side of guilt and therefore a proportional restitution (satisfaction). In the third stage, the Council of Trent confirmed a third, more spiritual and inner regime: private auricular confession with a strong emphasis on the authenticity of intentions and contrition (cf. the subtle distinctions between contrition and attrition). After a sifting of the complex history of the sacramental reconciliation, four building blocks remain: contrition of the sinner (Trent), an ecclesial-communitarian exteriorization of contrition (canonical penance), reparation of the harm (*satisfactio* – tariff penance), and – in the fourth place – a more or less official ecclesial intervention that symbolizes God's forgiveness (in every regime – but not limited to priests).

3.2. The ecumenical dialogue is brought forth an interesting evolution with immediate repercussions for our topic: can the *sacramenta maiora* be connected more closely to the *sacramenta minora*? Gisbert Greshake relates the anointing of the sick with baptism. He calls the sacrament of the sick a more explicit expression of the eschatological dimension of baptism at the moment a person is faced with the "real" possibility of dying (Greshake 1986). Francois Bourdeau connects confession through pilgrimage with the Eucharist (F. Bourdeau 1982). From earliest times on, reconciliation has been connected with baptism. Water, as a powerful symbol, could play a role in the sacrament of reconciliation and symbolize the relation between baptism and confession in a renewed liturgy of reconciliation.

3.3. Recent thinking in theological ethics criticizes the third penitential regime. Francois Bourdeau, and many other theologians, emphasize the process character of sin and, in a correlative way, the progress character of reconciliation: "*Quelle est la trajectoire et la courbe de ma vie?*" In the context of reconciliation during a pilgrimage, he talks about "*la gradualité du déplacement humain*" (Bourdeau 1982, 112). Jacques Pohier criticizes the anthropocentric hijacking of sin. The concept of sin has been reduced to a failure to achieve the dream images that humans constructed about themselves. He pleads for a religious-relational definition of sin where failure is related to the image that God has of man. (Pohier 1977, 39). Theological ethics also points out that sin is not a mere violation of the Law but is primarily about damaging relationships which ultimately hurt God; cf. the parable of the prodigal son: "Father, I have sinned against both heaven and you" (Luke 15:21).

3.4. Sacramental theology has undergone some interesting shifts that provide the theology of confession with new outlines. First of all, there is Louis-Marie Chauvet who describes the Christian identity as a triangle (*kerygma, leitourgia, diakonia*) within a circle (*koinonia*) (Chauvet 1995). Within this triangle of the Word that is proclaimed, celebrated, and lived, the sacrament is the keystone in the development of a Christian identity. A sacramental celebration contributes to this new identity by changing relationships. Grace means renewing identity by intensifying relationships. Grace doesn't give "something", but changes a person through a closer commitment with God and people. Francois-Xavier Durrwell is an author with similar thoughts (Durrwell 1971). Concerning the real presence of Christ in the Eucharist, he deals with a growing relationship with the eschatological expressive capacities of the real. This means that the presence of the Holy Spirit gives the Eucharistic bread its ultimate revealing meaning. In the Eucharistic breaking of the bread, the bread is not destroyed (this remains the prevailing idea of transubstantiation theory: a kind of cell amputation takes place). On the contrary, the bread becomes bread-er and bread-est, in order that the faithful become human-er and human-est, and the world world-er and world-est. Obviously, this can also be applied to the sacrament of reconciliation. The grace of reconciliation isn't an object (an antivenin) that eliminates the harm done; it changes the relational pattern of the sinner. Grace, through the Holy Spirit, brings the sinner closer to Christ. The relation becomes relation-er and relation-est, close, closer, and closest. And this new relationship changes the person.

A second input from current thinking in sacramental theology is the idea of spreading sacraments over a certain period (Depoortere 2000), giving sacraments more of a process structure. An inspiring example is the Roman Catholic *Rite of Christian Initiation for Adults*. The celebration of baptism is spread over a period of time. The baptism with water is the "crowning" moment of the extended ritual, but not the only moment of grace. Thus, liturgy becomes a process of grace, and what we used to call sacramentals are integrated into the sacramental event. They are no longer *pene nihil sed tamen aliquid*, but *humus* or moments of intensification in the sacramental process. Reconciliation in such a vision is a sacramental event that starts off with attrition-contrition, goes through penance until it receives its crowning in the official ecclesial absolution. We will return to this idea later on.

Although we used the word "crowning", the word "sealing" might be better to express the sacramental moment *sensu stricto*. The Ritual for the Anointing of the Sick is a good example. The highlight of the sacramental process confirms all the previous sacramental work, like a seal on a charter, and makes it authentic. It proclaims in public, through a pastor who speaks *in persona Christi Capitis et Pastoris*, that a caring God has always been present in all the care that was provided to the sick person (revelatory aspect of the sacrament). Secondly, the ultimate sacramental gesture brings the process of reconciliation to its fulfillment (*per-ficere*) through the *epiclesis*. Something new happens (operative aspect of the sacrament). Thirdly, the sealing also evokes a sending, a mission. The sacrament *sensu stricto* opens an eschatological perspective: at the end, God will be "all in all" (symbolic aspect of the sacrament). The ethical component of the sacraments is embedded in a mystical dimension: "You wouldn't search for Me if I hadn't found you already" (St Augustine). Again, this can be applied to the sacrament of reconciliation.

3.5. The sacrament of reconciliation can also be enriched from an ecclesiological point of view. L.-M. Chauvet is very clear about this: for a Christian, encountering God passes through the Church community. This is the core of the Easter Event: "Do you want to know if the risen Jesus lives? Then let go of the yearning to see, hear, or touch his earthly body. He is only to be seen, heard, touched in his body-of- the- word, where the Church integrates his message, gestures and life. The Church is the fundamental sacramental mediation, through her Christian faith is constituted." (Chauvet 1979, 86). Matthew 18, 15-22 shows that the mediation of the faith community is not only essential, but also very concrete. The text is an example of what we call conflict negotiating today. First, the sinner is seen in private. Then, two witnesses are called. Thirdly, an appeal is made to the love of the whole community and, finally, the severe warning is given that any decision on earth has consequences in heaven.

3.6. Behind a new understanding of guilt and sin lies a changed image of God. The concepts of "all-powerfulness" and "goodness" become conflicting terms. Since Kazoh Kitamori's *Theology of The Pain of God* (Kitamori 1966), one notices a significant shift towards a moved, sym-pathetic God: *a moved Mover* (Depoortere 1995, 91-92). This concept entails the risk that God's all-powerfulness is sacrificed to his goodness: a suffering God instead of a leading God. God is reduced to the ultimate, powerless victim described in Harold Kushner's *When Bad Things Happen to Good People* (New York 1981). Matthew 25, 31-46 is central in that discussion: Jesus stands fully behind the victims – and even identifies with them - and vice versa: "Truly, I say to you, as you did it to one of the least of these, you did it to Me" (Matthew 25, 40). We will discuss later how such a vision may deepen the concept of sin and, at the same time, offer a new perspective. The evil done by humans hurts God. But precisely because sin is radically placed in relationship, redemption becomes possible, unless God lost his all-powerfulness completely in the discussion. In the latter case, every significant other who judges humans beings and functions as a guarantor of fellow humans' liberty evaporates. However, this is one of the essential elements in monotheism.

3.7. Pastoral theology also offers a reflection towards more integrated sacramental celebrations. To put it bluntly: in the past, sacraments had a chance of being concluded with a conversation; now a pastoral visit has a chance of being sealed with a sacrament. This evolution is closely linked to the input of lay ministers in the Roman Catholic Church. Because lay ministers cannot celebrate sacraments, they discovered other ways to provide pastoral care, especially through counseling. Their ministry emphasizes the service of the Word. This has ecumenical repercussions. Because of the close working relationship between lay ministers and priests, questions are surfacing about the specificity of priesthood in the Roman Catholic Church. Does unfolding and spreading sacramentality also imply an unfolding of ministry? We think it does.

4. The input of the human sciences (evaluation II)

In the next part we will discuss some insights from the human sciences (criminology, psychology, psychotherapy, and philosophy) that offer a perspective on the concepts of guilt and forgiveness.

4.1. Concepts such as restorative justice originated in criminology. In the first place, restoring is a dynamic concept, bringing movement in a blocked situation (for example, through an encounter between victim and perpetrator). Secondly, restorative justice means repositioning: when victim and perpetrator look each other in the eyes, weak and strong switch sides. In the third place, restorative justice means personalization. It is discovering that both victim and perpetrator are human beings, for example, that the victim is a person (and not only a sexual part of a woman), and, concerning the perpetrator, a process of "de-monstering" might start. Fourthly, restorative justice means "responsibilization" (becoming aware of responsibility for the occasion, the event itself, and its consequences). Finally, restorative justice can, in some cases, lead to restoring the relationship (Bastiaensen 2000, 117-121). In the past decennia, a number of initiatives were taken within this context, for instance, the pilgrimages with prisoners. They aim at a certain restoring. They are often a profane form of doing penance.

4.2. Psychologists have studied the complexity of guilt and reconciliation extensively. Lytta Basset studied the relationship between *le mal subi* (the undergone harm) and *le mal commis* (the harm done) (Basset 1999, 14). The perpetrator is not infrequently also a victim. Basset points out how the harm experienced through complex mechanisms can lead to doing harm. She calls this the (sometimes) inevitable mechanism of *le mal original*. Studies like these question the radical division between perpetrator and victim.

Psychology also offers a better view on the difference between genuine and unauthentic feelings of guilt. Children sometimes feel guilty because of their parents are getting a divorce. Children who were abused often feel guilty later on ("I was walking around naked"). Taking the (undeserved) blame for situations like this often is an unconscious mechanism to get control of a disturbing reality ("If I avoid this kind of behavior, it will not happen again").

Psychoanalysis studied the difference between healthy and pathological feelings of guilt, and their blending (Vergote 1988). If the counselor or confessor does not have sufficient knowledge of the difference, a lot of harm can be done. In most cases of pathological guilt, a *tandem care* between the therapist and the pastor is advised. And last but not least, a great effort is being made to find new symbols and rituals in coping with guilt within the psychotherapeutic sector.

4.3. The findings of researchers in counseling and therapy have many far-reaching consequences for sacramental reconciliation. Although most studies start from the point of view of the victim, the insights of someone like Jean Monbourquette are very valuable. What is very interesting in his work is the turning point towards forgiveness when the victim realizes that she/he too has received forgiveness in the past. It can be a possible opening in growing towards forgiving. The growing "from below" is, in a certain sense, interrupted "from without" by an outer experience: "something I received without merits". When the focus shifts from "I'm hurt" to "I received forgiveness in the past", the process gets a new impetus. To name this turning point, Jean Monbourquette uses the words *"démarche du pardon"* (as opposed to *"le processus thérapeutique"*). The victim has to loosen her/his grip – beyond will power - and to become receptive to a gift. That inner change also has to happen in the perpetrator: one cannot claim or extort forgiveness but has to receive it. This turning point isn't easy for the victim or for the perpetrator if they never experienced unconditional love in the past. Only if there is a sufficient amount of self-esteem can the perpetrator accept that she/he needs forgiveness and that forgiveness is to be granted "for nothing". For those who lack basic trust, having to receive forgiveness means just another humiliation (Monbourquette 1994, 50).

Jean Monbourquette also makes an interesting distinction between forgiveness and reconciliation. The latter means a restoration of the relationship between the victim and the perpetrator. Monbourquette is convinced that this restoration is sometimes just not possible. The demand for complete reconciliation can even hinder the process of forgiveness. When the victim thinks she/he should trust her/his violator again after a serious infringement of this confidence, this idea can prohibit the growing towards forgiveness.

The same idea is found in the writings of Roger Burggraeve : "Forgiveness is a necessary condition for reconciliation but it is not a sufficient one" (Burggraeve 2000, 294). In therapy and on the anthropological level, the distinction between forgiveness and reconciliation is healthy. However, the question remains if – from a pastoral viewpoint - we don't have to continue aiming for reconciliation although we have to settle for forgiveness sometimes because of human weakness.

4.4. Extensive research has been done in philosophy on the performative dimension of language: talking "performs" something. Language is an existential (Martin Heidegger): the human *"kommt zur Sprache"*. Very important also are the philosophical reflections on corporality (*corporéité*) (e.g., the sinner has to "signi-fy" her/his guilt) and around the specific efficacy of symbols and rituals.

4.5. We could also refer to the input of liberation theology and sociology. They emphasize the structural dimension of evil and also present an entangling of *mal commis* and *mal subi*. But we want to focus on building up our model of "action".

5. A fourth penitential regime: principles (acting I)

5.1. First field of tension: the relationship between theology and the human sciences

The achievements of the human sciences should be integrated in a renewed theology of reconciliation. But a fundamental theological problem then arises: What is the relationship between creation and redemption, between grace and nature, between the human and the divine? L.-M. Chauvet asserts that "the most 'spiritual' happens through the most 'corporeal'" (Chauvet, 1995, 146) and that "The anthropolog(ic)al is the place of every possible theolog(ic)al" (Chauvet 1995, 152). Leonardo Boff speaks about the Transparent as the place of encounter between the Immanent and the Transcendent (Boff 1987). Henry Nouwen characterizes the pastor as a "living reminder" (Nouwen 1981). Tjeu van Knippenberg published "Between Two Languages" (van Knippenberg 1998). All these different expressions focus on the concept of experience-revelation in continuity-discontinuity.

Seen within the context of sacramental reconciliation, it means that there is the human process of growing towards forgiveness and there is grace that comes "from above", "from somewhere else". Grace meets human effort and essentially is a gift for nothing. One cannot merit Grace. Still, grace doesn't happen without human efforts or growth processes, but also not because of them. The relationship between the human (anthropological) and the divine (theologal) can only be expressed in a paradox, but it has many consequences for our research. The ultimate question is: What does God have to do with our human processes of forgiveness and reconciliation? The moment of Grace, in Jean Monbourquette's view, is when humans remember being forgiven themselves by another hurt human being in the past. This sudden realization is a breaking point in the process. But does this also translate into the relationship between God and humans? Can a human being hurt God? And how and where does God intervene in the process of human growth towards forgiveness? Or does the answer lie in the *"ubi caritas et amor ibi Deus est."* *"Est"* as it is. And God's being is "creative".

5.2. Second field of tension: between two (or more) images of God

A renewed theology of the sacrament of reconciliation will inevitably have to deal with the tensions between the image of an All-powerful and All-good God. Looking from the perspective of the victim, we like to hear that God is "*a moved Mover*". That means God is upset about the harm done to people. He objects, He identifies through Christ with the victims (Matthew 25). God is hurt and suffers with the victims. The question is whether a vulnerable God is able to act effectively against the evil that has been done. Is God capable of undoing evil? Concerning the perpetrator, theologians and the Magisterium of the Roman Catholic Church are hesitating between two images of God. Does he act as a physician, a healer, or as a judge. God as a judge, as the Other, as an Opponent of injustice and evil brings/forces the perpetrator to repent and, through punishment, does justice to the victim. If God acts as a physician, or as a shepherd, He offers forgiveness to the perpetrators, whether they deserve it or not (Luke 15). This ambiguous duality of terminology is clearly present in the Postsynodal Exhortation *Reconciliato et Paenitentia* (John Paul II 1984).

5.3. A third area of tension: the relationship between sacramentals and sacraments

The current multitude of celebrations for forgiveness is a good thing: private confession, celebrations of reconciliation, with or without personal confession, spiritual accompaniment by lay-persons, and so on. They are moments of grace that can accompany therapy in a *tandem care* or that constitute the humus for a sacramental reconciliation *sensu stricto*. On the other hand, the multitude of celebrations also poses a lot of questions: Does the specificity of the sacrament *sensu stricto* depend on the qualifications of the (ordained) minister? Or can L.-M. Chauvet's "*ecclesial mediation*" be seen in wider interpretation? Or do we have to take on a more objective view focused on the weight of the matter?

Can one claim that strictly sacramental reconciliation is necessary only when 1) harm is done that cannot be undone because of its gravity or because the victim cannot or will not reconcile (God already forgave the harm that is reparable and repaired, cf. daily sins), when 2) people are completely stuck in the position of the perpetrator and cannot/dare not live or love anymore, 3) in situations in which *mal subi* and *mal commis* are inextricably entangled with each other 4), when somebody actively participated or collaborated at structural evil, and 5) in order to take away the unavoidable "leftover" or sediment (pain, wounds, anxieties) that remains even after reconciliation?

Narrowing a definition of when to apply the sacrament of reconciliation *sensu stricto* could lead to the same deadlock that we find with the sacrament of the sick. The blessing of the dying runs the risks of currently replacing the sacrament of the anointing of the sick. A broader description of the sacrament's possibilities requires a high competence from both the priest and the penitent. Will those high demands and the shortage of priests make the sacrament of reconciliation disappear?

5.4. Field of tension IV: the relationship between the four elements of reconciliation

The four traditional components of sacramental reconciliation that we identified from history are not as separated from each other as they used to be. Contrition (1) *kommt zur Sprache* in confession (2). Penance (3) is an action of restoration that already started in confession. Ecclesial mediation (4) reaches its fulfilment in absolution, but it is already playing a part from confession on. Contrition and confession are only possible if the sinner knows that there is a chance for forgiveness. One doesn't confess evil if the other has already abandoned you for good. And what is the relationship between penance – the human reparation - and acquittal, God's gratuitous gift?

6. A fourth penitential regime: construction of the model (acting II)

The four traditional elements of reconciliation cannot be separated totally. Therefore, the following division is for research and didactic purposes only.

6.1. From remorse to contrition

Three actors play a part in the concept of repentance: the perpetrator, the victim (c.q. society), and God. "I'm sorry, I did it", says the perpetrator. Initially, it often expresses a consciousness about violating a law or taboo. In traditional theological language, this is called "imperfect contrition" (*attritio*) when it is mainly characterized by fear of punishment or revenge by the taboo. This feeling is very much linked with shame (I'm ashamed of myself). The façade has been stained. Vladimir Jankélévitch calls this feeling remorse rather then contrition. In the long run, remorse is a self-destructive feeling because of the lack of a relationship. He therefore describes it as the "tears of Judas" (Jankélévitch 1933).

In this framework, mechanisms that veil and disguise, or cheap excuses, can obstruct development from remorse to contrition: "In fact, I'm more victim than perpetrator" or "This was the least harm after all" and so forth (Burggraeve 2000, 287-288; Demasure 2002). This first form of repentance can turn into an impasse – the hell of guilt (*l'enfer de la culpabilité*), to quote Paul Ricœur

(1969, 140) – or become the beginning of true development. The growing process starts with the sense that one "receives" forgiveness.

The second moment in the evolution towards authentic repentance starts with the sinner realizing that she/he could have acted differently: "I did this, and I could have done it in a better way". All disguise or escape mechanisms stop here. The perpetrator is able to describe the evil done: "This is the abcess". Delineating the mistake and not mincing words is the only way to avoid septicemia and general blood poisoning. At that very moment, the perpetrator makes a fundamental distinction between what she/he *did* wrong and her/his very *being*: "I made a mistake here but that's not who I am".

In a third moment, the victim enters into the self-mirroring world of the perpetrator. "I did this to you. I was unfair towards you. You are stuck with the consequences of what I did. I violated a relationship. You didn't deserve that." The perpetrator now may become aware of the fact that something, which seemed to be a tiny injury has touched a very sensitive nerve of the victim (for example, reopening wounds from her/his early youth). The perpetrator now realizes she/he has to ask for forgiveness, knowing that forgiveness is a gratuitous gift, not something you can claim.

Finally, repentance can get a religious dimension and becomes contrition in the full sense of the word: "I did this also to You, my God". Here the words fault, guilt, or harm turn into "sin". Sinning is the damaging of relationships in a series connection, all the way to God. Thus, the penitent realizes that sin is an inclusive concept: one simultaneously sins against a fellow human being and against God. *"Le sens du péché est corrélatif du sens de Dieu"* (De Clerck 1983, 200). Matthew 25 expresses just that. Experiencing that you also sin against God deepens feelings of guilt in an abyssal way but, at the same time, opens a way out: "I sinned against the One who is nothing but Love". That is why Jankélévitch calls this perfect contrition "the tears of Peter". He refers to Luke 22, 61-62 where Jesus, upon leaving the Sanhedrin, looks lovingly at Peter after having been betrayed by him.

The whole process towards religious contrition demands long-term guidance. The pastor "symbolizes" the process of grace. He or she is an icon of love-in-spite-of for the perpetrator. Only in this way can the sinner heal from his narcissistic wound. The pastor respects confused feelings and grants time so the tale of suffering can become a tale of love. He doesn't jump to a premature absolution. Untimely forgiveness could hinder the process of deepening of contrition. The pastor also tries to prevent the victim from giving forgiveness too soon. It could turn into a "power pardon" (*pardon-pouvoir*) with a claim of ethical superiority ("Do you see how I give you forgiveness?"): that humiliates and blocks the perpetrator. Time is needed. Sin is a process and so is contrition. Louis-Marie Chauvet emphasizes the importance of the time factor with the sacrament of reconciliation. Scholastic theologians have pointed out that contrition is grace. Today we see it as a part of the sacramental process that allows the sinner to built up and get a new identity through renewed relationships. This requires time and guidance.

6.2. From admitting guilt towards the confession of sin

Confession cannot be separated from contrition or penance.
Admitting guilt is the first step. Confessing is a more relational and thus "corporeal" process. Confessing is a "signifier", an embodiment of contrition: "*offrir un corps a la contrition*". In principle, evil is confessed to the victim and forgiveness is asked from her or him directly. This can happen in various forms (written or orally) and also with symbols. It is important though that it be done in the "first person": "I did this to you". Writing down one's mistakes on a piece of paper and burning it is not a personal encounter with the victim and takes on the aura of magic.

Confessing is putting oneself in someone's hands and hoping. Confessing evil is being utterly vulnerable. Some people need a lot of time for that. Therapy has shown us how strongly events from the past can interfere. The ability to bluntly confess is grounded in the experience of not being rejected after a confession. On the contrary: "I love you much more after this unconditional story of your mistake". Growing towards an honest confession is a process. It's preferable that the spiritual guide gives the penitent time. It can occur that the victim grows towards forgiveness and reconciliation sooner than the perpetrator and longs to give it. On the other hand, it is hard for the perpetrator to make an honest confession if he/she suspects that the victim isn't willing to forgive. Strangely, a co-dependency between victim and perpetrator is shown here. Certain situations require a mediator. He or she acts as a third person, a negotiator in the meeting of victim and perpetrator. Why can this not be part of the "job description" of the pastor?

If the victim forgives (and the perpetrator has made restitution for most of the damage), then Scripture allows us to believe that God also forgives. "Truly I say to you, whatever things you may bind on earth will be things bound in heaven and whatever things you may loose on earth will be things loosed in heaven" (Matthew 18, 18). Here, admitting guilt/sin receives its full significance as confession. In Latin, *confessio* has a double meaning: confessing that one is a sinner and at the same time professing God's mercy: "He loved us first" (1 John 4, 11). This profession of the *gratia praeveniens* allows the sinner to confess.

However, sometimes confessing in front of the victim is unattainable because an encounter is impossible. Either the victim is unwilling or the perpetrator can't take a confrontation or confessing would hurt an unknowing partner too much... Is this another deadlock?

6.3. Penance: from restoring to reconciling

To my surprise, while searching for the different translations of the Dutch word *boeten* ("to do penance" in our context) I found an English play on words, which also exists in Dutch. *Boeten* means to repair. Fishermen "repair" their nets with big needles (*boetijzers* in Dutch). And there a specific word for this activity: "to mend nets". And "to amend for" is an equivalent of "to make reparation for". Even if it demands some linguistic acrobatics, it is very significant, and it avoids the masochistic connotations of doing penance. To do penance means to repair a broken net(work), broken relationships. It has no link with "soothing an angry God".
Penance is one more step in the process of embodying contrition and confession: "*offrir un corps à la contrition et à la confession*". Not that contrition and confession can be seen as "finished articles" which only need to be "clothed" with a corpse. Contemporary philosophy teaches us that it is an integrative process. In the restoration of relationships itself (penance), contrition and confession "take place" and are fully born.

Penance has a double orientation: towards the past and the future. Towards the past, penance means repairing the damage, for example, material damage. However, it also includes some more complex tasks such as taking into consideration - if necessary with a third person as a negotiator - the reasons and prejudices that caused the conflict. Such a restoring act is at the same time oriented towards the future. It is a turning-point in order to avoid making the same mistakes again or becoming addicted to them. Roger Burggraeve points out that this kind of penance can take on radical forms: moving, changing jobs, breaking off some relations, and searching for a more supporting social environment (Burggraeve 2000, 289).

Again, long-lasting pastoral accompaniment is needed. It also means that pastors have to approve and to cooperate with new governmental initiatives regarding restorative justice (Haers 1997). Pastoral care can include actual conflict negotiation in line with Matthew 18, for example, in feuds between parents and children, in marital conflicts, or where a last will is an attempt to take revenge beyond death. Professional behavior from the pastor is a condition to function in a position of "multidirected partiality". The concept occupies a central place in Nagy's contextual therapy. This means that the pastor attempts to understand the position of the victim (and her/his surroundings) as well as the position of the perpetrator and thus avoids a unilateral polarizing partiality, where every negotiation shipwrecks (Boszormenyi-Nagy 1986). Pastors have a spontaneous tendency to feel for the victim. But perpetrators can also be victims: victims of their past but also of the fact that they have a hard time forgiving themselves – even after contrition and confession. Diagnosing and counseling this is not a task for an amateur but for a trained pastor.

The concept of penance is enriched by this all. The concept of (Mc Donald's) fast penance (three Our Fathers and ten Hail Marys) becomes questionable. One can argue that such a condensed (i.e., almost "figurative") penance symbolizes the over-abundance of God's undeserved mercy, but we think it is a rather acrobatic theology. There is a high risk of minimizing guilt: "It's all over, I'm free…".

In this context, it becomes clear that, liturgically, we would prefer penance to take place before the absolution (the sealing of reconciliation in the Church community). We go back to the first millennium for that, the time of the canonical and the tariff penance. A liturgy like that is meaningful on the anthropological level as well. The "body" too has its own exigencies: one wants to "do" something in order to receive forgiveness. Changing the order of the sacramental reconciliation includes spreading out the liturgy itself. The time period between Ash Wednesday and Holy Thursday could offer beautiful liturgical support to that process.

However, one question remains: If one can do penance for all the evil done, isn't there always something that remains, a residue, after every harmful act that can in no way be repaired?

6.4. Absolution: from forgiveness to reconciliation

"Grace is like *manna*", writes L.-M. Chauvet. In Hebrew, *manna* means: "What is this? Where does it come from?" *Manna* is gratuitous; it is not situated within the commercial circuit. No one can claim it; no one can store it (Exodus 16, 15-19). *Manna* is "grace as a question, grace as a non-thing, grace as non-value" (Chauvet 1995, 45). Forgiveness is *manna*. The perpetrator can hope for a new future, has to work on it, but exactly in the hoping and restoring, dawns forgiveness from "elsewhere" and it opens a new future. Even if the perpetrator has done everything to do penance for his evil, forgiveness is not a right. It cannot be merited. There is no "law of reciprocity" regarding forgiveness (Burggraeve 2000, 290).

Manna falls whenever people forgive each other wholeheartedly, repair the damage and reconcile. Their growing towards each other is 'absolution'. There is no need for an official church minister. God forgives in the process of reconciliation. God is at work, incognito but effectively, in the interplay of contrition, confession, penance by the perpetrator and forgiveness by the victim, without any remains.

However, the process does not always evolve without remains. Penance, yes, but how do you heal the pain the victim underwent during the conflict? It's a sediment of suffering that cannot be taken away. Given the fact that repeated painful conflicts leave their marks on a relationship, even after forgiveness. Scratches on a friendship. In some cases, (at least a part of) the damage cannot be repaired. Receiving forgiveness is not easy either. In some cases, the perpetrator goes through the whole process of contrition, confession, and penance, and asks the victim for forgiveness. His or her request doesn't get an answer. Or it cannot get an answer because the victim passed away. Complete reconciliation, meaning, according to Jean Monbourquette, that the relationship is completely restored, is rather rare. Some relationships may not recommence, for example, after incest. In other cases, the relationship cannot return to its original form (for example, when the partner has remarried). Yet, attempting to restore the relationship, be it in another form, is an essential Christian value.

We pointed out earlier that the loss of a personal relationship with God caused the evaporation of the sense of sin. If sin can be described as a kind of breaking relations in a series circuit right up to God, as we did earlier, if sacraments essentially consist of a renewal of our Christian identity in an ecclesial context, if contrition emerges from the consciousness that a relationship is damaged, if forgiving is stimulated by the remembrances of the many times we have been pardoned in the past, if penance means mending net(work)s, and if the covenant is finally restored by Christ's death, then how can we not consider reconciliation as a Christian ideal?

"Forgiveness is often possible, reconciliation sometimes not", says Jean Monbourquette. The practice of pastoral care teaches us that we often have to settle for what is possible. Paul Ricœur calls it "le meilleur humain possible": a road between what is ideal and what is humanly possible at this time. The challenge is to keep an eye on the ideal and the other on the human being in front of you and to go for the optimum, even if it is not the maximum (Ricœur 1968, 26). Irreparable sediment and remains may provoke a perpetrator's despair. And we did not even mention the unbearable feeling of guilt a human being can carry towards God.

The intervention of the community of the faithful is a matter of life and death in these desperate cases. A mediator is needed, someone who officially represents God and the community at the same time. She/he acts in a vicarious or a substitutive manner. The mediation of the minister is grounded in the mediating role of Christ. It is founded on the 'for-you dimension' of the Last Supper: "Take this and eat it, this is my body, broken for you. Take the cup: this is my blood, poured out on behalf of many for forgiveness of sins." Matthew 25 represents Christ as the substitutive victim. However, this is but one side of the coin. He is also the Redeemer. In the liturgy of sacramental reconciliation, this aspect is expressed in the absolution: "... through the death and resurrection of his Son ... for the forgiveness of sins".

Sometimes people think that the evil done disappears through absolution. I don't think so. There is no magic removal of the consequences of an evil act. Sacramental reconciliation includes a grieving process over an unchangeable past which cannot be wiped away in too fast a rite. But this is not the aim of the sacrament of reconciliation. Sacraments are not magic. Sacramental reconciliation brings about or processes a change in the relationship of the perpetrator towards his/her evil. The perpetrator is torn away from the ballast of his/her irreparable past (*ab-solvere*). He/she is not chained to a paralyzing past anymore. The process of de-tachment takes place by a process of re-tachment with Christ. Sacraments aim at a renewed identity through restoring and strengthening relationships. That is reconciliation in its fullest meaning. This is not a question of successive stages. In the relationship with God, forgiveness (detachment from the past) and reconciliation (restoring the relation) do not happen in a chronological way. It is an interplay – or even a "coinciding": forgiveness happens in and through contrition-reconciliation. Referring to what we wrote above: Grace does not belong to a commercial circuit of reciprocity. The only "law" applicable here is the superabundance of God's Love. Paul Ricœur writes: "*En lui [le pardon] se découvre toute l'étendue de ce qu'on peut appeler l'économie du don, si l'on caractérise celle-ci par la logique de surabondance qui distingue l'amour de la logique de la réciprocité de la justice*" (Ricœur 1998, 198) The new identity consists of the fact that a human being may live because she or he is child of God, *despite* a lot of evil, even better: *because* of a lot of evil. A strange propensity of our God.

Therefore the sacramental absolution formula is performative ("I Absolve you from your sins in the name of the Father, and of the Son, and of the Holy Spirit") and not imploring or invoking ("May God forgive you..."). It is regrettable that the text isn't reversed: "In the name of the Father, and of the Son, and the Holy Spirit, I absolve you from your sins". Doing this makes the necessary condition of possibility of reconciliation before forgiveness clearer. It would also express that the pastor is only a substitute and that pastor and sinner are standing together under a Third Party: the forever re-creating Spirit.

In normal circumstances, God uses human interventions and mediators (we forgive each other). In extraordinary circumstances – in impasses - God shows us how much greater He is than human emergencies. In exceptional situations, God acts with authority through his authoritative representatives. He liberates the remorseful sinner, even when the victim is unwilling to forgive. It's called *manna*, grace.

7. Pastoral and liturgical consequences

The strategic proposals we sketched above have some consequences "on the bias". The sacrament of reconciliation *sensu stricto* is not a weekly or monthly event. Sacramental reconciliation is a very deep and therefore a rather exceptional event of grace.

The sacramental seal is not an instant or "punctual" event. It is the crown on a process of accompaniment through phases of remorse, contrition, confession, and penance. The care is given by professionals on a relational (c.q. therapeutic) and religious level. If pastors are not capable, a *tandem care* between a pastor and a therapist is preferable.

In this context, it doesn't seem necessary for the perpetrator to retell (with number and circumstances) the whole story in the sacramental reconciliation to the priest. This is done only if she/he needs to. If it means reopening the wounds, it would be in contradiction with the Gospel. In other cases, the priest can, after the whole process, seal the process and lay hands on both perpetrator and caregiver (pastor or therapist) with a clear conscience. He can, in the name of the relational God, signify and express de-tachment (absolution) and be a sign of it. Then it will be a liberating rather than a humiliating confession.
This means that the churches need to make serious investments in training therapists to collaborate with pastors and to make them conscious of the religious dimension of evil and sin. On the other hand, pastors also need to be trained in counseling and negotiating in conflicts.

It is meaningful to integrate sacramental reconciliation in the liturgical time of Lent between Ash Wednesday and Holy Thursday. The readings of the Sundays in Lent provide many openings for that. It is also the setting in which to do penance before absolution.

Many people today are very creative in finding new symbols and rituals to deal with failures. Some of them are very useful in the liturgy of reconciliation (for example: priest and perpetrator hold hands in streaming water at the time of the absolution). Some of them are useful at home (for example, lighting the wedding candle at the time of a conflict).

It is very meaningful to have celebrations of reconciliation in parishes in Advent or Lent. They are able to take care of the *"accidents de parcours"*, the smaller accidents on the path of life. And we think that's a good opportunity. But a life-orientating confession won't take place there. Life re-orientation requires long-term accompaniment and professional spiritual guidance. This could be a real challenge for the places of pilgrimage in our regions. Multidisciplinary teams could work together and take care of reconciliation. Those places of pilgrimage could become sites of advanced pastoral care.

Follow-up demands special attention. It is not only the task of an individual caregiver but of the whole faith community. They can prevent relapses.
The above places great demands on pastors. We face a contradictory situation today. Priests have sufficient theological and ecclesial formation, but they lack education on a relational and therapeutic level. Lay chaplains are very capable on a relational and therapeutic level, but often lack theological, spiritual, and ecclesial background. Again, we would like to stress the importance of teaming up and *tandem care*. To put it in a too lapidary manner: *Dieu a besoin des hommes* (God needs human beings) (Queffélec 1964)…and kleenex.

And yet… In the process of forgiveness and reconciliation, pastors and the faith communities act with care, counseling, guidance, confrontation, mediation, and restoration. God's forgiveness relies on the healing support of people carrying broken people. And yet God is greater than our sacraments. God doesn't need them to forgive. We do.

References

Basset, L. 1997. *Le pardon originel: de l'abîme du mal au pouvoir de pardonner.* Genève: Labor et Fides.

Basset, L. 1999. *Le pouvoir de pardonner.* Paris: Albin Michel.

Bastiaensen, R. 2000. De dader-slachtoffer tegenstelling in vraag gesteld. *Metanoia* (2): 117-121.

Boff, L. 1987. *Sacraments of Life: Life of the Sacraments.* Washington: Pastoral Press.

Boszormenyi-Nagy, I. 1986. *Between Give and Take: a Clinical Guide to Contextual Therapy.* New York: Brunner-Mazel.

Bourdeau, F. 1982. *La route du pardon. Pèlerinage et réconciliation.* Paris: Cerf.

Burggraeve, R. 2000. Stapstenen naar vergeving en verzoening tussen mensen. *Collationes* 30(3): 269-300.

Chauvet, L.-M. 1979. *Du symbolique au symbole. Essai sur les sacrements*. Paris: Cerf.

Chauvet, L.-M. 1995. *Symbol and Sacrament. A Sacramental Reinterpretation of Christian Existence*. Collegeville: The Liturgical Press.

Clerck, P. de 1983. Vers un quatrième régime pénitentiel? *Communautés et Liturgies* (2).

Demasure, K. 2002. Verhullend spreken bij seksueel misbruik van kinderen. *Tijdschrift voor Theologie* 42(1): 50-72.

Depoortere, K. 1982. *Klei en adem. Over leven, geloven, beminnen en hopen*. Tielt: Lannoo.

Depoortere, K. 1984. *Wij zijn van U met al ons kwaad. Over zonde, verzoening en biecht*. Tielt: Lannoo.

Depoortere, K. 1995. *A Different God. A Christian View on Suffering*. Leuven-Chicago: Peeters. Revised version 2000: *God anders. Een christelijke visie op het lijden*. Leuven: Acco.

Depoortere, K. 2000. From Sacramentality to Sacraments and Vice-Versa. *Questions Liturgiques. Studies in Liturgy* 82(1): 46-57.

Durwell, F.-X. 1971. *L'eucharistie, présence du Christ*. Paris: Les Editions Ouvrières.

Greshake, G. 1986. Extreme unction or Anointing of the Sick? A Plea for Discrimination. *Review for Religious* 45: 435-452.

Haers, J. 1977. Close encounters of the Third "Week". Enkele voorzichtige theologische overwegingen n.a.v. een gesprek over herstel en strafbemiddeling. Metanoia 4(1): 58-80.

Hostie, R. 1966. *Pastoral Counseling*, New York, 1966.

Jankélévitch, V. 1933. *La mauvaise conscience*. Paris: Alcan.

Kitamori, K. 1966. *Theology of the Pain of God*: London: SCM.

Knippenberg, T. van 1998: *Between Two Languages*. Tilburg: Tilburg University Press.

Knippenberg, T. van 2000 (second edition). *Tussen naam en identiteit. Ontwerp van een model voor geestelijke begeleiding*. Kampen: Kok.

Knobloch, S. 1996. *Praktische Theologie. Ein Lehrbuch für Studium und Pastoral*. Freiburg: Herder.

Kushner, H. 1981. *When Bad Things Happen to Good People*. New York: Schocken Books.

Lascaris, A. 1999. *Neem uw verleden op. Over vergelding en vergeving*. Baarn-Tielt: Lannoo.

Monbourquette, J. 1994. Processus thérapeutique et démarche du pardon. *Pastoral Sciences* 13: 25-54.

Monbourquette, J. 2000. *How to forgive: a step-by-step guide*. Ottawa: Novalis.

Monden, L. 1965. *Sin, Liberty and Law*. New York: Sheed and Ward.

Nouwen, H. 1981. *The Living Reminder. Service and Prayer in Memory of Jesus Christ.* New York: Seabury Press.

Pohier, J. 1977. Le péché à quoi ça sert?. *Le Supplément* 120-121.

Queffelec, H. 1964. *Un recteur de l'île de Sein.* Paris: Livres de Poche.

Ricœur, P. 1968. Sens et fonction d'une communauté ecclésiale. *Cahiers du Centre Protestant de Recherche et de Rencontres du Nord* 26.

Ricœur, P. 1969. *The Symbolism of Evil.* New York: Harper & Row.

Ricœur, P. 1999. Mémoire, oubli, pardon. In : *La religion, les maux, les vices,* edited by A. Houziaux. Paris.

Vergote, A. 1988. *Guilt and Desire: Religious Attitudes and their Pathological Derivatives.* New Haven: Yale University Press.

Vogel, C. 1982. *Le pécheur et la pénitence au Moyen Age.* Paris: Cerf.

Vogel, C. 1982. *Le pécheur et la pénitence dans l'Eglise ancienne.* Paris: Cerf.

Asymmetric Expectations of Church-leaders and Media-Professionals

Ernest Henau

In his inaugural address "Borderlines: the Pastoral Theologians' Workplace", Tjeu van Knippenberg posited that the workplace of theology is on the marchland between the Christian message and the ever-changing situation. This is equally true of practical theological reflection on the media's potential as an avenue of proclamation. This, too, is a marchland in which the communicator moves between content and form, between the expectations of church leaders and those of the audience. This article examines a problem with which Tjeu van Knippenberg, as member of the Dutch KRO's Advisory Council for Programming, would be familiar: how can justice be done to the legitimate expectations of both the church's leadership and media professionals? The first part of this article addresses the church's problematic instrumental view of the media. It then shows how this vision runs a foul of audience expectations as revealed by research. Finally, it argues the need for a change of perspective on the side of the church and on that of producers.

1. The Instrumental View of the Media

Christianity is very closely entwined with media. From its earliest days, the letter was used as a means to communicate the faith. And the reformation would have been unthinkable without the contemporaneous development of printing. But here, too, lie the roots of the church's ambivalent attitude toward the media, which was so characteristic of later developments. Both the book and the more modern media were looked upon with suspicion and their arrival was met with distrust. (Schmolke 1993). At the same time, there was awareness that the media could also be used to spread the gospel message. This last conviction led to the predominantly instrumental understanding, which is characteristic of the church leadership, as reflected in numerous official documents (Mediathec 1990; Eilers 1997). One familiar example of this is the frequently recurring quotation from Paul VI's 1975 apostolic exhortation *Evangelii nuntiandi* (Evangelisation in the Modern World) in which the media are depicted as an extension of the pulpit. *"The Church would feel guilty before the Lord if she did not utilize this powerful means that human skill is daily rendering more perfect. It is through them that she proclaims 'from the housetops' the message of which she is the depositary. In them she finds a modern and effective version of the pulpit. Thanks to them she succeeds in speaking to the multitudes"* (Eilers 1997, 319).

This instrumental view of the media and the expectations related to it are still present in the attitudes of church leaders, albeit in a milder and more qualified form. By way of illustration, we could refer here to an article by bishop Crispian Hollis of Portsmouth (Chairman of the European bishops' committee for the media) in *The Tablet*. In this article, which is revealingly entitled, "The Media as Pulpit", he states: *"Radio and television give us privileged access to the intimacy of people's lives and homes so that we are often actually talking and sharing our faith person to person, if not face to face. But we have to learn the skills to be able to speak that Word in an intensely personal way so that it can be seen to flow from the living of our faith and from our loving commitment to God. We use the mass media to speak the Word but it comes, in a typically Christian paradox, unseen yet powerfully, to individuals, telling each of them to share God's life"* (Hollis 1745).

In the literature, authors have tried to demonstrate that the attitude of the church's leadership toward the media depends on the model of the church that is espoused (Thorn 1996). In past years, the American theologian Avery Dulles examined the documents of Vatican II for potential triggers for a "communicating" church. In line with his principle work *Models of the Church* (Dulles 1978), he distinguishes five different models: the 'hierarchical-institutional model' the 'herald, sacramental and communion or community models' and the 'secular-dialogic model'. These models need not exclude one another, but studies show that the hierarchical model predominates. And this induces a particular view of communication: "Most of the communication within the Catholic Church appears to be a one-way, top-down, monological process. Communication in the Church is largely through pastoral letters, so-called 'guidelines', sometimes even 'orders' to be obeyed from above. These are often passed down as the Will of God for the faithful, based on unilateral interpretation of scriptures, traditions and teachings of the Church by those in authority. They are monological not only in their style of communication, but also in their process of formation" (Emmanuel 1999).

2. Audience expectations

This type of ecclesiological approach and the associated communication model ignores one of the most important patterns governing this closed system of communication: selective exposure. "Whether the viewer or listener 'exposes' him- or herself to a religious message, depends on his or her relation to the source of the communication. In general, religion elicits ambivalent feelings. It fascinates but also repels. Those who are dismissive of, or indifferent to, faith and religion do not watch, or listen to, religious programmes. And when they do watch sporadically or by chance, it does not mean that they perceive all that is communicated" (Henau 2002, 187). Church documents do indeed show that the proclamation religious messages are tacitly put first in the media. No one asks what the audience really expects; all eyes are focussed exclusively on the theoretical potential. Because media professionals do want to take these patterns into account, an asymmetric relation arises between the expectations of the church's leadership and those of religious programme producers. To explain this, we will use the results of a study carried out by the head of the, then, BRTN (public broadcaster of the Flemish community in Belgium), in cooperation with KTRO (Catholic Broadcast Organisation, Brussels). [1] This study included a qualitative component based on sixteen in-depth interviews and a measured examination of the perception of and the expectations regarding religious television. Further on in this article, we will limit ourselves to the results of the quantitative study, more particularly to the part that assesses the audience's view of what is called the "ideal religious television programme". The respondents were presented with a series of statements such as "The ideal religious programme is a programme..." and then they could accept or reject the theme that completed the statement. This is the result:

General Profile of the Ideal Religious Television Programme

Statements where the respondent agreed (completely)	Total	18-34 age group	35-54 age group	55-65 age group
(percentages)				
N =	240	93	98	48
The ideal religious programme is a programme ...				
that treats general social and human questions	94	96	94	92
that deals with average people	88	88	89	83
that leaves room for personal interpretation	83	83	85	77
that allows all views on a subject to be expressed	81	85	81	77
that sets me thinking	80	76	81	83
where other religions also have a place	74	73	78	67
that speaks about life in modern society	73	73	73	71
that treats religious themes critically and independently	72	73	72	67
in which no taboo is side-stepped	70	70	73	63
that is also addressed to non-believers	69	72	69	63
that emanates a clear commitment	68	62	71	71
that helps me to understand my conviction better	68	66	62	81
in which the family is in the forefront	65	56	77	60
that speaks more about Christian values than about the church	63	65	59	67
that lets me measure my convictions against those of others	62	54	65	71
that stimulates me in my conviction	60	52	59	75
that has appealing witnesses about believers	60	54	57	79
that combines information and entertainment	58	61	57	54
that helps me to hone my own conviction	58	55	57	69
that educates the viewer	57	48	57	71
than can move me emotionally	54	39	60	71

[1] This study was carried out by the "Centre for Systematic Diagnostics and Marketing" (Censydiam) in Antwerp. One of the results was a report entitled: Measured Research into the Perception and Expectations on Religion in Broadcasting in General and the KTRO in particular, Antwerp 1994.

that offers me certainty in today's chaotic world	51	35	59	63
that gives me the courage to go on	48	42	44	65
that sticks to Catholic traditions	40	31	39	58
that focuses strictly on the proclamation of the "gospel message"	39	25	38	69
that helps me to understand the bible	36	32	33	52
that "convinces" people, tries to "convert"	18	13	16	29

This table shows that the ideal religious programme must have a social and societal tenor, that it must leave room for the viewer's own opinion and for discussion and that it must confront other philosophies and religions. Of course, it is also important for our question to note which items receive low scores: 40% think that the programme should stick to Catholic traditions. 32% think that it should preach the gospel message. 36% think that it should help people to understand the Bible and 18% believe that the ideal programme should convince, i.e. try to convert, people. In sum: the ideal programme is a broadly social and societal programme based on a Christian inspiration. It examines social, ethical and religious themes critically. It should not stick strictly to Catholic traditions. It should not try to preach and convert. The study shows that there are differences between the young respondents under age thirty-four and older respondents between ages fifty-five and sixty-five. For the younger viewers, the ideal religious program has a broader and more social and societal orientation. For the older audience it is a more traditional and sheltering programme that speaks to the emotions.

What specific items should have a place in this ideal religious program?

Items that Should be Treated (Very) Frequently

(percentages)	Total	18-34 age group	35-54 age group	55-65 age group
N =	240	93	98	48
elucidation of general social themes	75	83	69	69
reports on many types of praiseworthy projects	66	63	66	69
portrayals of how average people experience their faith	60	56	63	63
elucidation of ethical themes	53	51	57	48
insight into the person behind the church official	40	39	43	35
broadcast of eucharistic celebrations	39	20	40	71
interviews with religious and philosophers	38	39	36	38
religious music (church choirs...)	37	27	39	52
introduction to other religions	36	41	31	38
specialists who speak about the meaning of faith	34	23	33	58
elucidation of strictly religious themes	31	23	28	54
elucidation of biblical figures	30	22	34	40
religious festivals	28	23	26	44
artistic, cultural and historical aspects of religious architecture	25	27	20	33
the lives of persons significant in the church	23	20	21	31
preaching the faith	22	11	19	48
reviewing religious publications	20	15	21	27
reviewing church documents	16	11	16	23

Here again the general social themes have high scores (75%). Other items considered important are: reports on all types of praiseworthy projects (66%), themes relating to how average people experience their faith (60%) and ethical subjects (53%). Among the items with the lowest scores are: cultural and historical aspects of religious architecture (25%), life's of significant church figures (23%), preaching of the faith (22%), reviews of religious publication (20%) and church documents (16%). Here again there is a difference between those under age thirty-four and those in the fifty-five – sixty-five age group. Specific religious items score lower among young people and higher among older people.

These research findings are confirmed by the viewing figures for religious programmes. While most of these programmes in Europe obtain figures between one and two percent, *Kruispunt* (a programme broadcast by the Dutch KRO) has an average of four to five percent (700.000 to 800.000 viewers). [2] A closer examination of the items in this programme immediately shows that it treats mainly the subjects that scored best in the study cited above: human interest, interesting projects, etc. [3] However, the bishops (who commission the programme) are not satisfied with this success because, in their view, too little attention is given to strictly church-related items. In the opinion of the church leaders, the programme lacks sufficient witness. Moreover, these broadcasts also offer a podium for people who often agitate against the church's positions. Here we face a classic case of asymmetric expectations between two groups, each with their own (inalienable) responsibility: church leaders and media professionals (Grond 2001). The latter consider themselves to be journalists in the first place, and not preachers or apologists. They will thus exercise objectivity and will act in accordance with the practices that govern the media (for instance, the above-mentioned selective exposure of viewers. And so they will consider the expectations of these latter very important. And this attitude is reinforced by recent developments in the media in which viewer ratings and market shares have become the most important factors. The religious programme producer (certainly within a general broadcaster) cannot ignore this, because the programme's place in the broadcast schedule depends on the number of viewers or the market share.

---

[2] NOS Audience Research, Information and Advice Department, postbox 26444; NL-1202 JJ Hilversum, The Netherlands.
[3] Bal, M. and T. Crijnen. 1999. De kijkcijfers van Kruispunt. Scoren met een kerkelijk programma, *Trouw* 14.; Oudejans, F. 1999. Religieuze TV met een hoog treurigheidsgehalte, *De Bazuin* 17, 22-24.; Pekelder, W. 1999. *Het geheim van Kruispunt.*

3. How is Religion Represented in the Media?

To find a solution to this dilemma, we must first ask why public broadcasters give broadcast time (and a large amount of it, at least in The Netherlands) to churches and religious communities. First a distinction must be made between religion as cultural and social phenomenon on one side, and broadcasts in which the message of one or other church community is put forward under the aegis of that same church community. In the first case, the presence of religion can be based on the fact that being religious is one of the most fundamental characteristics of humanity. When the media want to address all facets of being human, they cannot restrict themselves solely to entertainment. They must also provide information and education, and religion and church belong to these domains. For instance, to the extent that Christianity is the cultural-ethical substratum of our civilisation, it will be impossible to ignore biblical and Christian faith in many types of historical and cultural programmes. And to the extent that this faith still inspires people today and that this inspiration becomes visible in word and deed, it is still newsworthy and thus has a place in informative programmes.

However, the second way that religion is present rests on totally different considerations. This presupposes the argument that a society needs interpretive and value systems that are rooted essentially in faith and tradition, systems that cannot be created by a government (Henau 2000). Because of the separation of church and state, a pluralistic state cannot become identified with any faith, current or movement. It is never the state of one party or of one particular religion or philosophy. The government in a pluralistic state can never dogmatise attitudes toward ethical or religious questions or political theories. That the state has no religion or conviction is the price to be paid for, and is the negative aspect of, religious freedom. This means that the state is neither atheistic nor religious. This type of neutrality or institutional agnosticism is defined on the basis of the concept "abstention". That is why Ricoeur speaks in this context of "la laïcité de l'abstention" (Ricoeur 195,194). But beside the state there is also the phenomenon of civil society. And this, according to Ricoeur, is dynamic, active and polemical. It exists thanks to the public discussion between what Mark Elchardus calls the various "communities of discourse" in our society (Elchardus 1996). From this perspective, it is evident that the church and other philosophical communities should be present in the media.

But the church is a very specific community of discourse and it is only from this specificity that it can make its own contribution to the discussion that is essential for our own pluralistic society. This specificity is inseparably bound with the person of Jesus of Nazareth. Christians are people who refer Jesus of Nazareth as the Christ and who are willing to accept the value pattern that Jesus lived as normative for their lives. We only know this Jesus from the tradition that speaks of Him as the Christ. And the community of believers, which precedes every individual belief, buttresses this tradition. All of Christian faith has an ecclesial dimension, because it can only arise from the given faith that it receives from the Christian community and then contributes back to the same community. As community of discourse, the church knows it is bound to normative narratives and to the binding consensus interpretations that have arisen from continuous discussion. Within the community of believers there is also an agency (magisterium) whose duty is to ensure that the community today preserves its contact with the original narratives and the resulting presentations, which have been deposited in the Scriptures and the history of their explanation. Given this (theological) description, proclamation is the first duty of the community of believers. And this also has consequences for the latter's presence in the media. For a large part, the programmes – in the broad sense – will have to have a proclamatory character. In substance, the church's task remains the same, regardless of the context in which it must be carried out. It would seem that we are confronted here by two irreconcilable basic principles: on one side the leadership of the church community (which focuses above all on the message) and on the other the media professionals (who focus primarily on the audience). It is only possible to break this deadlock when both groups are willing to change their perspective. The last part of the article will address this point.

4. The Need for a Change in Perspective

Even when one is critical of the instrumental view of the media, which is characteristic of the church leadership, it will be necessary to share its concern for the explicit presentation of the Christian message. This concern is not only prompted by the Christian religious conviction, which necessarily results in proclamation: "Woe to me if I do not preach the gospel" (1 Corinthians 9,16). It also has to do with the legal grounds on which the church has access to the public broadcasting system. As was said, the government expects church communities to make their own inalienable contribution to the structure of civil society, which exists just thanks to the presence of the various communities of discourse. Religious programmes that present nothing more than what the general media also present, namely broadcasts on religion as cultural or social phenomenon, or documentaries on human-interest themes without explicit religious reference, undermines their reason for being. This need for explicit reference is also related to the essence of Christianity as the distinction between general religiosity and Christian faith. For even those who are not proponents of a radical distinction between faith and religion will have to admit that the transition from general religiosity to Christian faith presupposes a qualitative leap. The first case deals with an indeterminate sense of being rooted in a mystery that transcends and that we call God. This mystery reveals itself in the cosmos and in our deepest selves. But Christian faith is based not only on the idea that God is revealed in the cosmos and in ourselves, but above all in history: more specifically in the history of the people of Israel and in a definitive and unsurpassable manner in the figure of Jesus of Nazareth.

These insights (the legal grounds for being present in the media and the theological insights just expressed) lead to the church leadership's preference for explicit Christian and markedly proclamatory programmes. However, they must not forget that the media professionals usually start from other, equally legitimate considerations, prompted by their knowledge and experience. They are acutely aware of the, often, obsolete character of Christian language. They are probingly confronted with the fact that the Christian message is frequently at odds with what society considers obvious. As is evident from the study on what is expected of religious programmes, we know (at least intuitively) that our contemporaries prefer an a-dogmatic and socio-ethical religiosity. From their journalistic ethos, media professionals want to be objective, even when they produce programmes that are under the direct responsibility of the church leadership. They want to offer a forum for very diverse opinions, especially when controversial subjects are treated. For the sake of their credibility, they see themselves as more than the church leadership's megaphone. In their view, that is the task of spokesmen and press officers.

The church leaders will have to understand that all this leads to a more indirect and inductive method of "preaching". They will have to realise that because of the laws of the medium television, for instance, preference will have to be given to the portrayal of discernable experiences at the cost of direct proclamatory elements. When extensive broadcast time is available, as in The Netherlands, this can be more easily permitted, because there can also be programmes that are directly and explicitly proclamatory. But it will have to be accepted as part of the package that there will be fewer viewers for such broadcasts. It is also important for church leaders to realise that an open journalistic attitude need not necessarily lead to polarisation. Openness and criticism do not always mean that differences of opinion are driven to their extremes. Openness can also mean a fair and professional meeting, a satisfying of the need for information, a willingness to avoid sweeping differences under the carpet. When the endeavour to reach harmony arises from a need for mutual understanding, then this is a praiseworthy objective. But harmony can never be the result of concealing unpleasant aspects or obscuring or withholding any information. The price that will have to be paid for this is too high.

Programme producers will always have to remember that all attempts to attract the greatest possible number of viewers poses a danger that is particularly specific to television: "The problem for religious broadcasting is that in order to survive it may be forced to compromise some of the more traditional and thoughtful aspects of its broadcast content" (Harrison 2000, 11). Paradoxically enough, it is this attempt at survival that could lead to the downfall of religious programmes. They would then no longer comply with the legal grounds that justify their presence in the public broadcasting system as the most important forum for the public debate that is so essential for democracy.

Apart from the more legal questions of the grounds for the existence of religious programmes, there is also a problem of content. "Over-concentration on the criteria of relevance as being the key to attracting large audiences may predefine topics in a way which means that some important dimensions of religious affairs, which are not necessarily relevant to the majority, are in danger of being ignored because they are not perceived to be fitting into people's existing horizons. Religious programming needs to educate and expand viewers' horizons and not simply resort to showing what is either familiar or experiential" (Harrison 2000, 11). In the ideal situation in which the change of perspective, for which we argue, takes place, the media professionals are given the most difficult task. Here their creativity comes into play. If they are to produce explicitly proclamatory and witnessing programmes in addition to their "human interest" programmes, they will not be able to start from the question "what does the public want". They will also have to be aware "that the public has no idea what it wants until it sees it". [4]

References

Dulles, A. 1978. *Models of the Church*. New York: Doubleday.

Eilers, F.-J. 1997. *Church and Social Communication: Basic Documents*. Manila: Logos.

Elchardus, M. 1996. Complexiteit en diversiteit bewaren: waarden, vertooggemeenschappen en media. In *Media en Spiritualiteit*, edited by S. Bleeker and others. Leuven.

Emmanuel, D. 1999. *Challenges of Christian Communication and Broadcasting: Monologue or Dialogue*. London: MacMillan Press LTD.

Grond, A. 2001. Dichter bij de ziel dan de AEX-index: Gods come-back in de media. *De Bazuin* 16 november, 16-19.

Harrison, J. 2000. A Review of Religious Broadcasting on British Television. *Modern Believing* 41, 3-15.

Henau, E. 2000. De aanwezigheid van kerk en religie in de media. Een pastoraaltheologische benadering. *Collationes* 30, 315-328.

Henau, E. 2002. Religious Broadcasting and the construction of a just society. Pp. 185-196 in *Divine Justice - Human Justice*, edited by J.S. Dreyer and J.A. van der Ven. Pretoria.

---

[4] Quotation from David Liddiment, cited in B. McCarthy in "Can TV Get its Spark Back" *The Tablet* 8 September 2001, 1260.

Hollis, C. The Media as Pulpit. *The Tablet*, 1745.

McCarthy, B. 2001. Can TV Gets its Spark Back. *The Tablet* 8 september 2001, 1260.

Médiathec. 1990. *Les médias: Textes des Eglises réunis et présentés par le group Médiatec de la Faculté de Théologie de Lyon.* Paris: Centurion.

Ricoeur, P. 1995. *La critique et la conviction. Entretiens aves François Assouvi et Marc de Launay.* Paris: Calmann-Lévy.

Schmolke, M. 1993. Kirchliche Kommunikation in der entwickelten Kommunikationsgesellschaft. *Communicatio Socialis* 26, 26-37.

Thorn, W. 1996. Models of Church and Communication. In *Media, Culture and Catholicism*, edited by P.A. Soukup. Kansas.

The Pastor on the Boundary of Biography and Profession
The Courage to Continue

Sjaak Körver

Introduction

In his collection *Auf der Grenze* Tillich (1962)[1] opens with a contribution of the same name in which he describes how he has continually found himself both personally and professionally in boundary zones. He describes the way in which he lives on the boundary of the temperaments of his father and mother, how being in the boundary areas of city and country and of various social classes has influenced him. He also shows how he has coped in his life and work with the boundary between reality and imagination, how essential it has been for him to work on the boundary of theory and practice. He shows clearly how he struggled on the boundary between heteronomy and autonomy and how this has influenced his work. He also searches for his position on the boundary between theology and philosophy, on the boundary of church and society, on the boundary of religion and culture, on the boundary of Lutheranism and socialism, of idealism and Marxism and finally on the boundary of native country and being a stranger. In effect Tillich describes the development of his way of thinking from and in relation to his biography, and he discovers that the concept *boundary* is the most fitting symbol with which to describe his personal and professional development. Tillich quotes from earlier work: "The boundary is actually the most fertile place in which to gain knowledge" (Tillich 1930). He discovers this insight as a personal truth that he in turn is able to trace out in his scientific career. At the same time he also formulates this insight as the task for the (practical) theologian. It is this insight that has become (and still is!) the source of inspiration for Tjeu van Knippenberg during his academic career. This is clear from the speech he made on entering his office of professor in pastoral theology in Tilburg: "He [Tillich] can be a mirror for pastoral theologians who wish to do justice to the relation between faith and science, between ideal and reality, between the religious and political dimension of existence, between the vocational and professional aspect in pastoral actions" (Van Knippenberg 1989, 6).

---

[1] This publication with various contributions from the work of Tillich was composed on the occasion of the award of the peace prize of the German book trade in 1962. It concerns the introduction (*On the boundary*) from *The Interpretation of History* (Tillich 1936, 2-73).

In fact Tillich describes his *professional biography* in the collection mentioned above. This concept, professional biography, has been formulated by Tjeu van Knippenberg, in his capacity as chairman of the Executive Committee for Clinical Pastoral Education in the Netherlands, as the particular focal point of Clinical Pastoral Education (CPE). In the *Policy Plan 1999 – 2002* of the Committee for Clinical Pastoral Education the general objective of CPE training is indeed specified as: the re-gauging of the actions of the pastor with as particular focal point the relation between person and profession: *the professional biography*. Therefore, the starting point and objective of CPE training are in other words, insight into and reflection on the personal professional history of the pastor, on the interweaving of the biography on the one hand and the motivation to, satisfaction in and identity of the pastoral profession on the other.

The concept *professional biography* is – certainly in the framework of CPE training – extremely useful, for the very reason that it is a *boundary* concept. The concept lends itself for research into, purification of and making more manageable the complex relation between person and profession for the pastor. The same applies also to the relation between vocation and profession and the relation between the individual pastor on the one hand and his organisational framework and social and cultural context on the other. Reflection on the relations mentioned above invite the pastor and the theologian to move in various boundary zones in order to gain new insight and knowledge there. There is the boundary zone where the personal life story of the pastor and his professionalism affect one another. There is the boundary zone where on the one hand one's spirituality and motives meet and on the other professional standards. And there is the boundary zone where the personal motives of the pastor merge with organisational and cultural factors. Reflection is what helps the individual pastor to develop a better view on his or her personal and professional identity and position. It is also reflection that helps the (practical) theologian to produce a theology that is reality conscious and relevant. According to van Knippenberg it is there that the theologian finds himself in his workshop.

Henceforth, I will examine to what extent the concept *professional biography* is a significant contribution from practical theology, for the benefit of the reflections of others, apart from those who practice the pastoral profession, in the framework of the present developments that are taking place in many professions involving people. For this reason I will introduce a case involving the supervision of a manager from the health care sector. I place this case against the background of the analysis made by the American sociologist Richard Sennett who observes a number of – alarming – developments in work and opinions on work that all have to do with a strong orientation on the short term and with the loss of values that actually only have a chance to develop in the long term. I then ask myself whether the concept *professional biography* is suited to escape from fixation on the short term, and the contribution practical theology can offer with this concept for contemporary culture.

1. The middle manager

This past year I supervised a number of managers from the health care sector. On the hierarchical ladder they were the middle management, caught between strategy and operation, the group of managers threatened most by nervous exhaustion and burnout. The job responsibilities of this group of managers are becoming more and more complex. The expectations, of both senior management and employees, are on the one hand high and on the other strongly susceptible to change. They are expected to put policy and decisions made into practice, which they themselves have ultimately only had a marginal say in, and of which they know in advance that employees will only reluctantly and with passive resistance agree to. They hear complaints and objections from employees that the senior management turn a deaf ear to. They are expected to be some kind of jack-of-all-trades, from coaching employees via the management of budgets, to the marketing of the department product. They often go to pieces under the work pressure, the amount of their span of control and the complex number of tasks involved. Compared to 10 years ago when there were 7 or 8 layers of management within an organisation, nowadays there are only 3 or 4, whereby most of the pressure is on the middle managers. In the past years it is this middle management that has become the outcast in many organisations (Crooijmans 2001; Stoker and de Korte 2000).

This layer in an organisation, the middle management, and the experiences of these middle managers in management itself reflect, as if held under a magnifying glass, a number of developments in our society. The personal search and struggle of these managers not only give us a glimpse of the man or woman themselves, but at the same time of present views on work and the consequences of these views for modern man.

John was trained as a nurse in the eighties. From the beginning it was obvious that he was dedicated and had insight. He is particularly aware of the needs of older patients, who are regularly confused, and whose behaviour was classed as unreasonable by colleagues. John clearly feels the fear, desperation, despondency, homesickness and loneliness of these people. He has the ability to support his colleagues – to coach them as we would say now – in their approach to these confused elderly people. He is made deputy head and later head of what would be classed nowadays as a small ward. John is excellent in combining his direct work with the patients with management responsibilities. He is supported by a deputy head, who among other things draws up rosters and organises duty times. The tasks of the head and the deputy head are described in broad terms, and there is therefore room to interpret them to meet the needs of each ward.

The content of the work is most important. Budgetary affairs, care reform, quality policy, product consideration, marketing research: health care, let alone his ward have not yet reached this stage. In the meantime, he is intuitively aware that the work on his ward is of a high quality. He is not worried about the market and the budget is organised for him. In the past years there have been four rounds of reorganisations or mergers. He (just as his fellow-workers) hardly has time to recover from one merger or he has to begin to get used to the next. His job description changes time and again: assistant foreman, care co-ordinator, team co-ordinator, care manager. The trend is in any case that his span of control and the distance from the actual work is increasing, that the pile of paperwork on his desk is getting bigger, his direct involvement in care smaller, the absence through illness on his ward more and more worrying and that the quality of the care being offered is getting worse. He regularly warns his superiors of these developments, but to no avail. The study carried out by Stoker and de Korte (2000) on the middle manager in a number of Dutch companies underlines the above. John has sleepless nights, as opposed to, or so he suspects, the senior management that has in the past ten years changed more often than the number of reorganisations. He is offered a management course, which includes supervision.

During the supervision he takes stock of the events of the past years. He reflects, for the first time out loud, on these developments. He considers the effects these developments have had on him as a *Professional Person* (Van Kessel 1997), on him as a person, on his profession and on the connection between the two[2].

Halfway through the supervision series he reports sick. He is able to allow the realisation that he has been exploiting both himself and his family to enter his mind. He was always occupied with his work, not only literally but also psychologically. He felt that he had been let down by his superiors who were occupied only with their *curriculum vitae,* with reports that had to look perfect before being passed on to the board of directors or the subsidisers of so-called care reform projects. He felt let down by his colleague managers in the management team: each person was relieved to be able to keep his or her own patch running. He also felt let down by his fellow-workers, who more and more often – on the basis of collective labour agreements – started to calculate, were barely willing to stand in and who stayed at home at the slightest excuse. He had continually tried to fill the gaps himself. Worst of all for him was the fact that the care for the patients was being skimmed off more and more often: there was no time (read: no staff, no money) for a walk in town, a trip, a collective

---

[2] The term Professional Person was thought up by Van Kessel in order to be able to describe the necessary integration between the person and his/her values on the one hand, and profession and standards that apply within this on the other. This integration always takes place in a personal way, and is also determined by the specific work situation the person finds him/herself in as well as the surrounding culture (Van Kessel 1997).

activity. It was often lunchtime before everyone was out of bed and washed, and out of sheer necessity patients were put to bed at 6:00 PM, directly after dinner which was an hour earlier any way because that was easier for the kitchen and the transport department. Absolutely alienating were the notes on quality that landed on his desk with the regularity of clockwork: if you were to believe this, you would think that things had never been so good on his ward. In the meantime he was convinced that he would never admit his father or mother to this ward.

The supervision helped John to put things into perspective. Reflection helped him to gain insight in structural aspects; you see he had the tendency to blame himself in the first place: lack of management knowledge and experience, the wrong type of leadership, not bold or harsh enough, not able to play along with the managers. It helped him to think about the norms and values that for him formed the basis of working in health care, but that did not tally with the pressure that was put on him by his superiors to change constantly. There are two remarks John made I did not fully examine at the time, that I would like to mention in connection with the continuation of this story. In the first place, whilst reviewing the events of the past ten years of organisational changes he made a remark about his children. Both his children were at a difficult age. He said that he had not been a good example to them in the past years. Being committed to and involved with others was very important to him. "How can I show this if I have to keep changing my position, have hardly had a chance to get to know people before I have to move on, and am continually occupied with the question of whether all the paperwork is correct?" He attempted to convey involvement, whilst this was being undermined more and more often in his work. A second remark was one he made when he compared the beginning of his career with the present situation: "I have never really thought about religion, but when the hospital still worked with religion as a basis there was a greater feeling of solidarity and communality among the employees."

2. The flexible person

It was easier to place John's story against the background of the book *The corrosion of character. The personal consequences of work in the new capitalism* written by the American sociologist Richard Sennett (1998). Sennett points out that the emphasis lies on flexibility in the present economy and society. Rigid forms of bureaucracy, routine and formal procedures are under pressure. Workers should be flexible, be able to adapt to fast changes, continually take risks. This emphasis changes the meaning of work. A *career* no longer involves being connected to one company or one boss for life, but instead a chain of separate jobs. It is hardly surprising that this flexibility makes people restless, after all you never know what risks will bring with them. Sennett suggests that flexibility is in fact a disguise for a new type of capitalistic oppression. Flexibility suggests the freedom to give life structure, but is in fact in control in a way that is barely possible to comprehend (Sennet 1998, 59). The most confusing aspect of flexibility is the influence it has on someone's character or personality. Character has mainly to do with our emotional experiences on the long term, with loyalty and mutual commitment, the pursuit of long-term objectives, and with the delay of satisfaction with a future goal in mind. Character has to do with values and being appreciated by others, with involvement with others and with the world around us (Sennett 1998, 10). With the emphasis on flexibility questions arise with regard to our character:

- how do we decide what is of permanent value within ourselves, in an impatient society and one that is focused only on the moment itself?
- how can long term goals be pursued in an economy that is focused completely on the short term?
- how can we hold onto mutual loyalty and commitment within institutions that are continually falling apart or being reorganised?
- and how can a person develop a narrative identity and a life story in a society that is made up of short episodes and fragments? (Sennett 1998, 26).

Orientation on the short term in particular undermines within organisations the growth of informal confidence, mutual responsibility and commitment. Strong ties are actually dependent on lengthy relationships, and – on a personal level – on the willingness to be involved and committed. According to Sennett the short term affects mutual relationships, but also the consciousness of a coherent self. And Sennett also observes the negative consequences of this for relationships with family, relations and friends (Sennett 1998, 136-148). He asks himself whether long-lasting relationships can be maintained in this new capitalism. How can a person develop his/her life story, an individual identity, in a society that is made up of episodes and fragments? In the course of history people have come to accept that unexpected wars and disasters can suddenly change their lives. Orientation on the short term and flexibility add continual instability to this.

In the area of work the short term means continual reorganisation or in other words re-engineering. Although research shows that the efficiency of organisations rarely increases (on the contrary: often actually decreases) through reorganisation, consultants and senior managers like to uphold the myth, because it shows to the outside world (read: marketing and financial world) that the organisation is capable of change. The morale and motivation of employees plummet during continual reorganisations that in fact happen to be a series of reductions. Those who remain await the following blow. But the motto seems to be: any change is better than continuing on the same footing as before! In the framework of these changes employees are often unaware of the consequences. Subsequently it turns out that wrong decisions were made on the basis of inadequate information about a fluctuating environment. It thus becomes clear that one has moved sideways instead of forward. Older employees do not count at all in the game of changes. Experience is of no value. Knowledge of organisation and profession are namely more of a hurdle for the management than an aid in the framework of changes. Moreover, younger people are more flexible, in the sense that they can still be manipulated in terms of daring to take risks and subjection to the regime in power (Sennett 1998, 49-50; 91-97).

You have to have the courage to take risks, although only a few will succeed. If taking risks is the modern adage, then failure is the modern taboo. Popular literature is overflowing with recipes for success, but nothing at all is mentioned about how to cope with failure. Moreover it seems that failing is not only a normal prospect for the poor and less fortunate, but surprisingly enough, also for the middle class. Failing at work and thus letting one's family down is a pressure that many people are under and one that is subtly and strongly present (Sennett 1998, 84-91; 130-135).

Finally a quotation from Sennett's book, in which he among others describes a meeting with Rico, who has been very successful in the new economy and who has accomplished an amazing social climb. Sennett describes this Rico as the *Everyman* of the present. Rico's greatest worry is his children. "He (...) wants to set his son and daughters an example of resolution and purpose, ' but you can't just tell kids to be like that'; he has to set an example. The objective example he could set, his upward mobility, is something they take for granted, a history that belongs to a past not their own, a story that is over. But his deepest worry is that he cannot offer the substance of his work life as an example to his children of how they should conduct themselves ethically. The qualities of good work are not the qualities of good character." (Sennett 1998, 21).

3. Professional biography

Against the background of Sennett's analysis what appeared to be an individual case, John's story, turns out to be a story of our time. What John experienced at work, the loss of involvement and communality and that at all levels of the organisation, turns out to be a characteristic of an economy, of a society, of a culture that only thinks about the short term. Part of what happens to John, his burnout and the loss of himself as an example and model for his children, is a result of those cultural and economic changes.

What helped John to clarify things in particular was the interest in his life story, better still: interest in his *professional biography*. Sennett asks himself especially how a person is able to develop a narrative identity and a life story nowadays, in a society that is made up simply of episodes and fragments. Emphasis on the short term and the necessity for flexibility that is linked with this is initiated by changes in the modern economy. However, these changes have repercussions on the character and personality of modern man. Values and relations that flourish only in a climate that is characterised by a certain continuity come under pressure. Trust, mutual responsibility and commitment barely have a chance at all in flexible and continually changing organisations, work relations and teams. Solidarity is under pressure from developments on a micro-level (for example conflicting responsibilities and commitments in relation to labour organisation, housekeeping and the care for and bringing up of the children) and on a macro-level (for example the growing emphasis on flexibility) (Sanders 2000). In this framework solidarity can be specified in five ways of behaviour: contributing to the public interest, helping others in need, resisting the temptation to let others do most of the work, sharing costs and profits equally, and rectifying errors and misunderstandings (Sanders 2000, 12-13; Lindenberg 1998). Sanders indicates, just as Sennett does, that a lack of the long-term perspective within present economic relations and within many labour organisations discourages employees from committing themselves to their labour organisation. This leads to negative consequences for the development of a feeling of solidarity that can only succeed within a long-term perspective.

Sennett adds that the emphasis on the short-term and on flexibility has consequences for the character of modern man, for his/her narrative identity and life story. In his book Sennett describes the reactions of a group of employees who have been made redundant in the framework of a reorganisation within a large computer factory. They continue to meet regularly. In a number of steps they are able to bring their experiences together in a story that is connected to their person, their ambitions and their failures, to their opinions on their profession and their professional position. It is a story that tells more than just complaints about bad management, corruption or the disloyalty of their superiors. In small steps they rediscover their identity, as a person and as a worker (Sennett 1998, 130-135), as a Professional Person as Van Kessel (1997) would say.

During the supervision John noticed how strongly his person was involved in his work and in his profession. In the course of his career he had hardly thought about this. The discovery of this connection during the supervision allowed him to relate (again) the values that were most important in his work, with the way he functioned as a manager. Where in the past years his life had been led for him by the continually changing agenda of the senior management and by the repeated waves of reorganisations, he was able to distinguish the thread through the course of his career. One could also say that the supervision enabled him to put his *professional biography* into words. In actual fact this coincides with what Tillich (see above) did, when he reconstructed the connection between his scientific career and his personal development under the title of the *boundary*. Kelchtermans (1994; 1999) takes the *professional biography* or *career story* to mean the retrospective reconstruction by the worker of his/her career in story form. This reconstruction gives insight into the *critical incidents, phases and people* in the (run up to) career as key moments or structure points in that career. The career story points to the changes the worker – in Kelchtermans' study the teacher – experiences in thoughts and deeds. In the career story opinions of the worker on him/herself as a person play a large role. These opinions can be summarised in the concept *professional self-understanding*. In the professional self-understanding Kelchtermans distinguishes the *self-image, self-value, professional motivation, conception of one's job, and perspective*. At the same time the *subjective theory about work*, one's own theory in practice is prominent.

As has been said the supervised, John, actually had no connection with the world of religion and faith. Yet he chose me as his supervisor, whilst he could also have chosen for one of the other two supervisors of the course. He was aware of my background as theologian and pastor. He expected a different approach from me as supervisor than from a supervisor with a psychological or agogic background. He expected to be paid attention to as a person (and not only as the holder of an office) who attempts to actualise certain values in his work. He hoped there would be room for his story, and that he would not immediately be confronted with all the things he was not capable of doing or of learning during the management course. And when he was able to tell his story, his professional biography, it turned out not only to be an individual but also a collective story. Similar stories came up during the supervision of a number of his colleagues. All of them were surprised that their person was of importance in the setting of work. In the supervision course, fifteen one and a half hour-long meetings, once every two or three weeks, they gradually gained more and more insight in their person (their character in Sennetts words) in relation to their profession, their position and the context (organisational and social). Moreover, they gradually developed the realisation that the changes in their work situation were not possible without a great degree of continuity, and that this continuity was to a large extent to be found in their experiences, in their professional biography, and besides this in the mutual involvement of employees and through this commitment, in the values developed and maintained – such as integrity, trust, responsibility. Change does not exist without continuity, continuity not without change.

4. Clinical Pastoral Education

A tradition in which structural attention is paid to the *professional biography* is Clinical Pastoral Education. At present this is the most intensive form of in-service and continued education for pastors, ministers and pastoral carers in the Netherlands. The training includes approximately hundred daily periods and is divided into different blocks (in some training centres these are continuous, apart from the weekends) whereby the student stays in the course centre, and where he or she also sometimes carries out pastoral duties in a general or psychiatric hospital. In this training, that is not aimed at brief successes but at a lengthy and often radical learning process the pastor learns to reflect on his/her person in relation to the pastoral profession (Vossen 1991; Körver 1998).

Starting point and objective of CPE training is – as has already been mentioned – insight into and reflection on the individual professional history of the pastor, on the interweaving of the biography on the one hand, and the motivation to, satisfaction in and identity of the pastoral profession on the other. At the same time the reflection intended must take into consideration the institutional or organisational framework in which the pastor works, and the present social and cultural context that has an influence on faith, church and pastoral care.

The policy that the Council for CPE wishes to develop for the benefit of practices in the Netherlands is based on the tradition of Clinical Pastoral Education that has been applied and developed since 1925 in the United States, and since the '60s in the Netherlands.

In 1925 Anton T. Boisen invites five students of theology for work experience in the psychiatric centre where he is pastor. Against the background of the religious developments and conflicts in the 1920s in the United States CPE explicitly concentrates on individual pastoral contact and small groups. The objective is to prise students away from their purely cognitive oriented theological education and to come to an integration of head and heart through the alienating confrontation with the world of psychiatry (Hall 1992). The fact that Boisen brings students from the safety of the lecture-room and plunges them into a psychiatric hospital has to do with his own personal history. He spent a long period of time in a psychiatric centre at the age of about forty-four. He asks himself what the significance of his illness is, in his personal life story as well as in his professional biography. This leads him to a new understanding of religious experience, theology and the professional possibilities of pastors. It is only in the interaction between living human documents – patients and pastors – and theological models and concepts that real insight in those living human documents develops, and at the same time in theological models and concepts. It is only when pastors learn to perceive, interpret and deal with for example guilt and shame, providence and mercy, judgement and reconciliation in the concrete biography that these concepts gain reality value (Körver 2001).

The CPE philosophy thus distinguishes itself through its explicit interest in the influence of the person and the personal history on faith and theology. For Boisen and for the CPE tradition interest in the autobiography of the pastor and in the biography of clients is essential for the development of theological and pastoral competence. The success of the CPE philosophy worldwide and in particular in the Netherlands is an indication of the power of the concept. Zijlstra expresses it as such: "What help is it to the pastor if he learns every skill, but does not really 'come to him/herself'? He becomes no more than a dangerous 'narrow-minded specialist'." (Zijlstra 1973, 20) Explicit reflection on the professional biography makes it possible to do a strengths-weaknesses-analysis of the person in relation to his/her work, so as to discover the connections between the individual life history and the way things are dealt with in pastoral actions, in order to re-evaluate the motivation for, satisfaction in and identity of the pastoral profession, to learn to distinguish structural and subjective influences on work questions, and also to (re)discover the reality value of theological models and concepts.

There is evidence of a certain development in the tradition of CPE. In the 50s especially there was a reorientation. The patients are no longer the living human documents but the students themselves who from those years onwards struggle more and more with the rooting into and identity of the pastoral profession. Looking back on fifty years of CPE in 1975, Powell summarises the development of CPE as follows:

- in the period between 1925-1935 emphasis lay on the theoretical question 'What should I *do?*'
- from 1935-1945 on 'What should I *know?*'
- from 1945-1955 on 'What should I *say* in order to be of help to the patient?
- in the period 1955-1965 students and trainers asked questions like 'In order to be of help to the patient: who should I then *be?*'

5. Shared fate

Again I will use someone as an example. It involves Carla, pastoral worker in a psychiatric hospital. In accordance with the assignment in the framework of her application for CPE she writes a biography that includes attention for the factors that have had an influence on her development as pastor. She describes a chaotic situation at home. One specific memory she has is of the enormous pile of smelly, mouldy dishes on the draining board that had been there for days, and that at the age of eight she started to wash up herself in the end. A mother who was unable to cope with the tasks involved in a large family, a father who after being a postman became an office manager and who in the end was unable to find a connection with either social worlds. In her adolescence especially she sees herself as closed but also as eccentric. Various courses and jobs follow, until she seems to have found what she was looking for in theology. Working in psychiatry she feels like a fish in water, but she continually asks herself whether she is needed. In consultations she hardly says a word, in the presence of psychiatrists and therapists she is at a loss for words, overawed. In a number of work groups she becomes the negative vote against the continual reorganisations, that on the level of the work floor bring only cuts with them and that decrease the amount of care, despite all the promising words about *made to measure care, care that fits the demand* etc. But this negative vote is more the vote of the underdog, who offers passive resistance and who always falls into aggrieved silence when in the presence of executives. These circumstances lead to tension and cost her an enormous amount of energy. It is with this burden that she starts CPE. The training includes a number of verbal moments in which fragments from each person's life are analysed for strong and weak points, for blind spots and pitfalls, but also for opportunities. Besides this there are creative moments, sport and exercise, music, moments for exercises in spirituality. And all of this in a reasonably lengthy process embedded in intensive group dynamics. The group consists of no more than nine participants, who naturally get to know each other well in a course lasting nine to twelve weeks. The better they get to know each other, the better they are able to give each other feedback. One point during a meeting in the gymnasium led by a psychomotor therapist becomes the icon for Carla's development. This therapist who takes the group for one and a half hours of sport each week always starts off by giving the group a task to do together. At this particular meeting he gave the group the following task. The whole group is to get to the other side of the gym without any one of them touching the floor, via a kind of survival course of mats, cupboards and ropes. Out of the blue it appears that in a non-verbal situation she has a talent for improvisation, creativity and the ability to lead others. Qualities that have always remained below the surface, and that now appear. She is able to guide the group to the other side of the gym in record time. In the discussion afterwards (and in the following days and weeks) she discovers aspects of her life story that up till then had not been put into this category. It was chaos at home, which led to her developing the talent to improvise. She did not feel at home in many social contexts, but at the same time she developed her creativity. When improvisation and creativity are released, she is able to have faith in herself and the fear for and resistance against executives and therapists disappears.

What I describe here in a number of sentences is a process that took almost a year. Carla evaluated her professional biography in the framework of the training. She actually constructs a new story. She puts the fragments of her life story into a new context. A new configuration appears that challenges her to a new relationship in connection with herself, her profession and with her work situation. In the words of Ricoeur Carla develops her narrative identity in the dialectics of *idem* (sameness) and *ipse* (selfhood). And she does this in relation to the demands and needs of others, others that need her and that she knows need her through their mutual problems and failures (Ricoeur 1992, 113-168). These thoughts link with the continuity that Sennett (1998, 145-148) considers to be necessary as a counterforce against indifference and the lack of a shared story about problems and thus of shared fate, such as he has observed in the new capitalism with its one-sided emphasis on continual change and flexibility.

During the course of the training Carla reports on the changes in her work. She is able to voice the thoughts of the clients better on the hierarchical levels where decisions are made. Because she occupies a somewhat *eccentric* (Corveleijn

1996) position in the institution as pastoral carer, she is able to observe matters that others do not see or that they consider to be a matter-of-course. This gives her a much better position from which to observe the issues of the day, and she is able to put into words for the management the values that through scarcely uncritical and fashionable processes of change threaten to be affected.

6. Conclusion

What contribution can the tradition of Clinical Pastoral Education make to communication with modern society?

1. Attention for the *professional biography* helps professionals to gain a better insight in their life story in relation to their profession and the actual way in which they function.
2. This demands lengthy training and reflection, in which one should explicitly consider values such as involvement, trust and responsibility.
3. The training underlines the importance of continuity, of stability, as a counterpart to change. "Change and stability, apparently opposing points of view are, however, so close to each other that they are complimentary. Without the notion of stability we would have no notion of the concept of change. That these concepts have something to do with each other is obvious in the fact that when people want to change, they are often unsuccessful in putting their old, undesirable state behind them. Or, the other way round, in spite of their search for stability they are unable to find a certain line. Apparently, in a situation like this the longing for stability and the desire to change compete with each other" (van Knippenberg 1998, 100).
4. In our society, that is focussed more and more on the short term, attention for continuity requires courage. I have deliberately formulated a paraphrase of the title of a book by Tillich *The Courage to Be* (1952) in the title of my story. The courage to be is in conflict with not being. Not being is the fear of losing the essence of being human in the face of fate and death, is the fear of losing one's spiritual life in the face of emptiness and meaninglessness, and is the fear of losing one's moral self in the face of guilt and judgement. In the same sense it is the courage of continuity that is needed so that ultimately the most essential of being human is not lost.
5. The unique contribution made by CPE to society is the attention for the life story, for the professional biography. What is most unique about this is that this tradition has developed in the US, the cradle of CPE, and the Netherlands apart from the church. The aim has been to be ecumenical in the real sense of the word from the beginning. It has never been difficult to realise co-operation and commitment between Catholics and Protestants of all walks in the framework of the training. There is now also experience

with Islamic pastoral carers. The professional biography as an objective seems to aim its attention to the essence and at the same time it arouses mutual involvement and trust, which for that matter are processes of the long term and continuity.

It is in this workshop, in these boundary areas that a practical theologian, as Tjeu van Knippenberg imagines him/her to be, is able to function successfully and is not only able to contribute to theology but also to reflection in those professions and management positions that involve people. With this the practical theologian occupies a position in the cultural and social debate on the sense of work.

References

Corveleijn, J. 1996. Bedenkingen van een psychotherapeut over geestelijke verzorging van ernstig psychiatrisch gestoorde mensen. *Psychiatrie en Verpleging* 72(2): 93-104.

Crooijmans, H. 2001. Ken uw baas! Hij is sukkel en held tegelijk: de chef dreigt te bezwijken onder de omvang en complexiteit van zijn taken. *Elsevier* 05-05-2001.

Hall, C.E. 1992. *Head and Heart. The Story of the Clinical Pastoral Education Movement.* Decatur: Journal of Pastoral Care Publications.

Kelchtermans, G. 1994. *De professionele ontwikkeling van leerkrachten basisonderwijs vanuit het biografisch perspectief.* Leuven: Universitaire Pers.

Kelchtermans, G. 1999. Kwetsbaarheid en professionele identiteit van leerkrachten basisonderwijs. Een exploratie van de morele en politieke wortels. *Pedagogisch Tijdschrift* 24(4): 471-492.

Kessel, L. van 1997. Supervisie: noodzakelijke bijdrage aan de kwaliteit van maatschappelijk werk. Pp. 136-151 in *De levende professie. Hoofdlijnen van het maatschappelijk werk,* edited by H. Nijenhuis. Utrecht.

Knippenberg, M. van 1989. *Grenzen. Werkplaats van pastoraaltheologen. Rede in verkorte vorm uitgesproken bij de aanvaarding van het ambt van hoogleraar in de pastoraaltheologie aan de theologische faculteit Tilburg.* Kampen: Kok.

Knippenberg, M. van 1998. *Tussen Naam en Identiteit. Ontwerp van een model voor geestelijke begeleiding.* Kampen: Kok.

Körver, J., eds. 1998. *Corrigerende Ervaringen. Leren in Klinische Pastorale Vorming en Pastorale Supervisie. Bij het afscheid van Piet Zuidgeest.* Eindhoven: CVPE.

Körver, J. 1999. De organisatiecontext van pastorale supervisie. *Supervisie in opleiding en beroep* 16(2): 3-16.

Körver, J. 2001. Theologie in de Klinische Pastorale Vorming. *Praktische Theologie* 28(2): 182-191.

Lindenberg, S. 1998. Solidarity: its Microfoundations and Macro Dependence. In *The Problem of Solidarity: Theories and Models*, edited by P. Doreian and T.J. Fafaro. Amsterdam: Gordon and Breach.

Powell, R.C. 1975. CPE. Fifty Years of Learning through Supervised Encounter *with Living Human Documents*. New York: Association for Clinical Pastoral Education.

Raad voor Klinische Pastorale Vorming in Nederland 1999. *Beleidsplan 1999 - 2002*. Amersfoort: Raad voor KPV.

Ricoeur, P. 1992. *Oneself as Another*. Chicago/London: The University of Chicago Press.

Sanders, K. 2000. *Solidair gedrag binnen moderne arbeidsorganisaties. Rede uitgesproken bij de aanvaarding van het ambt van hoogleraar Personeelswetenschappen aan de Katholieke Universiteit Brabant*. Tilburg: Dutch University Press.

Sennett, R. 1998. *The Corrosion of Character. The Personal Consequences of Work in the New Capitalism*. New York/London: W.W. Norton et al.

Stoker, J.I. and A.W. de Korte 2000. *Het onmisbare middenkader*. Assen: Van Gorcum.

Tillich, P. 1930. *Religiöse Verwirklichung*. Berlin: Furche-Verlag.

Tillich, P. 1936. *The Interpretation of History*. New York/London: Charles Scribner's Sons.

Tillich, P. 1952. *The Courage to Be*. New Haven/Conn et al.: Yale University Press.

Tillich, P. 1962. *Auf der Grenze. Aus dem Lebenswerk Paul Tillichs*. Stuttgart: Evangelisches Verlagswerk.

Vossen, H.J.M. 1991. Klinische Pastorale Vorming als religieus-communicatief leerproces. *Praktische Theologie* 18(2): 176-196.

Zijlstra, W. 1973. *Klinische Pastorale Vorming*. Nijmegen: Dekker and van de Vegt.

Spiritual Guidance
What, Who and How?

Frans Maas

Introduction

Among the great diversity in counselling in our society, religious counselling has received good credentials in recent years again, considered as 'spiritual guidance'. It fell into the background at the end of the sixties when an aversion arose within the counselling sector to any association with religiosity. This seems to be diminishing. Even, recognition of the religious dimension is growing so long as it is not an institutional religion. Along that line, the term spiritual guidance is used again without a sense of shame. The term has been influenced since by the spirit of our age. The anti-authoritarian trends of the past several decades have caused the more vertical 'spiritual direction' to be replaced by 'spiritual guidance'. This is also the case in other languages: 'geistliche Führung' versus 'geistliche Begleitung' and 'direction spirituelle' versus 'accompagnement spirituel'.

In this article, I will consider the subject of spiritual guidance on the basis of three questions: *what* is spiritual guidance compared to other forms of counselling; *who* are the people involved in the process of spiritual guidance; and finally *how* should spiritual guidance proceed according to certain authorities in the field? My perspective will be that of Christian spirituality, acknowledging at the same time that spiritual guidance can also be based upon other (religious) traditions and that the inter-religious dialogue is of major importance in this area as well.

1. What is spiritual guidance?

Let me chance a definition by way of guideline. Spiritual guidance means providing someone with a sounding board for questions connected with the ultimate perspective of his or her life. The following paragraphs will deal with the nature of that sounding board.

1.1. The person who is guided, is asking

The client's request or question should be the starting-point. In spiritual guidance, the question comes first and is indeed the most important guideline. In this respect, it distinguishes itself from preaching or catechesis, in which the initiative lies with the offering rather than the request. Frequently this question is barely explicit. Someone can have a vague sense that life should have more to offer than has been apparent so far, or a person has difficulty dealing with a certain experience. In these situations, guidance consists of trying to zoom in on underlying questions and choices. Whenever specific questions are present from the beginning, the attention can be focused on these. The nature of these questions offers a starting-point for the external organization of spiritual guidance; duration, frequency, location, objective, means like a diary or an autobiography, finances, etc. The questions can become the basis for a contract that supplies spiritual guidance with an outline in order to keep expectations as clear and realistic as possible. Now that the traditional settings of spiritual guidance – such as belonging to a monastic order, preparation for ordination, etcetera – have mostly disappeared, many agree with Andriessen's assertion (1996, 131-139), that it is wise to apply a similar contractual framework.

1.2. The spiritual path of life

The word guidance evokes the image of a journey or a path. 'Path' is a much-used metaphor in the spiritual tradition, and in Scripture as well. Human growth to spiritual maturity or getting closer to God is often compared to a spiritual path. The image of a path implies a certain coherence and continuity instead of viewing life as a tangle of coincidences. It gives a sense of direction. This is of vital importance to mental health. The desire to discover this direction can cause someone to seek spiritual guidance. On the other hand the idea or even the claim of a coherence that is too encompassing or too convenient can be risky. Andriessen (1996) warns for this danger and often speaks of the 'extra' in spiritual guidance. This is a dimension that cannot be trapped in structures. Spiritual leaders teach this when people overemphasize coherence that causes stagnation. No room is left for the unexpected and the unforeseen on the part of God.

What is this path of life? One could say that people go several paths, each with its own destination. One follows a path at the basic level of earning a living and building a career. Getting an education, working on diplomas, improving a *curriculum vitae* and building a social network are all matters that are encountered on this path. There is also a path of psychological and social maturation. Additionally there is a path of forming relationships at the micro-level, finding a life companion and intensifying this relationship. Finally at the level of the relation with God or, more generally phrased, the relationship to what is of ultimate concern in life, one can speak of a path. All these paths cover different areas of life, but interact as well. What happens in one area often has an influence on developments in other areas. These paths not only have their own destination, but they especially have their own perspective. Van Knippenberg has paid a lot of attention to perspective in his book on spiritual guidance (1998, 70-94). Perspective is what characterizes spiritual guidance compared to other forms of counselling. He defines perspective as a network of affects, intentions and concepts, which causes reality to be perceived in a particular way. A hungry person will see tasty meals everywhere and a lonely person will find loving couples all around. It is of major importance to be aware of one's own perspective and its influence. Van Knippenberg describes the worldly perspective as one of self-interest, causing the person to become demanding to himself and to others. The Christian perspective, on the contrary, is that of Jesus. For example how he views Peter after his denial in such a way that he sees more than just betrayal. This view brings Peter home with himself and it opens the sources of repentance in his soul (Luke 22, 61). The Christian perspective does not deny reality. Betrayal and sin are not ignored, but they do not peg someone down to factual limitations. It looks further towards what someone's deepest destiny is in the eyes of God. This destiny, after all, has to be recognized as a possibility and has to be opened up.

1.3. The characteristic perspective of the spiritual path

Let us first establish the territory of the spiritual, by identifying the specific perspective of spiritual guidance. By spiritual perspective we mean the most fundamental level of human existence: who a person most profoundly or ultimately is, or better: what is ultimately possible in and for this person. The areas of the existential and the spiritual appear to be synonymous at first. They apply to the most profound level of the human self. Psychological perspectives, however, show that this level cannot be easily accessed. Mostly it is buried under several layers of a person's psyche in which people present themselves to others and themselves as different from whom they really are. People often act in such an impressive way, that they lose themselves in the process. Fortunately this can sometimes be felt. These moments of discomfort are really precious. A process is necessary of breaking away from identities to which one has become attached for all kinds of reasons. This can be done by letting personal feelings, needs, thoughts and fears surface without acting upon them and without identifying with them. One can get in touch with the self: the authentic principle of one's life. One becomes oneself, so to speak. There the mind finds its destination as a psyche, there the psychological process of life has succeeded. However, the development can progress one step further. The mind can rise above itself and become principle of not just the individual life, but also of the surrounding life: the social and the cultural. The mind takes responsibility for an existence that is larger than the individual's life itself. There the mind will turn out to be a reception area: the opportunity to be touched by something beyond. Philosophers, also the modern ones like Safranski, call this the human capacity for transcendence and they consider it essential for mental health. Here mind becomes spirit and reaches beyond the psychosocial into the existential process of life itself. Normally speaking, this mind as spirit is often referred to as 'self'. This 'self' is more than a strong ego. It has not only learned to deal fruitfully with its own limitations, but also finds openness and responsibility for a different reality. I would call guidance in this process existential or spiritual guidance having used the terms 'spirit' and 'self' synonymously. This guidance perspective regards the personal process of life from the perspective of the ultimate in order to orient the path of life towards the ultimate in return.

1.4. The religious perspective

Normally speaking, spiritual guidance has an immediate religious connotation. This is not without reason. For those who believe this intentional orientation into the ultimate reality, in order to find one's own strength, is not just a theoretical possibility, but has always had a clearly defined shape, as told in the Christian story. The human spirit is related to the Spirit. God's Spirit is regarded as the ultimate motive for our actions, in which basic trust is sought and found. The 'self' is linked to sources of existence that have a Name and a Story, which take shape in rituals and ethics. At the same time these sources are often far removed, hidden in the emptiness of the desert. In this respect, spiritual guidance is not merely synonymous to existential guidance. They are indeed situated at the same level, but spiritual guidance has a tradition at its disposal. The ultimate perspective has been interpreted. It concerns a Someone who transcends this self, Someone who is 'greater than our heart' or 'is closer to us than we are to ourselves' (Augustine). Who we are in the most profound sense, is not determined by our own spiritual size and weight, but by the promise that we are to God. The 'self' that unfolds, is noticed by God. It is called the soul. This soul is the 'self' in its openness towards and in its intentionality concerning God. Spiritual guidance can assist in reaching that 'self', the soul. It is therefore 'cure of souls' in the most authentic sense of the word.

The conclusion that spiritual guidance as a form of counselling concerns the specific area of the relation with God is justifiable so long as one does not think of a well-defined area in which the development of the relationship with God is separated from other areas of the self. They always interact. Becoming holy and remaining neurotic is an impossible combination - although even this may be subject to the condition that for God nothing is impossible. Great spiritual leaders have shown to be good 'psychotherapists' for that reason; we have put this word in quotes because they do not usually work with conventional psychological models, but with what they consider to be God's point of view. Usually, however, a good spiritual guide will direct the problem towards its own specific territory. In his book, Van Knippenberg (1998) elaborates on some striking examples of overlap and difference between different counselling perspectives. Revealing is his example of the man who suffers from an authority complex. He is burdened by the competence that he attributes to others. He enlarges them and diminishes himself to such a degree that he feels ashamed to be and to be noticed. The counsellor in the example works with him on that psychosocial level for a period of time, but tries, at a certain point, to translate the problem to religious terms: who makes and worships idols reduces himself to slavery. That is why, Scripture says, the gods have to be shattered from time to time to allow a person to be whoever he or she is. The counsellor introduces the word 'iconoclasm'. He sees a connection between idols at the psychological and at the religious level. On the one hand, he tries to extend the perceived need for iconoclasm at the psychological level to the broader area where people allow themselves to be made existentially unfree. Here psychotherapy blends into spiritual guidance. On the other hand, he tries to use religious motivations to open up psychological blockades. Here psychotherapy employs a religious field of force. Both perspectives interact. The skill of switching between idioms is crucial for a counsellor. However, he or she has to follow the lead of the client. Another example, also mentioned by Van Knippenberg, illustrates the importance of distinguishing between perspectives. A young man is upset as a result of dancing glasses at a séance. The counsellor states: "That does not surprise me, you are having an affair." In this case the counsellor puts spiritual matters in the perspective of psychosocial hygiene. A counsellor is able to offer this connection between social and spiritual experiences, because he or she can switch idioms. This switch can only be successful if the client is able to follow along.

2. Who are the people engaged in the process of spiritual guidance?

Usually two people are involved in the process of spiritual guidance: the person who is asking for guidance, the guided, and the person who is guiding, the guide. I will briefly mention two items for each role that catch attention in tradition. Subsequently I will address the relationship between guided and guide.

2.1. Discernment and openness in the guided

Traditionally dominant in spiritual guidance is the category of 'discernment of the spirits'. Directly related to this is the openness of heart. Discernment of the spirits is an unusual expression for present-day audiences. Since Origenes 'spirits' usually means states of mind that motivate a person. These states of mind were mostly associated with the activity of spirits or demons. It was important to distinguish between good and evil influences of spirits, or in more modern terms: to distinguish between states of mind that lead a person in a positive direction or impulses in the wrong direction.

The starting-point of spiritual guidance is the conviction that people are intrinsically capable of discernment of the spirits in their own life. This positive direction can be recognized in a profound feeling of consolation that is coupled with it. This feeling is considered as to be gratuitously given by God. People cannot cause it themselves. On the contrary, access to it is often hindered by self-created blockades. Mostly these blockades consist of different forms of egocentricity. It is important to recognize these secret shapes of egocentricity. Sometimes they can even be religiously camouflaged. For example the pride one could take in personal prayer or fasting; or fostering all kinds of altruistic ideals for the sake of personal peace of mind. The fact that this does not result in real peace of mind can actually be noticed or discerned by the person. The spiritual guide can assist the mobilization of this ability to discern. That spiritual guidance only acts as a sounding board can be illustrated by a story from the tradition of the anchorites, handed down as an apothegm of Abbot Sylvan. It is about a monk who has sinned so severely that he does not feel worthy to continue a monastic life. Something inside him, however, tells him to ask other monks for advice. He approaches them with the very general question 'if a person has committed such and such sin can he continue to be a monk?'. One after another responds negatively. No matter how discouraging this is, the young man does not give up. Finally he also puts the question to Abbot Sylvan who understands that it is not just a general question and answers that under certain circumstances a monastic life can certainly be continued. The book of apothegms states that by continuing the search, the young monk shows his capability of discernment of the spirits. Abbot Sylvan praises him for this (Wagenaar 1981, 41).

Besides registering the states of mind, informing the spiritual guide is vitally important as well. The guided must be willing to 'open his heart' and not conceal things out of shame or pride. "One has to arm the younger monks against this dangerous mistake and persuade them not to hold back any of the thoughts that trouble them, but inform an older brother from the moment they arise", says Cassian (Hausherr 1957, 1032 and following). By holding these thoughts in the devil who strikes with his seduction, since this shame about matters that a person, rightly or wrongly, judges as not optimal, makes him or her most vulnerable. Many secret forms of egocentricity can cause damage in this area. The spiritual guide can only function as a sounding board when an 'openness of heart' is present in the guided. It will allow this egocentricity to be perceived more clearly, to prevent pious deception.

2.2. Insight and experience of the spiritual guide

A spiritual guide has to respond to the openness of heart with respect, knowledge and insight. Great spiritual leaders such as Ignace, John of the Cross and Theresa of Avila all emphasized common sense and insight, but considered experience to be of crucial value, especially in the transition from the active works in the form of meditation and practice of virtues to a more passive attitude of contemplation. For Cassian, Benedict and Gregory the Great, the sensible insight of the discernment is found mainly in knowing the golden mean between extremes. The great danger of the spiritual path is fanatical exaggeration. This mean is never concretely known in advance. It can only be found by following the specific process of a particular person carefully and with respect (*discretio*). Thomas puts this central art of spiritual guidance in a managerial context and calls it *prudentia* and sometimes *providentia*. Within a systematic theory of virtues, the royal mean is developed (*media via regia via*). This path is not seen and found anew in people every time by way of level-headedness and experience, but it has been traced out neatly in the middle already. This shift has caused a great attenuation of spiritual life all through history.

There exist different styles of guidance. Since for discernment of the spirits - the central category of spiritual guidance - only very global 'objective' criteria can be given and even then sensible insight and experience turn the scales, it will be obvious that in the concrete form of spiritual guidance different emphases are possible. These differences are closely related to the personality of the guide. Andriessen (1996) distinguishes four styles, each with its own possibilities and limitations. (1) The achievement-oriented style, which emphasizes concrete actions and practical results; something has to come out of it. Precisely those impulses that lead to practical effects, are looked for, supported and tested. This results in a real commitment to daily life, but less of an emphasis on creativity. Feelings and experiences are questioned for their practical use and inner autonomy is only measured by behaviour. Spiritual life is mainly considered a matter of doing. The cognitive style (2) emphasizes insight, articulating the content and fitting insights into a broader perspective. The emphasis is on explaining, assuming implicitly that knowledge leads to action. The advantage of clear structure and understanding is offset by a diminished attention for feelings and experiences. The didactic style (3) emphasizes the educational aspect of spiritual guidance, in which a framework (a more or less worked out spirituality or rule of life) is given. In this approach, as in the first two, the spiritual guide takes a prominent role. This style offers an easy foothold, but in the interaction between guide and guided, the baggage of the guided is neglected. Finally Andriessen mentions the didactic experiential style (4), which he clearly prefers. In this style the experience of the guided is central, together guide and guided look for what is God's truth for the guided. This becomes the leading factor, in which other elements of the previous styles can be incorporated.

Reading present-day literature about spiritual guidance, one cannot overlook the large difference of style and the crucial role of the talents and tradition of the guide. The thread however is the search for who people are to God in the most profound sense, in order to make this the strength and the orientation of life. This is everyone's own task in life, but the spiritual guide can be of assistance.

2.3. The relationship between guided and guide

The relationship between these two people offers room for exchange of fundamental matters. It involves intimacy and care. What is characteristic for the relationship between guided and guide, is portrayed well by Waaijman (2000, 921-927), but I would like to sharpen one particular point. Waaijman agrees with the analysis of empathy that was made by the Jewish philosopher who later became a Carmelite nun, Edith Stein.

The guide has an empathetic relationship with the guided. Empathy means that one tries to project oneself into the 'inner world' of the other person, in which this particular person creates his or her own image of reality. The way that someone deals with his world is apparent in bodily expressions. Body is used here in the broader sense of animated body, which is the physical shape of a person's intentionality concerning the world outside. Bodily expressions are used to attempt to experience the way the other person deals with his or her world. This world, however, is at the same time my own world, with which I have my own intentional relationship. Therefore empathy is more than sensory perception, which only deals with the physical body that I register and explain. In that case I apply my own theory of perception but I do not project myself in the 'inner world' of the other. Empathy is not sympathy either, because in that case I focus on the object of the other person's experience, not on the experience itself. It is neither a feeling of unity, because in that case one 'me' develops, while empathy implies two; nor is it transfer, whereby I let the behaviour of a person evoke an experience in myself. The experience of the other person should be the focus of my attention. Another option is that I try to understand the inner experience from the way someone expresses himself by means of my own experience – how an expression of mine relates to a feeling in myself. Empathy exists only in the case that I transpose my experience into the inner world of another ego. The reality that is under discussion in spiritual guidance is divine reality. Neither the guide himself, nor his own relation with God is of interest; that one of the guided is. By means of empathy the guide can come closer in proximity to this. Waaijman puts major emphasis on empathetically projecting oneself into the God-relation of another person. This emphasis is right and primary. But that is not enough. When the guided himself in his own God-relation has not yet discovered his own dynamics – that is after all the reason why a sounding-board is needed – and the guide has, then this is because of the guide's insight and experience. Even though the guided has to get in touch with those dynamics in his own God-relation, the personal God-relation of the guide plays a certain role. The importance, however, of the term 'empathy' as an indicator for the relationship of spiritual guidance, is related to the fact that the Spirit is the true guide.

3. How should spiritual guidance proceed according to great spiritual leaders?

The substantial amount of issues worthy of consideration in the writings of great spiritual leaders makes arbitrariness in the selection inevitable. I will concentrate on certain aspects of Cassian, Augustine, Ignatius of Loyola and John of the Cross.

3.1. Cassian: the parable of the competent moneychanger

Cassian († 430/35) is of special importance to western spirituality, not only because he himself was a very creative spiritual leader, but also because the great spiritual riches of the Orthodox Church became available to the West through his writings. In his *Collationes* (I, 20 and following) he compares a good spiritual leader to a competent moneychanger. Becoming a sensible moneychanger he takes – maybe in accordance with Matthew 25,27 – as an order from Jesus. Just like a competent moneychanger can distinguish between real and fake coins, we can do something similar in spiritual guidance. Four criteria are available to the moneychanger. Cassian links each of these with an analogy to spiritual guidance.

The most fundamental criterion is whether the coin is of real gold or of deceptively shiny copper. A good moneychanger is not fooled by appearances. With a competent eye one has to discern the raw material of the spiritual path as well. Is it really something that turns us towards life, or is it something that leads us astray with nice words, sharp analyses or pious feelings? That is a fundamental decision, associated with what in most places in Scripture and in early Christian literature is presented as a choice between the way to life and the way to death. Cassian indicates only briefly what is crucial in relation to thoughts, feelings, rituals and behavioural patterns: have they been purified by the fire of the Spirit or do they merely belong to a package that, even with a religious flavour, is only meant to satisfy materially and mentally and thus strengthen a person's self-complacency? Golden things have been purified by celestial fire, they have to do with dynamics towards the Infinite and not with any type of established luxury.

Does the coin bear the right effigy or the wrong one, that of the king or that of the tyrant? This is the second criterion for the sensible moneychanger. Even golden coins can bear the wrong effigy. This means for spiritual life that convictions, life style, or even reading Scripture, though good in themselves, can nevertheless be oppressive like a tyrant instead of liberating like a king. The criterion is: Do we recognize the liberating king, the spirit of the Kingdom of God that bans all slavery and enables to enjoy God's presence in all worldly reality?

Important also is the question whether the coin has come from an acknowledged mint. Even the golden coin with the right effigy can originate from a counterfeit mint. This criterion concerns the legal stamp of the right tradition, that is the right context in which matters that are good in themselves do not work the wrong way as a result of exaggeration, such as immoderate fasting, irregular prayers, long wakes, abandoning a certain order because of higher motives, etc. Not only the coin itself, but also its origins determine the value. We need an environment that helps us keep the sensible mean, which is vitally important to practices and exercises that are good in themselves. This is not the same as mediocrity; it is exactly that measure that fits a specific person. Exaggerations, particularly in the right direction, are considered dangerous in the tradition of spiritual guidance. They are tricks of the devil.

The sensible moneychanger also knows the weight of the coin. He uses scales to gauge the weight. In this manner we should use the scales of virtuosity that has been gauged by Scripture and tradition. The moneychanger knows that sometimes a light coin will also suffice. If it has lost weight because of abrasions, the competent moneychanger can still recognize the coin as a legal means of payment. The weighing and testing should take place continuously. The goal is not rejection of the factual but establishing the relationship to the ideal full measure. If a spiritual guide tests and weighs, then the objective is to find the possibilities that God envisions. Even though it certainly happens that certain fragments need to be discarded, the testing and weighing is meant as encouragement rather than judgement.

Cassian's criteria are still valid nowadays. Any spiritual style – whether it be ecclesiastical or New Age, human resource management in large companies or ecologically inspired – should be questioned about its direction: Is it made of gold or shiny copper? Does it serve self-preservation and profit or does it guide people towards a secret that can no longer be defined in those terms and where Christians make mention of the Spirit? The effigy should be examined: Does it truly elicit a good feeling, does it lead to the freedom to enjoy all that is given or does it work only towards the satisfaction of achievement? Christians think this issue in terms of grace. Especially in the West even the noblest ideas and praxis risk being mutilated by compulsive achievement. The spiritual style is important, corresponding with the criterion of the acknowledged mint. Maybe tradition is not the crucial issue anymore – good things from other cultures can be grafted onto Christian stems quite well – but the socio-cultural context and its evidences should be examined critically. The last criterion is of interest nowadays as well. In this age of efficiency and perfectionism the spiritual domain should leave room for the (still or once again) imperfect. What is characterised by human defectiveness should not be rejected because of it. It should be respected in light of growth towards and community with the one full Life. A spirituality that excludes that perspective because of perfectionism should be mistrusted.

3.2. Augustine: development of the self and more than that

In what is perhaps his most famous book, his *Confessiones*, Augustine († 430) contemplates the most important moments in his life in the presence of God. It is one long prayer with his life story as raw material. Andriessen (1996, 64) has distinguished between the exterior and the interior path of life. The exterior is the story of the entire factual development including religious views. So, Augustine tells his exterior path of life. But he does more, he asks questions, hesitates, prays, and tries to distinguish between what gave life and what resulted in a dead-end. That is the interior life story, the notes in the margin. Here is the point of contact for spiritual guidance, where God's guidance in life can show itself.

One episode that is significant for questions of present-day spiritual guidance is the part in book X where Augustine contemplates the question whether happiness can be found in one's own life. He starts with a positive response. We actively look for happiness; it is a major part of our life. Especially in searching truth and community (X, 21) we find happiness in all sorts of ways, and we save it in our memory. Happiness and God are deeply connected. That is the reason, he says, that we find God inside our memory, and not outside. In the unfolding of our own life, in finding truth and community, God can be found (X, 24). That is why memory is so important. We don't have to look far, our own life story points towards God. Unfortunately, we often don't listen well: You were inside of me, but I was outside (X, 27).

First of all God cannot be found outside our own life, not outside our active search, not without our attempts to make it work. Nevertheless God does not coincide with what has succeeded in my life; there is also an outside and an above (X, 17). Augustine asks for happiness and for God also beyond the boundaries of our memory (X, 37). It turns out that in my attempts to make my life work I am not truly safely anchored in God or in happiness, because the light of my searching is finite while God is the ever-lasting infinite Light. My searching disperses. Only when God gathers me in my diverse searching, I converge. That is when I am inside myself, where not I do find God, but where God finds me. That is the moment that I realise that two things are true at the same time: on the one hand that only in self-realisation and my own search God can be found inside myself, and on the other hand that I am found there by God, who exceeds my life. My own searching merges into my being found by God. That is how God lets himself be found: inside and outside (VII, 10).

Augustine illustrates excellently in his own meditative life story what spiritual guidance is about: discovering on the one hand how my own human activity is indispensable in the encounter with God, but on the other hand how it is immediately taken over, as it were, by God who searches and finds me from beyond the human range. Spiritual guidance should concentrate on the concrete life, in its material, psychological, social and cultural forms in the first place.

That is where God can be found, says Augustine, doing justice to the Christian conviction that the Highest has not only created this world, but wants to be present in it to become human as well. Christian spirituality considers all earthly things not only as a starting-point for beginners (that should be left behind as quickly as possible) but also as the destination for adepts. If one pays too little attention to the concrete life, spiritual life evaporates into an almost unchristian spiritualism. Unfortunately spirituality has suffered of this type of anaemia on several occasions. To Christianity incarnation is a crucial issue. But the emphasis on divine incarnation in worldly reality asks also for the useful tension of being touched by the Transcendent One, by God beyond me, says Augustine. This opens spiritual growth towards an infinite perspective. Only then real justice is done to our searching. Without this opposite of being-touched by God's transcendence the incarnation of the God-relation in this world would not be done justice. Its perspective would be narrowed, instead of being extended and intensified beyond human limits, also beyond the limit of death. For many great spiritual leaders the eternal vision of God plays an important part, not as an isolated goal, but as an intensification of the happiness that is also sought and found on earth.

3.3 Ignatius of Loyola: Letting the deepest longing carry over into daily choices

The Spiritual Exercises of Ignatius († 1556) can be considered as a structure, consisting of texts, reflection and exercises, through which one can shape his or her deepest longing for God. It is about personal growth. One can of course apply that structure mechanically, aimed at achievement and result, but that makes a caricature out of them. They should be considered helpful in ordering one's own life and looking for the meaning and source of all life. It is a method to open oneself to God's workings in our own life. Beyond the standard of general moral principles, that still allow a range of possibilities, one looks for God's will in every day reality. God is to be respected not only in his hidden ness, but also in his relation to all things and occasions. A spiritual guide will assist in translating these exercises to the measure and the experience of a specific person. In such a specific situation they have been generated. They originated from Ignatius' own experience, on his path to the mystical experience of God. He is convinced that it is not the prerogative of a special, blessed elite, but that every person in search of meaning and happiness can attain it. A person's own experience and especially his or her deepest longing is starting-point of the exercises, which proceed according to a threefold rhythm: Wondering, reflecting and seeing which steps the developmental process needs. In regard to content the encounter with Jesus is central.
The complete exercises take four weeks. The first week focuses on the reflection of one's own broken existence and God's mercy, after which one

concentrates on the life of Jesus in the second week. The third week pictures the suffering of Christ and the fourth his resurrection. The spiritual guide will continually lead the guided to his or her most fundamental longing and to the choices that this requires. One alternative is not necessarily better than another; it is related to the personal path that someone has to go. As the most important criterion for judging the correctness of the choice, Ignatius takes the discernment of the spirits. The experience of consolation and peace is more than a reaction of one's own psyche, like relief or satisfaction. Even though these psychological reactions may accompany the consolation, the experience of peace is crucial. One knows that in this process of decision-making one is touched by God who knows and gauges our heart. Conversely, when experiencing negative feelings, like despondency and unease, one should consider that this might be a loud psychological reaction, which might drown the deeper feelings of peace as a result of the consequences that a certain decision implies. It appears therefore that the criterion cannot be applied mechanically. One has to devote all of one's natural capacity for discernment and common sense. All great spiritual leaders have warned for the tricks of the devil. He will constantly try to obscure the clear criteria that determine the choice. This difficulty however does not alter the fact that one keeps returning to this gauge of consolation as the most important indicator. In that sense also the spiritual guidance of Ignatius puts a lot of trust in natural feelings in which God's paths are shown. Making choices is the central category in the method of Ignatius starting at the fundamental level of deepest longing, but extending into making choices in concrete and even material matters.

It appears to me that Ignatius' search for the will of God concerning concrete choices is also a noteworthy theme in spiritual growth in our day and age. It is true that especially in a consumptive culture there are quite a few impulses to decide quickly and frequently, but much less so at the existential level. Here important decisions are put off more and more often as it seems. Moreover, dilemmas that cannot be postponed are often approached with standards that are valid in a certain well-defined domain. The current procedure for problem solving is: isolating and tackling. On both counts, Ignatius offers a complementary accent. He stimulates choosing and applies a standard that goes far beyond particular domains. He opposes an endless postponement of steps to be taken and relates the choice to the fundamental direction of the course of life. Of course this spirituality can also end up in a spiral that is dominated by an 'activist efficiency syndrome'. And of course one can manipulate 'God's will' in a manner that is degrading. But as long as spiritual guidance guards against such caricatures the Ignatian method seems very adequate for present-day attitudes.

3.4. St John of the Cross: about proper reserve on the part of the spiritual guide

Together with Theresa of Avila († 1582) St John of the Cross († 1591) is the most important exponent of sixteenth century Spanish mysticism. In his writings as well as in his personal pastoral work he is an excellent spiritual leader. Unjustly, he is regarded as an exponent of merely strict ascetism. He does indeed demand a degree of radicalism in active practicing of virtues, but even more strongly he displays an earnest concentration on the presence of God by not letting anything distract him and by not being satisfied with anything less than God himself. He emphasizes that not only active dedication is necessary but even more so the passive act of letting-things-happen. The actual work in the development of the relation with God is not done by a person but by God himself. This experience is crucial, but only few people dare to let it happen and the devil readily takes advantage of this situation. John of the Cross especially turns on those spiritual leaders who overwhelm people under their care with well-meant advice to try their best, while the time of being passive has come (Llama de amor viva III, 30-62). Spiritual leaders should know better, but unfortunately few good ones exist, he flatly states. For a beginner it is of course important that subjects are presented for meditation and for acquiring a taste for the spiritual. The human faculties, intellect, will, imagination and affect, must be addressed to get started. Virtues can be practiced to deliver the soul of egocentricity. Spiritual leaders know of exercises and methods to attain this. But at a certain point in time, when the soul has become detached, or even when this process of detachment can only be completed by detaching from the religious exercises themselves – for example because one searches a sense of safety and self-preservation in those exercises – that is when God takes over. He will allow the spirit of the free person to share in unprecedented beauty, or He will take away the taste for the spiritual, in order to free the spirit. But exactly then, when the Beloved takes over, many spiritual leaders do not know when to stop. They keep suggesting, advising and urging people on. By this lack of understanding, they can cause a lot of damage, St John says, because here reserve is called for: a time of holy 'doing-anything'. This is extremely vulnerable; it is openness and pure receptivity. Spiritual leaders who are not aware of this, should not guide people. However, often they are too vain to accept this. St John considers an attitude of reserve essential and states that one should be imbued with the necessity of accepting the lead of the Spirit in others.

This line of approach differs slightly from that of Ignatius. We should realize that John of the Cross focuses on spiritual leaders first and subsequently on those who are advanced on the spiritual path. His warnings are directed at a religious culture in which activity and productivity are central, while in religious development letting-things-happen is essential. In the West, however, exactly this is associated with neglect and irresponsibility. John reacts to the overestimation of oneself that is connected with it. He refers to fundamental trust that diminishes emphasis on human effort.

Conclusion: spiritual guidance and psychotherapy

We have looked at the style of spiritual guidance of four people only, thereby ignoring much wisdom. In conclusion, I would like to glance at one more subject: the possible worth in the renewed interest of spiritual guidance in psychotherapy circles. Concerning the relationship between spiritual guidance and psychotherapy, I am certain about the psychological skills of all spiritual leaders mentioned above, their ability to recognize, rate and point out unconscious motives. The unconscious often plays a more prominent part than conscious motives. Guidance at this level might not strictly be spiritual guidance, but the two are interwoven. The spiritual guide does not have to be a qualified psychologist, but he or she has to be able to understand how needs, old disappointments, fears, etc. interfere with spiritual longing. Spiritual growth will stagnate if one does not personally integrate such psychological processes. Spiritual leaders turn out to be excellent psychotherapists.

On the other hand – concerning the value of spiritual guidance for psychological counselling – I cannot offer more than suppositions. In the past decennia psychotherapists have been slightly allergic to any type of connection with the religious. The aversion may have something to do with meddling of the church that was often authoritarian, or maybe with religious patterns in the therapists themselves. Also the need to profile psychotherapy as a separate discipline called for a method cleansed of any religious colour. It looks like the tide is turning. Some factors might be involved, which might hypothetically indicate the value of the religious/existential field for the psychological. Spiritual/existential guidance taps sources of personal development outside the individual existence as well. First of all there is a narrative tradition that can help people find their destination. It does not substitute the search for a destination but facilitates it. A story that stimulates the process of finding one's identity can of course also serve psychological development. Subsequently in the religious dimension strength and motives are opened up that propel the process of changing and that belong to the strongest present in human existence. Mobilization of this force seems advantageous at the psychological level as well. Finally I think that spiritual/existential guidance is broader and sometimes deeper than the area in which psychosocial problems are handled. Spiritual/existential guidance looks for a thread that spans several psycho-therapeutical fields with their own specific methods. This fundamental *ductus* could possibly provide a non-methodological scope for different areas of development. However, it might be more important to establish a mutual open-mindedness between different forms of counselling, than to give an exact overview of the advantages that can be expected.

References

Andriessen, H. 1996. *Oorspronkelijk bestaan. Geestelijke begeleiding in onze tijd.* Baarn: Gooi & Sticht.

Barry, W., and W. Connolly, 1982-86. *The Practice of Spiritual Direction.* San Francisco: Harper Collins.

Bluyssen, J. 1999. Naar het model van Franciscus van Sales. Pp. 106-121 in *Steun en toeverlaat. Historische aspecten van geestelijke begeleiding*, edited by M. Montero, P. Nissen and J. De Raat. Hilversum.

Deenen, S.J., van 1999. De vraag, niet het aanbod. Geestelijke begeleiding volgens ignatiaanse traditie. Pp. 122-135 in *Steun en toeverlaat. Historische aspecten van geestelijke begeleiding*, edited by M. Montero, P. Nissen and J. De Raat. Hilversum.

Geestelijke begeleiding 1995. *Speling* 47(2).

Hausherr, I. 1957. Direction spirituelle en Orient. Pp. 1008-1060 in *Dictionnaire de la Spiritualité ascetique et mystique III.* Parijs.

Knippenberg, T., van 1998. *Tussen naam en identiteit. Ontwerp van een model voor geestelijke begeleiding.* Kampen: Kok.

Sheldrake, P. 1990. St. Ignatius of Loyola and Spiritual Direction. In *Traditions of Spiritual Guidance*, edited by L. Byrne. London.

Sudbrack, J. 1981. *Geistliche Führung. Zur Frage nach dem Meister, dem geistlichen Begleiter und Gottes Geist.* Freiburg.

Switek, G. 1972. Discretio spirituum. Ein Beitrag zur Geschichte der Spiritualität. *Philosophie und Theologie* 47: 36-76.

Waaijman, K. 2000. *Spiritualiteit. Vormen, grondslagen, methoden.* Kampen: Kok.

Wagenaar, C. 1981. *Woestijnvaders. Een speurtocht door de Vaderspreuken.* Nijmegen: Gottmer.

Secularisation and Catholicism
On the Identity of Catholic Social Organisations

Karl-Wilhelm Merks

Queries with regard to social organisations with a particular philosophical or religious identity are justly viewed in connection with the phenomenon of secularisation. The general marginalisation of religion in public life is often the basis for the increasing loss of recognition of identity-bound organisations' right to exist. Society is becoming increasingly – and it is felt, more and more effectively – structured on the basis of what is known as functional rationality. Every domain is managed and controlled by a specific rationality (Schramm 2001). Politics, the care sector, the medical world, the cultural sector, the leisure sector, etc., all have their own aims and laws. Their organisation is a matter of professionalism.

The entwinement of the professional approach with consideration for identity would only confuse the clear and efficient organisation. Social service is functional and should therefore be freed, as it were, from the burden of a worldview. Philosophical interpretation made from the perspective of a particular concept of humanity, world and God or from that of specific traditions in values is declared irrelevant for the functional-professional aims of the social organisation. Sport should be organised as sport, and not as Catholic sport; school should be organised as school and not as Catholic school. Thus, from this perspective, the preservation of specific (identity-bound) Catholic organisations for the promotion of social activities is no longer a matter of course.

This is, for that matter, a view that is not only imposed upon Catholics from the outside, but that many Catholics themselves have internalized. Generalisation has supporters not only amongst the non-religious. "Professionalism" is the catchword (even in pastoral care). The Christian-believer aspect is obviously a separate element that contributes little or nothing to that professionalism. In such a context, protecting those Catholic organisations that still exist is in danger of becoming more a matter of retaining power and defending interests than one of maintaining a professionally substantiated position. Those who interpret secularisation as the displacement of God from our existence and as the corruption of true Catholicism, which should aim to permeate society with a religious view on life, contribute to the establishment of such an image. It is therefore not surprising that, in reaction to this, the suspicion is again being expressed that Catholic organisations, where they still exist, are a mixture of social aims with their own interests that should be rejected.

Another element in this context is the disappearance of the traditional management structures of Catholic organisations. The "clerical leadership" of Catholic organisations has vanished. The issue of "ideological" guidance is a completely different matter. Who decides what is Catholic and what Catholics should (are allowed to) do? This matter came to a head with great vehemence in the German discussion (Thoma et al. 2001) on the "Schwanger-schaftskonfliktberatung" and (after all but one of the bishops had withdrawn their "cooperation" at the insistence of Rome) the foundation of the organisation "Donum vitae" – nota bene by lay people usually very active on the religious front. There is hardly a more obvious sign of change in "management structures" than in this ethically laden issue. It is also obvious from "official" religious reactions that people are fully aware of this. The material ethical issue is not the only thing involved. Also concerned in the definition of the role of Catholic organisations in a "civil society" is a change in leadership (Zentralkomitee der deutschen Katholiken 2001), whether we call this laicisation, democratisation, or whatever. In any case, the tide has turned.

In my opinion, this change is also reflected in a number of trends in the developments in theology in the past years. A number of decades ago most theologians would have considered the ideal of Catholic organisations quite normal; this could not have been otherwise in the context of the role of religion that was experienced as being natural, in public life too, that was expressed in the Netherlands in the phenomenon of (denominational) segregation. Other countries had, perhaps less perfect, but, in any case, similar social structures. Later a different generation of theologians appeared. Many opted for breaking open the Catholic inner culture. Various factors contributed to this, including the ecumenical movement, a revision of the role of the lay person in the church and the world, the revaluation of the everyday and the so-called autonomy of earthly realities during the Second Vatican Council, but certainly also the individual biography of many people who experienced the uniformity and the pillarized communality as stifling. I feel it is important to note how outdated various positions are: the question of the defensibility of identity-bound Catholic organisations has nothing to do with unchanging essential relations; rather, it concerns the history of culturally defined institutions.

In the meantime, the situation is again changing. The significance of the identity issue is now coming more subtly into view with nostalgia, on the one hand, and scepticism with regard to Catholic organisations, on the other: substantiated ideas need a social basis; the individual is by no means as individual as was thought; and pluralism can maintain itself, as such, only in cases where it is made up of separate elements, each of which has a distinct profile. There is a lively discussion taking place on this; however, it is not easy to persevere against the two traditional extremes, which still seem to be very appealing, namely liberalistic neutralisation views, on the one hand, and integral identity ideals that crop up in the form of all sorts of ancient and neo-fundamentalisms, on the other hand.

It is against this background that I would briefly like to deal with the following three points:

1) the theological significance of secularisation

2) the relation of the professional-functional aspect in social organisations and the (Catholic) identity aspect

3) the significance of identity-bound social organisations, particularly for a secularised society.

1. The theological significance of secularisation

Secularisation is often the banner under which it is argued that identity-bound social organisations no longer have a place in modern society. It is true that this can be explained historically and it is sometimes promoted by the church – yet it is a one-sided interpretation. The pretence that neutrality in the social order is a necessary consequence of secularisation goes beyond historical reality and sociological data and patterns. It is well known that secularisation is just as little as any other similar concept, a timeless definition of essence. It serves as a characterisation of particular historical developments that are typical of our history of Western culture. In that history, the tense relation between religion and politics forms a typical element (Merks 1987; 1989); modern secularisation is one way, our *modern* way, of expressing this tension. Even in situations in which the role of religion in public life is denied, this is an implicit reference to religion as an element that is related to public life. Secularisation does not therefore mean the expulsion of the religious from society, but a way of considering its position. Secularisation is criticism of particular cultural expressions of the relation religion/public life; it is the dispute of certain organisational entwinings of religion, society, and state, and, as such, a process of rearrangement.

Secularisation is, however, not only – negatively – the attempt to ban the undesirable entwinement of religion and public order; on the positive side, secularisation also opens our eyes to the specific rationality of the various areas of reality. The significance of the latter is sometimes underestimated; yet one should, in my opinion, consider it unambiguously as an advantage. Because of it, we now know that poverty should be combated with economic means, illness with medical means, and that differences in opportunities demand legal, social, and cultural intervention. We may not resort to a reference to a divine order; that road is now closed. Besides this concentration on the specific patterns of social structures, secularisation can be appreciated for another reason. Historically, it is secularisation, and not the political-religious unity of society, that creates the space for plurality in worldviews, in other words, for freedom of conscience. It is only through the disentanglement of social-political views and religious ideas concerning social order that society is able to organise itself in such a way that it offers a refuge for people who live by various convictions.

However, that this disentanglement should lead to complete neutralisation and colourless generalisation is definitely not the case. Secularisation determines, when looked at more closely, rather negative boundaries for religious influence; how society integrates religion within these boundaries, and the significance of identity-bound organisations is not indicated as such by the principle of secularisation.

People will possibly ask themselves what all of that has to do with theology. For me, it is a facet of what is known as the inculturation of faith (Merks 1998, 283vv.), the attempt to root faith – as has happened repeatedly in the history of Christianity – into our modern culture with its own experience of values, its difficulties, but also opportunities for a humane existence.

Therefore the secularisation and pluralisation of society becomes a learning process for theology and for faith (Merks 1997). The separation of an all too obvious entwinement of politics and the gospel, of church and state, of Christianity and society offers the opportunity for a "purer" commitment, in which it is not privileges that have been acquired and the actual institutional position of power that rules (and for that matter also not the benevolence due to a government because of the privileges it offers), but where the violence-free persuasiveness of the faith of Christians must prove itself (Merks 1987).

Catholic organisations within society should now create an unmistakably distinct profile as a provider of service to that society. It is only in the second instance, and through this provision of service, that "self-preservation" is involved.

Thus, one could conclude that secularisation and pluralisation force us to profile more distinctly the Christian social commitment as a service. In the following section, I wish to make it clear why this orientation towards service to society should also take place in this way, from a theological point of view. I will do this on the basis of the following question: Where does a commitment of faith get its actual standards. One would imagine from its own Scripture and tradition, or from an individual system of norms and values. Yet, this is an answer that needs to be nuanced.

Certainly, Christians live, at least when they do it well, with the message of the Gospel as their foundation; but what that actually involves cannot simply be traced back to the Gospel; this often only becomes apparent in the experiences with social reality and therefore has consequences for the question of identity.

2. The relation of the professional-functional aspect in social organisations and the (Catholic) identity aspect

In my opinion, it is important to start with the principle that Catholic social organisations should, in the first place, establish their identity with particular tasks in mind and not their self-preservation. Theologically, this could be elaborated as follows.

Concern for society that in the past century has gained a broader structural-social orientation, in particular in the social doctrine of the church, is not a matter of subordinate importance for faith. It is especially with the rise of this social doctrine of the church that the question of social justice and the commitment of Christians in the service of that justice is being more and more clearly interpreted as a determinant and integral part of faith itself and, with it, of the Catholic identity (Merks 1991a; 1991b).

As far as the content of that justice is concerned, it – as is becoming more and more obvious in the development of the social doctrine – cannot be traced back to faith, but becomes visible from social reality, in particular from people's wants and needs, suffering, worries and shortcomings. Social justice is therefore not specifically Christian.

When social justice is, on the one hand, an expression of a commitment of faith, and on the other, is not directly intrinsically determined by faith, then this means: Christian identity with regard to social commitment is partly determined by a by no means specifically Christian criterion. This is why recent moral theology has become convinced that "specific" Christian morality cannot be found in "exclusive" specific norms, values, and behaviour. Instead of "exclusively" Christian, the term "typically" Christian is preferred. This indicates that it is not of any particular interest whether Christians behave differently from others, but that they draw consequences from faith and that for a Christian an ethical commitment can typically be formed by faith.

What social justice actually involves, however, is not thought to come (specifically) from faith. Discovering the requirements of justice involves reasonable insight, based on reasonable effort, in which everybody can, in principle, take part.

This presents us with a remarkable fact. Whether we experience and actualise our faith in an authentic way is in large part determined from "the outside". Thus, faith itself can, as it were, be judged by a standard outside that faith. The result can be epitomised in a paradox: the true Christian identity is confirmed in doing something unspecific.

True, the Christian may be faced with the question of social justice and social commitment in the context of the Gospel, church and faith, which could motivate and stimulate him/her and also cause him/her to question the accepted views held by society. Still, the search for a more just structuring of society remains a task in which Christians, like all people, must develop reasonableness and creativity.

The history of the social doctrine shows that identity has nothing to do with obstinately maintaining a situation that has always been the same. What it says about property and work, about politics and economy, about church and state, and about human rights has visibly grown alongside social developments. It is in this light that the issue of the identity of Catholic organisations in the contemporary cultural context must be seen; that context is for us that of autonomy, secularisation, rationalisation, democracy, and pluralism (Merks 1998, 311-317). It is in this, and not against it, that Christian commitment takes place.

3. The significance of identity-bound social organisations for a secularised society

It is clear from what has been reflected upon till now that a) secularisation by no means has to exclude identity-bound social organisations; and b) these have to justify themselves precisely through a professional significance for the factual social problems (what in the discussions concerning these topics is indicated as the "quality aspect").

But the question now is: In a situation in which we find ourselves faced with this task in community with many other people, with all sorts of different views on faith and the world, why would a specific identity really be necessary?

In considering this, there are a number of elements that can be mentioned. On doing so, I make claim to neither completeness nor originality.

3.1. Running down wrong conceptions

a) The position of state/government
It is wrong to create an image that suggests that the state is responsible for everything and that it is thus the patron of observations of all public duties. While the government is stressing its limited responsibility as far as the content is concerned, at the same time it practically claims "full competence" via subsidy distribution.

The fact that particular organisations need government money is not an expression of the government's right to control, but of the fact that the government has to an increasing degree transferred the financial control from citizens and their associations to the centre. The state does not provide money but manages it. In other words, it is the government that is subsidiary, and not social organisations.

b) The actual efficiency of generalisation
Has anybody ever been able to prove what the actual economization effects, of expansion and generalisation are? Furthermore, are there any thoughts given to

what the price of generalisation is with regard to the *integral* quality of the provision of services? Moreover, the question should be asked whether organisational streamlining is not actually a case of new more complex coordination structures.

c) A narrower analysis of modern society

We have already discussed the one-sidedness of the interpretation of secularisation; such considerations should be adjusted with regard to other central concepts of our modern society such as individualisation, plurality, and democracy. What these concepts involve is not always clear.

d) The significance of a purely functional justification of organisations

Organisations must justify themselves functionally or through the quality aspect; but that is, as it were, only conditio sine qua non. Medical care should be medical care; education, education, etc. However, the question that does arise is whether, in the explanation of what is involved in medical care, or education, etc., purely technical answers are given that no longer take into consideration the integral aspects of these specific and specialised services: for example, that, in medical care, it is not a kidney, a broken arm, or a confused metabolism, but the whole person that is at issue, who, depending on the circumstances, also requires integral care. Or that in education it is not only information, but also an upbringing that may be included.

3.2. A careful formulation of the individual identity

a) Linked with the above, this would mean that Catholic organisations should make serious attempts – besides quality control – to explain time and again the additional value of their activities for an all-embracing care for people and society, and to be self-critical in doing so.

b) The significance of identity-bound organisations must be differentiated with regard to their own supporters and general public. The first aspect may also be emphasised in this: people are not, in the first place, general state citizens and then actors in all sorts of other roles.

c) The significance of identity-bound organisations concerns, in particular, those dimensions that, because of an ever increasing technical development in the provision of services, threaten to be lost: questions involving meaning, value consciousness, education in values. The meaning of suffering and death, guilt and forgiveness; the importance of solidarity, mercy, pity and many other questions are *not automatically asked* and kept alive in society.

d) I have already discussed avoiding a wrongly exclusive definition of identity on the part of the organisations themselves. The service offered must be made visible as one that is offered and not as a monopoly.

e) This includes creating structures (management structure; control; legitimisation; personnel management, etc.) within the organisation that are linked with the general democracy and sense of justice in our society.

3.3. Care for the material and institutional conditions of the social provision of services

a) Individual commitment can neither replace nor guarantee institutional presence.
b) Without social "status", one cannot expect a social effect.
c) Identity-bound organisations do not have to present themselves as an exception, but may present themselves as normal organisations; in the long run, a tolerated "status apart" of Catholic organizations (namely an exceptional position in the "normal case" of *general* organisations) is the beginning of the end of social relevance (Merks 1989).

Finally

In the light of the above propositions, I can draw some sort of conclusion:
As far as I can evaluate, one should not confuse two issues when it comes to the question of identity. Identity through setting up boundaries is one issue. Identity as a result of belonging somewhere, of having a group that you can lean on, people who think somewhat along the same lines as yourself; where a number of things are natural, where one can commit oneself in the same way for the same thing; is another issue.
I am of the impression that we sometimes forget the importance of having a recognisable group to which we belong and from which we take action. This is probably so because these groups often do not exist, at least as we would wish them to be, open and at the same time profiled, Christian and at the same time secularised. It is sometimes difficult for us to experience the church itself as that living context of people with whom we would *like* to form a community. Thus, this does not concern the limited determination of identity through being specifically different, but the concrete interpretation of identity within an active community that is able to function as a kind of natural breeding-ground for a self-assured commitment supported by trust.
People exist not as individuals, opposed to society as a whole, total entity. In reality, this is not the case. Therefore we do not have to be persuaded otherwise, whenever suitable on the grounds of ideology or, very primitively, for financial reasons.
A society that does not cherish intermediate structures, the midfield, robs itself of its substance. This is where the relative independence of sectoral and parcelled rationality can be integrated into the whole of human reasonability and "sympathy" as the foundation for a humane existence. Resistance of Catholic organizations against a fixation on sectorial rationality will, however, only be successful when it is possible to make transparent the value of the group identity, for the society as a whole. And in this regard Catholic organizations have to do a lot of work.

References

Merks, K.-W. 1998. *Gott und die Moral. Theologische Ethik heute.* ICS-Schriften 35. Münster: LIT.

Merks, K.-W. 1997. Zur Situation der Moraltheologie. Plädoyer für eine "säkularisierte" Theologie. *Bulletin ET* 8(1): 115-121.

Merks, K.-W. 1991a. Nieuwe fase in sociaal denken van de kerk. *1-2-1 Informatiebulletin* 19: 25-29.

Merks, K.-W. 1991b. Van sociale leer naar sociale ethiek. *1-2-1 Informatiebulletin* 19: 11-16.

Merks, K.-W. 1989. Voorbij symbiose en separatie: over de publieke rol van de kerk in een moderne staat. Pp. 47-60 in: *Kerk en Staat. Actuele ontwikkelingen belicht,* edited by J.A.F. Peeters. Zwolle: W.E.J. Tjeenk Willink.

Merks, K.-W. 1987. Kerk en Staat - sociaal-ethisch gezien. Pp. 40-72 in: *Kerk en staat. Hun onderlinge verhouding binnen de Nederlandse samenleving,* edited by S.C. den Dekker-van Bijsterveld, E.M.H. Hirsch Ballin, K.-W. Merks and G.J.M. van Wissen. Baarn: Amboboeken.

Schramm, M. 2001. Systemtheorie und Sozialethik. Methodologische Überlegungen zum Ruf nach Verantwortung. Pp. 105-132 in: *Verantwortung - Ende oder Wandlungen einer Vorstellung? Orte und Funktionen der Ethik in unserer Gesellschaft,* edited by K.-W. Merks. Münster: LIT.

Thoma, M.E., B. Fraling, A. van Kalmthout and J. Schuster. 2001. Beratung statt Strafe. Neue Beziehungen zwischen Ethik und Strafgesetz am Beispiel der Schwangerschaftskonfliktberatung. Pp. 257-271 in: *Verantwortung - Ende oder Wandlungen einer Vorstellung? Orte und Funktionen der Ethik in unserer Gesellschaft,* edited by K.-W. Merks. Münster: LIT.

Zentralkomitee der deutschen Katholiken 2001. *Berichte und Dokumente 113.* Bonn.

The Liturgical Profile of the Pastor and the Dynamics of Cultus and Culture

Louis van Tongeren

Introduction

The process of secularisation and the influence of various (post) modern trends have in the past decades led to great changes in the position and significance of the institutionalised church in the West. The natural and communal faith of the people's church has been transformed into individual forms of faith and religion. In his overview of this development, Hans van der Ven makes a distinction between shifts in the macro-level of society, the meso-level of the church and the micro-level of the individual (Van der Ven 1998). In all three of these levels pastors are confronted in their work with shifts in the area of religion. A univocal frame of reference with regard to the church and faith has been replaced by ambivalence, a diversity in the way faith is experienced and church views and sometimes even conflicting ideas. This pluralisation within the church, theology and faith has made the work of the pastor much more complicated. Moreover, pastors are faced with an increase in work pressure, due to the decline in the number of available pastors. Although there has been a great decline in the number of churchgoers over the past decades, this has not resulted in more time or less pressure for pastors. The workload has not been reduced by any means.

It is therefore hardly surprising that both the structure and the organisation of the parish as the position and work area of the pastor have recently come under review in the Netherlands. As a rule the staffing in pastoral care receives particular attention. On the parish level this has led to various forms of co-operation, in the area of management as well as pastoral care. Meanwhile various alternatives have been tried and tested, from personal unity in a collective team of pastors, to inter-parochial links or the complete merger of parishes (see for a complete overview Huysmans 1998a). Figures show that there was a 1 to 1 situation in the year 2000; that is to say that there was on average one pastor available for each parish, a pastoral worker, deacon or priest. The tendency to restructure coincides with the prognoses that show that the integration of parishes on a managerial level and increased co-operation will expand in the coming years. At a rough estimate the number of managerial units will be reduced to approximately 500 or 600 in five years time, according to the expected number of available priests, that in comparison to now will be halved (Bernts 2002).

The concern for the future of the parish and pastoral care has recently been given a new impulse due to the fact that on a national as well as diocesan level policy plans are being developed, whereby more parochial expansion is linked with the structure of larger pastoral teams, made up of a number of pastors each with his/her own speciality or profile (Eerste Ontwerp 2000; Tweede Ontwerp 2001; Profileren 2001). Tasks among pastors themselves can be defined more clearly by means of profiling, and moreover, profiling should offer sufficient guarantee for a personal investment in the various task areas that are traditionally distinguished within parochial pastoral care: *kerugma, diakonia, leitourgia* (see for an overview of other classifications of specific jobs or task areas within pastoral care, Van der Ven 1998,125-135). Although these tasks are essentially the essence of a parish, and the promotion of them determines its vitality (Huysmans 1998b, 55-56), liturgy is the most important area of attention for the pastor. Research shows that pastors, in comparison to other tasks, spend most of their time on liturgy, independently from their consecration abilities (Beroepsprofiel 1999). The introduction of pastoral workers and deacons who work together with priests has not led to a differentiation in task areas and job profiles. They all perform the same tasks and all of them spend a large amount of time on liturgy. In reality it is clear that liturgy is the greatest – and for many also the most important – area of attention in pastoral care. In connection with this a differentiation of tasks is proposed in the distinguished profiles in the policy documents mentioned, but liturgy forms a part of each profile.

This means that pastors are able to develop the competence they require for their specific work areas or field of attention, but that all of them should have sufficient liturgical expertise. Because of this liturgy earns a prominent place in the curriculum of pastoral training, in accordance with its importance in the work area of pastors. Moreover, the content of the liturgical part of the curriculum will have to be given form in the light of the complex and dynamic interaction between religion and culture pointed out above. The liturgical profile of the pastor demands an expertise that is aimed at the dynamics between cultus and culture. Before I enter into the consequences this has for the training of pastors, I will consider two elements in which these dynamics manifest themselves, and what the pastor is confronted with in the pulpit. In the first place this is the community within which and the type of service in which the pastor takes the pulpit. Both the composition of congregations and liturgical practices are in a state of flux. Liturgy has become more divergent and more multiform, and the type of people who make up a congregation can vary from service to service. With regard to the liturgy, supply and demand no longer correspond automatically. The differentiation that has arisen requires continual adjustment to the actual congregation that gathers for a service.

1. Break down of parish structure

The drop in church attendance, the decline in institutional church involvement and the decreasing number of available pastors have resulted in more and more pressure on the traditional parish structure. The intricate network of parishes can no longer be maintained. Expansion and the formation of teams are applied in order to relieve dwindling parishes. The drop in the number of churchgoers does not, however, mean that they do not remain the most important gauge in the parish, the leaders of which are linked to liturgical leadership. This relation between congregational leaders and liturgical leadership has, however, become a problem, just as taking the pulpit in liturgy has become more complex due to the fact that the congregation that gathers for the liturgy is continually changing. I have entered into more detail on the consequences of this shift and the possibilities and opportunities for liturgy elsewhere (Van Tongeren 2002a).

1.1. Community of believers and congregational leaders

According to the present Codex dating from 1983, it is the community of believers that determines the essence of a parish (CIC c. 515, 1; Eysink 1995, 3). The congregation is the essential factor that makes a parish a parish. Although this sounds quite natural to us now, for a long time it was a carefully defined territory that determined what a parish was, and the church building in this territory or the parish priest formed the legal body (Huysmans 1998b, 35; see for a historical overview Eysink 1995, 22-28). Following along the lines of the theological principle of the *communio* or the *koinoonia* and that of the ecclesiology of the people of God, emphasis is now placed on the communal aspect of the parish. Constitutive are the believers; in the canonical definition they form the first and foremost characteristic of the parish (Eysink 1995, 4-5; Huysmans 1998b, 56). A similar shift has taken place in the parish as in liturgy: just as the congregation has been rediscovered as the subject of liturgy, so is the congregation also the subject of the parish.

The priest is responsible for the leadership of the parish, due to his liturgical competence (Huysmans 1998b, 49; Karrer 1998, 274). Therefore, parish leadership is closely connected to liturgical leadership, through ordainment. The ministry represents, as a service of parish leadership, the church that in turn is essentially connected to liturgical leadership (Koch 1998, 67). In the meantime in practice this link between parish leadership, liturgical leadership and the ministry has been so stretched that this connection still exists officially, but in actual fact it is extremely artificial. Officially many deans carry the final responsibility for a number of parishes, but it is impossible for them to carry out their liturgical tasks to the full in all of these parishes. In reality pastoral workers led those parishes, have final responsibility and take the pulpit in liturgy. Because they have gained sufficient experience in liturgy, they are generally competent enough to take the pulpit; however, they lack official competence (Karrer 1998, 265). They are crippled pastors because they lack ministerial qualifications meaning that they do not have the same liturgical, or in other words, sacramental authority as the priest. As a result of this priests are hired from elsewhere or a liturgy is adjusted to the competence of the pastoral worker, which results in the reduction of sacramental services to a minimum. Because of this a situation has arisen where in many places there is a separation of on the one hand parish leadership and liturgical leadership, and on the other the ministry. In reality a division is arising between a sacramentally based leadership structure of the parish, and a purely functional parallel structure, according to the German theologian and bishop Walter Kasper (as quoted in Koch 1998, 80). Even in Reformed Churches where proclamation, parish leadership and sacramental administration are emphatically connected to the ministry, there is no evidence of this kind of disconnection (Koch 1998, 78). The purest way to maintain and guarantee this link appears to be the liberalisation of admittance to the ministry. And since this is an unmentionable subject, it is hoped that it can be avoided through means of expansion. Parishes coalesce and form pastoral units with a collective pastoral team consisting of at least one priest, which means that the number of available priests is the deciding factor in the number of teams that can be formed (Huysmans 1998b, 49-53).

As long as pastoral workers are not given the same liturgical authority as priests, however, the connection between parish leadership and liturgical leadership will remain a problem, and many liturgical services in which they take the pulpit will officially be given another name, but the way in which they are experienced, their form and content will continue to resemble the services of which they are a surrogate, such as celebrations of the Word with Communion and the blessing of the sick as alternatives for the Eucharist and extreme unction respectively. Although believers are the most important and supportive pillar of the parish, and it is the primary task of the parish to guarantee public access to faith as well as the full celebration of secrets of the faith (Huysmans 1998b, 35-36), it is not the salutary meaning that the celebration of the sacraments can have for the religious life of the parishioners that is predominant. The importance for parishioners to take part in these services is merely respected in so far as it is subordinate to the specific interpretation assigned to priesthood in the second half of the Middle Ages.

1.1. Incidental community

The territorially defined parish still exists, but its borders are increasingly being crossed. Churchgoers have become church-hoppers as it were. People swarm and are less dedicated to their own parish; they tend either incidentally or permanently to seek elsewhere what is offered liturgically in the way of a choir, a minister or the atmosphere of a building. As a result the neighbourhood character of a parish or the connection to a district is reduced and is also less felt and experienced as being less important. Just as people have become more mobile in all areas of social life, the same applies to church involvement. The composition of the congregation has thus become variable and changes from Sunday to Sunday. This is enhanced by the fact that going to church each Sunday is no longer a matter-of-course. This not only applies for those who live somewhat on the verge of church life, but also for those who feel very involved in the church and faith. The long maintained distinction between main members or the main congregation and the non-practising or marginals has become much more diverse. Nowadays there are many more gradations in church involvement and participation in liturgy. The dedicated churchgoer who, till not long ago, took part in the celebration of the liturgy every weekend, now does not mind missing a service every now and then. The size of the parish does not therefore coincide with the number of participants in a regular weekend service, but is generally considerably greater. The obligation to go to Sunday Mass, a requirement for participation in the Eucharist, still exists it is true (CIC c. 1246, 1; c. 1247; see also c. 1248, 1-2), but this applies to few people nowadays, and it seems to clash with the idea of Sunday as a day off, that is to say a day that is free from obligation (Nissen 1992). Up till a number of decades ago, going to church was one of the few leisure activities outside the home on a Sunday, nowadays the Sunday liturgy has become less and less of a rival amongst the enormous supply in the leisure sector. Although the Sunday liturgy has come under a lot of pressure, among other things due to the shifts observed above (see for a more detailed argumentation Van Tongeren 2001a; 2001b), many still participate regularly; the regularity with which this occurs, however, varies greatly.

This more varied participation in liturgy seems to correspond with broad post-modern culture, in which club life in general is under pressure. People are finding it increasingly difficult to bind themselves and enter into regular obligations (Janssen s.a [2000], especially 73-77). The parish also no longer functions within the present social context as a social binding agent, at least not as strongly and naturally as it did for a long period of time. Such developments require a review of the concept community (of faith), as it is becoming increasingly obvious in practice that we should really refer to communities as what I would like to call: incidental communities, the composition of which can vary from service to service.

That the community that celebrates liturgy varies and is incidental in composition, is most obvious in occasional liturgy (Jespers 2000a; 2000b), especially services concerning life-cycle liturgies, that is to say: liturgy on the axis of life or liturgy on special occasions such as baptisms, weddings and funerals (Van Tongeren 2003), but also the celebration of anniversaries and of the first Communion (Post and van Tongeren 2001), that are celebrated in particularly in the more intimate circles of family, friends and acquaintances.

The number of parishioners that takes part in such services is in general small. Demographic developments show that we move house more often, and that families live further apart than they used to. Such services are thus experienced as more of a reunion; family members meet again and many ex-colleagues and old friends see each other for the first time in years, whilst these groups hardly know each other at all. The binding factor is not the mutual relationship between those present and a communal faith or Christian orientation, but the way in which each is involved with the person or people whose party it is or whose farewell is being celebrated. An incidental community forms itself around this person or these people, in which every imaginable gradation in church involvement is usually represented. In the German language this is known as a *Kasualgemeinde*, in correspondence with the type of liturgy that is called *Kasualliturgie* in German (see for example Wagner-Rau 2000).

Changes in the fields of church and society have caused churchgoers to become pilgrims or nomads, according to a description of the present-day believer given by Louis-Marie Chauvet during the international liturgy colloquium in October 2001 in Leuven. Along the same lines as the shift I described briefly above, he gives a number of profiles of today's believer on the grounds of which he reaches the indication pilgrim or nomad. He brings forward the following aspects (Chauvet 2002). The believer participates in liturgy and parish life on a *voluntary* basis. There is no longer any social pressure, and religious compulsion is no longer experienced. Everyone is free to choose whether or not he/she participates in church life. The people's church has become a church of choice, as sociologists impressed on us in the past. At the same time this implies a certain degree of *conviction*, because without motivation there would be no reason to participate. This motivation could also be based on external factors and instead of a personal conviction. As said this applies in particular to occasional liturgy when non-religious people go to a funeral for example, because of the personal relationship they had with the deceased or relatives of the deceased. If this voluntary attendance turns out to be a positive experience, then the degree of involvement becomes *optional*. The frequency of participation is after all not fixed, but can vary. For many participation is *exceptional* and the call for liturgy only arises incidentally and at particular times. People desire a liturgical framework at Christmas, when they get married or are in mourning, or when a child is born or does his/her first Communion. Incidental church attendance results in *brief* liturgical involvement. As irregularity increases so does familiarity decrease. Rituals do not have the chance to sink in and it will be more difficult to get to the very heart of the subject. Due to *mobility* church facilities have become accessible outside the territory of the domestic parish and these locations are visited either once in a while or regularly. The believer as an *individual* is central in all these profiles. Personal choice and preference define attitude and behaviour: I myself decide whether to join a parish and to participate in liturgy; I myself decide when, where and how often I go to a service.

The churchgoer has thus become much more of a nomad or transient. Not only has the community celebrating liturgy become smaller, but it is also becoming increasingly variable.

2. Liturgical practice

Just as the dynamic interaction between religion and culture not only has its effect on the meaning, function and composition of a parish, but in all areas of church life, so does it also not leave liturgy unaffected. Besides the official renewal of liturgy since Vatican II, the praxis and the way liturgy is experienced have changed drastically in the past decades due to sociocultural shifts. In order to indicate how drastic these changes are, Chauvet compares their impact not with a storm, where the damage done can be cleared, but with an earthquake that changes the landscape permanently (Chauvet 1999, 202). Because liturgy is essentially connected to a living faith, it also has a part in the complexity of religion and faith, so that there is likewise a case of a dynamic relationship between cultus and culture. These changes have caused various fields of tension and discrepancies to develop which Gerard Lukken and Louis-Marie Chauvet have already listed (Lukken 1987; 1998; Chauvet 1999). These are largely related to the difference that has grown between the professed rituals of the church as laid down in official liturgical books, and the experimentally designed liturgy in which an individual contribution and creativity play a large part. The inviolable liturgical structure that indicates the direction of personal faith, that steers experience and in which one can take shelter or flee, was replaced by a liturgy from below. Liturgy was put together on the spot by oneself, giving it an experimental character. Experience has become an important starting point; liturgy was expected at least to link up with this. Churchgoers had to feel that they were being approached personally so that there was room for doubt and uncertainty. Liturgy became more human, or as the critics call it, horizontality. This probably explains the multiform and heterogeneous liturgical repertoire that was created; a broad spectrum developed that was geared to various target groups: youth liturgy, children's liturgy, family services and services in Latin or in vernacular, with or without Gregorian hymns, Taizé services, etc.

The shift that took place caused tension between a deductive and an inductive approach to liturgy, or between a view on liturgy as a *katabasis and an anabasis*. Whilst in the past decades emphasis has been on an inductive approach to liturgy, now signs point to its one-sidedness and the need for a broadening. At present the value, inner dynamics and the coherence of the prescribed ritual from the perspective of spirituality is being reviewed (De Keyzer 2001). However, in a number of other recent publications, distance has expressly been taken from inductive liturgy (Kunzler 1995; Torevell 2000;

Ratzinger 2000). As opposed to a rational view on liturgy and one aimed at active participation, the mystery of liturgy is emphasised in a plea for a review of the liturgy renewal of Vatican II, and the transcendental dimension in particular is illuminated by a call for attention for the experience of the sacred as the most characteristic of liturgy. Due to a disregard for the cultural embedding of the church and faith there is, however, a danger that liturgy will also be considered as an upper-historic and upper-cultural greatness. By ignoring the dynamics of cultus and culture and in this way nostalgically harking back to the liturgical form of the past, there is a danger of taking on a reactionary position and of liturgical fundamentalism.

Of the many areas of tension that have developed over the past decades as a result of the liturgical earthquake, I will only enter into one: the changed relationship between the demand for liturgy and what can be offered, and the consequences of this for the view on liturgy and for liturgical policy in a parish.

2.1. Shift between supply and demand

The liturgical repertoire of parishes is on the one hand dominated by the regular weekend liturgy and on the other by the celebration of an occasional liturgy. This rough division of the liturgical supply partly corresponds with a division that can be made in relation to the demand for liturgy. There is a group that participates in the whole supply and besides this there is a group that almost exclusively calls upon the parish in connection with occasional liturgy. For many years both groups were referred to as the main congregation and marginal members. The description I give above of the parish as a community that celebrates liturgy in a variable, incidental composition distances itself from this rough distinction. After all, the main congregation has also become less homogenous and shows more divergence; nowadays there are many gradations in the level of liturgical participation here too. So a division can be made in the demand for liturgy as well, despite this differentiation.

That the division that can be made with regard to the liturgical supply corresponds to a certain extent with the division with regard to the demand for liturgy, seems to be connected to a difference in orientation of both types of liturgy. The weekend liturgy stems primarily from a salvation history line (Auf der Maur 1983, 223-228). On the basis of a semi-continual reading of one of the gospels, Jesus' salutary work is celebrated in a service linked to the reading each week. Because the weekly visit to the church is declining, this cohrence of the church year is, however, becoming more and more fragmented and the effect of the inner dynamics of the readings schedule is put into perspective. Liturgy plays an increasingly smaller part in the structuring of the rhythm of the day, week and year, and the same applies to the forms of devotion and (domestic) customs connected to that rhythm. The daily visits to Mass and the collective evening prayer or chaplet together as a family have disappeared.

Weekly church attendance is no longer a matter-of-course. The annual cycle is no longer supported by religious celebrations and liturgical services at Advent, Christmas, Lent, Easter, Pentecost and holy days, and by processions and moments of prayer. These celebrations structure the year in so far as they have a general sociocultural significance, in which the specific Christian interpretation has been pushed into the background. Advent and Christmas have transformed the month of December into a period wherein the end of the year feeling is cherished with the celebration of New Years Eve as the climax. Lent has been reduced to the enthusiastic celebration of carnival that precedes it. And Easter is in particular a celebration that marks the beginning of the holiday season. Participation in these liturgical celebrations that mark the passing of the year form a hindrance in social life, so in many cases they are set aside and therefore play a smaller and smaller role.

On the other hand in occasional liturgy it is not so much the history of salvation that forms the starting point but the individual life history. Liturgy offers a framework that leads to fundamental experiences of existence and questions of meaning, through the personal biography. At the hinge points in life there is room for religion and at times like these one is receptive to a religious interpretation of existential questions. At times like these rituals come into view, both old and new ones, to give form to deeply human desires and experiences, whereby new rituals are often grafted onto elements from the Christian tradition. This connection with the personal biography could explain why many still ask for this type of liturgy even though they no longer take part in the regular services; incidental participation in occasional liturgy is for many the last link they have with the parish and with religious liturgy.

2.2. Double strategy as liturgical policy

The request for occasional liturgy is experienced as problematic in many parishes and by many pastors, especially when people who are barely, or not at all linked to the parish, make the request. Baptism, mourning and marriage take up, in comparison to the regular liturgy more and more time and make a demand on the pastor's overfull diary. It is for this reason that the request for these types of services is considered more critically and sometimes not honoured. For example, there are places where it is policy that a church service must precede a parting at the cemetery or at the crematorium before a pastor may be approached to take part. One is faced with the dilemma of whether or not one can and should honour every request.

So how should the dilemma between supply and demand as this manifests itself in particular with regard to occasional liturgy be dealt with? This field of tension is the realisation of the more general question of how one as a church and as a pastor can and should relate oneself to the great diversity in church involvement. In a recent article Kees de Groot gives a plural answer to the question on how the church or a parish can organise themselves in a situation where participation and involvement are no longer a matter-of-course (De Groot 2001). Although his line of approach does not specifically concern liturgy, there is a lot of common ground and his method of approach seems to me to apply to liturgy too.

In his analysis he distinguishes two types of religious organisations, one of which is based on membership (like a club), and the other which is aimed at the provision of services (like a company). Both types of organisation have their own aims. In a membership organisation these are especially aimed at recruitment in order to increase the number of supporters, whilst the objective of the service organisation lies in the improvement of the services it offers, so that through the improvement of services and supply it is able to increase its numbers or range. He also makes a distinction with regard to the target group, the churchgoers, that is made up of those strongly and those moderately interested in religion. He only takes into consideration those who are actually reached and not the intended target group. Under those strongly interested in religion, the religious virtuosi, he considers "pastors, members of religious orders, people who are actively in search of ways to form their spirituality, and actively involved members of religious communities" (De Groot 2001, 12). He classes the religiosity of those who are moderately interested as popular religiosity, in which the material and instrumental aspect play an important role. Rituals play a major role here, especially those related to the ups and downs of life (problems in relationships, the concern for children, illness) and those that take place on the hinge points in the biographic and personal growth (life and death, maturity).

The various aims and target groups result in a typology which one can relate oneself to in different ways. One can choose to increase the number of members by approaching each incidental visitor or newcomer as a potential member, or by attracting and binding those interested through an explicit characterisation of the individual identity. And from the viewpoint of the provision of services one is able to apply oneself to intensifying an existing interest, or to meeting every need as sympathetically as possible in an accessible way. In liturgy this typology can be realised in the following way as an example. With regard to the recruitment strategy of the membership church, it is on the one hand impressed upon incidental churchgoers at Christmas that they are welcome to come every weekend, and during many first Communion services the hope is expressed that the first Communion will not be the last. And on the other hand there is evidence that both the more distinctly traditional and the explicitly experimental parishes add to their appeal by strengthening their own liturgical profile. With regard to the provision of services of the service church visits to monasteries and their liturgy by people who are interested in faith and religion can be pointed out on the one hand, and on the other the one-off request for the rituals of life.

Clearly the boundaries between the different types overlap. In practice the membership church and the service church often overlap each other and there is a whole range of nuances between those with a moderate and those with a strong interest in religion. However, most parishes fulfil for a large part a position as service church, and this situation confronts them with the question of what the limits of the provision of services are. Is it necessary to be available for everyone and should every request be honoured in so far as is physically and materially possible? Is this possible for pastor and parish? Does this not suppose a balance? After all, in order to be able to offer adequate services and be open and receptive with regard to various questions and wishes, a parish must have sufficient energy. The incidental liturgical provision of services also supposes a wide scope and continuity, an embedment in other activities and in the involvement of others. At the same time the question arises on the grounds of which intrinsic motives can and may limits be drawn? In short: a hospitable congregation needs a strong group of people at its centre. In Kees de Groot's typology this means that the service church and the membership church should in a sense join together, which implies the choice for a double strategy, whereby it is attempted to strengthen one's own organisation as well as to invest in the provision of services (De Groot 2001, 20).

Within such a double strategy it is, in view of liturgy, essential that there is a differentiated supply. With this in mind it would seem to me to be important to approach the liturgical experiment large-heartedly. In the past years much creative and inspiring work has been done along the same lines as the liturgy renewal, whilst maintaining respect for tradition in the search for a contemporary form. A recognisable link between liturgy and the dimension of faith in the personal life was sought after. These experiments could be expanded. With reference to the regular complaint that the liturgy has become very verbal, rational and intellectual, it might be an idea to develop the sensory dimension of the liturgy that is missed by many. In relation to this a review of the use and design of church buildings also plays and important role (Richter 1998; Gerhards 1999; Van Tongeren 2002b).

The importance of an experimental approach plays a particular role with regard to occasional liturgy. The churchgoer, that as a transient or nomad makes an appeal to the parish as a service church for this type of liturgy, is often unfamiliar with the liturgy and has a limited liturgical reference. The same applies to a large group of the incidental community that gathers in the church for that occasion. It seems more obvious to look for and express openings to religiosity experimentally and by way of feeling, rather than to offer and perform a massive ritual. It does not have to be argued that this is not a simple task. After all, there is a danger of superficiality or of bantering, whilst tradition and conviction also have to be taken seriously. Navigating in this field of tension thus asks a lot of the sensitivity of those who take the pulpit.

3. The ritual-liturgical profile of the pastor

The pluralism with regard to the church and faith that has manifested itself in the past decades in the composition of the community celebrating liturgy, and that has had an effect on liturgical practices, also has repercussions on the functioning of pastors. Their expertise is appealed to in various ways. They are expected to execute the regular liturgical supply, and at the same time to have a feel for reality and all sorts of concrete situations whereby services have to be approachable and should have existential relevance. Moreover, the changed relationship between cultus and culture has led to the growth of new rituals or to a changed significance and experiencing of existing rituals (Barnard 2001; Post 1995; 1999c; Post, Pieper, and Nauta 1998, 119-121). This means that the liturgical competence of pastors has to be more and more versatile. One has to be professional with regard to both the official religious rituals as well as the repertoire that is developing around these (Post 1999a; 1999b). Therefore it is important that the dynamic relationship between cultus and culture is also taken into account in the training in which this competence is acquired. In connection with the broad interest for rituals the past years have seen an increasing interest for a broadening as well as a deepening of the ritual-liturgical profile of the pastor.

3.1. Renewed interest for the *ars celebrandi*

When in the second half of the last century the renewal of the liturgy was carried through, most attention was paid to the sobering down and simplification of the liturgy, to translations, new texts and music, to the sermon and to making the liturgy more understandable and providing more insight, and to encouraging the participation of all; less attention was paid to form and style. At present there seems to be a reaction to this. Symbols and non-verbal elements are becoming more popular, and statues and attributes from the past are being brought from the attic or the cellar, cleaned and cherished and put back into the church building. And because a measured and balanced ritual requires a set (but invisible) direction, much attention is paid to form, the execution and the dramaturgy of services. Requirements as to quality are also made with regard to liturgy. Well-meant intentions are not enough. The choir should sing well and the lector is expected to read well and audibly. A good presentation and stylisation are essentially connected to ritual, and can make of break a service.

This shift fits in with the increased interest over the past years for the *ars celebrandi*. Attention varies from the concrete form, to flower arranging. Significant here is the publication of a thick hardback sexton's book (Kostersboek 2000), as well as the beautifully executed German and French editions in which all the ins and outs of the liturgical rituals that take place during the year are explained in detail, suitable for a broad public of pastors, liturgical work groups and volunteers (Gottesdienstgestaltung 2000; Renier 2000). And in the past years the *ars celebrandi* has also been a favourite subject for theme issues of scientific magazines and for symposiums (Acteurs 1998; Voorganger 1999; Vieren 2001; Lamberts 2003). As children of their time many of the present generation of pastors and pastors-to-be are no longer automatically liturgically socialised. They have not grown up with an intensive church programme, where they got to know the rituals as choirboy and as acolyte from close quarters and inside out; they have not learnt to play the serious game of liturgy with dedication from childhood. Therefore many feel the necessity and the need to familiarise themselves with the performance of the liturgy. They often feel literally inconvenienced when it comes to the practical liturgical area. They have difficulty moving in the large space, feel ill at ease during baptisms or when using the aspergillum and censer. They do not know the musical repertoire of the choir and liturgical books are often unfamiliar.

There are two dimensions of the *ars celebrandi* that seem especially to attract interest: familiarity with the given rituals of the church that have been laid down in a plan in liturgical books, and the execution of these rituals and their concrete form. But most of the attention for the *ars celebrandi* lies in the practical liturgical area and strives for the improvement of quality or for the optimisation of the competence to act. This competence to act, that is aimed mainly at the exterior form of the liturgy, can be broadened by linking it up with the inherent dimension of spirituality that calls for attention to the inner dynamics of the liturgical ritual, and for personal experience of this (De Keyzer 2001).

3.2. Expertise aimed at context

Liturgy is not an isolated greatness, but something that takes place again and again amongst a living community of people who seek God, and who have the desire to meet Him in a world that is continually in motion and in a state of development. It was mentioned briefly above that sociocultural shifts have repercussions on the place and way of believing, and also what the consequences are for parochial liturgical practices. The liturgy is also a part of the complex dynamics of religion and church. And the altered demand for liturgy is an exponent of these dynamics that brings to light not only the changed attitude of many with regard to the church and faith, but also the different position rituals and sacraments have in (religious) life and experience. As history has shown more than once, faith also takes on a contemporary form in the social and cultural context of the present. Many new forms and patterns have evolved besides those that are familiar. Not long ago it was as though religious ritual life was extinct, but now there is evidence that it is flourishing and abundant (Lukken 1999), both within and outside the church (religious liturgy). Signs, initiatives and shifts can be observed especially in the margin, in the direct vicinity of the parish, whereby rituals and liturgy are connecting with surrounding culture (Post, Pieper, and Nauta 1998). This inculturation shows that where traditional relations have disappeared, there is a search for a new anchorage of liturgical rituals in culture. In relation to culture, forms of expression in which faith manifests itself are transforming, and the same applies to the liturgy. It is not easy to relate to this development, but it would seem one-sided to speak of horizontality or of a loss or thinning out of the sacramental consciousness in this context (Danneels 2002). True such qualifications shed light on an aspect of the shifts observed, but they do not do sufficient justice to their complexity. Such an approach ignores people's search nowadays for a particular form of their religiosity, their faith and their notion of God. It is therefore important for pastors and for the way in which they function liturgically that they take note of, and develop an eye for the position of rituals in the broad social and cultural context. When liturgy is situated in a broad ritual environment then connections can be made from that basis with religion and faith and with the Christian tradition. The demand for religious rituals implies at least a trace of consciousness with regard to religion and faith, even when these rituals are not desired in their traditional form. Finding the right words, forms and actions demands a sensitivity from the pastor that does justice to sociocultural shifts and their relationship with religion and faith, as well as to the tradition of faith.

The contextual embedding of the liturgy demands more than practical capabilities from the pastor. They should also be capable of acting on the cutting edge of cultus and culture, a capability that I would also like to grade under *ars celebrandi*. In order to gain and develop this expertise it is for the good of pastors that during their training they not only approach the liturgy from a historic and theological point of view, but also from (cultural) anthropology and hermeneutics. Moreover, because of the disappearance of the uniformity and the communality of faith, the language of faith and religion, continual reflection is essential, in relation to the ritual that has been performed as well as one's own ritual acts, and in relation to developments that present themselves on the dynamic cutting edge between cultus and culture.

3.3. Equipment and training

The practical liturgical training of pastors will in the first place be aimed at mastering the basic attitude that concentrates largely on liturgical performance. One must become familiar with books, objects and ritual acts. Under the guidance of an experienced colleague actual practice is excellent training. However, *ars celebrandi* has become a much broader concept so that competence aimed at dramaturgy is no longer enough. For a liturgy that involves people and the divine, it is of growing importance that pastors learn to notice developments on the cutting edge of religion and society, of cultus and culture, of theology and anthropology, of sacraments and rituals, and that they are able to make a connection between all these domains. Other abilities are desired that require an *éducation permanente*. There are few programmes or curricula developed in connection with a continual type of liturgical training (in Van der Ven 1998 liturgical training is part of a broad pastoral selection).

One initiative being developed within the Liturgical Institute attached to the Tilburg Faculty of Theology has a four-point basis and emphatically has reality as its starting point by connecting with the actual experience of the pastors who participate. Observation, analysis, reflection and creation are key words. Participants observe each other's liturgical performance, analyse orders of service, and are presented with elements on the basis of which they learn to reflect on the way they themselves function liturgically. In turn this reflection results in points of learning with a view to the composition and performance of services in the future. Orientation on reality is supplemented with new theoretical insights and developments in connection with the anthropology and theology of rituals and sacraments. For example, the implications and complications of the many developing initiation rituals are made a subject in relation to the practice of baptism. The interference between cultus and culture has made the question of the Christian identity of the ritual more urgent, a question that thus plays an important role in continual liturgical training. The *éducation permanente* offers pastors a framework in which to mould their liturgical role. By confronting and integrating an intrinsic reflection of developments with regard to the ritual domain within and outside the church with and in their own liturgical acts, their liturgical competence will be expanded.

References

Acteurs 1998. Acteurs et ministères dans la liturgie. *La Maison Dieu* 215, special issue.

Barnard, M. 2001. Dynamiek van cultus en cultuur. Pp. 47-62 in *Ritueel bestek. Antropologische kernwoorden van de liturgie*, edited by M. Barnard and P. Post. Zoetermeer.

Bernts, T. 2002. Samengaan en samenwerking van parochies: een noodzaak voor de liturgie? *Tijdschrift voor liturgie* 86(4): 194-206.

Beroepsprofiel 1999. *Beroepsprofiel parochiepastor. Verslag van een onderzoek naar beroepsprofielen in het parochiepastoraat.* Utrecht, Federatie VPW Nederland.

Chauvet, L.-M. 1999. La liturgie demain: essai de prospective. Pp. 201-229 in *La liturgie, lieu théologique*, edited by P. de Clerck. Paris.

Chauvet, L.-M. 2002. La présence liturgique dans la modernité. Les chances possibles d'une crise. *Questions liturgiques. Studies in Liturgy* 83(23): 140-155.

CIC. *Codex iuris canonici*. Liberia editrice Vaticana 1983.

Danneels, G. 2002. Rituelen in, sacramenten out? *Tijdschrift voor liturgie* 86(5): 306-322.

Eerste ontwerp 2000. Eerste ontwerp beroepsprofiel parochiepastor. *Kontaktblad federatie vpw [vereniging van pastoraal werkenden]* 3:10-11.

Eysink, A. 1995. *Hartslag van de kerk: de parochie vanuit kerkrechtelijk standpunt*. Part 1. Leuven: Peeters.

Gerhards, A., eds. 1999. *In der Mitte der Versammlung. Liturgische Feierräume*. Trier: Deutsches Liturgisches Institut.

Gottesdienstgestaltung 2000. *Gottesdienstgestaltung. Eine Arbeitshilfe für die Sachausschüsse Liturgie der Pfarrgemeinderäte im Bistum Aachen und für alle, die an der Gestaltung von liturgischen Feiern mitwirken*. Aachen: Bischöfliches Generalvikariat.

Groot, K. de 2001. Religieuze organisaties in meervoud. Mogelijkheden voor 'de kerk' in de huidige Nederlandse samenleving. *Praktische theologie* 28(1): 5- 24.

Huysmans, R. 1998a. Kerkrechtelijke inventarisatie van het parochie-beleid van de R.-K. bisdommen in Nederland. Pp. 3-34 in *De parochie van de toekomst* (= Scripta canonica 2), edited by A. Meijers. Leuven.

Huysmans, R. 1998b. De parochie in de Nederlandse R.-K. bisdommen voorbij? To close or to cluster? Pp.35-60, in *De parochie van de toekomst* (= Scripta canonica 2), edited by A. Meijers. Leuven.

Janssen, J. s.a. 2000. Individualiteit en engagement. Religies en relaties in de hedendaagse cultuur. Pp.64-102 in *Het informatieparadijs*, edited by H. Evers and J. Stappers. Nijmegen.

Jespers, F. 2000a. Gelegenheidsgelovigen. Bewust genieten van genereuze tradities. *Tijdschrift voor theologie* 40(2): 111-121.

Jespers, F. 2000b. Gelegenheidsliturgie van en voor gelegenheidsgelovigen. *Tijdschrift voor liturgie* 84(6): 339-348.

Karrer, L. 1998. Der liturgische Leitungsdienst im Kontext der Gemeindepastoral. Pp. 264-281 in *Wie weit trägt das gemeinsame Priestertum? Liturgischer Leitungsdienst zwischen Ordination und Beauftragung* (= Quaestiones disputatae 171), edited by M. Klockener and K. Richter. Freiburg/Basel/Wien.

Keyzer, A. de 2001. *Ga met ons jouw weg. Opbouw, betekenis en vormgeving van de eucharistie*. Kampen: Gooi en Sticht.

Koch, K. 1998. Der Zusammenhang von Gemeindeleitung und liturgischem Leitungsdienst. Ein ekklesiologischer Beitrag. Pp. 65-85 in *Wie weit trägt das gemeinsame Priestertum? Liturgischer Leitungsdienst zwischen*

Ordination und Beauftragung (= Quaestiones disputatae 171), edited by M. Klockener and K. Richter. Freiburg/Basel/Wien.

Kostersboek 2000. *Kostersboek. Een wegwijzer voor kosters in de Kerk van de Romeinse ritus.* Nijmegen: Centrum voor parochiespiritualiteit.

Kunzler, M. 1995. *Die Liturgie der Kirche.* (= Amateca 10) Paderborn: Bonifatius.

Lamberts, J., eds. 2003. 'Ars celebrandi'of de kunst van het waardig vieren van de liturgie. Leuven/Amersfoort: Acco.

Lukken, G. 1987. De voorganger in het spanningsveld van de liturgie. *Tijdschrift voor liturgie* 71(5): 259-278.

Lukken, G. 1998. Op zoek naar een nieuwe stijl van voorgaan. *Tijdschrift voor liturgie* 82(6): 341-351.

Lukken, G. 1999. *Rituelen in overvloed. Een kritische bezinning op de plaats en de gestalte van het christelijke ritueel in onze cultuur.* Baarn: Gooi en Sticht.

Maur, H.J. auf der 1983. *Feiern im Rhythmus der Zeit 1. Herrenfeste in Woche und Jahr* (= *Gottesdienst der Kirche. Handbuch der Liturgiewissenschaft 5).* Regensburg: Pustet.

Nissen, P. 1992. De geschiedenis van het zondagsgebod. Pp. 68-83 in *De zondag. Een tijd voor God, een tijd voor de mens,* edited by E. Henau and A. Haquin. Brussel.

Post, P. 1995. Zeven notities over rituele verandering, traditie en (vergelijkende) liturgiewetenschap. *Jaarboek voor liturgie-onderzoek* 11: 1-30.

Post, P. 1999a. Rol en rite: over liturgisch voorgaan. *Praktische theologie* 26(2): 128-147.

Post, P. 1999b. Leidende kwaliteiten in het spel. Over liturgisch voorgaan. Pp. 57-78 in *Over leiden. Dynamiek en structuur van het religieus leiderschap,* edited by H. Beck and R. Nauta. S.l. [Tilburg].

Post, P. 1999c. Rituele dynamiek in liturgisch perspectief. Een verkenning van vorm, inhoud en beleving. *Jaarboek voor liturgie-onderzoek* 15: 119-141.

Post, P., J. Pieper, and R. Nauta. 1998. Om de parochie: het inculturerende perspectief van rituele marginaliteit. *Jaarboek voor liturgie-onderzoek* 14: 113-140.

Post, P., and L. van Tongeren. 2001. The Celebration of the First Communion. Seeking the Identity of the Christian Ritual. Pp. 581-598 in *Christian Feast and Festival. The Dynamics of Western Liturgy and Culture* (= Liturgia condenda 12), edited by P. Post, G. Rouwhorst, L. van Tongeren, and A. Scheer. Leuven/Paris/Sterling.

Profileren 2001. *Profileren in het parochiepastoraat.* Utrecht: Aartsbisdom.

Ratzinger, J. 2000. *Der Geist der Liturgie. Eine Einführung.* Freiburg/Basel/Wien: Herder.

Renier, L.-M., eds. 2000. *Exultet. Encyclopédie pratique de la liturgie.* Paris: Bayard.

Richter, K. 1998. *Kirchenräume und Kirchenträume. Die Bedeutung des Kirchenraums für eine lebendige Gemeinde.* Freiburg/Basel/Wien: Herder.

Tongeren, L. van 2001a. De zondag. Pp. 69-76 in *Ritueel bestek, Antropologische kernwoorden van de liturgie,* edited by M. Barnard and P. Post. Zoetermeer.

Tongeren, L. van 2001b. The squeeze on Sunday. Reflections on the changing experience and form of Sundays. Pp. 703-727 in *Christian Feast and Festival. The Dynamics of Western Liturgy and Culture* (= Liturgia condenda 12), edited by P. Post, G. Rouwhorst, L. van Tongeren, and A. Scheer. Leuven/Paris/Sterling.

Tongeren, L. van 2002a. Schaalvergroting van parochies: uitdagingen en kansen voor de liturgie. *Tijdschrift voor liturgie* 86(3): 222-243.

Tongeren, L. van 2002b. Vers une utilisation dynamique et flexible de l'espace. Une réflexion renouvelée sur le réaménagement d'églises. *Questions liturgiques. Studies in Liturgy* 83(1-2): 156-178.

Tongeren, L. van 2003. Individualizing Ritual. The Personal Dimension in Funeral Liturgy. *Worship* 77 (in preparation).

Torevell, D. 2000. *Losing the Sacred. Ritual, Modernity and Liturgical Reform.* Edinburgh: T&T Clark

Tweede ontwerp 2001. Tweede ontwerp beroepsprofiel parochiepastor. *Kontaktblad federatie vpw [vereniging van pastoraal werkenden]* 3: 3-9.

Ven, J. van der 1998. *Education for reflective ministry* (= Louvain Theological and Pastoral Monographs 24). Louvain: Peeters.

Vieren 2001. Vieren in schoonheid. *Tijdschrift voor liturgie* 85(1/2), special issue.

Voorganger 1999. *Voorganger in de liturgie. Praktische theologie* 26(2), special issue.

Wagner-Rau, U. 2000. *Segensraum.Kasualpraxis in der modernen Gesellschaft* (= Praktische Theologie heute 50). Stuttgart/Berlin/Köln: Kohlhammer.

Bibliography M.P.J. van Knippenberg
1971-2002

Plaatselijke oecumene. Onderzoek naar de oecumenische situatie in Nederland, Utrecht, Interuniversitair Instituut voor Oecumenica, 1971.

Religiositeit in Spelinggroepen: tussen gescheidenheid en verbondenheid, in *Speling* 27 (1975) 2, 60-72.

Werken binnen de kerk: tussen droom en werkelijkheid, in *Speling* 27 (1975) 4, 54-61.

In de Ashram van Bagwan Shree Rajneesh, in *Ons Geestelijk Leven* 57 (1980) 3, 126-132.

Mogelijkheden en gevaren uit het Oosten, in *Critic* (1980) 1, 3-6.

De dood kiezen als levenspartner, in *Speling* 34 (1982) 4, 43-52.

Onze verhouding met de dood, in *Ecclesia* 37 (1983) 4, 18-21.

Meditatio Mortis: een pastorale herijking, in J.A. van der Ven (ed.), *Toekomst voor de kerk? Studies voor Frans Haarsma*, Kampen, Kok, 1985, 272-286.

Oriëntatie op de dood in het pastoraat, in J.A. van der Ven (eds.), *Pastoraal tussen ideaal en werkelijkheid*, Kampen, Kok, 1985, 35-48.

Geloofsidentiteit en levensgrens, in J.A. van Belzen & J.M. van der Lans (eds.), *Rond godsdienst en psychoanalyse*, Kampen, Kok, 1986, 185-195.

Het uiteindelijke als pastoraal perspectief, in *Kosmos en Oecumene* 20 (1986) 185-195.

De stilte vertrouwen, in *Speling* 38 (1986) 4, 42-47.

Dood en religie. Een studie naar communicatief zelfonderzoek in het pastoraat, Kampen, Kok, 1987.

Pastorale competentie: de erfenis leren delen, in *Praktische Theologie* 14 (1987) 35-48.

De dood als levenspartner, Kampen, Kok, 1988.

Grenzen. Werkplaats voor pastoraaltheologen, Kampen, Kok, 1989.

Preken over Job. Pastoraaltheologische reflecties, in *Praktische Theologie* 17 (1990) 272-284.

Pastorale communicatie, in A.F.A. van Ierland en R. Schulte (eds.), *Onze kerk: postadres van Gods Rijk in de wereld?,* 's-Hertogenbosch, Vereniging van Pastoraal Werkenden, 1990, 10-17.

Pastorale spiritualiteit, in *Vincentiaanse Cahiers* 27 (1990) 1-5.

Lijden en geloven. Het gesprek in een groep, in *Praktische Theologie* 17 (1990) 146-166.

Clinical and Empirical Theology: An Ambivalent Relationship [Paper 4th International Conference on Clinical Pastoral Education], Noordwijkerhout, ICCPE, 1991.

Communicative self-examination [Paper 4th International Conference on Pastoral Care and Counseling], Noordwijkerhout, ICCPC, 1991.

M. Vasalis, een confrontatie met de grens, in W. Kusters (ed.), *In een bezield verband. Nederlandstalige dichters op zoek naar zin,* Baarn, Gooi & Sticht, 1991, 236-251.

M. Vasalis en grenservaringen, in H. Rijksen (ed.), *Dichter bij de dood,* Tilburg, Faculteit Educatieve Opleidingen, 1991, 10-20.

Levensbeschouwingen in therapie, in *Qohelet* 1 (1991) 6, 10-11.

Commentaar bij oecumenisch pastoraat in het ziekenhuis, in *Kosmos en Oekumene* 25 (1991) 149-150.

Vasalis en grenservaringen, in *Verbum* 58 (1991) 137-144.

Zin en voorzienigheid, in *Geest en Leven* 68 (1991) 103-112.

Together with J. Jacobs, N. Schreurs, B. Vedder en W. Weren (eds.), *Zin tussen vraag en aanbod. Theologische en wijsgerige beschouwingen over zin* (TFT-Studies 18), Tilburg, TUP, 1992.

Zingeving en levensbeschouwing, in *ibid.,* 211-215.

Christelijk geloof en communicatie van zin, in *ibid.,* 216-226.

Existentie en zingeving. Bezinning op het bestaan in tijd en ruimte, in *Arts en existentie,* Nijmegen, Post-academisch Onderwijs Geneeskunde, 1992, 6-14.

Oud en nieuw. Omgaan met pluraliteit, in *Oude boodschap in een nieuwe tijd,* Amsterdam, Leger des Heils, 1992, 6-12.

Pastorale dienst. Functie en existentie, in *De herder en de macht,* Utrecht, VGVZ, 1992, 33-40.

Pastorale dienst. Functie en existentie, in *Praktische Theologie* 19 (1992) 494-506.

Art. Dood, in H. Willemsen (ed.), *Filosofisch woordenboek,* Assen, Van Gorcum, 1992, 110-111.

In het spoor van het verhaal. Ouderen en pastoraat, Kampen, Kok 1993.

Inleiding, in *ibid.,* 1-4.

Ouderen en pastoraat, in *ibid.,* 5-19.

De (on)mogelijkheid van het helpen, in R. Nauta (ed.), *Helpen. Zin en onzin. Over de zin en de betekenis van helpen,* Kampen, Kok, 1993, 101-108.

Ouderenpastoraat, in *Praktische Theologie* 20 (1993) 201-217.

Communicatie met fundamentalisten, in *Tijdschrift voor Theologie* 33 (1993) 61-77.

De vuursalamander. Gelouterd pastoraat, in W. Claessens, L. Jansen en G. van Tillo (eds.), *Echo's uit een ander dal. Landschap in taal en wording,* Tilburg, Gianotten, 1993, 107-115.

Vragen naar zin: achterhaald of actueel?, in *SAW. Tijdschrift voor Welzijnszorg en Christelijke Zingeving* 4 (1993) 6-10.

De pastor als grensganger, in *Speling* 45 (1993) 2, 27-33.

Together with R. Nauta, *Diakonie als zielzorg. Vraag en aanbod,* in J.A. van der Ven & A. Houtepen (eds.), *Weg van de Kerk. Reflecties op 'De pastorale arbeid in de 90er jaren' van bisschop H.C.A. Ernst*, Kampen, Kok, 1994, 139-159.

Grensgangers worden voorgangers. Helpen bij zinverlies, in *Tijdschrift voor Geestelijk Leven* 50 (1994) 273-289.

Ontwikkelingen in de poimeniek, in *Praktische Theologie* 21 (1994) 294-309.

Communicatie over de dood, in *Schrift* 152 (1994) 39-45.

Het collectieve en het gezamenlijke in de zingeving, in *SAW. Tijdschrift voor Welzijnszorg en Christelijke Zingeving* 6 (1995) 1, 26-40.

Zinvraag en geloofsantwoord, in Y. Kuin e.a. (eds.), *Levenservaringen en zinvragen* (Annalen van het Thijmgenootschap 83,1), Baarn, Ambo, 1995, 109-130.

Een poging tot plaatsbepaling: André Zegveld, Tot vrijheid bestemd. Spiritualiteit en geloofsbelijdenis, in *Monastieke informatie* 26 (1995) 204-208.

Veranderen bij het leven, in *SAW. Tijdschrift voor Welzijnszorg en Christelijke Zingeving* (1995) 2, 1-2.

Pastoraat en zingeving, in *Praktisch0e Theologie* 22 (1995) 365-376.

Pastoral Group Work, in J.A. van der Ven & E. Vossen (eds.), *Suffering: Why for God's sake? Pastoral research in Theodicy* (Theologie und Empirie 23), Kampen, Kok, 1995, 25-42.

Together with Th. van Reen, P. Dogge & M. de Nobel-Andriessen, *Hierna. 31 liederen voor afscheid en rouw, om te zingen, om te zeggen. Partituur*, Baarn, Gooi en Sticht, 1995.

Together with J. Munnichs, C. Knipscheer & N. Stevens, *Ouderen en zingeving* (KSGV-cahier 2-47), Baarn, Ambo, 1995.

De vraag naar zin en de beleving van continuïteit bij ouderen, in *ibid.*, 63-74.

Ontwikkelingen in de poimeniek. Een literatuurbericht, in *Praktische Theologie* 23 (1996) 76-89.

Identity claim and the homosexual movement, in *Case studies*, Université de Sherbrooke, 1996.

Troost en ambivalentie, in A. Baart (ed.), *Het troostrijk. Cultuur tussen maakbaarheid en eindigheid*. Baarn, Gooi & Sticht, 1996, 44-56.

Voorwoord, in F. van Iersel (ed.): *Religie, geweld, verzoening*, Baarn, Gooi & Sticht, 1996, 7-8.

Continuïteit en verandering, in J. Jans (ed.), *Bewogen theologie, theologie in beweging. Symposium bij het afscheid van Mgr. H.C.A. Ernst en ter verwelkoming van Mgr. dr. M.P.M. Muskens, bisschop van Breda, aan de Theologische Faculteit Tilburg*, Tilburg, 1996, 8-10.

Geestelijke leiding als pastorale kerntaak, in K.-W. Merks & N. Schreurs, *De passie van een grensganger. Theologie aan de vooravond van het derde millennium*, Baarn, Ten Have, 1997, 267-288.

The quest for meaning from the perspective of creation, in *Bijdragen. Tijdschrift voor filosofie en theologie* 58 (1997) 381-398.

Together with K. Sonnberger, *Pastor Pontifex,* in *Praktische Theologie* 24 (1997) 221-235.

Between Two Languages. Spiritual Guidance and Communication of Christian Faith, Tilburg, TUP, 1998.

Introduction, in *ibid.,* 9-12.

Perspectives and Languages, in *ibid.,* 15-24.

Together with H. Zondag, *Dynamics of Bilinguality,* in *ibid.,* 125-139.

Ontwikkelingen in de poimeniek. Een literatuurbericht, in *Praktische Theologie* 25 (1998) 85-99.

De pastor als theoloog, in *Praktische Theologie* 25 (1998) 191-205.

Tussen naam en identiteit. Ontwerp van een model voor geestelijke begeleiding. Kampen, Kok, 1998.

Pastoraat tussen oude bronnen en nieuwe feiten, in J. Körver (ed.). *Corrigerende ervaringen. Leren in Klinisch Pastorale Vorming en Pastorale Supervisie,* Eindhoven, CVPE, 65-84.

Oorsprong en toekomst, in *Bisdomblad Breda* 12 (1998) 12, 15.

Together with G. Heitink, *Inspirerend leiderschap. Themanummer Praktische Theologie,* 26 (1999) 2.

Charis en charisma, in *ibid.,* 513-519.

Compassie. Over leiden en lijden. In H.L. Beck & R. Nauta (eds.), *Over leiden. Dynamiek en structuur van het religieus leiderschap,* Tilburg, Syntax, 1999, 205-219.

Tussen naam en identiteit. Een model voor geestelijke begeleiding, in M. Monteiro, P. Nissen & J. de Raat (eds.), *Steun en toeverlaat. Historische aspecten van geestelijke begeleiding,* Hilversum, Verloren, 1999, 157-172.

Een regisseur van het verschil, in Th. Beckers (ed.), *Los uit het zadel. Beschouwingen van veertien decanen bij gelegenheid van het afscheid van prof. dr. L.F.W. de Klerk als Rector Magnificus van de Katholieke Universiteit Brabant,* Tilburg, TUP, 1999, 61-65.

Zin in straftijd, in *Zandschrift: contactblad voor het justitiepastoraat* 4 (1999) 2, 3-22.

Verkenningen in de poimeniek, in *Praktische Theologie* 27 (2000) 86-100.

Together with E. Jonker, *De ziel onderwijst, het zelf leert. Interview met Tjeu van Knippenberg over leren,* in *Praktische theologie* 27 (2000) 129-134.

Pastoraat tussen godsdienst en gezondheid, in *Praktische Theologie* 27 (2000) 480-488.

The Structure of Prayer. A Practical Theological Perspective, in *Journal of Empirical Theology* 13 (2000) 2, 55-67.

Tussen naam en identiteit. Een model voor geestelijke begeleiding, Kampen, Kok, 2000[2].

Zielzorg. Spel tussen tijd en eeuwigheid, in H. Beck, R. Nauta & P. Post (eds.), *Over spel. Theologie als drama en illusie,* Leende, Damon, 2000, 246-259.

Geestelijke verzorging en de ziel, in *Tijdschrift voor geestelijke verzorging* 15 (2000) 4, 19-27.

Inleiding, in *Een dak boven de ziel. Over zielzorg en media,* Lelystad, Omroeppastoraat, 2000, 13-29.

Persoon en professie in de Klinisch Pastorale Vorming, in *De spelers en het spel. Over de spanning tussen professionaliteit en het eigen van verhaal van de pastor,* Amersfoort, KPV, 2000, 4-8.

De theologische dimensie van rouwverwerking: de betekenis van religie, in P.A.M. van den Akker (ed.), *Rouwbegeleiding: verwoorden en verantwoorden van religieuze zin,* Tilburg, IVA, 2000, 9-17.

Op verhaal komen in de biechtstoel, in *De Bazuin* 83 (2000) 5, 18-20.

Zin en ziel, in *Herademing. Tijdschrift voor spiritualiteit en mystiek* 8 (2000) 14-19.

Transcendence and Personal History, in H.-G. Ziebertz e.a. (eds.), *The Human Image of God,* Leiden, Brill, 2001, 263-285.

Rouwbegeleiding: de religieuze dimensie, in *Praktische Theologie* 28 (2001) 316-328.

De ziel van zielzorg, in *Zandschrift: contactblad voor het justitiepastoraat* 6 (2001) 3, 31-38.

Competence for Spiritual Guidance in Pastoral Ministry. A Theological Educational Programme, in B. Roebben & M. Warren (eds.), *Religious Education as Practical Theology. Essays in Honour of Professor Herman Lombaerts,* Leuven/Paris/Sterling, Peeters, 2001, 307-333.

Gestalte van een christelijk zinsverband, in K. Sonnberger & H. Zondag (eds.), *Redden pastores het? Religieus leiderschap aan het begin van de 21ste eeuw,* Budel, Damon, 2001, 83-96.

Biechten: een weg tot narratieve identiteit, in R. Nauta e.a. (eds.), *Excuus. Pardon, vergeef me, het spijt me. Exercities in de excuuscultuur,* Nijmegen, Valkhof Pers, 2001, 34-59.

Zin en ziel, in K. Bouwman & K. Bras (eds.), *Werken met spiritualiteit,* Baarn, Ten Have, 2001, 95-102.

A Ambivalencia na Vida de Vicente de Paulo, in *Caminho Verdade Vida,* Recife, 2001.

Trouw proberen. Teksten om te zeggen en te zingen, Kampen, Gooi en Sticht, 2002.

Towards Religious Identity. An Exercise in Spiritual Guidance (Studies in Theology and Religion 4), Assen, Van Gorcum, 2002.

Viver em Meio de Contrastes, in J. Pubben (ed.), *Reflexoes sobre São Vicente de Paulo,* Recife, 2002, 13-16.

Together with J. Strijards, *De relatie tussen godsbeeld en zelfbeeld,* in *Praktische Theologie* 29 (2002) 426-475.

Poimenische Verkenningen, in *Praktische Theologie* 29 (2002) 487-506.

Melancholie: zonde of ziekte, in R. Nauta e.a. *Zonde en zonden – Opstellen over de tragiek van het bestaan,* Nijmegen, Valkhof, 2002, 229-241.

Geestelijke begeleiding en de ziel, in *Proeven van het spirituele.* Rotterdam, DPC, 2002.

Sources of Spiritual Guidance. An Exercise in the Cure of Souls, in *Practical Theology in South Africa* 17 (2002) 2, 154-169.

[Bibliography closed October 1, 2002 – Final compilation by Bert Roebben]

List of contributors

Dick Akerboom is Assistant Professor of Patrology and History of Church and Theology at the Faculty of Theology of Tilburg University. Topics of interest: transformation processes in the history of theology, especially the transformation from the Late Middle Ages into the Reformation period. Recent publications: Akerboom, D. 1995. *Vrije wil en/of genade. Een theologie-historisch onderzoek naar het dispuut tussen Erasmus en Luther over de (on)vrijheid van het menselijk willen.* Nijmegen: S.l.; Akerboom, D. 2002. Ecumenism of the future – the future of ecumenism. A balance of global ecumenical developments in the second part of the twentieth century. *Grace & Truth. A Journal of Catholic Reflection* 19: 5-20.

Karlijn Demasure is Research Assistant in Pastoral Theology at the Catholic University of Leuven. Recent publications: Demasure, K., and K. Depoortere. 2002. *Pastoor zijn: geven wat je ontvangt.* Antwerpen: Halewijn.; Demasure, K. 2002. Verhullend spreken bij seksueel misbruik. *Tijdschrift voor Theologie* 42: 50-72.

Kristiaan Depoortere is Professor of Pastoral Theology at the Catholic University of Leuven. Recent publications: Depoortere, K. 2000. *God Anders. Een christelijke visie op het lijden.* Leuven: Acco.; Depoortere, K. 2001. From Sacramentality to Sacraments, and Vice-versa. Pp. 51-62 in *Contemporary Sacramental Contours of a God Incarnate*, edited by L. Boeve and L. Leijssen. Leuven.

Leon Derckx is Research Assistant in Practical Theology at the Faculty of Theology of Tilburg University. Recent publication: Derckx, L. 2001. Zonde en narcisme. De invloed van narcistische kwetsbaarheid op de hedendaagse religieuze communicatie. Pp. 114-130 in *Redden pastores het? Religieus leiderschap aan het begin van de eenentwintigste eeuw,* edited by K. Sonnberger, H. Zondag and F. van Iersel. Budel.

Veerle Draulans is Assistant Professor of Practical Theology and Deacony at the Faculty of Theology of Tilburg University and Lecturer in Gender Studies at the Catholic University of Leuven. Topics of interest: leadership, gender and leadership. Recent publications: Draulans, V., and J. De Tavernier. 2002. Sorge für die Umwelt als Quintessenz öffentlicher Güter in einer Dynamik der Globalisierung. Pp. 152-178 in *Der Globalisierungsprozess. Facetten einer Dynamik aus ethischer und theologischer Perspektive*, edited by G. Virt.

Freiburg-im-Breisgau.; Draulans, V. 2003 (forthcoming). The Glass Ceiling: reality or myth? A gender analysis of leadership. *Ethical Perspectives.*

Stefan Gärtner is Assistant Professor of Practical Theology at the Faculty of Theology of Tilburg University. Topic of interest: poimenics. Recent publications: Gärtner, S. 2000. *Gottesrede in (post-)moderner Gesellschaft. Grundlagen einer praktisch-theologischen Sprachlehre.* Paderborn et al.: Schöningh.; Gärtner, S. 2000. *Zwischenbilanz. Eine Auswertung zum Dialog um den Sexualitätsbrief der Deutschen Bischofskonferenz.* Düsseldorf: Verlag Haus Altenberg.

Marcel Gielis is Assistant Professor of the History of Church and Theology at the Faculty of Theology of Tilburg University. Recent publications: Gielis, M. 2002. Johannes Driedo. Anwalt der Tradition im Streit mit Humanismus und Reformation. Pp. 135-153 in *Theologen des 16. Jahrhunderts. Humanismus – Reformation – Katholische Erneuerung*, edited by M.H. Jung and P. Walter. Darmstadt.; Gielis, M. 2002. De zeven hoofdzonden. Pp. 17-38 in *Over zonde en zonden. Opstellen over de tragiek van het bestaan*, edited by R. Nauta. Nijmegen.

Ernest Henau is Professor Emeritus at the Department of Empirical Theology of the Catholic University of Nijmegen and director of the Catholic Radio and Television Station in Brussels. Topics of interest: church and media, homiletics, community development. Recent publications: Henau, E. 2002. Religious broadcasting and the construction of a just society. Pp. 185-196 in *Divine Justice – Human Justice*, edited by J.S. Dreyer and J.A. van der Ven. Pretoria.

Jan Jacobs is Professor of the History of Church and Theology at the Faculty of Theology of Tilburg University. Topics of interest: history of Dutch Catholicism, Vatican II, the ecumenical movement. Recent publications: Jacobs, J. 2001. Beyond polarity. On the relation between locality and universality in the Roman Catholic Church. Pp. 49-68 in *Of all times and of all places. Protestants and catholics on the church local and universal*, edited by L.J. Koffeman and H.P.J. Witte. Zoetermeer.; Jacobs, J. 2002. Van losse hulptroepen naar een welgeordend leger. Over de samenwerking tussen de priester-religieuzen bij de wederopbouw van katholiek Nederland na 1853. Pp. 215-232 in *Staf en storm. Het herstel van de bisschoppelijke hiërarchie in Nederland in 1853: actie en reactie*, edited by J. Vis and W. Janse. Hilversum.

Jan Jans is Assistant Professor of Moral Theology at the Faculty of Theology of Tilburg University. Topics of interest: research on becoming neighbour as characteristic for Christian moral identity, images of God in contemporary medical and media ethics. Recent publications: Jans, J. 2002. E-vangelization. A theological reflection on the relation between the internet and Christian faith. *Bulletin ET* 13:59-65.; Jans, J. 2002. 'Sterbehilfe' in den Niederlanden und Belgien. Rechtslage, Kirchen und ethische Diskussion. *Zeitschrift für evangelische Ethik* 46: 283-300.

Sjaak Körver is a staff member of the Center of Religious Communication at the Faculty of Theology of Tilburg University and supervisor and trainer in Clinical Pastoral Education. Recent publications: Körver, S. 2001. Theologie in de Klinische Pastorale Vorming. *Praktische Theologie* 28(2): 182-191.; Körver, S. 2001. Geestelijke verzorging en gedrag. *Tijdschrift voor Geestelijke Verzorging* 21: 25-34.

Wiel Logister is Professor of Fundamental Theology at the Faculty of Theology of Tilburg University. Topics of interest: the understanding of the truth and believe in God. Recent publications: Logister, W. 2003. *Die Spiritualität der Divina Commedia. Dantes Gedicht theologisch gelesen.* Münster: LIT Verlag.; Logister, W. 2000. Jesus Christ as Source of Assertiveness and Plurality. *Studies in Interreligious Dialogue* 11: 25-36.

Frans Maas is Assistant Professor of Systematic Theology at the Faculty of Theology of Tilburg University and Radboud Professor at Utrecht University. Topics of interest: spirituality and fundamental theology. Recent publications: Maas, F. 2000. Beauty and Religion. Being touched by a sense of openess and underlying unity with all things. Pp. 275-291 in *In Quest of Humanity in a Globalising World. Dutch Contributions to the Jubilee of Universities in Rome,* edited by W. Derkse, J. van der Lans and S. Waanders. Leende.; Maas, F. 2001. Spirituality and Postmodern Philosophy. Emptiness as an Opportunity for Esteem. *Studies in Spirituality* 11: 6-27.

Karl-Wilhelm Merks is Professor of Moral Theology at the Faculty of Theology of Tilburg University. Topics of interest: fundamental ethics, political ethics, Thomas Aquinas. Recent publications: Merks, K.-W. 2001. *Verantwortung – Ende oder Wandlungen einer Vorstellung? Orte und Funktionen der Ethik in unserer Gesellschaft.* Münster: Lit.; Merks, K.-W. 2001. Über Schuld und Autonomie. Plädoyer für den Aufbruch aus der Innerlichkeit. *Bijdragen. International Journal in Philosophy and Theology* 62: 249-279.

Rein Nauta is Professor of Pastoral Psychology and Psychology of Religion at the Faculty of Theology of Tilburg University. Topics of interest: the dynamics of religious leadership, playfulness and seduction, excuses and forgiveness, heroes and sinners, prayer and confession. Recent publications: Nauta, R. 2002. Not practising theology. *Pastoral Psychology* 50: 197-207.; Nauta, R. 2001.

The performance of authenticity: vocation and profession in pastoral care. Pp. 101-109 in *Education for ministry in the Church of Sweden. Tro und Tanke,* edited by P. Hanson. Uppsala.

Bert Roebben is Associate Professor of Practical Theology and Religious Education at the Faculty of Theology of Tilburg University. Topics of interest: religious education, ministry with youth and young adults, ethics of education, theology and cultural change. Recent publications: Roebben, B., and M. Warren. 2001. *Religious Education as Practical Theology. Essays in Honour of Professor Herman Lombaerts* (ANL 40). Leuven/Paris/Sterling: Peeters.; Roebben. B. 2001. The Vulnerability of the Postmodern Educator as Locus Theologicus. A Study in Practical Theology. *Religious Education* 96: 175-192.

Louis van Tongeren is Assistant Professor of Liturgical Studies at the Faculty of Theology of Tilburg University. Topics of interest: the history of liturgy, especially the Middle Ages, themes related to the current liturgical praxis. Recent publications: Tongeren, L. van 2000. *Exaltation of the Cross. Toward the Origins of the Feast of the Cross and the Meaning of the Cross in Early Medieval Liturgy.* Leuven: Peeters.; Tongeren, L. van 2001. Contributions about the medieval calendar, the first Communion and the Sunday. Pp. 287-317, 581-598 and 703-727 in *Christian Feast and Festival. The Dynamics of Western Liturgy and Culture,* edited by P. Post, G. Rouwhorst, L. van Tongeren and A. Scheer. Leuven.

Leo van der Tuin is Assistant Professor of Practical Theology and Religious Education at the Faculty of Theology of Tilburg University. Topics of interest: religious education, teacher training, religious attitudes of youth and young adults. Recently publications: Tuin, L. van der 2002. Hoogmoed. Pp. 194-211 in *Over zonde en zonden: opstellen over de tragiek van het bestaan,* edited by R. Nauta. Nijmegen.; Tuin, L. van der 2003 (forthcoming). Jugendliche und Religion. *Religionspädagogische Beiträge.*

Marinus van Uden is Professor of Clinical Psychology of Religion at the Catholic University of Nijmegen and the Faculty of Theology at Tilburg University and he is a clinical psychologist-psychotherapist in Heerlen. Topics of interest: religion, world view and mental health. Recent publications: Mulder, A., J. Pieper, and M. van Uden. 2001. *From myth to act. Modern Pilgrimage to Santiago.* Pp. 729-745 in *Christian Feast and Festival. The Dynamics of Western Liturgy and Culture,* edited by P. Post, G. Rouwhorst, L. van Tongeren and A. Scheer. Leuven.; Pieper, J. and M. van Uden. 2002. Klinische Religionspsychologie. Ein Trainingsmodell. *Wege zum Menschen* 54: 241-253.

Anne Vandenhoeck is Research Assistant in Pastoral Theology at the Catholic University of Leuven. Recent publications: Bulckens, J., and A. Vandenhoeck et al. 2000. *Al de dagen van ons leven.* Averbode: Altiora Averbode.; Debroey L., and A. Vandenhoeck. 2001. *Ik word gedoopt.* Averbode: Averbode.

Anton Vernooij is Professor of Liturgical Music at the Faculty of Theology of Tilburg University. Topics of interest: musical services and functions in liturgy. Recent publications: Vernooij, A. 2002. Muziek en liturgie. Pp. 95-112 in *Nieuwe wegen in de liturgie*, edited by M. Barnard and N. Schuman. Zoetermeer.; Vernooij, A. 2003. *Music and liturgy in movement.* Pp. 115-157 in *Liturgy and Muse*, edited by A. Vernooij. Leuven.

Myriam Wijlens is Assistant Professor of Canon Law at the Faculty of Theology of the University of Tilburg and teaches in the Canon Law Institute in Münster (Germany); staff member of the tribunal of the diocese of Münster. Recent publications: Wijlens, M. 2000. *Sharing the Eucharist: A Theological Evaluation of the Post-Conciliar Legislation.* Lanham MD: University Press of America.; Wijlens, M. 2001. *The Ordinary Contentious Trial: A Revised Schematic Overview.* Losser: Wijlens.

Hessel Zondag is Assistant Professor of Psychology of Religion and Culture at the Faculty of Theology of Tilburg University and the Catholic University of Nijmegen. Topics of interest: narcissism and religion, the pastor. Recent publications: Zondag, H. 2000. Motivation for the pastoral profession in the Netherlands. *Journal of Psychology and Theology* 28:109-118.; Zondag, H. 2002. Involved, Loyal, Alienated, and Detached. The Commitment of Pastors. *Pastoral Psychology* 49:311-323.

Theologie

Stephan H. Pfürtner;
Ulrich Schoenborn (Hg.)
Der bezwingende Vorsprung des Guten
Exegetische und theologische
Werkstattberichte (Festschrift für Wolfgang
Harnisch)
Bd. 1, 1994, 450 S., 30,90 €, br., ISBN 3-8258-2060-2

Martin Pöttner
Realität als Kommunikation
Ansätze zur Beschreibung der Grammatik
des paulinischen Sprechens in 1 Kor 1,4 – 4,21
im Blick auf literarische Problematik und
Situationsbezug des 1. Korintherbriefs
Bd. 2, 1995, 360 S., 24,90 €, br., ISBN 3-8258-2687-2

Karl-Horst Matthes
**Abraham, Isaak und Jakob geraten in die
Geschichte der Väter**
Eine Studie
Bd. 3, 1997, 280 S., 24,90 €, br., ISBN 3-8258-2655-4

Hans-Michael Wünsch
**Der paulinische Brief 2 Kor 1 – 9 als
kommunikative Handlung**
Eine rhetorisch-literaturwissenschaftliche
Untersuchung
Bd. 4, 1996, 352 S., 30,90 €, br., ISBN 3-8258-2603-1

Nélio Schneider
**Die "Schwachen" in der christlichen
Gemeinde Roms**
Bd. 5, 1996, 176 S., 17,90 €, br., ISBN 3-8258-2762-3

Ulrich Schoenborn
Dialog und Offenbarung
Zur Strategie literarischer Vergewisserung in
Krisenzeiten
Bd. 6, 1996, 96 S., 10,90 €, br., ISBN 3-8258-2763-1

Nam-Shin Cho
**Das Spiel des Geistes mit dem Wort:
Rudolf Bohren**
Bd. 7, 1996, 224 S., 24,90 €, br., ISBN 3-8258-2784-4

Martin Sieg
Vorweggenommen in ein Haus aus Licht
Sinnerfülltes Leben aus dem Vertrauen und
der Zuversicht heraus. Mit einem Geleitwort
von Landesbischof i. R. Prof. Dr. Eduard
Lohse
Bd. 8, 2., veränd. Aufl. 1997, 280 S., 15,90 €, br.,
ISBN 3-8258-2917-0

Gol Rim
Gottes Wort, Verkündigung und Kirche
Die systematisch-theologischen Grundlagen
der Theologie Eduard Thurneysens
Bd. 10, 2000, 248 S., 24,90 €, br., ISBN 3-8258-2991-x

Dieter Baltzer
Alttestamentliche Fachdidaktik
Gesammelte Studien
Bd. 11, 3., erweiterte. Aufl. Frühj. 2003, ca. 280 S.,
ca. 20,90 €, br., ISBN 3-8258-3002-0

Ulrich Johannes Plaga
"Ich bin die Wahrheit"
Die theo-logische Dimension der Christologie
Hans Urs von Balthasars
Bd. 12, 1998, 480 S., 50,90 €, br., ISBN 3-8258-3424-7

Karl-Horst Matthes
**Schöpfung und Sündenfall von Kain und
Abel bis Lamech**
Umgestaltete Überlieferungen
Bd. 13, 1998, 88 S., 15,90 €, br., ISBN 3-8258-3605-3

Stefan Brandenburger, Thomas Hieke (Hg.)
**WENN DREI DAS GLEICHE SAGEN –
Studien zu den ersten drei Evangelien**
Mit einer Werkstattübersetzung des Q-Textes
Bd. 14, 1998, 272 S., 25,90 €, br., ISBN 3-8258-3673-8

Andreas Leinhäupl-Wilke;
Stefan Lücking (Hg.)
Fremde Zeichen
Neutestamentliche Texte in der Konfrontation
der Kulturen
Bd. 15, 1998, 176 S., 15,90 €, br., ISBN 3-8258-3674-6

Günther Wied
**Prophetie im Spektrum von Theologie,
Psychiatrie und Parapsychologie**
Bd. 16, 1998, 208 S., 20,90 €, br., ISBN 3-8258-3760-2

Sabine Manow
**Textpläne für Kindergottesdienste – ent-
wicklungspsychologische und soziologische
Kritik**
Bd. 17, 1999, 344 S., 25,90 €, br., ISBN 3-8258-4113-8

Klaus Neumann
**Das Fremde verstehen – Grundlagen einer
kulturanthropologischen Exegese**
Untersuchungen zu paradigmatischen
mentalitätengeschichtlichen, ethnologischen
und soziologischen Zugangswegen zu
fremden Sinnwelten
Bd. 18, 2000, 1128 S., 61,90 €, br., ISBN 3-8258-4261-4

LIT Verlag Münster – Hamburg – Berlin – London
Grevener Str./Fresnostr. 2 48159 Münster
Tel.: 0251 – 23 50 91 – Fax: 0251 – 23 19 72
e-Mail: vertrieb@lit-verlag.de – http://www.lit-verlag.de

A. Autiero, K. H. Menke (Hg.)
Brückenbauer zwischen Kirche und Gesellschaft – A. Rosmini, J. H. Newman, M. Blondel und R. Guardini
Bd. 20, 1999, 360 S., 30,90 €, gb., ISBN 3-8258-4178-2

Dirk Chr. Siedler
Paul Tillichs Beiträge zu einer Theologie der Religionen
Eine Untersuchung seines religionsphilo-sophischen, religionswissenschaftlichen und theologischen Beitrages
Bd. 21, 1999, 296 S., 25,90 €, br., ISBN 3-8258-4203-7

Gerhard Tenholt
Die Unauflöslichkeit der Ehe und der kirchliche Umgang mit wiederverheirateten Geschiedenen
Bd. 22, 2001, 296 S., 30,90 €, br., ISBN 3-8258-4353-x

Lothar Becker
Rebe, Rausch und Religion
Eine kulturgeschichtliche Studie zum Wein in der Bibel
Bd. 23, 2000, 288 S., 25,90 €, br., ISBN 3-8258-4516-8

Wolfgang Fenske
Und noch ein Jesus!
Jesusbücher unter die Lupe genommen
Bd. 24, 2000, 192 S., 15,90 €, br., ISBN 3-8258-4565-6

Volker Lubinetzki
Von der Knechtsgestalt des Neuen Testaments
Beobachtungen zu seiner Verwendung und Auslegung in Deutschland vor dem sowie im Kontext des 'Dritten Reichs'
Bd. 26, 2000, 488 S., 40,90 €, br., ISBN 3-8258-4679-2

Christoph Recker
Erzählungen vom Patriarchen Jakob – ein Beitrag zur mehrperspektivischen Bibelauslegung
Bd. 27, 2000, 440 S., 40,90 €, br., ISBN 3-8258-4828-0

Heinz Georg Lederleitner
Erlösung erschließen – Wahrnehmungen gewaltloser Gottesmacht nach Georg Baudler
Bd. 28, 2000, 264 S., 30,90 €, br., ISBN 3-8258-4969-4

Reinhard Richter
Nationales Denken im Katholizismus der Weimarer Republik
Bd. 29, 2000, 440 S., 35,90 €, br., ISBN 3-8258-4991-0

Peter Dschulnigg
Jesus begegnen
Personen und ihre Bedeutung im Johannesevangelium
Bd. 30, 2000, 360 S., 20,90 €, br., ISBN 3-8258-5042-0

Klaus Schwarzwäller
Fülle des Lebens
Luthers Kleiner Katechismus. Ein Kommentar
Bd. 31, 2000, 360 S., 20,90 €, br., ISBN 3-8258-4934-1

Matthias Kopp
Pilgerspagat: Der Papst im Heiligen Land
Eindrücke, Analysen, Wirkungen zur Reise von Papst Johannes Paul II. (März 2000). Mit ausführlicher Dokumentation der Ansprachen und der wichtigsten Schritte vatikanischer Nahostdiplomatie
Bd. 32, 2001, 240 S., 15,90 €, br., ISBN 3-8258-5220-2

Jürgen Heise
Auslegen durch Nachdenken
Exegese johanneischer Texte und hermeneutische Überlegungen
Bd. 33, 2001, 128 S., 17,90 €, br., ISBN 3-8258-5267-9

Olaf Lezinsky
Der Laienbegriff in der Katholischen Kirche
Eine Betrachtung aus historischer und dogmatischer Sicht
Bd. 34, 2001, 168 S., 15,90 €, br., ISBN 3-8258-5273-3

Reinhard Nordsieck
Maria Magdalena, die Frau an Jesu Seite
Zur Frage nach der Identität der Maria Magdalena, der "großen Sünderin" und der Maria aus Bethanien und ihrer historischen Bedeutung
Bd. 35, 2001, 88 S., 12,90 €, br., ISBN 3-8258-5289-x

Peter Schwanz
Unterwegs zu einer anderen Theologie
Zur Weiterentwicklung genuin christlichen Denkens im Anschluß an Paul Tillichs philosophische Theologie. Aufsätze
Bd. 36, 2002, 256 S., 25,90 €, br., ISBN 3-8258-5311-x

Volker Keding
Theologia experimentalis
Die Erfahrungstheologie beim späten Gottfried Arnold
Bd. 37, 2001, 304 S., 30,90 €, br., ISBN 3-8258-5334-9

Dominik Bohne
Friedrich Wilhelm Hopf
(1910 – 1982) Pfarrer, Kirchenpolitiker, theologischer Publizist, Mann der Mission

LIT Verlag Münster – Hamburg – Berlin – London
Grevener Str./Fresnostr. 2 48159 Münster
Tel.: 0251 – 23 50 91 – Fax: 0251 – 23 19 72
e-Mail: vertrieb@lit-verlag.de – http://www.lit-verlag.de

Bd. 38, 2001, 344 S., 20,90 €, br., ISBN 3-8258-5338-1; 35,90 €, gb., ISBN 3-8258-5337-3

Eugene Dike
The Role of Mass Media for the Pastoral Development of the Catholic Church in Nigeria
Bd. 40, 2001, 344 S., 25,90 €, br., ISBN 3-8258-5367-5

Wolfgang Pfüller
Die Bedeutung Jesu im interreligiösen Horizont
Überlegungen zu einer religiösen Theorie in christlicher Perspektive
Bd. 41, 2001, 224 S., 20,90 €, br., ISBN 3-8258-5382-9

Walter Vogel
Religionspädagogik kommunikativ-vernetzt
Möglichkeiten religionspädagogischer Arbeit im Internet
Bd. 42, 2001, 240 S., 20,90 €, br., ISBN 3-8258-5332-2

Kenneth Nwokolo
Inculturation in Pastoral Care of the Sick
A study in the liturgy of anointing and pastoral care of the sick
Bd. 44, 2002, 456 S., 35,90 €, br., ISBN 3-8258-6142-2

Jutta Siemann
Jugend und Religion im Zeitalter der Globalisierung
Computer/Internet als Thema für Religion(sunterricht)
Bd. 45, 2002, 80 S., 15,90 €, br., ISBN 3-8258-5886-3

Walter Gerwing
Die Gottesherrschaftsbewegung Jesu
Die Phasen des Wirkens Jesu sind: Gewinnung einer Anhänger- und Jüngerschaft, Aussendung der Zwölf und Hinaufzug zum Passafest in Jerusalem. Jesus deutet sie durch die gegenwärtige, sich entwickelnde und vollendende Königsherrschaft Gottes, die final auf den Termin des Passafestes 30 n. Chr. bezogen ist. Mit Jesu Auferstehung wird sie diesseitig-irdisch weitgehend verwirklicht. Jesus hat sich also weder in ihrem Wann noch ihrem Wie geirrt.
Bd. 46, 2003, 288 S., 24,90 €, br., ISBN 3-8258-6299-2

Gesine Jost
Negro Spirituals **im evangelischen Religionsunterricht**
Versuch einer didaktischen Verschränkung zweier Erfahrungshorizonte
Negro Spirituals – ergreifende Gesänge der afro-amerikanischen Sklaven des 17./18. Jahrhunderts, Dokumente des christlichen Glaubens und musikalische Überlebensstrategien. Von diesem Erfahrungspotential ausgehend führt die Autorin zu einer einfühlsamen Begegnung mit der Erfahrungswelt heutiger Jugendlicher. Über Analogien in den Bereichen der Heimatlosigkeit und Unfreiheit hinaus wird die rhythmusbetonte Musik als affektive bzw. religiöse Bewältigungsform der Wirklichkeit zum Bindeglied zwischen Sklaven damals und Jugendlichen heute – eine Chance, *Negro Spirituals* religionsdidaktisch neu wahrzunehmen und jungen Menschen ganzheitlich zu begegnen.
Bd. 48, 2003, 224 S., 19,90 €, br., ISBN 3-8258-7329-3

Peter Haigis; Doris Lax (Hg.)
Brücken der Versöhnung
Festschrift für Gert Hummel zum 70. Geburtstag 2003
Die versammelten Beiträge zu Ehren Gert Hummels verstehen sich als Anknüpfung an die vom ihm gelebten Gedanken christlicher Existenz kraft von Gott geschenkter *Versöhnung*. Biographischen Erinnerungen folgen historisch orientierte „Brückenschläge zu Philosophie und Theologie" und an Grundsatzfragen interessierte „Brückenschläge zu gegenwärtigem Denken und Handeln". „Brückenschläge zur politischen Ethik" und „Brückenschläge zur angewandten Ethik" thematisieren christlich verantwortliches Handeln und „Brückenschläge zur kirchlichen Praxis" die Aufgabe, Kirche Jesu Christi *in der Welt* zu sein.
Bd. 49, 2003, 424 S., 24,90 €, br., ISBN 3-8258-6396-4

Karl-Wilhelm Merks (éd.)
Modèles d'unité dans un monde pluriel
Actes du Colloque international de Tilburg (décembre 2001) organisé par la Faculté de théologie de Tilburg (Pays-Bas) et des enseignants du Centre Sèvres (Paris)
Bd. 50, Frühj. 2003, ca. 104 S., ca. 14,90 €, br., ISBN 3-8258-6473-1

Friedrich Daniel Ernst Schleiermacher
Christliche Sittenlehre
Vorlesung im Wintersemester 1826/27. Nach großenteils unveröffentlichten Hörernachschriften herausgegeben von Hermann Peiter
Bd. 51, Frühj. 2003, ca. 1104 S., ca. 65,90 €, br., ISBN 3-8258-6535-5

LIT Verlag Münster – Hamburg – Berlin – London
Grevener Str./Fresnostr. 2 48159 Münster
Tel.: 0251 – 23 50 91 – Fax: 0251 – 23 19 72
e-Mail: vertrieb@lit-verlag.de – http://www.lit-verlag.de